Britain Decides

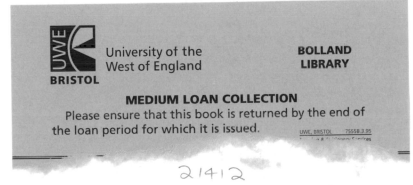

British General Election Series
General Editors: **Andrew Geddes**, Department of Politics, University of Sheffield, UK and
Jonathan Tonge, School of Politics and Communication Studies, University of Liverpool

The British General Election series provides timely, authoritative and incisive analyses
of British electoral politics. It brings together leading experts to comprehensively assess
election results, campaigns and the issues that animate contemporary political debate.
The series provides indispensable guides to the dynamics of British electoral politics, the
performance of political parties and the fortunes of governments.

Titles include:
Andrew Geddes and Jonathan Tonge (*editors*)
BRITAIN DECIDES
The UK General Election 2005

British General Election Series
Series Standing Order ISBN 1–4039–9981–3 (Hardback) 1–4039–9982–1 (Paperback)
(*outside North America only*)

You can receive future titles in this series as they are published by placing a standing order. Please
contact your bookseller or, in the case of difficulty, write to us at the address below with your name
and address, the title of the series and the ISBN quoted above.

Customer Services Department, Macmillan Distribution Ltd, Houndmills, Basingstoke, Hampshire
RG21 6XS, England

Britain Decides

The UK General Election 2005

Edited by

Andrew Geddes
University of Sheffield

and

Jonathan Tonge
University of Liverpool

palgrave
macmillan

First published 2005 by
PALGRAVE MACMILLAN
Houndmills, Basingstoke, Hampshire RG21 6XS and
175 Fifth Avenue, New York, N.Y. 10010
Companies and representatives throughout the world

PALGRAVE MACMILLAN is the global academic imprint of the
Palgrave Macmillan division of St Martin's Press LLC and of
Palgrave Macmillan Ltd.
Macmillan® is a registered trademark in the United States,
United Kingdom and other countries. Palgrave is a registered
trademark in the European Union and other countries.

ISBN-13   978–1–4039–4656–0 hardback
ISBN-10   1–4039–4656–6 hardback
ISBN-13   978–1–4039–4657–7 paperback
ISBN-10   1–4039–4657–4 paperback

This book is printed on paper suitable for recycling and
made from fully managed and sustained forest sources.

A catalogue record for this book is available
from the British Library.

Library of Congress Cataloging-in-Publication Data

10 9 8 7 6 5 4 3 2 1
14 13 12 11 10 09 08 07 06 05

Printed and bound in Great Britain by
Antony Rowe Ltd, Chippenham and Eastbourne

Contents

Acknowledgements

We wish to thank a number of people for their input to this book. Firstly, each contributor deserves our gratitude for producing their chapter so quickly after the election, without our emails ever becoming unduly terse. We owe a large debt to Alison Howson and Steven Kennedy at Palgrave Macmillan for their commissioning of the book and infectious enthusiasm. This is our third work on general elections in the UK and we wish to record thanks to Dr Bill Jones of Manchester University, who stimulated and backed the idea. For this volume a post-election seminar was held at Sheffield University. We are grateful to all those that attended, to Sylvia McColm of the Sheffield University Politics department for her organisational support and to the Institute for the Study of Political Parties at Sheffield University (particularly Dr Charles Lees), the Department of Politics at Sheffield University and the European Studies Research Institute at Salford University for their financial backing.

Jon Tonge would like to thank Dr Jocelyn Evans and Professor Steven Fielding who provided valuable input within the European Studies Research Institute at Salford University, whilst a Faculty-awarded sabbatical year in 2004–05 was very helpful. Jim Hancock and Jim Clarke at the BBC Politics Show in Manchester provided stimulating discussions among fellow-obsessives. On a personal note, Jon thanks Maria for her unstinting patience, plus Andy, Dermot, Anita and Neil. Jon was particularly gratified by the interest in the election shown by his nine-year-old son Connell. Hopefully his question: 'Why did Tony Blair win after starting the war dad?' has been answered adequately in this volume. Andrew Geddes would like to thank Federica and Jacopo for their support and deep abiding interest in British electoral politics.

List of Abbreviations

AM	(Welsh) Assembly Member
AWS	all-women shortlist
BES	British Election Study
BME	black and minority ethnic
BNP	British National Party
CBI	Confederation of British Industry
CCS	Constituency Campaign Services
CON	Conservative Party
CSI	City Seats Initiative
DUP	Democratic Unionist Party
EU	European Union
GDP	gross domestic product
GFA	Good Friday Agreement
GNP	gross national product
ICD	International Commission on Decommissioning
ICT	information communication technologies
IDS	Iain Duncan Smith
IFS	Institute of Fiscal Studies
IND	Independent
IRA	Irish Republican Army
ISG	Iraq Survey Group
LAB	Labour Party
LD	Liberal Democrats
MEP	Member of the European Parliament
MSP	Member of the Scottish Parliament
PC	Plaid Cymru
PLP	Parliamentary Labour Party
PP	Pensioners' Party
PPERA	Political Parties, Elections & Referendums Act
PR	proportional representation
PSA	public service agreement
SDLP	Social Democratic and Labour Party
SDP	Social Democratic Party
SF	Sinn Fein
SNP	Scottish National Party
Soc Lab	Socialist Labour
SSP	Scottish Socialist Party

STV	single transferable vote
UKIP	United Kingdom Independence Party
UUP	Ulster Unionist Party
WMD	weapons of mass destruction

List of Figures

List of Tables

Notes on Contributors

Jonathan Bradbury is Senior Lecturer in politics at the University of Wales Swansea. He is author of a number of articles and books on British politics, devolution and territorial politics and local government. He is co-convenor of the PSA British and Comparative Territorial Politics group.

Gavin Cameron is an Associate Professor in the Department of Political Science and a Fellow of the Centre for Military and Strategic Studies at the University of Calgary, Canada. He previously taught Politics and Contemporary History at the University of Salford. He is the author of *Nuclear Terrorism: A Threat Assessment for the 21st Century* (1999) and co-editor of *Agro-Terrorism: What is the Threat?* (2003).

Sarah Childs is Lecturer in Politics at the University of Bristol. She has published articles on women's representation in a range of journals, including the *British Journal of Politics and International Relations* and *Parliamentary Affairs*. She is author of *New Labour's Women MPs: Women Representing Women* (Routledge 2004).

Philip Cowley is Reader in Parliamentary Government at the University of Nottingham and runs <www.revolts.co.uk>.

David Cutts is a Simon Research Fellow at the University of Manchester. He completed his doctorate, examining the effects of constituency campaigning, at the University of Bristol.

David Deacon is Senior Lecturer in Communication and Media Studies, Department of Social Sciences, Loughborough University. He is currently investigating British news media coverage of the Spanish Civil War.

David Denver is Professor of Politics at Lancaster University. He is author of the widely used text, *Elections and Voters in Britain* (Palgrave 2003).

Edward Fieldhouse is Professor of Social and Political Science at the University of Manchester. He is co-author (with A. Russell) of *Neither Left not Right? The Liberal Democrats and the Electorate* (Manchester University Press 2005) and has published a wide range of journal articles.

Steven Fielding is Professor of Contemporary Political History at the University of Salford. He has written widely on the Labour Party, most recently *The Labour Party. Continuity and Change in the Making of 'New' Labour* (Palgrave 2003) and *The Labour Governments, 1964–70. Volume One. Labour and Cultural Change* (Manchester University Press 2003). He is also co-editor (with Jocelyn Evans) of *Parliamentary Affairs*.

Justin Fisher is Senior Lecturer in Political Science at Brunel University. He is co-author of Central Debates in British Politics (with D. Denver) (Longman 2002) and was lead editor of a special issue of *Party Politics* (2004) comparing campaign finance across democracies, a subject on which he has published a wide range of journal articles.

Andrew Geddes is Professor of Politics at the University of Sheffield. Recent books include *The European Union and British Politics* (Palgrave 2004), *The Politics of Migration and Immigration in Europe* (Sage 2003) and *Immigration and European Integration: Towards Fortress Europe?* (Manchester University Press 2000).

Jane Green is a doctoral student at Nuffield College, Oxford.

James Mitchell is Professor of Government at the University of Strathclyde. His most recent book is *Governing Scotland: The Invention of Administrative Devolution* (Palgrave 2003).

David Richards is a Reader in the Department of Politics at the University of Sheffield. Recent books include *Governance and Public Policy in the UK* (with M. Smith) (Macmillan 2001) and *Changing Patterns of Governance in the UK* (with D. Marsh and M. Smith) (Oxford University Press). He is currently preparing a co-written book with Palgrave on *Whitehall under New Labour*.

Martin J. Smith is Professor of Politics at the University of Sheffield. Recent publications include *Changing Patterns of Governance in the UK* (with D. Marsh and D. Richards) (Macmillan 2001), *Governance and Public Policy in the UK* (with D. Richards) (Oxford University Press) and *Governing as New Labour* (eds with S. Ludlam 2003) (Palgrave Macmillan).

Jonathan Tonge is Professor of Politics at the University of Liverpool. Recent books include *The New Northern Irish Politics* (Palgrave 2005), *Sinn Fein and the SDLP* (Hurst/O'Brien 2005, with Gerard Murray), *Northern Ireland: Conflict and Change* (Pearson 2002). Recent articles include pieces in *Political Studies*, *Party Politics* and *Contemporary British History*. He is co-editor of *Irish Political Studies* and Chair of the Political Studies Association of the UK, 2005–08.

Stephen Ward is a Research Fellow at the Oxford Internet Institute, University of Oxford. Recent publications include *Political Parties and the Internet: Net Gain*, co-edited with Rachel Gibson and Paul Nixon (Routledge 2003) and *Electronic Democracy*, co-edited with Rachel Gibson and Andrea Roemele (Routledge 2003).

Tony Wright is Labour MP for Cannock Chase, having been first elected for the seat in 1997. He was previously a Professor at the University of Birmingham. He chairs the Commons Select Committee on Public Administration and chairs the Constitution and Citizenship Associate Parliamentary Group.

Dominic Wring is Senior Lecturer in Communication and Media Studies at Loughborough University. His most recent book is *The Politics of Marketing the Labour Party* (Palgrave Macmillan 2005).

1
Introduction

Andrew Geddes and Jonathan Tonge

British politics has been dominated for more than ten years by Tony Blair. The 2005 general election was, however, Blair's last campaign as Labour leader. For him, this may well be a relief. Labour saw its majority slashed, as its vote fell, barely 36 per cent of voters prepared to endorse New Labour. On a turnout of just 61.3 per cent, fewer than 21.5 per cent of the electorate voted for the government. Blair himself was portrayed as an election liability, while his credibility was battered by an election campaign that saw him pilloried as a liar because of the Iraq war and forced to rely on his Chancellor Gordon Brown as a human shield to give some credibility to his campaign. 'A kick in the ballots' was how the *Sun* put it on the morning after.

Or that's one way of looking at it. Another is that Blair secured an historic third term for Labour with a workable Commons majority of 66. The Conservatives were consigned to a third consecutive election defeat for the first time in the party's history and with a share of the national vote that had barely shifted since 1997. Blair also saw off his fourth Conservative leader. Michael Howard became one of only four Conservative leaders not to have become Prime Minister. The fact that two of these four were his immediate predecessors William Hague and Iain Duncan Smith indicates the Conservatives' plight.

The 2005 campaign contest was hardly the most enervating or elevating, although British electoral politics has rarely been a venue for spiritual uplift. By the end of the campaign the appeals from the Parties had been stripped to their most basic core messages. Don't let the Tories back in was Labour's rallying cry, and don't vote Liberal Democrat either because that might have the same effect, or so Labour claimed. From the Conservatives the call was to give the Prime Minister a bloody nose, or to wipe the smirk off his face. The Conservatives called for an anti-Blair vote and had no compunction in labelling him a liar. Note that this Conservative tactic, developed partly by its imported campaign strategist, Lynton Crosby, was less about voting *for* a Conservative government than *against* a Labour one. The Liberal Democrats sought to clamber to the moral high ground, which, so far as they could work out, seemed to be to the left of Labour. Trust and allegations of broken promises were central to the Lib Dem campaign too with the Iraq war and tuition fees for university students central to their campaign. Neither Labour nor the Conservatives turned their fire on the Liberal Democrats until towards the end of the campaign. This allowed Charles Kennedy to overcome a rather muddled start to his campaign, when he was unable to explain his showpiece policy of local income tax, which the Liberal Democrats offered as a replacement for council tax. That said, the odds on Kennedy becoming Prime Minister were the same as those of his baby son born during the election campaign. We may live in an era of three-party politics in England and four-party politics in Scotland and Wales, but given the disjuncture between voting and representation, the battle for power was still a Labour versus Conservative run-off.

The leaders also faced a sceptical and, at times, hostile electorate. As the campaign went on, it became ever clearer the extent to which Britain is no longer a deferential society. Moreover, the public mood seemed one of ennui. Politics are boring, was the fashionable refrain in the run-up to and during the election. Sky News set an 'interest index' showing the balance between those interested and those uninterested in the election. The result was resoundingly negative for the duration of the campaign. Research for the Electoral Commission suggested that disengagement rather than apathy was the issue. The ideological gap between the main parties has closed, political leaders tend not to be trusted and membership of political parties has plummeted. In many parts of the country the 2005 campaign was invisible with scarcely a campaign poster to be seen. The real campaign was fought in marginal seats where the resources of the parties were focused.

Disengagement was not helped by the way in which British politics seemed to be conducted in a media bubble into which real voters rarely intrude. An encounter between a political leader and a random member of the electorate can often be front-page news. Each morning the party press conferences would be relayed and then chewed over by a commentariat for the hidden messages and 'real' meanings. Television viewers watching the nightly news bulletins would get the impression of the party leaders touring the country because that was the impression the parties wanted to give. Leaders could rely upon coverage in regional news bulletins. In reality the leaders helicopter in and out before a small, invited audience and the media pack. An urge to 're-connect' saw party leaders take their jackets off, roll up their shirt sleeves and address a carefully selected audience.

In defence of the politicians, they submitted themselves to gruelling question times, in front of national and regional television audiences and presenters. Ennui and the triumph of marketing aside, politics do matter. Often it can be local politics that animates people. In Bethnal Green, Kidderminster, Blaenau

Gwent and countless other seats this maxim was proved accurate once again. The closure of Rover in the West Midlands, council tax levels in Wales, health care in Scotland, immigration in the M62 corridor and Kent, tuition fees in student areas, were all burning election issues with an uneven local impact. Foreign policy is rarely a campaign theme, but the war in Iraq was refracted as an issue of trust in the Prime Minister and brought foreign affairs decisively into domestic politics. The 2005 general election was the Iraq election in the sense that trust in the Prime Minister had been badly corroded.

As was the case in 1997 and 2001, this was a Blair election. It was about him, his past and his political future, the latter most indeterminate. Soon after his election in 1997 Blair asked voters to trust him because he was 'a pretty straight sort of guy'. The credit in the bank had long since been exhausted for many voters. The fact that he would not re-stand was actually seen by many as a vote winner. As soon as the election results were in, senior Labour MPs such as Robin Cook and Frank Dobson were calling for him to resign.

What had changed to so dramatically undermine trust in the Prime Minister? The answer is to be found in the aftermath of the September 11, 2001 attacks on New York and Washington. British politics changed after 9/11 when Blair decided to stand foursquare behind the Americans in their 'War on Terror'. He led Britain into a war in Afghanistan to topple the Taliban and into an invasion of Iraq in search of Weapons of Mass Destruction that, it turned out, no longer existed. Domestically, the 'War on Terror' turned security into a key issue. Identity cards were mooted while detention without trial for terrorist suspects alienated many Labour voters and civil libertarians. While four separate inquiries cleared the Prime Minister of wilfully misleading the British people over the war, an inner circle of confidants and advisors was revealed. Labelled as 'denocracy' after Blair's small office in 10 Downing Street, a 'shift of sovereignty from Parliament to the Downing Street sofa' had occurred, according to the *Observer* (1 May 2005).

Labour had been re-elected in 2001 on a pledge to make good on a commitment to public services and to 'deliver'. The domestic agenda was, however, overshadowed by foreign policy. There were some achievements to be trumpeted. Labour could point to a huge increase in health spending, rising to 9 per cent of national income, spending per pupil in education doubled, the introduction of a national minimum wage, the attainment of near full employment. There had been redistribution of income too. Since 1997, according to the Institute for Fiscal Studies, the bottom 10 per cent of society became 10.8 per cent better off while the top 10 per cent were 4.4 per cent worse off. However, the delivery message was crowded out by the issues of trust and Iraq.

Labour found itself fighting the 2005 election on a number of fronts. In the north they were confronted by the Liberal Democrats on their left, anxious to hoover protest votes against the war, top-up fees and Blair himself. In the south the Conservatives were hopeful of a revival in some of their former heartlands, based upon a populist campaign playing on issues such as concern about immigration. Although Conservatives hoped for 1970, when the voters defied the pollsters to deliver a majority to the Conservatives, they got a performance worse than Labour's in 1983 in terms of number of seats. Yet the Conservatives went into election day having conducted a more focused and disciplined campaign than many had expected. It was the Conservatives that set the campaign agenda on issues such as immigration and hospital cleanliness. This effective campaign, reminiscent in some ways of Labour's in 1987, might provide some solace, although it should be recalled that it took ten years and root and branch reform of the party after 1987 before Labour were to win again. Even with trust in Blair at low levels, he was still more popular than Michael Howard and still seen as the most likely party leader to be effective as Prime Minister. Moreover, Labour had seized and maintained a reputation for economic competence over the Conservatives ever since Black Wednesday in September 1992.

For the Liberal Democrats there was much at stake in 2005, given the convergence of a range of favourable political forces. They possessed the capability to make some inroads into Labour support, but underestimated the risk of losses to the Conservatives in the south. Although over-hyped by the media as a decapitation strategy, the Liberal Democrats did believe they could claim important Conservative scalps. Yet the aspiration of capturing the seats of such prominent figures as Theresa May, Oliver Letwin, David Davis and perhaps even Michael Howard proved merely that, the only notable Conservative victim being the shadow education spokesman, Tim Collins in Westmorland. In Scotland and Wales, where four-party politics is the rule, Labour hegemony was further dented as the Liberal Democrats made some further inroads, but the nationalists and the Conservatives stalled. Northern Ireland saw a hardening of the sectarian divide with the Democratic Unionists and Sinn Fein making gains, the SDLP holding on, and the Ulster Unionists going into meltdown.

The plan of the book

In many ways this book is the story of a rather dull campaign that produced some rather intriguing results. It is the story of the end of Labour's landslide politics, or at least those presided over by Tony Blair in 1997 and 2001. Chapter 2 details the election result and the key voting variables that produced a somewhat altered political landscape. The following three chapters provide a detailed assessment of the campaign and fortunes of the three main parties, after which Tony Wright, returned as Labour MP for Cannock Chase, offers some personal reflections on the election battle.

The 2005 election was a story of a complex and fluid election campaign where local variations were the key. This is reflected in the emphasis in this book upon sub-UK state variation. Individual chapters are dedicated to the contests in Scotland and Wales, which differ markedly from that in England, whilst the very distinctive contest in Northern Ireland also merits a chapter. Moreover, the changes in vote share varied considerably across and within each country. The interplay of national and local factors prompting such variation is covered in a series of individual constituency profiles located between chapters.

After the analysis of results, parties and territory, the book turns to some of the key issues that dominated the 2005 election and explains why others, such as Europe, failed to register. The book also assesses potentially salient aspects such as finance, media coverage and the growing use, if not necessarily impact, of the Internet. At times the campaign appeared to be stuck upon the issues of immigration, asylum and Iraq, yet these might be regarded as 'noises off'. Labour's victory owed much to continuing economic prosperity which obliged the Conservatives to fight on alternative terrain.

The 2005 campaign focused on the integrity of a Prime Minister in a forensic and perhaps unprecedented way. This book is an attempt to make sense of the election results, the party campaigns and the issues that animated the 2005 British general election. It is the story too of Labour's third victory. This is an achievement that does require some reflection. After the 1992 Conservative victory some heralded the 'Japanisation' of British politics with a ruling Conservative Party apparently permanently in government. Labour now holds a commanding position. It is seen as the economically competent party, it is seen as the party of the public services and, what is more, benefits from an electoral system that is stacked in its favour. It also has an anointed leader waiting in the wings, while the Conservatives have once again plunged into a leadership contest. The 2005 campaign showed that while New Labour has lost much of its lustre and remains a party within a party, the Conservatives – the natural party of government for much of the twentieth century – still have a mountain to climb.

2
The Results: How Britain Voted

David Denver

Throughout the period between the 2001 and 2005 general elections almost all commentators and politicians, including some Conservatives, appeared to assume that Labour would win a third term in the next election and do so fairly comfortably. In some ways this is surprising. Figure 2.1 shows the trends in party support over the period according to opinion polls.

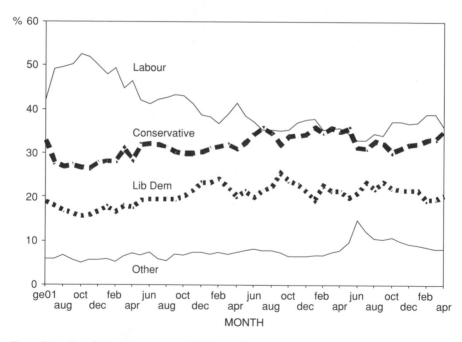

Figure 2.1 Trends in party support, 2001–April 2005

Note: 'ge01' = general election 2001. For each month the graph shows the mean percentage intending to vote for each party on the basis of all published polls. The data for April 2005 are derived from four polls undertaken before the date of the election was announced.

Labour experienced the usual 'honeymoon' with the electorate after the 2001 election but then its support fell. Support for the Conservatives, on the other hand, held steady throughout and was, indeed, on a slow upward trend. As a result, although Labour was usually in the lead, the gap between the two main parties was relatively small from about the middle of 2003 and had almost closed entirely by the beginning of April 2005, just before the date of the election was announced. The Liberal Democrats, meanwhile, also held steady and were generally at a slightly higher level of support than they had achieved in 2001. Small parties – in particular UKIP – experienced an upsurge of support at the time of the European elections in June 2004 but this faded in the following months.

Overall, there is nothing in the poll figures to suggest a runaway Labour victory. Moreover, there is plenty of evidence that the Iraq war cost Labour support – the best estimates suggest about three percentage points net of all other factors – and contributed to a marked decline in the popularity of Tony Blair and trust in his leadership.

One reason for the assumption that a second Labour victory was almost certain was the belief that the major opposition party ought to have been doing a lot better. From about the 1960s onwards, commentators became accustomed to a familiar electoral cycle. Between elections, governing parties would lose a great deal of support and the main opposition would benefit – having large leads in the opinion polls, making numerous gains in local elections and taking seats from the governing party in by-elections. As the next general election approached, however, support would flow back to the government. Midterm 'blues' would be forgotten and the big opposition leads previously recorded would be whittled away. To have a chance of winning, the main opposition party had to be very far ahead in the midterm.

Between 2001 and 2005, however, despite the manifest unpopularity of the government, the Conservatives clearly failed to establish any such lead in the polls. Moreover, their performance in by-elections was dismal. They failed to take any seats and fell into fourth place behind UKIP in one (Hartlepool) even although support for Labour plummeted.

Expectations based on past experience of election cycles may be misplaced, however. Recent cycles have not conformed to the 'familiar pattern'. Between 1992 and 1997 support for the Conservative government fell very steeply but, although it bottomed out, there was hardly any upswing as the election approached. With Labour in power between 1997 and 2001 there was indeed a decline and surge of support for the government but the surge came very late in the day, in the last few months before the election. The cycle of support between 2001 and 2005 was again unusual – as can be inferred from Figure 2.1, there was a decline in the government's popularity but no increase at all in the last few months before the election was called. If anything, there was a further decline.

It would seem, then, that a rather out-of-date view of electoral cycles is a rather shaky basis on which to base expectations about how a forthcoming election will turn out. On the other hand, a second reason underlying confidence about Labour's election prospects is more solidly based: the operation of the electoral system. For a variety of reasons, the first-past-the-post system is currently biased against the Conservatives to the extent that, before the 2005 election, it was calculated that if the two major parties emerged with the same percentage of the votes and the swing required to achieve that were uniform across constituencies, then Labour would still have many more MPs than the Conservatives. In 2001 Conservative-held seats had, on average, larger electorates and a higher turnout than seats won by Labour. In addition, seats won by the Liberal Democrats were mostly taken from the Conservatives. These factors meant that the Conservative share of the popular vote was not reflected in seats won.

Although the operation of the electoral system is not a subject that usually attracts much interest, the uphill task facing the Conservatives in attempting to convert any increase in popular support into seat gains came to be well understood by political professionals and media commentators. If this is what underlay pessimism about the Conservatives' chances then such pessimism was well founded and the electoral system did, in the event, produce a convincing Labour majority in the House of Commons despite a relatively close result in terms of votes.

Trends in party support during the campaign

Trends in voting intentions from the announcement of the election (5 April) over the four and a half weeks of campaigning through to the actual result on polling day on 5 May are charted in Figure 2.2. Four pre-election polls based on fieldwork undertaken from 1 April to 3 April (ICM, NOP, MORI and Populus) constitute the starting point. The mean voting intentions in these four polls were 35.3 per cent for the Conservatives, 36.0 per cent for Labour and 20.5 per cent for the Liberal Democrats. The figure then shows the average share of voting intentions in each week of the campaign (based on all published polls) and the parties' actual shares of the vote in Great Britain in the election itself.

As can be seen, Labour opened up a lead over its main rivals in the first three weeks of the campaign. In the last two weeks, however, the gap narrowed a little and on polling day itself the Conservatives did slightly better and Labour slightly worse than the last polls suggested they would. (It should be said, however, that, overall, the final polls were remarkably accurate, especially given the difficulties caused by uncertainties about turnout.) The Liberal Democrats achieved a small but discernible increase in support over the campaign. This was nothing like as dramatic as the increase achieved during the 2001 campaign, however, amounting to only two percentage points from the beginning of April to polling day. This

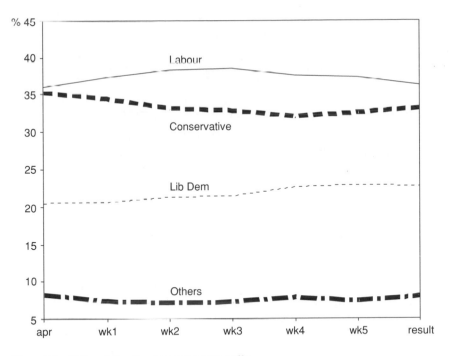

Figure 2.2   Voting intentions in campaign polls

Note: The data – mean share of voting intentions for each party – are derived from the 'headline' figures in all published polls with each poll being assigned to the week in which most of the fieldwork was carried out.

may be explained by the fact that the Liberal Democrats entered the campaign already at an unusually high level in the polls so that it was more difficult for them to make further advances.

During and after the election there was much media criticism of the Conservative campaign, largely on the grounds that it was 'negative' and focused on the 'wrong' issues. The Liberal Democrat campaign and the performance of Charles Kennedy, on the other hand, attracted generally favourable comment after an uncertain start. The voters appeared to share (or perhaps reflect) these perceptions. At the end of the campaign British Election Study (BES) respondents, by wide margins, believed that the Liberal Democrats had fought the best campaign and the Conservatives the worst. They also thought that, of the party leaders, Charles Kennedy had been the most effective campaigner and Michael Howard the least effective. Whether these perceptions matter very much is open to doubt. As we have seen, the Liberal Democrats did not improve their position by very much as the campaign progressed and Conservative support remained fairly stable. Labour ended on top despite the fact that BES respondents gave a slightly negative rating to Tony Blair as a campaigner and were only just positive about

Labour's campaign as a whole. Perhaps more significantly, there was virtually no change in the extent to which voters liked or disliked the party leaders. The BES asked voters to indicate this on a scale ranging from 0 (dislike) to 10 (like). Kennedy went from 5.2 at the outset to 5.5 at the end, Blair from 4.0 to 4.1 and Howard from 3.7 to 3.4.[1]

There may be a temptation when looking at Figure 2.2 to conclude that all the campaigning efforts made by the parties were a waste of time. Once things got going there were no dramatic changes. It should be remembered, however, that the graph is based on aggregate voting intentions and although these suggest that there was considerable stability over the five-week period, individual voters were constantly switching between parties or coming off the fence in favour of one party or another. Aggregate stability does not mean that the voting intentions of individuals were unwavering.

Turnout in the election

The 'big story' of the 2001 general election had been the fact that the turnout (59.1 per cent) was the lowest in a general election since 1918 and the decline from 1997 was the largest between any two elections in modern times. Subsequently, there was much hand-wringing over this on the part of the chattering classes and numerous investigations into what could be done about it. Various experiments using different methods of voting – including compulsory postal voting – were tried at local elections. In 2005, however, there were no innovations in voting methods although, controversially, there was a large increase in the number of people applying for postal votes (from 3.9 per cent of the electorate in 2001 to a reported 12 per cent). Whether or not this had any effect, turnout appears to have increased a little in 2005 as compared with the previous election (Table 2.1).[2]

Table 2.1   Regional and national turnout in 2005

	Turnout (%)	Change 2001–05
North East	57.2	+0.7
North West	57.3	+1.4
Yorkshire/Humber	58.9	+2.2
East Midlands	62.4	+1.5
West Midlands	60.9	+2.4
Eastern	63.7	+1.7
London	57.9	+2.7
South East	64.4	+2.9
South West	66.3	+1.4
Wales	62.4	+0.8
Scotland	60.6	+2.5
Great Britain	61.7	+2.6

Over the country as a whole, turnout increased by 2.6 per cent and there were increases in every region ranging from 0.7 per cent in the North East (where there may have been some 'voting fatigue' following the referendum there on a regional assembly in November 2004) to 2.9 per cent in the South East. In trying to explain the low turnout in 2001 many commentators suggested that one contributory factor was that the result of the election was thought by almost everyone to be a foregone conclusion. A Labour landslide was expected and duly transpired. In 2005, however, the polls consistently reported that – at least in terms of votes – the result would be much closer and it is difficult to resist the conclusion that this is what explains the slight increase in the willingness of the electorate to go to the polls.

The data in Table 2.1 indicate that across England there was clearly something of a north–south pattern to turnout in 2005. Excluding London, the three northern regions had the lowest turnouts while the South East, South West and Eastern regions recorded the highest figures. There was much greater variation, of course, in both the level of turnout and the change in turnout from 2001 at constituency level.

Taking change in turnout first, across England and Wales (Scotland is excluded from all analysis of turnout change because constituency boundary changes make calculations of turnout for 2001 unreliable) the provisional figures show that turnout increased in 466 seats and fell in 102. The biggest fall was in Norwich South (–4.7 per cent) and the biggest rise was in Maidenhead (+9.7 per cent) where the high-profile Conservative incumbent, Theresa May, was thought to be under threat.

Labour campaigners feared that some of their supporters might vent their displeasure with the government – especially over Iraq – by not turning out to vote in the election but the aggregate turnout data suggest that these fears were not realised. Turnout did increase slightly more in Conservative-held seats (mean change +2.3 per cent; N = 164) than in those that were Labour-held (+1.9 per cent; N = 357) but the increase was smallest in Liberal Democrat seats (+1.6 per cent; N = 42). In any event, these differences are not statistically significant. Even in the safest Labour seats (majority over 30 per cent) turnout was up by 1.8 per cent. Overall, there was no significant association between variations across constituencies in the strength of support for any of the three parties in 2001 and the change in turnout between 2001 and 2005. Nor, indeed, did the marginality or safeness of constituencies in 2001 have any significant impact on the change in turnout.

On the other hand, there is some evidence that Labour was harmed by the general increase in turnout. There was a slight but significant tendency for Labour's vote share to decline more the larger was the increase in turnout (correlation coefficient = –0.194) but turnout changes were not systematically related to changes in the Conservative and Liberal Democrat shares of votes. This is easy to understand since in different constituencies one or other of these two parties would have been the main beneficiaries of Labour's discomfiture.

To summarise this section, it appears that there was a small across-the-board increase in turnout in 2005 that was not clearly related to regional or constituency factors. This suggests that it was a product of nationwide factors and it seems likely that there was a generally increased determination to vote against the government. The lack of pattern to the changes is also consistent with the suggestion made above that it was simply the case that at least some electors recognised that the election outcome was going to be closer than in 2001 and on that basis took more trouble to cast a ballot.

Turning to actual turnout in 2005, we encounter a much more predictable and familiar pattern of variation across constituencies. The lowest turnout, as in both 1997 and 2001 was in the Liverpool Riverside seat (41.5 per cent) while the highest was in Leominster (77.3 per cent). Also as in 2001, turnout was higher in seats won by the Conservatives (mean of 65.3 per cent; N = 197) than in those that Labour won (57.9 per cent; N = 355) and that difference is statistically significant. (For Liberal Democrat seats (N = 62) the figure is 64.8 per cent.)

The general pattern of constituency variations in turnout is most effectively described by correlation coefficients which measure the strength of association between turnout and variables indicating the socio-economic characteristics of constituencies and the electoral context. This is done in Table 2.2. The socio-economic variables are derived from the 2001 census and they are all strongly and significantly related to turnout. Turnout was higher in constituencies with more professional and managerial households, owner occupiers, people aged 65 and over, people employed in agriculture and people with degrees. Turnout was lower the more manual workers, social and private renters, young voters, persons per hectare, people from ethnic minorities and households without a car. The latter is an indicator of the general level of poverty and deprivation and it has the strongest correlation with turnout of all the variables listed. In general, then, – and it is nothing new – turnout was strongly related to the socio-economic character of constituencies. In broad terms, Britain divides into relatively low turnout and relatively high turnout constituencies and the two are very different in social terms.

The closeness of the contest in a constituency in the previous election (marginality) is also regularly associated with turnout levels. Parties put greater campaign efforts into more marginal seats (and, these days, virtually ignore those that are either very safe or hopeless for the party concerned) and unsurprisingly these efforts bear fruit in higher turnouts. The 2005 election was no exception. As Table 2.2 shows, previous marginality was strongly related to turnout (even although the marginality of Scottish seats could only be estimated) with a correlation coefficient of +0.712. This is, indeed, the strongest correlation between marginality and turnout in any post-war general election and reflects the intense targeting of party efforts into marginal seats. Finally, there were a large number of minor party candidates in the election – UKIP, BNP, Respect, Green, Veritas and assorted others. It might be thought that the larger the array of candidates that were available the more people would be inclined to vote, since it would be more difficult to use the excuse that there was no one to vote for. In fact, the better 'others' did in a constituency, the lower was turnout.

Table 2.2   Bivariate correlations between turnout in 2005 and constituency characteristics

% Professional & managerial	0.538	% In agriculture	0.452
% Manual workers	–0.569	Persons per hectare	–0.541
% Owner occupiers	0.700	% Ethnic minority	–0.402
% Social renters	–0.723	% With degrees	0.235
% Private renters	–0.157	% With no car	–0.788
% Aged 18–24	–0.423		
% Aged 65+	0.429	Constit. marginality 2001	0.712
		Minor party vote 2005	–0.242

Note: All coefficients are significant at the 0.01 level. Glasgow North East (Speaker's seats) is excluded from all calculations and Wyre Forest (Independent victory in 2001) from those involving 2001 marginality and minor party vote.

While bivariate correlations are interesting and important in themselves, they constitute only a first step in analysis. One problem in interpreting them is that the various measures of the social composition of constituencies are themselves highly inter-correlated. Thus, areas in which a large proportion of households are owner occupiers tend also to have large proportions of professional and managerial workers and small proportions of social renters. Secondly, bivariate analysis provides no clue as to the joint impact of a number of variables or to the impact of any single variable once others are taken into account. Thus, we might want to know how much of the variation in turnout is explained by class and housing tenure together or whether constituency marginality affects turnout once the class composition of the constituency is taken into account.

We can begin to deal with these problems by undertaking multiple regression analysis. This enables us to sort out which variables are the most important influences on turnout, see whether a particular variable remains significant when all others are held constant and evaluate how successfully combinations of variables explain turnout variations. The results of a stepwise regression show that just six of the variables account for 79 per cent of the variation in constituency turnouts. The most important predictors by some way are percentage with a degree, previous marginality and percentage with no car, the others being percentage aged 65+, persons per hectare and percentage of private renters. Each of these has an independent effect on turnout even when scores on the other five are taken into account. So, the pattern of constituency turnouts in the 2005 election is very satisfactorily explained by a combination of a small number of socio-economic characteristics and the level of marginality in the previous election.

Votes and seats won

The shares of votes and the number of seats won by the major parties in 2005 (in Great Britain) and changes from 2001 are shown in Table 2.3. The Conservatives made only a small advance in terms of vote share, but there was significant drop in Labour support to produce a net swing of 3.2 per cent from Labour to the Conservatives. This was enough to enable the Conservatives to take 31 seats from Labour (while also winning five from, and losing three to, the Liberal Democrats). In addition to the seats lost to the Conservatives, Labour lost twelve to the Liberal Democrats, two to the SNP and two to 'others'. The Liberal Democrats increased their share of the vote significantly but, as usual, found it difficult to convert popular support into seats won. Nonetheless, their total of 62 is the largest number won by a third party since before the Second World War. The most successful of the 'other' parties were UKIP with 2.3 per cent of votes (up 1.1 per cent on 2001), the Green Party (1.1 per cent, up 0.4 per cent) and the BNP (0.7 per cent, up 0.5 per cent) although all three had many more candidates than they had in 2001. The 'others' to win seats, apart from the Speaker, were George Galloway of Respect, who took Bethnal Green and Bow from Labour, Peter Law who won Blaenau Gwent standing in protest at Labour's imposition of an all-women shortlist of candidates on the usually very safe Labour constituency and Dr Richard Taylor who again won Wyre Forest as an independent candidate.

Table 2.3   Share of votes and number of seats won (Great Britain) and change from 2001

	Share of votes (%)	Change 2001–05	Number of seats	Change 2001–05
Conservative	33.2	+0.5	197	+32
Labour	36.2	−5.8	355	−47
Liberal Democrat	22.6	+3.9	62	+11
SNP/Plaid Cymru	2.2	−0.4	9	+1
Other	5.8	+1.9	4	+2

Note: The Speaker, who was not opposed by the Conservatives or Liberal Democrats, is treated as an 'other'. The election in Staffordshire South was postponed due to the death of a candidate. The change in seats calculations use the notional 2001 results in Scotland, where the total number of constituencies was reduced by 13 by the boundary revisions.

It is tempting to deduce from the figures in Table 2.3 that what happened in the election was that the Conservatives held on to their voters but that Labour leaked support to the Liberal Democrats and others. That may have been the main story but it cannot be inferred from the election results alone. It is likely that the 'flow of the vote' between 2001 and 2005 was more complex – with voters switching in all directions and moving into and out of non-voting – but in order to describe the ebbs and flows of voters which produced the final result individual level survey data are required. Only a partial 'flow-of-the-vote' table is available at the time of writing (from MORI) based on recall of 2001 vote and vote intention in 2005. The figures are shown in Table 2.4 and show that Labour had the lowest retention rate of the major parties, losing support to the Liberal Democrats but also to the Conservatives and others. This was partially balanced by switching from the Liberal Democrats to Labour but there was also significant movement from the Liberal Democrats to the Conservatives. The Conservatives themselves had a high retention rate (90 per cent) but also lost voters to the Liberal Democrats. Overall, the picture is clearly more complex than a simple reading of the election results suggests.

Table 2.4   Flow of the vote, 2001–05

	Vote 2001		
	Con	Lab	Lib Dem
Vote 2005	%	%	%
Con	90	8	12
Lab	2	72	6
LibDem	6	15	78
Other	2	5	4

Source: MORI aggregated campaign polls.

Table 2.5 gives a regional breakdown of shares of votes and seats won. With the exception of London, there remains a broad north–south division in terms of party support. Labour's strongest areas were the three northernmost English regions and its weakest the three southern regions – Eastern, South East and South West. In the latter two, indeed, Labour was third in popular support. The Conservatives were weakest in Scotland, Wales and the North and strongest in the South. Support for the Liberal Democrats was much more even across regions but they were relatively weak in Wales and the Midlands and strongest in the South West. A north–south division is even more apparent in terms of seats won. In Scotland, Wales and northern England the Conservatives won only 23 seats, compared with 210 won by Labour and 25 by the Liberal Democrats. In the south of England outside London, in contrast, Labour won only 45 seats compared with 120 for the Conservatives and 25 for the Liberal Democrats.

Table 2.6 shows changes in party support across regions. As can be seen, Labour declined across the board but did particularly badly in London and Eastern England. The Liberal Democrats advanced in every region, with especially notable increases in votes in the North East and Scotland. On the other hand there appears to be a 'ceiling effect' to Liberal Democrat support in that they made little further headway in the South East and South West – the two regions in which they were strongest in 2001. The Conservative share of the vote declined slightly in the North and Midlands but these losses were offset by increases in support elsewhere.

Table 2.5   Party shares of votes and seats won in regions, 2005 (%)

	Con	Lab	Lib Dem	SNP/PC	Other
North East	19.5	52.9	23.3	–	4.3
Seats	1	28	1		
North West	28.7	45.1	21.4	–	4.8
Seats	9	61	6		
Yorkshire/Humber	29.1	43.5	20.7	–	6.7
Seats	9	44	3		
East Midlands	37.0	39.0	18.5	–	5.5
Seats	18	25	1		
West Midlands	34.9	38.9	18.6	–	7.6
Seats	15	39	3		1
Eastern	43.3	29.8	21.8	–	5.0
Seats	40	13	3		
London	31.9	38.9	21.9	–	7.3
Seats	21	44	8		1
South East	45.0	24.4	25.4	–	5.3
Seats	58	19	6		
South West	38.6	22.8	32.5	–	6.1
Seats	22	13	16		
Wales	21.4	42.7	18.4	12.6	5.0
Seats	3	29	4	3	1
Scotland	15.8	38.9	22.6	17.7	5.0
Seats	1	40	11	6	1

Table 2.6   Change in shares of votes 2001–05, in regions

	Con	Lab	Lib Dem	SNP/PC	Other
North East	–1.8	–6.5	+6.6	–	+1.7
North West	–0.6	–5.6	+4.7	–	+1.5
Yorkshire/Humber	–1.1	–5.1	+3.6	–	+2.7
East Midlands	–0.3	–6.1	+3.1	–	+3.3
West Midlands	–0.1	–5.9	+3.9	–	+2.1
Eastern	+1.5	–7.0	+4.3	–	+1.6
London	+1.4	–8.5	+4.4	–	+2.6
South East	+2.1	–5.0	+1.7	–	+1.2
South West	+0.1	–3.5	+1.3	–	+2.1
Wales	+0.4	–5.9	+4.6	–1.7	+2.7
Scotland	+0.2	–4.4	+6.0	–2.4	+0.3

Although changes in party support were broadly similar across regions this was not true across constituencies. Indeed, as the results came in and in the immediate aftermath of the election, most commentators were struck by the extent to which the pattern of change varied from constituency to constituency. Writing in the *Daily Telegraph* (7 May), Anthony King began his analysis by saying that making sense of the election 'is like trying to discern patterns in a shattered mosaic'. The absence of uniformity is illustrated by the fact that all three major parties managed to increase their share of votes in some seats while declining in others. Excluding Scotland, the Conservatives were up in 323 seats but down in 245, Labour up in 31 and down in 537 and the Liberal Democrats up in 489 but down in 78. The differences between each party's best and worst performances are huge. The Liberal Democrats, for example, increased by more than 20 percentage points in four constituencies but dropped by more than nine points in five.

Variations in changes in party support across constituencies reflect the important role that local factors can play in general elections – the pattern of electoral competition in the constituency, variations in campaigning intensity, the popularity of the incumbent MP, whether there has been an intervening by-election, and so on. The effects of different patterns of competition are illustrated in Table 2.7 which shows how mean changes in support for the major parties varied according to which were in the top two places in 2001 and the presence or absence of UKIP and BNP candidates in 2005.

Table 2.7 Change in major party vote shares in constituencies (England and Wales), 2001–05

| | Top two parties in 2001 | | | UKIP Cand | | BNP Cand | |
	Con/Lab	Con/LD	Lab/LD	Yes	No	Yes	No
Con	+0.3	+1.1	−1.1	+0.5	−0.3	−1.0	+0.7
Lab	−6.8	−2.1	−7.1	−6.0	−6.0	−6.6	−5.8
Lib Dem	+4.1	0.0	+7.0	+3.4	+4.9	+3.4	+3.7
(N)	(401)	(97)	(46)	(470)	(92)	(116)	(445)

Note: The six seats in which there were by-elections between 2001 and 2005 are excluded.

The Conservatives did significantly worse in seats where Labour and the Liberal Democrats were the two leading parties – in other words, in constituencies where it did not really matter how they did – than in those where they were in contention but whether Labour or the Liberal Democrats were their main opponents made no significant difference to their performance. Labour did least badly in Conservative–Liberal Democrat contests, where it had less support to lose, but had similar losses where it was in contention with either the Conservatives or the Liberal Democrats. The differences between the changes in the Liberal

Democrat vote share in the different categories of seat are all significant. They did best when in contention with Labour, but made no headway in seats in which they were competition with the Conservatives.

On the face of it, it might be expected that UKIP represented something of a threat to the Conservatives. People who voted for UKIP, it seems not unreasonable to suppose, would otherwise have voted for the Conservatives, clearly the most Euro-sceptic of the major parties. Given that in 14 seats the number of UKIP votes exceeded Labour's majority over the Conservatives while in a further nine the Liberal Democrats' majority was smaller than the UKIP vote, it is tempting to conclude that UKIP cost the Conservatives a number of seats. The data in Table 2.7 suggest, however, that, if anything, the Conservatives did slightly better in seats where there was a UKIP candidate than in those where there wasn't. It appears, indeed, that it was the Liberal Democrats who suffered most from the UKIP presence – their advance where there was no UKIP candidate was significantly greater than in seats where there was one. Similarly, the Conservatives and Labour, on the whole, did slightly worse where a BNP candidate was in the field but this made no real difference to change in Liberal Democrat support.

The data in Table 2.7 give only a rough guide to patterns of change in party support. A fuller picture would require other variables, such as region, to be taken into account. We can explore changes in party support in more detail, however, by looking at correlation coefficients measuring the associations between changes in parties' shares of vote and a variety of social and political variables. Table 2.8 shows the relationships between changes in the parties' shares of the votes on the one hand and their former strength in the constituency concerned and the performance of UKIP and the BNP in the election on the other.

Table 2.8   Correlations with changes in party vote shares, 2001–05

	Change in % Con	*Change in % Lab*	*Change in % Lib Dem*
Con % 2001	0.240	0.264	−0.354
Lab % 2001	−0.226	−0.504	0.448
Lib Dem % 2001	–	0.457	−0.373
UKIP % 2005	–	0.155	−0.157
BNP % 2005	−0.325	−0.289	–

Note: Scottish constituencies and those having by-elections between 2001 and 2005 are excluded. The numbers for coefficients involving UKIP and the BNP are 470 and 116 respectively. In other cases they are 562 and 561 (for coefficients involving the Liberal Democrats). Only significant coefficients are shown.

The stronger the position of the Conservatives in 2001, the more they advanced in 2001. If the Conservative strategy was to solidify their core support, therefore, it was relatively successful. In contrast, Labour clearly lost most heavily where it had previously been stronger (coefficient –0.504). Moreover, it was in the strongest Labour seats that the Liberal Democrats increased their share of the votes most sharply (coefficient +0.448). These figures are consistent with the view that the Liberal Democrats were successful in detaching support from Labour, possibly due to discontent among the latter about the Iraq war. On the other hand, the 'ceiling' problem encountered by the Liberal Democrats is further illustrated here since the stronger their previous position the less they were able to improve in 2005 (coefficient –0.373).

Finally, this analysis also confirms the suggestions above relating to the impact of UKIP and the BNP. The level of support for UKIP had no effect on Conservative performance but tended to weaken that of the Liberal Democrats, while the better the BNP did, the poorer were the results for both the Conservatives and Labour.

When changes in party support are correlated with socio-demographic variables two particularly interesting results emerge. The first relates to the percentage of full-time students in a constituency. Labour's policy on university tuition fees was widely believed to have alienated students and contrasted sharply with the proposals of the Liberal Democrats. Possibly as a consequence of this, the more students there were in a constituency the more sharply Labour's vote share fell (correlation coefficient = –0.260) and that of the Liberal Democrats rose (coefficient = +0.350). Similarly, the Iraq war was thought likely to lead to a withdrawal of support from Labour on the part of Muslim voters. The data are certainly consistent with this speculation since the correlations between the percentage of the population who are Muslims and the change in Labour's vote share is –0.429 while for the Liberal Democrats it is +0.309.

It is certainly true to say that the patterns of changes in party support across constituencies between the 2005 and the 2005 general elections were complicated but they were not quite as bewildering as they might have appeared at first. Some sense can be made of them. What has been shown here is that the Conservatives maintained their vote most successfully in their stronger seats but were somewhat affected by increased support for the BNP (although not UKIP); Labour lost support almost everywhere, most heavily where the party was previously stronger and especially in seats with many students or Muslim voters; the Liberal Democrats generally increased support but hit a ceiling in their strongest areas while making most inroads in previously strong Labour constituencies and seats with large student and Muslim populations.

As with turnout, when we turn from change between elections to variations in absolute levels of support for the parties across constituencies we reach much more familiar territory. The patterns are very similar to those evident in previous elections. The correlations measuring the strength of association between the parties' vote shares in all British constituencies in 2001 and 2005 (using estimates for the Scottish constituencies in 2001) are +0.976 for the Conservatives, +0.972

for Labour and +0.915 for the Liberal Democrats (numbers for Conservative and Labour are 626 and for the Liberal Democrats 625). Moreover, the constituencies which deviated most sharply from what would have been expected in 2005 on the basis of 2001 performance are easily explained. Thus, Labour underperformed hugely in Blaenau Gwent for reasons already touched on; the Liberal Democrats most exceeded expectations in Brent East where they had won a by-election; the Conservatives had a greatly increased vote share in Brentwood and Ongar where in 2001 Martin Bell, standing as an independent, obtained more than 30 per cent of the votes.

Correlation coefficients measuring the associations between the shares of the vote obtained by the parties in the constituencies and a standard set of socio-demographic variables are shown in Table 2.9 and the data contain few surprises.

Table 2.9   Bivariate correlations between party shares of vote in 2005 and constituency characteristics

	Con	Lab	Lib Dem
% Professional & managerial	0.566	−0.570	0.316
% Manual workers	−0.621	0.625	−0.332
% Owner occupiers	0.612	−0.455	0.040*
% Social renters	−0.681	0.609	−0.185
% Private renters	0.014*	−0.156	0.266
% Aged 18–24	−0.386	0.233	0.106
% Aged 65+	0.307	−0.368	0.137
% In agriculture	0.310	−0.502	0.223
Persons per hectare	−0.311	0.311	−0.022*
% Ethnic minority	−0.224	0.237	−0.051*
% With degrees	0.188	−0.359	0.351
% With no car	−0.731	0.646	−0.163
(N)	(626)	(626)	(625)

Note: All coefficients are significant at the 0.01 level except those asterisked.

The Conservatives, as might be expected, had a larger share of the vote in constituencies where there were more professional and managerial workers, owner occupiers, older voters, people with degrees and in more rural areas. They performed less well where there were more manual workers, social renters, younger people, people belonging to ethnic minorities, those having no car and in more urban areas. The pattern of Labour support was almost a mirror image of that for the Conservatives while that for the Liberal Democrats was, broadly, a paler reflection of it. It is worth noting, however, that while Conservative support was negatively related to the size of the ethnic minority population the correlation coefficient in the case of the Liberal Democrats was not significant whereas in 2001 and previous elections it had been significantly negative.

Regression analyses reveal that for the Conservatives all of these variables except percentage of private renters are significant and together they account for 80.6 per cent of the variation in the Conservative vote across constituencies. In Labour's case, all except persons per hectare are significant and 75.8 per cent of variation is accounted for. Only five variables are significant in explaining constituency variations in the Liberal Democrat vote (proportion with a degree and without access to a car, employment in agriculture and the two variables indicating the age structure of the population) and they account for only 23.2 per cent of the variation. Even without taking region into account, it is clear that the distribution of support for the Conservatives and Labour remains highly structured by the social and demographic characteristics of constituencies. This is much less true of Liberal Democrat support and partially explains the difficulty that the third party faces in winning seats under the first-past-the-post system. A few comments on the operation of the electoral system conclude this discussion of the election results.

The electoral system

As noted above, the seats won by the Conservatives in 2001 did not reflect their national share of the vote and they entered the 2005 election at a severe disadvantage even although one source of their problems in this respect – the over-representation of Scotland – had been reduced in importance by the reduction in the number of Scottish MPs from 72 to 59. In this election, as in 2001, Conservative-won seats, on average, had larger electorates (a mean of 72,960) than those won by Labour (66,817) or the Liberal Democrats (69,451) and, as already described, a significantly higher average turnout. In addition, it was the Conservatives who suffered most from Liberal Democrat success. Of the 62 seats won by the Liberal Democrats the Conservatives came second in 42 while Labour was runner up in 19 (and Plaid Cymru in one).

The effect was that the Conservatives won 31.4 per cent of the seats for 33.2 per cent of the votes. On the face of it, this does not appear an unreasonable rate of return and two developments help to explain why it does not look as bad as it might have been. While the Conservatives won 17 of the 23 seats that they should have taken from Labour on a uniform 3.2 per cent swing, they also won a further 14 seats with a larger swing. In addition, they took three seats from the Liberal Democrats despite the national tide in the latter's favour. Nonetheless, the Conservatives' success in winning seats compares unfavourably with Labour's haul of 56.6 per cent of the seats with only 36.2 per cent of the votes. The ratio of votes for the two parties was approximately 52:48 in Labour's favour but the ratio of seats was 64:36. The first-past-the-post system is supposed to exaggerate the lead of the winning party when votes are translated into seats but the exaggeration in this case is far greater than even the 'cube rule' would predict. The Conservatives could feel particularly aggrieved that in England they outpolled Labour (35.7 per cent to 35.5 per cent) but won 93 fewer seats.

The electoral system remains biased against the Conservatives. On current constituency boundaries, if they achieved a swing of 1.5 per cent from Labour at the next election, which would bring the two parties level in terms of vote share, then (assuming that the Liberal Democrats and others held all of their current seats and that the swing was more or less uniform) that would still leave Labour with about 112 more seats than the Conservatives (and an overall majority in the House of Commons). To draw level in terms of seats the Conservatives need a swing of approximately 5.5 per cent (which would put them eight points ahead in share of the popular vote). Constituency boundaries in England and Wales are under review, however, and new boundaries should be in place by the next election. By making constituency electorates more equal in size this should reduce the bias in the system and the size of swing the Conservatives need to win more seats than Labour.

Explaining the outcome

Interesting though the analysis of election results is, it cannot take us very far in explaining the outcome of the election. For that, survey data are required and full accounts will appear in due course. For the moment, however, it is worth attempting preliminary answers to what appear to be the two key questions. Why, despite the government's difficulties with the issue of the Iraq war, did Labour beat the Conservatives? Why did the Liberal Democrats increase their vote share significantly?

The most recent volume in the BES series (Clark et al. 2004) argues that party choice in modern elections is to be understood as a consequence of two main factors – the electorate's evaluations of party leaders and evaluations of the relative competence and performance of the parties, especially in running the economy. On this basis there is no real difficulty in explaining Labour's victory over the Conservatives. Using YouGov data, Figure 2.3 shows the electorate's preferred Prime Minister from January 2003 (when YouGov began to ask the 'best Prime Minister' question on a regular basis) to March 2005. As can be seen, apart from a short period at the start of 2004 Tony Blair was the clearly preferred Prime Minister. During the campaign, YouGov continued to monitor opinion on this matter but little changed. Over five surveys, the proportion preferring Blair varied between 34 per cent and 37 per cent while Michael Howard's scores were always between 23 per cent and 25 per cent and Charles Kennedy's between 15 per cent and 18 per cent. Blair's leads were much smaller than those he had recorded over William Hague in the 2001 election – and that, no doubt, helps to explain Labour's decline in popularity – but they were clear and sustained. Whatever their misgivings about the Labour leader, the electorate clearly believed that he would be a better Prime Minster than either of his rivals and that goes a long way in explaining why Labour won.

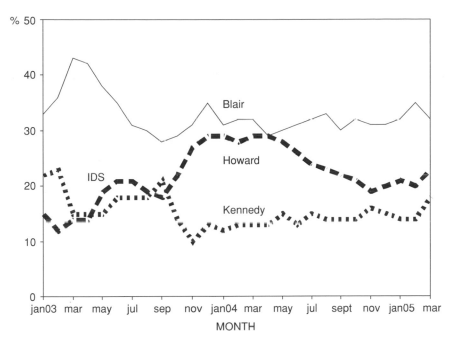

Figure 2.3 Best person for Prime Minister, January 2003–March 2005

Source: YouGov monthly polls for the *Daily Telegraph*.

Secondly, during the campaign YouGov regularly asked their respondents which party they thought was more likely to run the economy well. Over five surveys the proportion opting for the Conservatives averaged 28 per cent while those choosing Labour averaged 47 per cent. The economy may not be the only thing that matters in an election, but it does matter a lot and Labour's record in this respect put the party in a very strong position. As Helmut Norpoth (1992: 1) puts it, 'Prosperity spells r-e-e-l-e-c-t-i-o-n for governing parties'.

As for the Liberal Democrats, although Charles Kennedy once again made a favourable impression on voters (and also became a father at the start of the campaign) it seems likely that their improved performance can be largely attributed to their stance on the Iraq war. They were the only major party to oppose the war outright and called for the immediate repatriation of British troops. Towards the end of the campaign, YouGov reported that 25 per cent of respondents intending to vote Liberal Democrat said that they would probably have voted Labour but for the Iraq war. Unless this figure is very wide of the mark then it would appear that the Iraq issue accounts for almost all of the increase in Liberal Democrat support.

Conclusion

The Labour government could not have been happy with the outcome of the 2005 general election. To be sure, it was re-elected for a third term (an unprecedented achievement for Labour) with a solid overall majority in the House of Commons, but this was on the basis of the support of only 36 per cent of voters and 22 per cent of the electorate (and these figures would be even smaller if Northern Ireland were included). This outcome clearly evidences considerable disenchantment with the government and it remains to be seen whether the impending departure of Tony Blair as Prime Minister provides a fillip to party fortunes or causes significant electoral problems.

The Liberal Democrats, despite increasing their vote and making a net gain of ten seats might also have been somewhat disappointed. Although a total of 62 seats is far from negligible, it still represents a relatively poor return for almost 23 per cent of the votes and is nowhere near some of the more exaggerated claims that some Liberal Democrats were reported as making during the campaign about their likely successes. Moreover, the loss of five seats to the Conservatives is an ominous sign. The Liberal Democrats came first or second in 252 seats but that means that in the remaining 374 that they fought they came third or worse – usually by some distance. Three-party politics may have arrived in some parts of the country, but not all of it.

Writing in the aftermath of the 2001 election (Denver 2002: 25) I said that 'in 1997 the Conservatives were cast out into the electoral wilderness to wander for a time. Like the Israelites in the Old Testament, they needed a leader – a Moses – to take them to the promised land (electoral revival).' William Hague did not prove to be such a leader in 2001 and he resigned the Conservative leadership on the morning after the general election. Iain Duncan Smith replaced him, but proved unable to make much of an impact on the voters and was in turn replaced by Michael Howard in November 2003. Howard stemmed the tide in 2005 and inched the party forward on the road to recovery. Nonetheless, he immediately indicated that he would step down and the party began the process of choosing a new leader. Clearly, the Conservatives are facing a period of renewal and reinvention. In modern circumstances it is hugely important in electoral terms for parties to ensure that they have a popular leader able to 'connect' with the voters. To a considerable extent, therefore, the future electoral fate of the Conservatives is tied up with the leadership succession.

Notes

1. The BES data discussed in this paragraph are available on the BES website: <www.essex. ac.uk/bes>.
2. Turnout figures are provisional as there is some debate about the accuracy of the constituency electorate figures on which turnout calculations are based. To a large extent the difficulty arises because of the recently introduced system of 'rolling registration' whereby people can be added to the electoral register up to just a short time before an election.

References

Clarke, H., Sanders, D., Stewart, M. and Whiteley, P. (2004) *Political Choice in Britain*, Oxford: Oxford University Press.

Denver, D. (2002) 'The results: how Britain voted (or didn't)', in A. Geddes and J. Tonge (eds) *Labour's Second Landslide*, Manchester: Manchester University Press.

Norpoth, H. (1992) *Confidence Regained*, Michigan: University of Michigan Press.

Liverpool Riverside

Liverpool Riverside achieved infamy in 2001 as the constituency with the lowest ever turnout in a general election, a shockingly low 34.1 per cent. In 2005, the constituency achieved a hat-trick, returning the lowest turnout of any constituency at three successive general elections. The *Daily Mail* ran an April Fool's Day joke that Cherie Blair wanted to stand here at the next election; it is doubtful whether many in the constituency would notice her candidature.

Contrary to popular myth, Liverpool Riverside is not merely a run-down inner-city constituency. Along the regenerated waterfront, it contains some of Liverpool's most affluent professionals, working in a city widely regarded as undergoing a revival.

Moreover, there were signs of political life in the constituency in 2005. Turnout rose to 41.5 per cent, three times the size of the national increase in turnout of 2 per cent. The Liberal Democrats made some inroads into Labour's huge majority, cut from 13,950 to 10,214. Although nearly 6,000 more voters went to the polls, Labour's actual vote fell. The Liberal Democrats hold two-thirds of the seats on the city council and lie in second place, albeit mostly at a distance, in all Liverpool constituencies.

The Conservatives, thought to have expired in these parts, killed off in the 1980s by Thatcherism, increased their vote by 700, whilst the Greens performed well, saving their deposit. The Conservative candidate, Gabrielle Howatson, a product of Cheltenham Ladies' College and Cambridge University, brought unbridled enthusiasm to her party's campaign, even claiming 'affinity with the city' on the basis that 'my grandfather worked in Liverpool before the war as a captain for the James Moss shipping company' (*The Times*, 1 May 2005). Not all voters admired the Conservative chutzpah, the *Sunday Times* (29 April) reporting derision at the sight of blue rosettes in a pub ('Have Everton won?') and even one threat of violence.

For Labour's Louise Ellman, a high-profile MP in the region, the result was never a worry; the reputation of her constituency nonetheless remains cause for concern.

Result		%
Ellman, L. (Lab)	17,951	57.5
Marbrow, R. (LD)	7,737	24.8
Howatson, G. (Con)	2,843	9.1
Cranie, P. (Green)	1,707	5.5
Marshall, B. (Soc Lab)	498	1.6
Irving, A. (UKIP)	455	1.5
Lab hold		
Lab majority	10,214	32.7
Swing: Lab to LD		11.0

Turnout: 41.4%

3
Labour's Campaign: Neither Forward nor Back

Steven Fielding

Toward the end of 2004 Labour's Campaign Co-ordinator, Alan Milburn, predicted the forthcoming election campaign would 'be a clash of ideals and beliefs' in which the party's aims of 'social justice' within a 'fair society', of its desire to overcome poverty through unlocking individual aspiration could at last become fully manifest. Labour's election theme would be unlike that of 1997 ('it's time for a change') or that of 2001 ('give us more time'). For in 2005 it had 'to win on its merits' so Tony Blair's ministers were 'finally liberated to govern on our own terms' (Milburn 2004a, 2004b). Milburn's claims were infused with especial urgency because Blair had announced he would serve just one more term as Prime Minister. This would be his final campaign as leader. For allies like Milburn it was their last chance to, as he had earlier put it, 'transform New Labour from a strand of the Labour party to a movement that transforms the party itself' (*Guardian*, 16 December 2003).

As a consequence, in 2005 Blairites – and their opponents in the party – conducted two campaigns. The first and, most presumed the easiest, was to ensure the party's return to office by defeating the Conservatives; the second was to determine the government's direction during Blair's final term. These campaigns were necessarily interrelated: the bigger Labour's Commons majority, the greater would be the impetus behind the Prime Minister. In fact, Labour's election slogan, 'Forward not back', was suitable for both. It was ostensibly designed to exhort voters to support Labour's tax-funded improvements to the public services and its successful economic management and disavow returning to Conservative tax cuts and 'boom and bust'. However, it also echoed Blair's 2003 Labour conference speech when, facing calls to resign, he took on his many critics and urged those present:

> Get rid of the false choice: principles or no principles. Replace it with the true choice. Forward or back. I can only go one way. I've not got a reverse gear. (Blair 2003)

It was this second campaign – to define what Milburn meant by governing 'on our own terms', indeed to finally determine New Labour's identity – that consumed most attention in the months prior to Blair's announcement of the general election date.

As we know, Labour was re-elected, but with a much-reduced Commons majority and a considerably smaller share of the popular vote. Blair returned to Downing Street with calls for his resignation echoing about his ears: the election had turned out to be a referendum on the Prime Minister and his pursuit of one particular policy. Speaking immediately after his count, George Galloway, the newly elected Respect MP in the hitherto solidly Labour constituency of Bethnal Green and Bow declared:

> Mr Blair, this is for Iraq. All the people you have killed, all the lies you told, have come back to haunt you ... This defeat that you have suffered, and all the other defeats that New Labour has suffered this evening, is for Iraq.

Blair's support for President George Bush's toppling of Saddam Hussein in 2003, under cover of a 'War on Terror' that followed al-Qaeda's attack on the United States, overshadowed both campaigns to an unexpected extent. It set Blair against public opinion, dramatically undermining their trust in him personally, if not the government in general. Iraq also compounded doubts amongst Labour MPs about Blair's leadership, crystallising discontent even amongst former supporters. Many now looked to the Chancellor Gordon Brown to provide them with what they hoped would be a new direction.

The 2005 campaign was, then, an important moment in the party's development. If it did not point clearly to the future it denied Blair a firm platform on which to build what he had hoped would be an 'unremittingly New Labour' third term (BBC 2005a). As one of the Prime Minister's advisors ruefully remarked, after the election: 'Our slogan was "Forward not back". Three words, but we didn't talk enough about the first one' (*The Times*, 7 May 2005).

A lack of direction?

The idea of New Labour had never been fully accepted within the party (Fielding 2003: 1–17). As articulated by Blair it was extraordinarily successful at winning general elections, but many still questioned its substantive character. For a significant proportion in Labour's ranks thought his pursuit of votes in 'Middle England' had turned their party into an uncritical enthusiast for the free market with little regard for reducing inequality. Some long-established critics, notably the ex-Communist Martin Jacques, believed this trade-off between votes and principles was inherent to New Labour, that its advocates were all adherents of a milder form of Thatcherism (*Guardian*, 20 July 2004). Others, like Neal Lawson of the left-wing pressure group Compass, who had initially seen Blair as a vital means of winning over key voters, believed that while compromises had been necessary they did not have to include abandoning long-established ideals. They were however increasingly troubled by the alacrity with which Blair diluted the party's commitment to egalitarianism to maintain the party's electoral position (*Guardian*, 2 April 2005). Adherents of this latter view believed Brown would allow New Labour to recapture its social democratic potential while retaining its grip on national office.

Concerns about Blair's lack of radicalism were largely suppressed during Labour's first term, which was dedicated to ensuring the electoral coalition that gave Labour victory in 1997 was secured for a second period in office. That had meant maintaining economic growth while outlining plans to significantly increase government spending on the public services. Labour regained power in 2001 aiming to apply its 'invest and reform' programme in health and education, believing this would improve the services and help reduce inequality.

If that looked like a fairly ambitious programme, according to the Cabinet minister Robin Cook, from the outset 'caution rather than idealism' marked Labour's second term (Cook 2004: 1–2). Cook had never fully embraced New Labour but others, such as Peter Hain his successor as Leader of the Commons, were similarly concerned about the government's lack of radicalism, especially in relation to income redistribution. Much to Blair's annoyance Hain even called for a public debate on the merits of raising direct tax, bemoaning the fact that the party's 'vision of a progressive society' was a long way from realisation (*Independent*, 17 September 2003). Authoritative analysts claimed that while, since 1997, child and pensioner poverty had fallen overall Britain remained a starkly unequal society (Hills and Stewart 2005; Institute for Fiscal Studies 2005). Popular views about social justice had also changed little during Blair's time in office. If many believed inequality was too great and some supported redistribution such views were weakly held and few considered the issue important (Taylor-Gooby 2005). The denizens of Middle England remained particularly opposed to tax-funded measures they thought would only help the poor (*Guardian*, 22 April 2003; Opinion Leader Research 2003). Not wishing to undermine his support in the suburbs, the Prime Minister shied away from actively campaigning for greater social justice (Taylor-Gooby 2005: 16; Oppenheim 2004).

Even those close to Blair expressed their (mostly) private frustration with the government's lack of direction. Yet for much of his second term Blair saw no need to change a formula that had already won two elections. This reluctance was compounded by the Prime Minister's preoccupation with the 'War on Terror' and the subsequent invasions of Afghanistan and Iraq (Cook 2004: 10, 44, 76, 120–1, 126–7, 245, 302–5; Mulgan 2005: 28). In contrast, partly due to his frustrated desire to replace Blair, Brown began to articulate an alternative version of New Labour. For example, in opposition to tuition fees, Brown thought a graduate tax was the preferable way to finance the universities, as it would fall less heavily on the poor. The Prime Minister, however, feared antagonising Middle England by expecting them to pay more and insisted on fees (Peston 2005: 309–15). More broadly, although usually through surrogates (such as the junior minister Douglas Alexander), the Chancellor spoke of the need for government to refashion popular opinion and create a 'progressive consensus', by appealing to voters' morals as well as their financial self-interest (*Guardian*, 9 November 2004).

Public service reform

Improving the performance of the state-funded health and education services was critical to the government's fortunes as 'invest and reform' was designed to appeal to all parts of Labour's electoral coalition. Consumer-centred reforms were meant to address Middle England's concerns while spending more on provision would, it was believed, find favour with 'traditional' working-class voters. This was at once idealistic – aiming to reduce inequalities through government action – and ostensibly pragmatic – relying on private providers if they enhanced efficiency. It was also potentially very popular. For if measures designed to just help the poor alienated the better off, most voters endorsed improving those public services from which all could benefit (Taylor-Gooby 2005: 7, 11–12). Finally, some hoped, if successful the programme would rebuild social cohesion by restoring faith in government intervention on behalf of the collective interest.

Despite Brown not raising the basic rate of income tax, Britons still paid more in tax during Labour's first term, given the Chancellor's skill at finding covert ways of raising revenue. In 2002, however, Brown increased National Insurance contributions, openly redistributing income from rich to poor, albeit under the auspices of financing improvements in the NHS. Brown's Spending Review of the same year also committed government to augmenting public spending as a share of the gross domestic product from 39 per cent in 2001–02 to 42 per cent in 2005–06. No wonder Lady Thatcher attacked New Labour's 'reversion' to Old Labour's 'irresponsible policies of tax and spend' (*Independent*, 1 May 2003). Despite this, Brown's popularity rose to well above Blair's while his tax-raising Budget was approved by up to two-thirds of those polled. Those concerned about Blair's apparently uncritical support for US preparations to invade Iraq began to look to the Chancellor as a left-wing alternative to the Prime Minister (Bower 2005: 394–5).

Taking their lead from Brown, ministers claimed they spent wisely. Front-line staff was better paid and the numbers rising, while a variety of measures indicated standards and efficiency were improving. Yet as they also conceded, not everything was perfect. In the NHS waiting lists remained problematic while hospital cleanliness was an issue; in the schools discipline was imperfect while poverty still strongly influenced pupil performances. Blair was conscious that voters in Middle England, the ones paying more in tax, would expect a noticeably improved service and feared Labour would pay an electoral penalty if they thought it had not (*Observer*, 28 September 2003). There was in fact a popular prejudice against government spending. In 2002 only 35 per cent thought the state could spend money 'wisely', something the Conservatives exploited by highlighting instances that encouraged the impression rising taxes were being wasted (Taylor-Gooby 2005: 13). This was why Blair believed 'reform' had to accompany 'investment'. By 'reform' he meant the introduction of market mechanisms (and in some cases private companies) into theoretically public provision to improve efficiency and give the 'consumer' (in other words the parent or patient) greater 'choice'. While claiming to be pragmatic on this matter, some believed the Prime Minister was prejudiced in favour of such innovation and dogmatically ill-disposed to non-market solutions.

Blair's emphasis on market-based reforms led to problems with public sector trade unions: they feared redundancies and worsening pay and conditions. It also raised questions within the party about the extent to which 'choice' would undermine the egalitarian impact of improved public services. Despite that Blair encouraged Milburn (when Health Secretary) in his enthusiasm for 'foundation' hospitals – non-profit public interest companies independent of Whitehall that would enjoy financial freedom to expand – as both men saw them as vital to the future of the NHS. However, many MPs feared they would create a two-tier health system in which the better off would disproportionately benefit. The Chancellor shared their misgivings, but was mostly concerned about how these hospitals would increase public spending free of Treasury (and so his) control. In the subsequent struggle Brown prevailed, denuding foundation hospitals of many of their freedoms, much to the relief of party members. Having been thwarted on such a key issue Milburn chose to return to the backbenches. Brown, again spurred on by his own alienation from Blair, went on to develop an argument about the need to limit public service reform. He defended the virtues of the 'public service ethos' against the imposition of contracts and markets. While not an unqualified friend of public service unions, there were, he suggested, parts of the state sector that should always remain free from the kind of reform favoured by Number 10. In any case, he believed, greater efficiency did not always depend on the market (Peston 2005: 295–309). As a consequence, Blairites became convinced, their kind of changes would only come about once Brown had been removed from the Treasury.

The political consequences of Iraq

Blair was preparing to persuade the TUC of the need to accept public service reform when he heard of the attacks on the Twin Towers and the Pentagon. From that point the 'war on terror' dominated his horizons and led the Prime Minister to support the US invasion of Iraq, a decision that destroyed his credibility with many voters, provoked the resignation of two Cabinet ministers, gave energy to long-standing critics within his party and ended the possibility of an 'unremittingly New Labour' third term.

The principal cause of Blair's difficulties was a dossier he presented to the Commons in September 2002, which claimed Iraq could deploy weapons of mass destruction within 45 minutes. There were many other similarly dubious claims made during this period, but the provenance of that single assertion became critical. It was, in fact, based on one uncorroborated source, although Number 10 gave the impression it was indisputable fact. This led the BBC journalist Andrew Gilligan to assert that Alastair Campbell (Blair's director of communications) had pressured the security services to 'sex up' the dossier so it would better impress a public sceptical of the need to end Saddam's regime. Matters were complicated by the suicide of the government weapons advisor David Kelly after he was exposed as Gilligan's source.

The Parliamentary Security and Intelligence Committee, Commons Foreign Affairs Committee, the Hutton Inquiry into the circumstances surrounding Kelly's death and the Butler Inquiry into the use of intelligence all looked at different aspects of the matter. Each investigation questioned the veracity of the intelligence published prior to the war but none directly argued Blair had deliberately exaggerated the threat posed by Saddam. Campbell nonetheless resigned, hoping to draw a line under the issue, while Number 10 claimed the era of 'spin' was over. Few in the public, however, believed the Prime Minister had told the truth – certainly none of the 2 million or so who protested against the war in London in February 2003. Most considered Britain had gone to war not, as Blair argued, to disarm a rogue state that had consistently defied the UN but as a participant in an illegal war launched by the reactionary Bush administration for its own imperial reasons.

According to the pollsters ICM, support for Labour dropped significantly after the first twelve months of its second term: in 2001–02 it reached a maximum of 47 per cent, but during 2002–03 it never exceeded 42 per cent and throughout 2003–05 the party rose no higher than 39 per cent. Yet even at Labour's lowest point, in June 2004 when only 34 per cent of those polled said they would vote for the party, it still enjoyed a 3 per cent lead over the Conservatives (ICM 2005). Moreover, biases inherent to the electoral system, including outdated constituency boundaries, meant even that slim lead would be enough to see Blair retain a comfortable Commons majority.

The main reason for the party's decline was the invasion of Iraq: some claimed the war was responsible for the loss of three percentage points. Ironically, some of Blair's advisors had hoped for a 'Baghdad Bounce', a projected massive rise in the Prime Minister's popularity after a rapid and bloodless victory, during which they aimed to push through far-reaching changes in the public services and sideline Brown. As the war concluded quickly and British casualties were slight Blair did enjoy a brief upsurge in support. However, the failure to find weapons of mass destruction, a widening belief Blair had lied and the worsening security position in Iraq ensured there was no 'Bounce'. Indeed, by the eve of Labour's 2003 conference one poll indicated that half the public (and even 40 per cent of party members) wanted the Prime Minister to resign (Cronin 2005: 469–72). Such were the depths to which Blair had sunk in November 2003 that he discussed with Brown the possibility of resigning before the next election. After so long waiting, the Chancellor convinced himself his chance to become Prime Minister had finally come (Bower 2005: 434–7).

The local and European elections held in June 2004 persuaded Blair to stay on: despite Labour doing very badly the Conservatives also performed disappointingly. Strategists hoped that having – as John Prescott put it – given the party 'a kicking' over Iraq, in the forthcoming general election voters would focus on domestic matters. Polling evidence suggested Iraq did not figure as an issue that would influence how many people would vote – unlike the economy, health and education on which Labour enjoyed a striking lead over the Conservatives. A 'protest' vote was acceptable in minor contests but they rationalised, when it came to determining the occupant of 10 Downing Street voters would return to Labour. Brown took the Prime Minister's change of heart as a betrayal, feeling he had been duped, and that did nothing to improve the two men's fraught relationship (Bower 2005: 455–9).

Iraq also weakened Blair within his own party. In January 2004 he was faced with an unprecedented backbench revolt over tuition fees: despite Brown's reluctant support, the government's majority fell to five. At the last National Policy Forum meeting before the election, in July 2004 the unions also extracted various concessions from the leadership, most notably to review its attitude to pay and conditions in the public services (*Guardian*, 7 August 2004). Disillusion with Blair also accelerated the decline in party membership: official figures showed that by the end of 2003 there were 214,952 in the party, which meant the number had almost halved in size since 1997. The most obvious collapse was in the inner cities, where it was not unusual to find Constituency Labour Parties with only 200 members, most of who were ageing, inactive and unenthusiastic about their leader (*Guardian*, 27 July 2004; ICM 2004). Indeed, it was two Labour members who described Blair as: 'a man we believe to be the slipperiest, most profoundly disliked politician to hold the office of prime minister in our lifetime' (*Guardian*, 22 March 2005). It was unlikely such people would want to help their leader win an 'unremittingly New Labour' campaign.

The 'pre-campaign'

In September 2004 Blair reshuffled the Cabinet, laying the foundations for his 'unremitting' third term. He brought Milburn back as Campaign Coordinator, having some months before asked him to write an early draft of the manifesto. In January 2005 Campbell also returned as Head of Strategic Election Communications, second only to Milburn in the campaign hierarchy. Brown was left in the cold, even though he had assumed Milburn's lead role during the two earlier campaigns. This, Blairites anticipated, was to be the Prime Minister's election and his victory because, even as late as March 2005 Milburn believed: 'Nobody better expresses what the modern Labour Party stands for, what the country wants' (*Independent*, 28 March 2005).

The 'politics of aspiration' was Milburn's 'big idea', which he claimed would 'renew New Labour for a third term' and imbue the party's campaign with a positive message (Milburn 2004a, 2005; *Independent*, 28 March 2005). Labour, he said, should commit itself to building 'an opportunity society where the chance to get on is extended from a privileged few to all who are prepared to work hard and play by the rules, so that Britain becomes a nation based on merit, not class'. Recognising that income inequality had increased since 1979 and that Labour had reduced it, but only slightly, Milburn argued government could address the problem by fostering greater social mobility through equalising opportunities. That meant enhancing state support for skills training; extending a welfare state that improved employability; improving access to education; and building public services around personalised care. Such measures would enable 'hard-working families' to achieve their individual ambitions and from that all would benefit. Fairer access to opportunities would result in less poverty, lower unemployment and crime and a better-developed sense of social cohesion. Unlocking hitherto frustrated talents amongst the less well off would also have significant economic returns: fairness, Milburn asserted, meant a more efficient economy.

For observers of Labour's 2001 campaign this 'big idea' was familiar: Blair had outlined it during speeches largely overlooked by the media (Fielding 2002: 33–6). Milburn, like Blair, argued for the reduction of inequality in terms acceptable to Middle England while mining themes developed by post-war social democrats and chiming with Brown's own attempt to reinvent Labour's purpose for the twenty-first century. Yet as with every ideological vision, there were significant differences over how it should be achieved: it was clear that Milburn and the Prime Minister still looked on market-style reform of the public services as critical to the 'opportunity society'.

This 'big idea' was in any case obscured by Blair's desire to address public concerns over immigration, asylum and policing: as a result 'safety and security' lay at the heart of the Queen's Speech of November 2004. Popular fears did not reflect reality – crime was falling and asylum applications declining – but the Prime Minister's object was to neutralise one of the Conservatives' few strengths. The Prevention of Terrorism Bill in particular, which included proposals for identity cards and restricting the movements of those merely suspected of terrorist activities – was primarily meant to prevent the Conservatives outflanking Labour.

That it might also compromise civil liberties with no guaranteed reduction of the terrorist threat was, cynics suggested, beside the point.

During the early New Year Labour brought out posters underlining its economic achievements and warning of the Conservatives' threat to stability, the main emphasis being on the latter. This was deliberately 'negative', for while claiming to want to make the campaign forward-looking Milburn also needed to prevent it becoming a referendum on Labour's record. He knew that would be disastrous: instead strategists wanted to present voters with a choice between Labour and the Conservatives, believing they could only win from the comparison. That meant, paradoxically, making the Conservatives look more of a threat than they were and then discrediting them, by claiming the party was incompetent and still Thatcherite. In other words it involved convincing doubtful voters that there was something worse than another Blair term: an administration led by Michael Howard.

Attempts to undermine the Conservative leader and his Shadow Chancellor misfired, however, when one proposed poster placed on Labour's website depicted them as flying pigs over the slogan 'The Day the Tory Sums Add Up'. Showing a hitherto unsuspected adherence to political correctness Conservatives claimed they were offended by this weak visual gag, saying it was anti-Semitic given both men were Jewish. The posters were quickly withdrawn. More seriously, when Blair claimed a Conservative government would impose £35 billion of cuts on public services he was exposed as disingenuous, thereby reinforcing his post-Iraq reputation. For while the assertion sounded ominous (it was the equivalent of sacking every teacher, GP and nurse) rather than being a cut it was in fact a projection of how much less the Conservatives would spend by 2011–12 compared to Labour.

In February Labour produced a new pledge card, which Blair launched by travelling the country by helicopter to six different locations (all marginal seats) to unveil each promise. The Prime Minister also appeared on a variety of what were, for politicians, unusual television outlets. He was interviewed on Channel 4's youth strand T4 and on the same channel's late-afternoon *Richard and Judy* show, which was popular with housewives and older voters. He also spent much of one day on Channel 5. These appearances were supposed to allow Blair to discuss with studio audiences issues of importance to viewers in a direct and informal way. It meant the Prime Minister was sometimes told he was talking 'rubbish' and forced to admit fallibility when confronted by individual problems. Such occasions nonetheless also enabled him to put his case, most usually about the Iraq war, in the run-up to which this 'masochism strategy' had been developed to let him confront objections to invasion. This was an intriguing device, which Blair hoped would reconnect him with a sceptical public for whom 'politics' was an alien domain: 'It's the modern equivalent of Gladstone doing his public meetings', he claimed (*Observer*, 6 March 2005). Whether Gladstone would have allowed himself (as did Blair) to be interviewed on a Saturday night ITV show by two 10-year-old boys, and forced to endure their impertinent remarks about his wife's underwear is something historians may never be able to confirm.

Despite these efforts, Labour's poll lead fell. That was partly due to the Conservatives' enthusiastic embrace of a number of populist issues – such as travellers' sites – and their highlighting of poignant individual cases they claimed showed spending on the NHS and schools was not working. These efforts took Labour strategists aback by grabbing the headlines and preventing them getting their own message across. Some, however, blamed the party's 'negative' campaign, claiming Labour needed to give voters a positive reason to come out and vote. 'Simply saying we are not the Tories will not be good enough to secure victory', Hain told the Welsh Labour Party. Instead Labour needed to convince voters 'we have the positive policies to meet the challenges of the future' (*Daily Telegraph*, 19 March 2005). If there were genuine concerns about its tone, Brown supporters attacked the campaign for other reasons.

Brown's absence from the centre of activity became especially obvious when he presented the Budget in mid-March in which the Chancellor dispensed modest benefits to pensioners, homebuyers and low paid workers with children. If it included nothing dramatic, the Budget confirmed the economy's strength and underlined Brown's role. It was well received by the public who continued to give Labour a two-to-one lead over the Conservatives in economic policy. Thus when Howard claimed Brown would again increase National Insurance after the election he made little impact – because most voters assumed Labour would do that anyway and trusted Brown to run the economy better than his Conservative counterpart.

The Budget confirmed Brown's position as Labour's most popular and trusted leader, his appeal being strongest with those Blair's pollster Philip Gould termed 'Labour doubtfuls'. These were people who could give the party a healthy Commons majority – if only they were persuaded to vote, and avoided the attractions of the anti-war Liberal Democrats or any other 'protest' party. Accordingly Blair felt obliged to give Brown a leading role in the campaign and reluctantly abandon his 'unremitting' strategy. For Brown, not Blair, could persuade such voters to overlook their misgivings about Labour's record on tuition fees, public service reform and Iraq.

After protracted negotiations Brown was given the lead on economic and public service issues and became responsible for the campaign in the marginal seats. Prominent Brownites Ed Balls and Douglas Alexander were appointed to the main strategy committee. Blair was also to be accompanied by his Chancellor to numerous public events, so each had equal billing. Labour's economic achievements, rather than the promise of further public service reform, now became the bedrock of the campaign. Despite brave words to the contrary Blair was simply too damaged to lead the kind of forward-looking campaign Milburn had hoped to engineer. Indeed, while retaining a role at Labour's London headquarters, it was hard to see what of importance the Campaign Coordinator had left to do.

A 'quintessentially New Labour' campaign

When Blair took the short but long-anticipated journey to Buckingham Palace on 5 April, ICM gave Labour a three-point lead over the Conservatives, although MORI showed that, amongst those who said they were certain to vote, Labour trailed by five points. This confirmed the party's need to convince the 'doubtfuls' to vote and meant, as one Blair aide admitted, the campaign 'is not about middle Britain anymore ... for the first time in a long time we are focusing on our traditional supporters' (*Sunday Times*, 10 April 2005). Thus on 6 April the *Daily Mirror* – which had opposed the Iraq war under its previous editor and was read by many long-standing Labour supporters – published a 'personal letter' from the Prime Minister. He rehearsed the party's main themes: the economy was stronger; schools and hospitals had improved; more were in work; mortgages were cheaper; and Britain was a fairer country in which pensioner and child poverty had fallen. Forced to acknowledge disagreements over Iraq, Blair claimed that unless *Mirror* readers actually voted Labour they would give the Conservatives the chance to reverse all that had been achieved since 1997. Labour strategists continued to play up this Conservative threat, hoping Howard on his own might scare doubtfuls into supporting Blair, resulting in him featuring heavily on posters and being the subject of Labour's second election broadcast.

Technologically, Labour's campaign was much like the previous two. Most of the party's £15 million war chest was spent on those 800,000 voters in the 60 battleground marginal constituencies who usually determined the outcome of general elections. Employees at Labour's national call centre were meant to phone 500,000 of them between January and polling day. Like its opponents, Labour used Mosaic software to send material tailored to these voters' individual interests. DVDs were also despatched; these included an address by the local candidate as well as warnings about Howard and a message from Blair. It was said that the Prime Minister would communicate more directly with voters than hitherto, sending targeted emails and running a video diary on the party website. He also held 'surgeries' in shopping centres with invited members of the public. Presented by aides as a better way of engaging with the public than press conferences, in reality Prime Ministerial events were tightly controlled, usually with only photogenic 'rent-a-crowds' in attendance. In fact, the main comparison with 1997 and 2001 was how little the 2005 campaign was built around Blair. His smiling face, previously omnipresent, was absent from party propaganda unless juxtaposed against Howard or accompanied by Brown – and, when he appeared, Blair's expression was invariably serious and 'statesmanlike'.

The story was the same when Labour launched its manifesto: in contrast with the past there was no glitz, no glamour, and no personality cult. Blair was flanked by six colleagues on the platform and behind them sat the rest of the Cabinet: the Prime Minister was presented as one member of a bigger team. The manifesto itself was also deliberately 'un-spun', containing as many as 300 pledges and comprised 23,000 words with but one black-and-white picture of the Prime Minister. In terms of its substance Blair described the manifesto as 'quintessentially New Labour', the more aggressive 'unremittingly' having now been abandoned. He had been forced to compromise on a number of issues. The education section for example had been watered down because Ruth Kelly objected to the number of schools Blairites wanted to be allowed to select by ability and was sceptical about the projected role ceded to private companies. Blair even felt obliged to claim Labour's programme 'will embed a new progressive consensus', a hitherto Brownite phrase (Labour Party 2005: 5–7). The manifesto nonetheless echoed Milburn's 'big idea', with the devil necessarily residing in the detail. How far this was a Blairite manifesto written in Brownite language or a Brownite manifesto written in Blairite language would only become apparent once power had been regained.

According to the opinion polls, by the mid-point in the campaign, Labour's vote had solidified: those supporting the party were now saying they were more likely to turn out and vote than they had been on 5 April. As the party enjoyed a consistent if unspectacular lead over the Conservatives, Labour could now be confident of securing some sort of Commons majority. If it had inflicted any damage, Howard's focus on immigration and asylum had done its worst. Some even suggested he had helped shore up Labour by forcing anti-racist 'doubters' to back Blair. The security of Labour's modest lead was confirmed by the limited impact a series of unfortunate events occurring during the campaign had on the party. The closure of the troubled car manufacturer MG Rover; the conclusion of the trial of an illegal immigrant involved in terrorist activities who had murdered a police officer; and the stabbing of a young mother in front of her son in a Surrey village had failed to dent Labour's ascendancy over the Conservatives.

Labour's leaders were no longer anxious about retaining power (if they had ever been), as was confirmed by their enthusiastic manoeuvrings in anticipation of a post-election Cabinet reshuffle. They remained concerned however about the size of Labour's majority. As polling day approached turnout remained the key issue, especially in marginal constituencies, where contests were, as usual, closer than national opinion poll figures indicated. Thus, when the last week of the campaign came to be dominated by Iraq, strategists became concerned. It was known that the Liberal Democrats would highlight the war but the alacrity with which Howard took up the issue took many by surprise: Howard rather than Charles Kennedy accused Blair of lying over weapons of mass destruction. Up to this point, Iraq had been nowhere and yet it had been everywhere, underpinning as it did Blair's unpopularity. If few told pollsters the war was an issue that would influence their party choice, for many it gave coherence to more disparate doubts about the Prime Minister.

During the last week Labour wanted to discuss the economy and education and adopt a more positive tone in the run-up to polling. Instead Blair had to respond to the leak of the Attorney General's unpublished advice regarding the legality of the war. Lord Goldsmith had told Parliament he believed the invasion was legal so far as international law was concerned. This draft suggested that in private he was more equivocal. The implication drawn by many was that Blair had pressured Goldsmith to fall into line, and that the invasion was, as critics alleged, illegal. Howard and Kennedy used the issue to draw voters' attention to why they should no longer trust the Prime Minister's words on any issue.

Having previously refused to publish the Attorney's full advice, Blair relented on 28 April to prove that he had not forced him to change his mind. This failed to convince many and was just the start of his darkest day of the campaign. Along with Brown the Prime Minister had wanted to launch the party's business manifesto but was forced to defend his integrity. Journalists put Blair under so much pressure that Brown issued what was effectively a vote of confidence: 'I not only trust Tony Blair', he said, 'but I respect him for the way he went about that decision involving all members of the cabinet.' The day concluded on an even more dispiriting note when members of a BBC studio audience booed Blair before he had taken his seat to take their questions. Sweating profusely he looked embattled and out of touch, being unable to answer complaints about GP waiting times.

As polling day loomed, Labour returned to the 'threat' of a Conservative government, claiming that if one in ten of its supporters failed to vote for the party then Howard would get into Downing Street. Most experts ridiculed the claim and few voters believed it: most assumed a Labour government was a certainty. There was it seemed little that could be done to deter Labour 'doubters' from casting a 'protest' vote, even in marginals where the Liberal Democrats (rather than the Conservatives) were causing concern. Labour had spent most of its energy attacking Howard and had let Kennedy off the hook: it began to look like strategists had miscalculated. In any case, attention was again brought back to Iraq after the announcement of the 87th British fatality there, followed by emotional television interviews with the soldier's distraught widow, who blamed Blair for his death. The party was now so desperate, it even drafted in the 80-year old Tony Benn, a long time New Labour bogeyman, who phoned doubtfuls to reassure them they could oppose the Iraq war and still vote Labour.

Results and reactions

Despite all its efforts, Labour's share of the vote was similar to the one indicated by opinion polls on the eve of the campaign. Overall, Labour won 3 per cent more votes than the Conservatives, retaining a lead over Howard's party in all gender, class and age categories, apart from the middle class and retired, although amongst lower-middle-class voters the parties were virtually level pegging (see Table 3.1). Notwithstanding its place in the popular vote, Labour once again benefited from the lopsided nature of the electoral system, gaining 356 Commons seats, 55 per cent of the total, and a majority of 67.

Table 3.1   The Labour vote

	%	*Lab lead over Con*
Men	38	5
Women	38	6
AB (middle class)	32	–5
C1 (lower middle class)	35	1
C2 (skilled manual)	43	11
DE (unskilled manual)	45	17
18–24	42	18
25–34	42	18
35–64	38	5
65+	35	–7
Home owners	39	9
Council Tenants	56	40
All	36	3

Source: BBC (2005b).

If there had been a notional 3 per cent swing from Labour to the Conservatives since 2001, it was only in London and adjacent parts of the South East that Labour lost a significant number of seats in straight fights with Howard's party. Elsewhere Labour saw the Liberal Democrats and parties as diverse as the Greens, the British National Party and Respect all benefit from its unpopularity. In some cases, this shift in support allowed the Conservatives to win seats, despite a drop in its own vote. There were nonetheless some massive shifts of support from Labour to the Liberal Democrats, allowing Kennedy's party to take constituencies like Cardiff Central, Hornsey and Wood Green, Cambridge, Bristol West and Manchester Withington. Respect also did well at Labour's expense in London's East End and Birmingham, although only in Bethnal Green and Bow did a seat fall into their hands.

Most post-war Prime Ministers would have been happy with a majority of 67, but things looked very different after two terms with three-figure leads. Most interpretations of the result echoed that of the *Sun* headline of 6 May, which claimed Blair had been 'Kicked in the ballots'. For anecdotal evidence suggested Labour had fallen foul of the much-feared 'protest' vote, cast by those who continued to doubt the Prime Minister until the last. Numerous candidates claimed they had endured the same experience, meeting people who said they would have voted Labour had it not been for Blair and Iraq. When an apparently chastened Prime Minister returned to Downing Street he claimed to have 'listened and learned', but obviously not to MPs like Cook who led calls for him to resign 'sooner rather than later' (*Guardian*, 7 May 2005).

The 2005 campaign had seriously weakened Blair and most doubted he could remain in office for a full parliamentary term. Indeed, within hours of the result one Labour MP predicted his days in power would be few in number as the 'arse-lickers' in the party were already 'looking for a new arse to lick' (*The Times*, 7 May 2005). Blair's Cabinet reshuffle confirmed his lack of power. Brown was confirmed at the Treasury even before the campaign had begun while Milburn had announced his intention of returning to the backbenches on election night. Moreover, Brown's support for Jack Straw meant he remained as Foreign Secretary, despite Blair's intentions, while the Prime Minister's plan to put David Miliband and Andrew Adonis in charge of Education were stymied.

The Queen's Speech outlined a superficially ambitious programme of 45 Bills but its substance gave little sign of the promised 'unremittingly New Labour' agenda. It was underpinned by Blair's desire to 'foster a culture of respect', meant to address the perception that Britain's social fabric was fraying due to declining morality and deteriorating standards of behaviour, especially amongst the young. If that echoed many Conservative election themes, it was also one of the Prime Minister's own long-standing preoccupations. In fact on the morning of 6 May Blair had already identified the public's dislike of 'disrespect', 'whether it is in the class-room or on the street or in the town centres on a Friday or Saturday night'. The rest of the Queen's Speech was a mixture of 'reactionary' and 'progressive' policies designed to appeal to Middle England and the party's working-class supporters. It did not mark, as some hoped the end of New Labour, but nor was it 'unremittingly' New Labour: it was instead a familiar, indeed, 'quintessentially' New Labour programme for government.

Forward to a fourth term?

How this programme would influence Labour's chances of winning a fourth term was unclear: that in any case depended on many other factors, most notably the economy. Having made so much of economic stability, if (or rather when) the economy took a negative turn Labour would be especially open to Conservative criticism. There were in any case signs that even if the economy continued on a steady course the threat of a return to Conservative 'boom and bust' would produce diminishing returns. Events before 1997 were passing into history. Labour posters in 2005 recalling the unemployment and repossessions that occurred during the early 1990s slump were addressed to voters who had been children at the time. Various opinion polls taken during the campaign also indicated that the public was equally divided over whether health and education provision had got better or worse. However the government chose to 'reform' the NHS and the schools, improving the public services remained a pressing task.

On current constituency boundaries, a national swing of 1.9 per cent to the Conservatives would be enough to deny Labour a Commons majority at the next election. These boundaries were, however, imminently due to be redrawn and any change would reduce Labour's advantage. Despite the Liberal Democrats being second to Labour in 100 of its seats, 2005 had actually made the party more vulnerable to a relatively modest Conservative recovery. In any case Kennedy's party would be unable to exploit the Iraq war and anti-Blair sentiments in any forthcoming contest. Most of the 44 Labour-held constituencies that could be taken on a swing of less than 2.5 per cent had the Conservatives in second place. Moreover, nearly half of these seats were in London and the South East, where Howard's party had done best in 2005. The *Sun*'s half-hearted endorsement of Labour – 'One Last Chance' – was therefore a possible sign of worse to come, given its popularity with key voters in that part of Britain. While reflecting owner Rupert Murdoch's decision to back the expected winner, it actually contradicted the paper's position on immigration, asylum and travellers, all of which echoed Conservative policy (or, some alleged, vice versa).

MPs like Cook hoped Prime Minister Brown would help Labour regain votes lost in 2005 by taking the party in a more left-wing direction (*Guardian*, 7 May 2005). The party had, after all, lost 4 million votes since 1997 and studies suggested one reason was that many of those who had switched to Labour had become disillusioned. Women especially felt the Prime Minister had let them down by failing to live up to promises to restore 'trust' (Lawson 2005: 8–12; *Observer*, 20 February 2005). Blair had certainly become the scapegoat for disparate discontents, not all of them due to Iraq or his lack of radicalism. If some blamed him for tuition fees others bemoaned his supposed failure to control bogus asylum seekers entering Britain. Undoubtedly damaged by his enthusiasm for invading Iraq, Blair was, then, a lightning rod for numerous other criticisms of the government as a whole, not all of which would evaporate on his departure. Moreover, despite the public's many misgivings, when pollsters asked who would be the best Prime Minister respondents gave him large and consistent leads over Howard and Kennedy. If they mistrusted Blair, voters apparently considered him more competent than his rivals: despite everything he would be a hard act to follow.

Depending on when and in what circumstances Blair finally leaves Downing Street, he will give his successor at least the chance to renew New Labour in office. That was something Blair had hoped to do himself, albeit in an 'unremittingly New Labour' manner. If, as seems likely, Brown eventually becomes Prime Minister, it is unlikely that he will diverge too far from the direction set down after 1994: he was, after all, one of the chief architects of New Labour. If, during the second term, he had evolved a Brownite version of New Labour, it was not as different from Blair's as some wanted to believe. The diverse nature of Labour's electoral coalition also meant Brown, like Blair, would have to attend to contrasting demands, not all of which are amenable to left-wing solutions. If he is serious about it, Brown would already know that constructing a 'progressive consensus' is easier said than done.

References

BBC (2005a) <www.news.bbc.co.uk/1/hi/uk_politics/4171779.stm>, accessed 14 January 2005.

BBC (2005b) <www.news.bbc.co.uk/1/hi/uk_politics/vote_2005/issues/4520847.stm>, accessed 10 May 2005.

Blair, T. (2003) <www.politics.guardian.co.uk/speeches/story/0,11126,1052844,00.html>, accessed 25 May 2005.

Bower, T. (2005) *Gordon Brown*, London: HarperCollins.

Cook, R. (2004) *The Point of Departure*, London: Simon and Schuster.

Cronin, J. (2005) *New Labour's Pasts. The Labour Party and its Discontents*, Harlow: Longman.

Fielding, S. (2002) 'No-one else to vote for? Labour's campaign', in A. Geddes and J. Tonge (eds) *Labour's Second Landslide*, Manchester: Manchester University Press.

Fielding, S. (2003) *The Labour Party. Continuity and Change in the Making of 'New' Labour*, Basingstoke: Palgrave.

Hills, J. and Stewart, K. (eds) (2005) *A More Equal Society? New Labour, Poverty, Inequality and Exclusion*, London: Policy Press.

ICM (2004) <www.icmresearch.co.uk/reviews/2004/guardian-labourmembers-feb-2004.asp>.

ICM (2005) <www.icmresearch.co.uk/reviews/vote intention-reports/guardian-report.asp>.

Institute for Fiscal Studies (2005) *Poverty and Inequality in Britain: 2005*, London: IFS.

Labour Party (2005) *Britain Forward Not Back*, London: Labour Party.

Lawson, N. (2005) *Dare More Democracy*, London: BGMS.

Milburn, A. (2004a) <www.ippr.org.uk/articles/>.

Milburn, A. (2004b) <www.labour.org.uk/ac20004news?ux_id=milburnfabian>.

Milburn, A. (2005) <www.fabian-society.org.uk/press_office/>.

Mulgan, G. (2005) 'Lessons of power', *Prospect*, May.

Opinion Leader Research (2003) *Student Funding. Findings From a Two-Stage Programme of Qualitative Research on the Funding of Higher Education*, <www.education.guardian.co.uk/higher/news/story>.

Oppenheim, C. (ed.) (2004) *The Inclusive Society: Tackling Poverty*, London: IPPR.

Peston, R. (2005) *Brown's Britain*, London: Short.

Taylor-Gooby, P. (2005) *Attitudes to Social Justice*, Oxford: Oxford University Press.

Crosby

Labour's comfortable retention of its seat in Crosby highlighted the problems of the Conservatives in urban areas in northern England. Although only six miles north of Labour-dominated Liverpool, Crosby was held by the Conservatives at every post-war election until 1997, apart from a brief by-election with Shirley Williams and the SDP in 1981. Labour's landslide in 1997 transformed a normally safe Conservative seat into a constituency with a Labour majority of over 7,000, achieving the second largest Labour vote increase (22.4 per cent) in the entire country.

By 2005, the Conservatives faced an even bigger task, Labour's Claire Curtis-Thomas having increased her majority with a 3.1 swing to Labour in 2001. The 11.3 per cent swing required for a Conservative victory at the following election thus looked an impossible task. Instead, the Crosby result broadly matched the national picture, with a 3.2 per cent swing from Labour to the Conservatives and a sizeable increase in the Liberal Democrat vote, up by 6.3 per cent.

A sizeable number of voters were searching for an alternative to Labour. This was the first time that Curtis-Thomas has failed to win an overall majority of the vote. However, electors were still not prepared to transfer to the Conservatives, whose vote fell despite a slight increase in turnout. In contrast, the Liberal Democrats gained 2,600 votes, whilst their core support was certainly not prepared to back the Conservatives as a tactical ploy to oust Labour.

Labour ran an efficient campaign, backed by a visit from Cherie and Euan Blair on the eve of polling day. Claire Curtis-Thomas is widely credited as a good constituency MP and is making an impact at Westminster, sitting on two important select committees. These factors were necessary but insufficient conditions for her success, as wider voting considerations prevailed. Labour's vote held up in affluent parts of the constituency where the Conservatives remain unappealing and those settling in Formby from Liverpool may be bringing Labour values with them.

The Conservatives ran a vigorous campaign, having selected the energetic Debi Jones, a local radio broadcaster, to fight the seat. Her campaign had strengths and drawbacks of personality politics – moderately high profile but novice status. The Conservatives could not blame UKIP for stealing their votes. The party's bizarre decision to field the same candidate across eight constituencies backfired, John Whittaker attracting only 1 per cent of the vote.

The result left the Conservatives still needing a swing of 8 per cent to win a former natural seat next time. Boundary commission proposals to hive off the south part of the seat into solidly-Labour Bootle, whilst moving the more Conservative parts of the constituency into a new Sefton Central seat, should lift Conservative morale. Curtis-Thomas, who might reasonably prefer to fight the proposed new Sefton South seat, rather than the more risky battle to the North, described the Commission's proposals to split Crosby as 'baffling' (*Crosby Herald*, 12 May 2005).

Result		%
Curtis-Thomas, C. (Lab)	17,463	48.3
Jones, D. (Con)	11,623	32.1
Murray, J. (LD)	6,298	17.4
Whittaker, J. (UKIP)	454	1.2
Bottoms, G. (Communist Party of Britain)	199	0.6
Braid, D. (Clause 28)	157	0.4
Lab hold		
Lab majority	5,840	16.1
Swing: Lab to Con		3.3

Turnout: 66.7%

Bristol West

Bristol West was a rare entity, a genuinely three-way marginal. Backed by affluent supporters in Clifton and Redland, the Conservatives held the seat until 1997, when it was captured by Labour's Val Davey. Labour entered the 2005 contest 4,426 votes ahead of the Liberal Democrats, who led the Conservatives by a mere 39 votes. All three parties proclaimed confidence and it is indeed possible to come from third place to win; Labour did this in ten seats in 1997, although a landslide shift in their favour was hardly likely for the Conservatives in this contest. The potential closeness of the battle gave it a high profile, with visits from party leader and a regular focus on the seat on BBC1's *Breakfast*.

The outcome was, however, a comfortable victory for the Liberal Democrat candidate, Stephen Williams, who won with a majority of over 5,000 votes. The outcome meant that all three main parties have held the seat over the last two decades. The growth in size of the student and academic population in the city, many based in the constituency, offered advantages to the Liberal Democrats. An oft-quoted statistic during the campaign was that the constituency was the brainiest in the country, containing more PhDs per head than any other.

The Liberal Democrat candidate, Stephen Williams, had fought the seat in 2001, when his party failed to make any inroads into Labour's lead. This time, however, he held the advantages of the unpopularity of the Iraq war with some constituents and the hostility to Labour's introduction of £3,000 per year university tuition fees.

The defending MP had opposed the Iraq war, despite dubious claims to the contrary from the Liberal Democrats. Echoing the campaigning line of the national leadership, Davey attempted to ward off the Liberal Democrat threat by reviving the spectre of the old enemy: 'Our vote needs to the recognise the threat from the Tories. The Tories have been revitalised. We need every vote' (*Guardian*, 3 May 2005).

The truth is that the Conservative vote is in retreat in the constituency, as tends to be the case in areas with high numbers of academics and students. Despite an impressive increase in turnout of 5 per cent (postal voting trebled) to 70.5 per cent, the Conservative vote fell. Only four wards within the constituency are held by Conservative local councillors, one-fifth of the total of two decades earlier. The Conservative candidate, David Martin, a credible former MP, whose credentials, the *Guardian* (3 May 2005) told us, included Coldplay's frontman as a nephew, ran a solid campaign, but there remains no sign of a Conservative revival in this type of 'intellectual' seat.

Result		%
Williams, S. (LD)	21,987	38.3
Davey, V. (Lab)	16,859	29.4
Martin, D. (Con)	15,429	26.9
Quinnell, J. (Green)	2,163	3.8
Muir, S. (UKIP)	439	0.7
Kennedy, B. (Soc Lab)	329	0.6
Reid, D. (Baths)	190	0.3
LD gain from Lab		
LD majority	5,128	8.9
Swing. Lab to LD		0.4

Turnout: 70.5%

4
New Leaders, Same Problems: The Conservatives

Philip Cowley and Jane Green

Election night 2005 was the first for over 20 years in which the phrase 'Conservative gain' had been heard regularly on British TV and radio. Having effectively stood still in 2001 – when they had made a net gain of just one seat – the Tories ended the 2005 campaign up by a more respectable 33 seats. The Parliamentary Party increased in size by 20 per cent, the party won seats in the three countries of Great Britain for the first time since 1997, and (although not all their own work) they saw the government's majority fall from over 160 to a much more assailable 66. They also almost entirely repulsed the expected assault on Conservative seats from the Liberal Democrats. It was not just that the Liberal Democrats' much-discussed 'decapitation' strategy – targeting high-profile Conservative MPs in marginal seats – was a flop, but also that the Liberal Democrats' more general attack on Conservative marginal seats failed almost entirely. The Liberal Democrats took just three seats off the Tories, but lost five in return. In short, most Conservatives were feeling much more chipper when they woke up on 6 May 2005 than they had been four years previously.

But any Conservative who sprang out of bed filled with the joys of life had obviously not looked too closely at the election results. It was a sign of how bad things had got that the result could be seen as a success. Despite the increase in seats, 2005 remained the fourth worst Conservative performance at a general election for 100 years. Winning a total of 198 seats (including South Staffordshire) was a worse performance than Michael Foot's (frankly dismal) Labour Party had managed in 1983, and only the elections of 2001, 1997 and 1906 had seen the Tories win fewer seats. In share of the vote, the Tories gained just 0.6 per cent on 2001, itself thought to be a catastrophe, up to 32.3 per cent. This was a *smaller* increase than had been achieved by William Hague in 2001, and represented the third worst Conservative performance in terms of share of the vote for 100 years (beating only 1997 and 2001). In the North of England, the Conservative share of the vote actually fell; in other parts it increased just microscopically: up, for example, just 0.1 per cent in the Midlands, by just 0.2 per cent in Scotland. The electoral system rewarded the Conservatives' rather meagre improvement because in several key seats Labour's vote fell, not because there was any substantial Conservative revival. In London, for example, the reported swing 'to' the Conservatives of 4.9 per cent was caused much more by Labour's vote dropping 8.4 per cent than by the rather meagre increase of 1.4 per cent in the Conservative vote. Even in the South East, where the Tories did best, their share of the vote only went up by 2.1 per cent.

It was also the first time for almost 100 years that the Tories had lost three elections on the trot. At the beginning of the twentieth century, they had lost in 1906 and in two elections of 1910 – but by the end of those three elections (and in the space of just four years) they had achieved parity in terms of seats with the then government; by 1910, there were 272 Liberals, 272 Conservatives. The election of 2005 – eight years after their first landslide defeat – found the Conservatives still 158 seats behind Labour.

The period from 2001 to 2005 therefore constituted the journey from the third worst Conservative performance for 100 years to the fourth worst Conservative performance for 100 years. It had involved two different leaders – Iain Duncan Smith and Michael Howard – with Howard announcing the day after the 2005 election that he intended to resign the leadership. He thus became the fourth Conservative leader to have been seen off by Tony Blair and the third in a row not to make it to Prime Minister. Prior to William Hague, the party had only ever had one leader, Austen Chamberlain, who had failed to become Prime Minister. In the eight years from 1997, that figure increased to four.

This chapter is an examination of the attempts of the Conservative Party to improve its position under both Iain Duncan Smith (IDS) and Michael Howard. We show that whilst the change in leadership might have been necessary – and whilst it brought some benefits to the party's fortunes – the belief that a change in leadership could be sufficient to restore Conservative fortunes was always unrealistic: new leaders simply find themselves facing the same old problems. We begin with the selection of Iain Duncan Smith as party leader, and then discuss his performance in the role, and subsequent dismissal. We then examine Michael Howard's approach, and examine Conservative strengths and weaknesses during the election campaign. We highlight the obstacles the party must overcome if it is to return to being anything other than the natural party of opposition.

The selection of IDS

When Michael Howard announced, the day after the 2005 election, that he would be standing down as Tory leader, he also said that he would remain in post until the procedures for electing the party's leader had been reformed. There were two possible explanations for Howard delaying his resignation in that way. The first and more cynical explanation (denied, obviously, by Mr Howard) was that he was attempting to alter the rules in a way that would stymie those would-be leaders of whom he did not approve whilst giving an advantage to candidates he backed (David Davis was the name usually mentioned as an example of the former, with David Cameron being usually mentioned as an example of the latter). More generally, his move was believed to relate to the outcome at the beginning of the 2001 Parliament, when Iain Duncan Smith had emerged victorious.

The leadership rules had last been reformed under William Hague's leadership, giving the grassroots membership some involvement in the selection of the leader for the first time, and many MPs (along with plenty of commentators) blamed this innovation for Duncan Smith's success; the grassroots were accused of having selected IDS ahead of (what others argued were) more competent and electorally appealing candidates. The choice of IDS had demonstrated, so the argument went, the foolishness of giving the grassroots membership any significant say in choosing the leader. The grassroots chose IDS over Ken Clarke simply because the former shared their opinions (prejudices?) on Europe, rather than choosing a leader with the necessary skills. This has now become the widely accepted view of the 2001 leadership election – and is one of the key motivations of those who wanted to alter the leadership election rules after 2005.

It is, however, almost completely wrong. William Hague's reforms did end the Parliamentary Party's monopoly in leadership selection, but the parliamentarians remained extremely important, far more so than in other British political parties. The process involved the party's wider membership in the country, but only once the incumbent leader had resigned or been ejected by the MPs – at which point the wider membership were merely offered a choice between the two candidates most favoured by the Parliamentary Party. Indeed, there was no compulsion on the Parliamentary Party to put two candidates forward to the members at the final stage – as some more prescient observers pointed out at the time – and as came to pass.

Five candidates stood for the leadership in 2001: Ken Clarke, Iain Duncan Smith, Michael Portillo, Michael Ancram and David Davis. A multiple ballot system was used to choose the final two candidates to go through to the ballot of the party membership, with the bottom placed candidate being eliminated after each round.

Unfortunately the first round (see Table 4.1) saw two candidates – Davis and Ancram – share the wooden spoon, leading to the vote being held for a second time. The party's rules were widely criticised for not foreseeing such a possibility ('Can't they get anything right?', asked the *Daily Mail*; 'Chaos', said the *Sun*), with surprisingly little criticism focusing on the two candidates themselves for failing to withdraw from the race in the interests of the party, given their somewhat pitiful performance. The re-run contest, two days later, saw both Davis and

Ancram lose votes, whilst the front three candidates improved their positions slightly. Ancram was then eliminated from the contest; Davis withdrew (albeit after initially attempting to stay in the running). Both urged their supporters to vote for Duncan Smith.

Table 4.1   Changes in support between rounds, 2001 Conservative Party leadership contest

	Round 1	*Round 1 (re-run)*	*Change*	*Round 2*	*Change*
Clarke	36	39	(+3)	59	(+20)
Duncan Smith	39	42	(+3)	54	(+12)
Portillo	49	50	(+1)	53	(+3)
Davis	21	18	(−3)	−	−
Ancram	21	17	(−4)	−	−

The second round proper saw Clarke top the poll (59 votes), followed by Duncan Smith (54). Portillo – who had been in front in the first two rounds, and who was widely seen as the frontrunner – came third by one vote and was therefore eliminated.

Portillo's problem was easily summed up. Unlike Hague (in 1997), or Clarke and Duncan Smith (in 2001), Portillo was unable to attract supporters from defeated candidates. As Table 4.1 shows, after the first round his support went up by just one vote (compared to three each for Clarke and Duncan Smith). In the second round – when Clarke's support went up by 20 and Duncan Smith's by twelve – Portillo's support went up by just three, and not enough to keep him in the race. He was almost no MP's second choice. Indeed, there was a sizeable group of Conservative MPs who wanted to stop Portillo at any cost. The size of Clarke's final lead – which surprised Clarke himself – was at least partly due to a handful of Duncan Smith supporters who, thinking that Duncan Smith was himself going to top the poll, decided to vote for Clarke in order to block Portillo. Too clever by half, their actions almost had disastrous consequences for their candidate. Portillo himself summed his problem up well: 'I seem to unite people against me in antagonism' (Walters 2001: 207).

The sources of this antagonism were various. Portillo suffered from accusations that he (or, more often, his aides, supporters and assorted hangers-on) had been disloyal to William Hague (and, prior to 1997, John Major). Such accusations appeared repeatedly during the campaign but these were merely the public manifestations of widespread ill-feeling amongst parts of the Parliamentary Party. As one of the key 'modernisers' within the party, and an advocate of symbolic liberal changes in the party's policies, he also suffered both from a sense amongst some MPs that he had shifted his beliefs (to the chagrin of those who had kept the faith) and – just as importantly – that there was still no clear sign of exactly what his new beliefs were. As one journalist put it to him when he addressed the Parliamentary Press Gallery on the day of the second ballot: 'Are you still on a journey or are you just refuelling?'

It is this ballot that is the source of the view that Clarke somehow won the MPs' ballot – and that the grassroots membership were therefore overruling, or overturning, the judgement of the party's (oh-so-wise) parliamentarians in selecting Iain Duncan Smith. Yet the ballot of MPs that Clarke led was a penultimate, not a final, ballot. Had the decision been left solely to Conservative MPs, with no subsequent ballot of the grassroots membership, Portillo would have been eliminated from the contest and there would then have been a final run-off between Clarke and IDS. In those circumstances, who knows where Michael Portillo's backers would have gone? It is far from certain that many of them would have gone to the pro-European Clarke; and it is therefore quite possible that IDS would have won any ballot confined solely to the party's MPs. Moreover, it was, as Peter Lilley pointed out in a letter to the *Guardian* (9 May 2005), Conservative MPs who had drawn up what he described as 'the dismal shortlist of Kenneth Clarke and Iain Duncan Smith' in the first place. If IDS really was so terrible a candidate, why had he managed to finish in the top two places?

There is equally little evidence that IDS emerged victorious from the resultant run-off between him and Clarke solely because of the zealotry of Conservative activists. It is clear from the surveys that were carried out that one fear that Conservative members had was that Clarke would not help the party present a united front: according to one survey, 60 per cent of Conservative members thought Clarke would split the party. To be sure, this is evidence of Clarke's views on Europe counting against him, but given that disunity is thought to be a certain vote-loser, the party members were making a more strategic decision than many gave them credit for. More anecdotally, Conservative grassroots members were also swayed by the performance of the candidates at the various hustings that were arranged; Clarke appeared under-prepared at several of the meetings, whereas IDS performed better at the hustings than many people had expected, receiving largely positive reviews.

There is therefore no evidence whatsoever that the grassroots membership somehow overruled the MPs in a fit of ideological zealotry. It is quite possible that the grassroots chose the same candidate that the MPs would have chosen, had they been forced to make that decision, and for the very same reasons.

IDS as leader

Equally misunderstood was IDS's strategy once he became leader. For many observers, the election of a right-wing Eurosceptic – and a former Maastricht rebel to boot – was proof that the Conservative Party would move further to the right, and become even more obsessed by Europe in the process.

This criticism proved wide of the mark. For sure, one of IDS's first acts as leader was to harden the party's European policy. Under Hague, the policy had been to rule out the euro for two Parliaments – effectively eight years. Under IDS, the party ruled out membership for good. IDS was helped in making this move by changes in the composition of the Parliamentary Party in the four years since Hague became leader, the number of pro-European Conservative MPs having diminished yet further at the 2001 election. But this hardening of policy was not a sign that the party was ever more obsessed about Europe; rather, the shift in policy was designed to ensure that the party did not spend any longer discussing the issue. By 'closing' the issue in this way – and by arguing that it should not be an issue for a general election but for any forthcoming referendum – IDS was determined to escape the criticism levelled at Hague in 2001 for running a single-issue campaign on Europe. IDS was also hoping to avoid the criticisms that had been levelled at Hague for having a policy that ruled out membership of the euro – but only for the time being. (Such a tactic would also have enabled him to escape the subsequent criticisms levelled at the Howard campaign for its apparent narrow focus on immigration.)

This was also clear in his wider policy shifts. IDS attempted to broaden the party's commitment to issues more commonly associated with parties of the left. 'A Fair Deal for Everyone' (March–June, 2003) suggested that the Conservatives would govern for 'the whole country' and the strategy consciously moved from campaigning on tax, crime, Europe and asylum – issues where the Conservatives were traditionally strong, but which then ranked relatively low down the public's list of salient issues – to pensions, social services, inner-city deprivation, and health and education.

'A Fair Deal for Everyone' was an attempt to get Conservatives talking about their softer side – to make them look less harsh and to challenge the image of them as the 'nasty party' (Theresa May's now infamous observation in her October 2002 Conservative Party Conference speech). It attempted to address the opinion of voters that the Conservative Party stood for the rich rather than ordinary people. As part of the campaign, IDS conducted a programme of visits to some of Britain's most socially deprived inner cities whilst advocating centre-right policies for improving them. Instead of talking about being tough on criminals, the strategy involved 'tough love' solutions to helping them – such as Oliver Letwin's 'conveyer belt to crime' policies increasing spending on young offender and drug addiction programmes. By so doing, the aim was to reposition the Conservatives in the centre ground of British politics, at the same time forcing Labour back onto its heartlands, creating a more equal contest for the centre ground. Thus IDS tried to promote a brand of 'Compassionate Conservativism' which would reposition the party and provide Conservatives with a *raison d'être* beyond merely Thatcherism and Nationalism.

This was a strategy that only a right-winger like IDS could have undertaken (as it was, it attracted considerable criticism from some on the right of the party), but because it didn't fit easily with his reputation as a staunch right-winger or with the media's pigeonholing of the Conservative Party as a right-of-centre party, it did not receive the attention it deserved. It may, of course, be debatable whether he would have been able to continue with such a strategy as the election approached: Hague had variously attempted to 'reach out', as did Howard when first elected leader, only for both to be forced to fall back somewhat onto their relative strengths when faced with an imminent campaign. But it was at least a serious attempt to reposition the party, and one which predated some of the solutions widely discussed after Howard's resignation in 2005.

At times, such efforts at repositioning ran into difficulties with the Parliamentary Party. For example, in January 2002 the Shadow Cabinet came out in support of a largely elected Second Chamber (to be called the Senate), in which 80 per cent of its 300 members were to be elected, with just 20 per cent appointed. It was the exact opposite of the government's proposals, and, at first, it appeared that the new policy was a tactically sophisticated piece of repositioning, turning the Conservatives into the more 'democratic' party, and outflanking Labour on the issue. The problem for the Conservative leadership was that a belief in the wisdom of the party's position was not shared by all of its parliamentarians. When it came to voting on Lords reform in February 2003, over half the Conservative MPs who voted rejected the position advocated so publicly by the leadership (Cowley and Stuart 2004).

But perhaps the most notable clash came over an issue where (some of) IDS's backbenchers felt he had not repositioned the party enough: the Adoption and Children Bill (see Box 4.1). The rebellion over the Adoption and Children Bill resulted in a renewed focus on the issue of the Conservative leadership, made even more intense when Duncan Smith held a press conference at Conservative Central Office the following day (5 November 2002), during which he claimed that 'for a few, last night's vote was not about adoption but an attempt to challenge my mandate to lead this party'. He then told his party – in one of his few memorable quotes as party leader – that it had to 'unite or die'.

Yet the split – and the subsequent crisis – was almost entirely self-inflicted and eminently avoidable. It is quite common to see occasions when one major party allows a free vote, but the other enforces a whip. But it is almost always the other way round from the Adoption and Children Bill: governments, who need to get their legislation through, often enforce a whip, even if this reveals division, whilst the opposition can allow a free vote, thus disguising any division. This is one – indeed, perhaps the only – luxury of opposition.

Box 4.1 The Adoption and Children Bill

The Adoption and Children Bill began life as a fairly uncontentious piece of legislation. But mid-way through its passage it had been amended by backbench Labour MPs to include clauses allowing adoption by unmarried couples. Although the Bill made no distinction between heterosexual or homosexual unmarried couples (and although single gay people were already able to adopt), the issue was thereafter nearly always referred to as one of 'gay adoption' – and it caused division on the Conservative benches.

The government granted its MPs a free vote on the issue. After much discussion in Shadow Cabinet the Conservatives, by contrast, decided to issue a whip, telling the party's MPs to vote against the legislation, although Conservative peers were allowed a free vote. Faced with opposition from a vocal minority of Conservative MPs, the leadership let it be known that they would allow MPs to be absent from the Commons if the issue caused them difficulties (what became known, somewhat oxymoronically, as a 'soft three-line whip').

The issue reached the floor of the Commons in May 2002 and four Conservative MPs defied their party's whip and voted in favour of the legislation. Several others, including four Shadow Cabinet members, found convenient reasons to be absent from the Commons. After amendment in the Lords the Bill then returned to the Commons in November, with more damaging consequences. At the second time of asking, the numbers voting against the whip climbed to eight. A further number of Tory MPs also abstained. In quantitative terms, this was not especially damaging: eight MPs constituted just 5 per cent of the Parliamentary Party. But there was an important qualitative dimension to the Conservative rebels. They included John Bercow, absent from the vote in May but who now resigned from the Shadow Cabinet in order to vote and speak against the party's line. Michael Portillo and Kenneth Clarke – both of whom had stood against IDS when he won the leadership - also voted against their party whip. The other five - David Curry, Julie Kirkbride, Andrew Lansley, Andrew Mackay and Francis Maude – included four former members of the Shadow Cabinet.

Writing in *The Times* (5 November 2002), Peter Riddell called IDS's decision 'both wrong and tactically inept'. It is not obvious that the first part of Riddell's complaint is valid – in many ways issuing a whip was the more logical and consistent position to take – but the second part is certainly accurate. To impose a three-line whip when there was no pressing need to do so, and when it was clear that there were serious divisions within the party, was crass in the extreme.

The fall of IDS

Unfortunately for Duncan Smith, there was very little evidence that any of this attempted repositioning did the Conservatives any good with the public. IDS's own polling ratings, for example, were almost consistently poor, bordering on disastrous. Table 4.2 shows the findings of a Populus poll published in January 2003, giving comparisons between IDS and the two other party leaders. On almost every measure, IDS fared the worst of the three, with his scores on being a strong leader (14 per cent) and a good potential Prime Minister (18 per cent) being particularly poor. There were also frequent claims that Central Office kept the results of their focus groups from the leader, so damning was the public's view of him and (as Figure 4.1 shows) under his leadership the party still appeared to be flatlining in the opinion polls.

Table 4.2   Views on the party leaders, 2003

	Blair (%)	IDS (%)	Kennedy (%)
He is a strong leader	58	14	43
He understands the problems of people like me	37	29	49
He just says whatever he thinks people want to hear	63	47	38
I could never vote for that party while he is its leader	38	44	28
He is/would be a good Prime Minister	50	18	40

Source: Populus/*The Times*.

As a result of both such poor performances in the polls and some distinctly uninspiring performances by IDS, both at Prime Minister's Questions and in various media interviews, there were persistent rumours about a leadership challenge. Relatively few Conservative MPs (or peers) went public with their criticisms, although discontent surfaced occasionally, such as when Crispin Blunt, the MP for Reigate, described Duncan Smith as 'the handicap of a leader whom Conservatives in Parliament and outside feel unable to present to the electorate as a credible alternative prime minister'. Blunt's timing – coming on the evening that the Conservatives gained more than 500 seats in the 2003 local elections – was somewhat unfortunate (and led to him being widely mocked), but his views were more widely shared than was publicly acknowledged at the time.

Eventually, on 27 October 2003, IDS called on his would-be challengers to 'either bring it on or draw the line' – only to find that they intended to bring it on. The following day it was announced that the requisite 25 signatures of MPs had been delivered to Sir Michael Spicer, the Chairman of the 1922 Committee, to initiate a vote of confidence. And on Wednesday 30 October, IDS lost that vote of confidence by 90 to 75, a result that was closer than some had predicted, but still an overwhelmingly negative verdict on an incumbent leader. It was, in the end, a breathtakingly quick defenestration. With equally breathtaking speed, Michael Howard then appeared as the 'unity' candidate for the leadership. All the potential rival candidates declared that they would be supporting Howard. With just one candidate, there was no need for a ballot of MPs, let alone the grassroots, and Howard became party leader.

The whole process had been initiated, and then decided, by the party's MPs, within less than a week, with no grassroots involvement at all. Parliamentarians remain in an extraordinarily privileged position in most British political parties – and nowhere is that more obvious than in the Conservative Party.

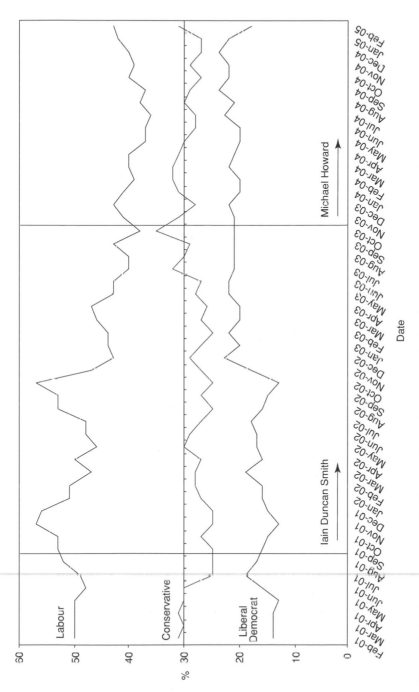

Figure 4.1 Voting intentions 2001–05, according to Conservative leader

Source: MORI.

The party under Howard

Michael Howard's assumption of the leadership appeared to transform the Conservative Party. It seemed to acquire some vim and vigour. Howard's appearances at Prime Minister's Questions were substantially better than those of IDS, with the result that Howard bettered Blair frequently. When he was on form – as with his charge that as a grammar school boy he would be taking no lessons on education from a public school educated Prime Minister – he landed blows way beyond those IDS could have dreamt of, with the result that his backbenchers were enthused almost overnight. His one conference speech made as party leader before the 2005 election was also much better received. Howard's performances also helped bring back into the fold influential financial donors – several of whom had stopped giving money whilst IDS was party leader – and helped reinvigorate the grassroots membership of the party.

One reason for this last point was that Howard was rated much more highly by Conservative supporters than either of his predecessors had been. As Figure 4.2 shows, both William Hague and Iain Duncan Smith had been viewed negatively even by Conservative supporters, with more dissatisfied than satisfied by their performance.

The exception – as is clear from Figure 4.2 – was IDS early on in his period as leader in 2002, when many Conservative supporters instead said that they didn't know how to judge him. Once Conservative supporters got to know IDS, then his ratings also became negative, just as Hague's had been. Whereas for every Conservative supporter dissatisfied with Howard, there were two who were satisfied with his performance.

The public also saw differences between the two leaders. Howard was more likely to be rated as understanding the world's problems, understanding the problems facing Britain and as a capable leader. But he was also more likely than IDS to be perceived as being rather narrow, tending to talk down to people, inflexible, and, most of all, out of touch with ordinary people.[1]

And there was also little obvious sign that the Conservative Party overall poll ratings improved under Howard's leadership. Despite an initial boost when he became leader, the Conservative Party failed to move significantly above its 30 per cent plateau in the opinion polls under Howard, just as it had done under IDS (see Figure 4.1). And whilst Howard may have been liked by Conservative supporters, his ratings with members of the general public (see Figure 4.3) were almost as poor as those of IDS. His overall satisfaction ratings with members of the public were almost uniformly negative: that is, more people said that they were dissatisfied with him than were satisfied.

However, leader evaluations are driven by perceptions of the party just as perceptions of the party are driven by perceptions of the leader (see Andersen and Evans 2003). The problem for the Conservative Party

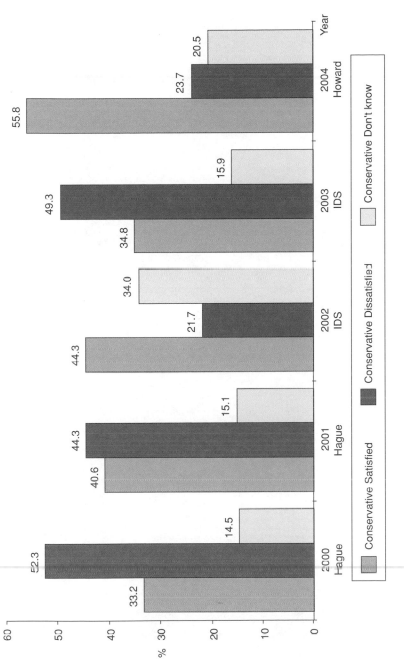

Figure 4.2 Satisfaction with William Hague, Iain Duncan Smith and Michael Howard among intended Conservative voters (% satisfied)

Source: MORI.

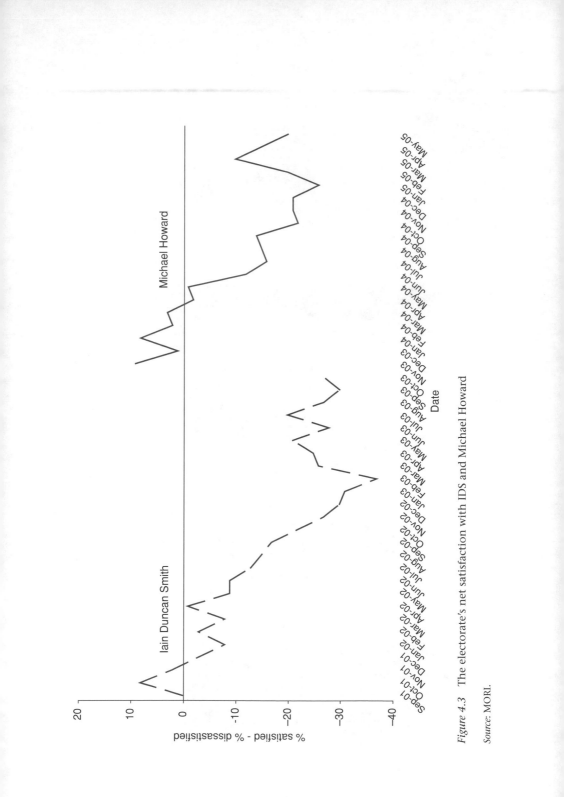

Figure 4.3 The electorate's net satisfaction with IDS and Michael Howard

Source: MORI.

throughout this period remained its inability to shift significantly from poll ratings of 30 per cent or just above – a situation it has now been stuck in since late 1992 – regardless of who has been in charge.

The Conservative approach

The overall Conservative strategy for the general election was predicated upon two pieces of knowledge. First, that the public did not think very highly of the government. Second, the party also knew that if instead of asking people to judge the government you asked them to choose between Labour and the Conservatives, they chose Labour.[2] Similarly, who did people think would make the better Prime Minister – Blair or Howard? Answer: Blair. The Prime Minister's ratings may have taken a knock over the last four years, but he was still preferred to Michael Howard.[3] One reason for this was that whilst people didn't think much of Labour, they had equally low, or lower, expectations of what a Conservative government would deliver. This meant that there was relatively little value in the Conservatives presenting themselves as an alternative government, because it was not an outcome that many people anticipated or relished. But there was value in presenting the party as a vehicle through which Tony Blair could be given a bit of a kicking.

This lay behind much of the Conservative language used in posters and adverts. For example, these are the words used by Michael Howard when launching the Conservative manifesto:

Imagine waking up on May the sixth to see Mr Blair re-elected. Imagine how you'd feel. You don't have to settle for that. Use your vote to tell Mr Blair that it's just not good enough. Use your vote to take a stand.

Similar words were then used almost consistently until the election. The following (all from Michael Howard) are just illustrative examples rather than a comprehensive list:

- So if you think that crime's too high, our asylum system is out of control and Mr Blair has hit you with too many stealth taxes – then you need to send him a very clear message. Enough is enough. (15 April 2005)
- Students cannot afford any more stealth taxes. They can either reward Mr Blair for eight years of broken promises, and vote for another five years of talk. Or they can vote Conservative, to support a party that's taken a stand and is committed to action on the issues that matter to hard working Britons. (21 April 2005)
- If you stay silent, you will send him a clear message: 'Carry on, you're doing just fine'. (23 April 2005)

- Why don't you take a stand? Isn't it your duty to take a stand? Your duty to yourselves and your duty to our country. So think carefully about the message you want to send. In twelve days time, you have the chance to take a stand – in fact it'll be your last chance to take a stand on Mr Blair. (23 April 2005)

All of these messages indicated that the election was a chance for voters to 'take a stand', and to 'send Tony Blair a message' by 'supporting' (but never by 'electing') the Conservatives. The unspoken implication of the latter was that Labour would still be in power after the election, and so it was especially important to use the election to send a message to the Prime Minister. A similar message came in Howard's comparison of the election to a football match in which one team was 2–0 down at half time (although the comparison was made in the context of teams being able to come back from 2–0 down).[4] The aim of such tactics was to depress the Labour vote (by appearing, at least de facto, to accept that Labour were going to win the election) whilst encouraging Conservative voters to turn out to send their message.

The Conservatives did occasionally talk about what they would do if elected to government, but such references were less common and were very carefully framed. The party knew that the electorate was highly disenchanted and turned off by Westminster village politics. Trust for politicians was low, many voters couldn't tell the difference between the parties, few people knew what the Conservative Party stood for, many people thought the party out of touch with the problems facing the country, and a general disillusionment with political rhetoric had taken root. Therefore the tactic chosen by the Conservatives was 'action not words' and a simplified message – so simple it initially involved only ten words – on 'the issues that matter': 'more police, cleaner hospitals, lower taxes, school discipline, controlled immigration'. ('Accountability' was later added to the list.) At times, it was like listening to a focus group recording being played back to the electorate. 'What do people say about Labour? They're all talk. What will the Conservatives do? Less talk. More action.' Hence when the party did talk about tasks for a Conservative government, they all had a set time frame. For example, within the first day, the Conservatives would set out plans to give head teachers the power to expel disruptive pupils and they would set a date on the referendum on the European Constitution to campaign for a 'No' vote. Within the first month they would start the recruitment of an extra 5,000 police officers each year, bring back matrons to take charge and deliver clean and infection-free hospital wards, introduce a waste-cutting budget and set in train 24-hour surveillance at ports of entry to Britain.

Much of this was similar to tactics used by the Conservative strategist, Lynton Crosby, an Australian brought in by Howard to mastermind the Conservative campaign. Crosby had been involved in several campaigns in Australia in which the opposition sought to give the impression that they could not win, and to encourage people to use their vote as a protest or a way of sending a message. Three specific phrases – 'enough is enough', 'send a message' and 'take a stand' were all direct imports.

Another Crosby tactic was a relentless focus on the marginal seats. Crosby once argued that 'targeting has become the key to electoral activity. Focusing on the seats that are critical, focusing on the people within those seats who are critical, and focusing on the critical issues within those seats', and in 2005 the Conservatives' targeting of marginal seats was regimental. The party expanded its target seat list to demonstrate confidence going into the election, and some money was spent on seats where they had a minimal chance of success, but the most marginal seats received relentless attention.

On Crosby's arrival, the Conservatives established a campaigning nerve centre for target seats, Constituency Campaign Services (CCS), in Coleshill, Birmingham (the location was itself said to be a statement of the party's determination to redirect its focus away from the South of England). Candidates could get support as and when needed, and were provided with a more professional array of centrally designed resources. Furthermore, with Coleshill came the innovation of a more sophisticated direct marketing database 'Votervault', apparently procured by the Party Chair, Dr Liam Fox, from the US. Votervault used consumer-based 'Mosaic' data combined with locally held canvassing returns to predict voters' intentions. This enabled the party to send targeted messages to key individuals in marginal constituencies, also enabling the party to spend precious campaign resources centrally (thus relieving candidates of pressure on their controlled campaign expenditures). These direct mailshots were complemented by the Geneva call centre in the newly situated Conservative Campaign Headquarters in Victoria Street, London, from which volunteers spoke to hundreds of thousands of voters.[5] These efforts were directed at just over 800,000 voters in around 100 constituencies. It left the rest of the country feeling like the general election campaign was happening on a distant planet whilst leaving targeted voters deluged. The eventual increase in the Conservative vote between 2001 and 2005 was about half the number targeted, at just over 410,000.

Conservative strengths – and weaknesses

Much controversy surrounded the choice of Conservative campaign issues – specifically the party's focus on immigration. But the Conservatives had little choice. In 2005, the Conservative Party had two advantages which were absent in 2001. The first was the self-evidently weakened Labour support caused by a loss of trust in the Prime Minister and general disillusionment with Labour. But the second was a significant increase in the salience of an issue on which the Conservatives were judged the best party.

Figure 4.4 shows which party was considered best able to handle issues considered to be important problems, listed in order of Conservative advantage relative to Labour.[6] The Conservatives led on five issues – asylum and immigration, defence, crime, Europe and taxation – whilst Labour led on the other five. This was actually a very similar set of rankings to those four years before. But four years before, the problem for the Conservatives had been that those issues where the public thought the Conservatives were strong, the public also judged largely unimportant, whereas on issues that the public thought important, they trusted Labour (Cowley and Quayle 2001: 58).

What had changed over the preceding four years was that in 2005 the public saw one of these issues – asylum and immigration – as far more important than they had four years before. Figure 4.5 shows the striking increase in the number of people claiming that asylum and immigration was 'the most important problem facing the country today'. For much of the 2001 Parliament, asylum and immigration was considered to be as important an issue as education and (at times) more important even than health care. It was, therefore, hardly surprising that the Conservative Party made asylum and immigration one of their campaign slogans. By focusing on this issue the Conservatives' strategy was consistent with saliency theory: to raise the salience of your own issue strengths and neutralise or downplay the strengths of your opponent (Budge and Farlie 1977). As one Conservative advert said apropos something else entirely: it's hardly rocket science, is it?

It was often said that by doing so the Conservatives were targeting their 'core vote' – but this is too simplistic a claim. Conservative voters were, in fact, only 3 per cent or 4 per cent more likely to rate this issue as the most important, when compared to undecided voters. The image of hordes of Conservative voters, all foaming at the mouth and morbidly obsessed by immigration, is a caricature. The Conservative 'core vote' has pretty much the same interests and priorities as most other voters. The policy was designed to help stave off the threat posed to the party by UKIP. The first test of Michael Howard's leadership had come in the European elections on 10 June 2004; and they had been a disaster for the Conservatives. The Tories achieved only 27 per cent of the vote, dropping almost nine percentage points since 1999. By contrast, UKIP's vote share increased from 7 per cent in 1999 to just over 16 per cent in 2004. The UKIP surge was a worrying signal to the Conservatives that even their core vote could desert them, and the period was one of deep dismay at Central Office. Polling evidence in Central Office showed that UKIP voters were not noticeably more Eurosceptic than other Conservative voters – but they were particularly motivated by immigration. The party's stance on immigration was therefore as much about fighting off the UKIP threat as it was about engaging with Labour or the Liberal Democrats; Kilroy-Silk's departure from UKIP (to set up his own party, Veritas) was one of the best

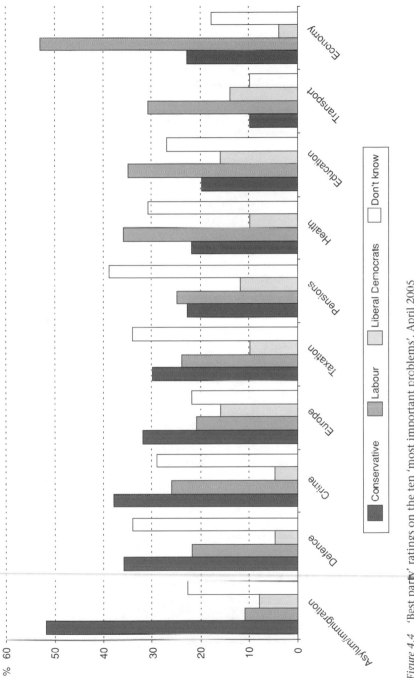

Figure 4.4 'Best party' ratings on the ten 'most important problems', April 2005

Source: MORI.

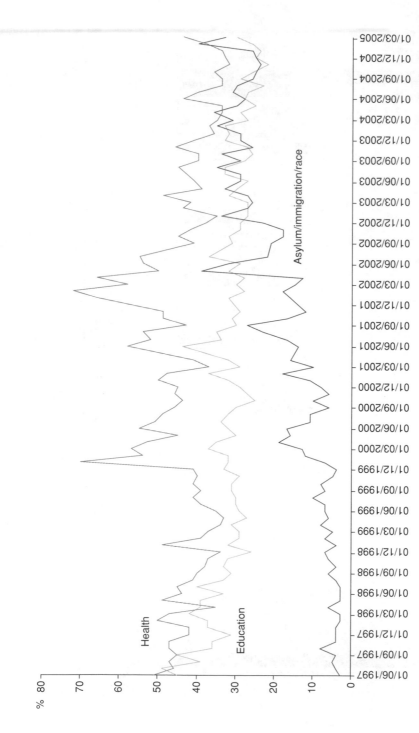

Figure 4.5 Proportions of respondents identifying race/immigration/asylum as the 'most important problem', compared to health and education, 1997–2005

Source: MORI.

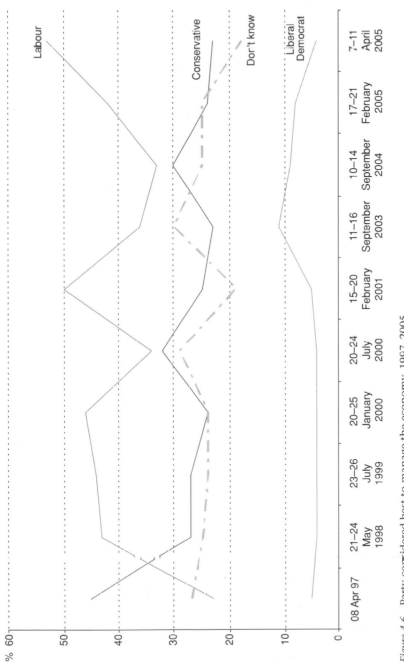

Figure 4.6 Party considered best to manage the economy, 1997–2005

Source: MORI.

pieces of news to arrive on Michael Howard's desk in the planning stages of the general election campaign.

The polling data also show one serious continuing weakness for the Conservatives. Of the ten issues listed as important problems or important in deciding how to vote, the economy was the one where the Conservatives were judged furthest behind Labour; and as the election approached (see Figure 4.6), Labour's advantage on this crucial issue increased, leaving the Conservatives even further behind. The overriding problem for the Conservative Party therefore was this: despite 13 years passing since 1992 when Black Wednesday resulted in plummeting poll ratings, the Conservatives have failed to demonstrably improve their position on this key issue. This is such a reversal of the normal state of British politics (prior to 1992) that it now sometimes goes without comment – but since 1992 the Tories have fought three elections in which they have been without the trump card that they used to be able to deploy so successfully throughout most of the twentieth century. Hence one of the key battles in the campaign was which party would shape the agenda onto or away from the economy.

Conclusion

By the end of 2005, it is likely that the Conservative Party will have elected their fifth leader in 15 years. If the period from 2001 to 2005 teaches them anything, it is that changing the leader is, on its own, not enough to solve the problems the party faces; and that short-term fixes are no substitute for long-term change.

There is little doubt that the replacement of Iain Duncan Smith with Michael Howard reinvigorated the party, but it also had its costs. The belief that a change in leadership was sufficient – and that the arrival of Michael Howard would therefore be enough to restore the party's fortunes – meant that the party avoided the big issues that remained associated with the party's image. The process of examination that Iain Duncan Smith began, at least hesitatingly, may be painful, but it remains essential. The lesson from 2001 to 2005 is that simply changing the leadership – and/or importing clever campaigning tactics – will not be enough. New leaders are simply faced by the same old problems.

The reliance of the Conservatives on their loyal base has only staved off disaster because the Conservatives have been contesting relatively low-turnout elections. Any new leader must address ways of reaching beyond the third of the electorate who voted Conservative in the last three elections – beyond core voters in the countryside and in the south and east of England and out into the urban areas and the Celtic fringe, where levels of Conservative support is currently dismal.

Yet one of the greatest difficulties for any new leader is that new solutions are hard to find. Just as replacing a leader is not enough, there is similarly no magic bullet for Conservative strategists. The Conservatives remain stuck between a rock and a hard place. If they campaign on their strengths they reinforce old images of the party. If they campaign on Labour's issues – issues which also enjoy higher salience with the public – they risk damaging the party even more in the short term. The challenge is to grow the range of relative strengths, but until the party's image improves, and until they resist the temptation of focusing only on imminent campaigns, it is unlikely that the party will be seen as more likeable or more competent on the issues that matter to most people.

It is also difficult to overstate the damage done to the Conservatives by their loss of reputation on the economy – and, concomitantly, by Labour's lead on this key issue. This is only likely to be reversed when the present government's record on the economy turns sour via some sort of recession. The Conservative MP John Bercow is right that the Conservatives can't afford to wait for the economy to fail – but that may still represent one of their best chances of regaining power.

The Conservative Party is, as we write, embarking on a potentially divisive disagreement on the required depth, breadth and meaning of its 'modernisation'. Such reform is hard to sustain for two reasons. First, because Blair has successfully occupied much of the Tories' traditional policy space for over a decade and it has proved extremely difficult for the Conservatives to repel these boarders. And second, many traditionalist Conservatives (both MPs and members alike) do not believe such changes are necessary. For all the talk of a large influx of modernisers among the 2005 intake, they still constitute a minority in the Parliamentary Conservative Party: for every Michael Gove, there is an Andrew Rosindell. Any attempts at radical change could simply result in renewed factional infighting between the 'mods' and 'rockers' within the party, which is unlikely to help it regain power.

Notes

1. As the Conservative Party campaigned, so Howard's own evaluations altered; his positive attributes became more positive, whilst his negative attributes became more negative. So, whereas between 2004 and 2005 Howard improved on ratings of understanding the world's problems (from 9 per cent saying so in 2004 to 12 per cent in 2005), understanding the problems facing Britain (from 17 per cent to 21 per cent) and being seen as a capable leader (15 to 18 per cent), he was also more likely to be perceived as being rather narrow minded (13 to 22 per cent), tending to talk down to people (17 to 22 per cent), and be out of touch with ordinary people (22 to 30 per cent).
2. The precise statistics varied, depending on the polling company, the question used, and the timing – but figures of around 50 per cent (Labour) to 35 per cent (Conservative) were not unusual. When people were given a slightly more nuanced choice, around a quarter would choose a hung Parliament, but even then those who'd prefer Labour to win outnumbered the Conservatives.
3. Again, the precise figures varied – but a ratio of 40 per cent (Blair) to 25 per cent (Howard) was not unusual.
4. Specifically, Howard was discussing the Carling Cup final, in which Liverpool (one of the several football teams Howard supports – along with Folkestone Invicta, Swansea

City and Llanelli) had been leading 2–0 only to lose. The interview in which he made this observation was also the first time (to our knowledge) that any party leader has used the word 'screwed' (in anything other than its purely mechanical meaning) whilst campaigning to be Prime Minister: 'we were ahead until the last 10 minutes and then we got screwed'.

5. One of Michael Howard's first decisions as leader was to move the party headquarters from Smith Square to the more modern and less maze-like Victoria Street offices. As well as a cost-saving measure, the move was an attempt to end the old Central Office culture and turf wars.

6. Respondents choosing an issue as the most important then choose which party would handle the problem best. The proportions rating the issues as the most important problem varied only marginally depending on which party respondents favoured.

References

Andersen, R. and Evans, G. (2003) 'Who Blairs wins? Leadership and voting in the 2001 election', *British Elections and Parties Review*, 13.

Budge, I. and Farlie, D. (1977) *Voting and Party Competition: A Theoretical Critique and Synthesis Applied to Surveys From Ten Democracies*, London: John Wiley.

Cowley, P. and Quayle, S. (2001) 'The Conservatives: running on the spot', in A. Geddes and J. Tonge (eds) *Labour's Second Landslide*, Manchester: Manchester University Press.

Cowley, P. and Stuart, M. (2004) 'Still causing trouble?', *Political Quarterly*, 75.

Walters, S. (2001) *Tory Wars*, London: Politicos.

Enfield Southgate

Were you still up for Stephen Twigg? The question was a predictable response to the downfall of the Labour candidate who had famously ousted potential Conservative leader Michael Portillo in 1997 and prompted a book title. As Twigg's victory in 1997 symbolised the arrival of New Labour and Blairism, so his defeat in 2005 indicated a turning of the electoral tide, a potential peaking of the Blair project.

Like Portillo, Twigg accepted defeat with dignity. Similarly, Twigg, a Labour minister, had not anticipated defeat. Although Enfield Southgate was never going to become a safe Labour seat, it appeared that Twigg had nurtured the seat sufficiently to prevent anything like the 6.6 per cent swing needed by the Conservatives for its recapture. Given that there had been a 5 per cent swing in Labour's favour in 2001 and the party had won an overall majority of the vote, it appeared the seat was secure for at least one more election. Twigg ruefully conceded a few days after the 2005 verdict that 'The first I knew I was in trouble was when the telly said so' (*The Times*, 13 May 2005).

Enfield Southgate provided one of several Conservative gains in the South East, where a strong revival was underway. The seats 'loaned' to Labour in 1997 and 2001 began to return, as 4,644 voters deserted the party. Meanwhile Portillo texted Twigg with some helpful advice: 'I recommend a by-election' (*The Times*, 13 May 2005).

Result		%
Burrowes, D. (Con)	18,830	44.6
Twigg, S. (Lab)	17,083	40.5
Kakoulakis, Z. (LD)	4,724	11.2
Doughty, T. (Green)	1,083	2.5
Hall, B. (UKIP)	490	1.2
Con gain from Lab		
Con majority	1,747	4.1
Swing: Lab to Con		8.7

Turnout: 66.4%

5

The Liberal Democrats: Steady Progress or Failure to Seize the Moment?

Edward Fieldhouse and David Cutts

The Liberal Democrats won 62 seats in the 2005 general election, making it the best performance by a Liberal party since 1923, polling nearly 6 million votes in the process. In terms of vote share, at 22.6 per cent this constituted the best performance since the Alliance in 1987. However, despite this, the result was somewhat of a disappointment for the party. Part of the reason for this lies in the obvious disparity between the vote share and the share of the seats in Parliament (less than 10 per cent). More than this, however, the disappointment stems from the feeling that this was an opportunity lost.

The Liberal Democrats entered the election campaign buoyed by poll ratings consistently above their 20 per cent goal of 2001. On the basis of their 1997 and 2001 experiences, the party expected an improvement in their position as the campaign progressed. Disillusionment with the government and trust in Tony Blair's leadership had propelled Kennedy as the most honest, principled of the three main party leaders in the eyes of the electorate. And then there was the Liberal Democrats' opposition to the war in Iraq, which promised to make them the main beneficiaries of an anti-war vote. But had the Liberal Democrats progressed fast enough to benefit from the fallout of Labour discontent and ineffective Conservative opposition? On the face of it, the 2005 general election represented an ideal opportunity for the Liberal Democrats to achieve that elusive electoral breakthrough. As Matthew Parris put it, 'when a governing party and its leader have run out of ideas and lost our affection and when a principal Opposition has only fear to trade on – is the hour of your enemies' weakness. Now is the hour when a rising third party must strike. Now or maybe never' (*The Times*, 16 April 2005).

In this chapter we explore where and why the Liberal Democrats capitalised on those favourable conditions, and likewise where they did not. We argue that this was a fundamentally uneven performance, and that unevenness reflects local conditions together with the vagaries of a disproportional electoral system. As anticipated by Russell and Fieldhouse (2005) the Liberal Democrats continued to build incrementally on historical and local success, but also reached out into new areas thanks to support from specific sections of the population.

Pre-election period, 2001–05

On the back of an anti-Conservative electoral strategy, and an improved vote share of 18.3 per cent, the Liberal Democrats won 52 seats in the 2001 general election. Furthermore, 51 of the 110 seats the party finished second in were Labour held, reflecting a long-term strategy of developing previously non-winnable seats in Labour heartlands, and thus lending credibility to its claim to be the main alternative. Between 1997 and 2001, the Liberal Democrats had only made one gain (Romsey) in 16 parliamentary by-elections. However, the electoral climate changed during Labour's second term in government with the Liberal Democrats being the main beneficiaries of Labour disillusionment particularly over the war in Iraq. The Liberal Democrats won two traditional safe Labour seats, Brent East (29 per cent swing from Labour) and Leicester South (21 per cent swing from Labour), and narrowly failed to win Birmingham Hodge Hill and Hartlepool.

Outside of Westminster, the Liberal Democrats remained coalition partners in the Scottish Parliament and continued to occupy a respectable number of seats in the Welsh and London Assembly.[1] The party also performed relatively well in the 2004 European elections, increasing its number of MEPs by 2 to 14, and its national vote share by 2.3 percentage points to 14.9 per cent. That said, the party's proportion of the national vote was much lower than opinion poll ratings for UK parliamentary elections. Yet in local government, the party continued to place great emphasis on building a strong local base which could then be used as a stepping stone to make parliamentary inroads. Winning more seats locally and gaining control of more local councils would enable the Liberal Democrats to build electoral credibility and diffuse any electors' suspicions of political inexperience which could hinder further parliamentary advances (Russell and Fieldhouse 2005). From 2002 to 2004, the Liberal Democrats achieved an overall net gain of 345 councillors. Generally, the Liberal Democrats made the vast majority of their gains in the North of England (for example, Durham City and Newcastle) and lost ground to the Conservatives in the South of England (for example, in Richmond upon Thames). This partly reflected the Liberal Democrats' strategy of strengthening their local base in traditional Labour strongholds to the possible detriment of areas where they had previously benefited from Conservative disillusionment.

As the Liberal Democrats approached the pre-election period, the party's average opinion poll rating was above 19 per cent, roughly 7 per cent higher than at the same period in 2001. Expectations were high with Lord Razzall, chair of the Campaigns and Communications Committee, claiming that the 2005 general election outcome would be 'the best Liberal Democrat result in 95 years'.

The pre-election campaign

Liberal Democrat strategists were well aware that party policies often took longer to reach the electorate given the focus on the two main parties during the non-election period. Hence they decided to unveil their key slogan 'The Real Alternative' and highlight specific policy pledges (50p top rate of tax for those earning over £100,000; policy to replace the council tax with a local income tax; abolition of student tuition fees) well in advance of the election campaign. Kennedy used his Spring Conference as the starting gun for the election campaign, yet even then, private polling indicated that the Iraq war was not top of voters' concerns. Consequently, the pre-election focus was on domestic policy pledges to secure disaffected Labour voters and persuade undecided Conservatives in key Conservative–Liberal Democrat marginals. As the phoney election campaign gathered pace in the last weeks of March, the Liberal Democrats became increasingly sidelined as the media focused on the traditional bitter battle between the Conservatives and Labour. The Conservatives' guerrilla-style tactics allowed them to monopolise media attention. In response, the Liberal Democrats hastily unveiled the most expensive advertising campaign in the party's history. The campaign featured Charles Kennedy along with ten reasons to vote for the Liberal Democrats. Party strategists focused on the honest, approachable style of the party leader and the party's positive message as the more credible alternative to Labour.

The electoral strategy

The Liberal Democrats' electoral strategy still had the long-term ambitions of increasing their proportion of the national vote, thus securing more second places, and portraying themselves as the only viable alternative in Labour's regional heartlands. However, circumstances necessitated a much more offensive strategy than in 2001 with Liberal Democrat insiders before the campaign openly discussing the possibility of 15–25 net gains (G. Hurst, *The Times*, 6 April 2005). With public trust in Tony Blair's leadership in freefall, the Liberal Democrats decided to shift their emphasis to an increasing number of Labour-held seats. The Liberal Democrats' twin targeting approach involved concentrating efforts in around 35 key targets, both Conservative and Labour. These targets were not based on marginality alone, but on developments since 2001 (for example, promising results in local government) and the efforts of local constituency parties. Neither were targets fixed: Chief Executive Chris Rennard likened target seats to the football Premiership, with constituencies being liable to move up or down depending on performance. Within this was the well publicised and unfortunately named 'decapitation strategy' where the Liberal Democrats were targeting high-profile Shadow Cabinet members such as Oliver Letwin, David Davis, Theresa May and Tim Collins. At the same time the party also poured resources into seats that it held with 'water thin' majorities. As in previous elections, the Liberal Democrats sought to vigorously defend their successes in by-elections and were prepared to operate a defensive strategy in a number of marginally held seats. Many of the key targets and a number of the so-called 'development seats' stemmed from Liberal Democrats' success at the sub-national level where the party had attempted to bridge the credibility gap (Russell and Fieldhouse 2005). Indeed there was optimism among party officials that significant recent local gains in development areas such as Watford, Norwich South and Luton South could result in shock victories, despite their third-place positions in 2001. More generally, the Liberal Democrats expected to benefit from retiring Conservative incumbents (Surrey South West), a disillusioned student population angry at top-up fees and the war in Iraq (Cardiff Central, Leeds North West and Cambridge) and a disgruntled Muslim vote (Rochdale).

The election campaign

The Liberal Democrats' national election campaign was a story of two halves. Primarily, the party sought to show that it was the more credible and effective opposition to Labour, by highlighting honesty and integrity in a political climate that had been marred by the electorate's growing distrust of their opponents. Two main themes emerged. First, the party's key weapon was the 'down to earth' and honest approach of its leader Charles Kennedy. Second, the main thrust of the Liberal Democrats' political strategy was to offer credible policy alternatives to both Labour and the Conservatives. Aware that they could be branded a 'one-trick pony' by allowing their opposition to the war in Iraq to dominate their election campaign, the Liberal Democrats used the first two weeks to promote other policies on the economy, education, health and local taxation. Just as the party began to focus its campaign on the war, events dictated that it would dominate the final two weeks, much to the party's benefit.

The first half

Buoyed by consistently high trust ratings, Kennedy embarked on an exhaustive campaign. After the morning conference at 7.30 am in London, Kennedy would then use a combination charter flights and the traditional campaign battle bus to target seats across Britain. The main aim was to maximise his exposure on regional evening television and radio. This gruelling tour of Britain took the Liberal Democrat leader to around 150 constituencies during the campaign.

Yet around one week into the election campaign, Kennedy's wife gave birth to their first child. Kennedy postponed the publication of the manifesto and took two days off the campaign, leaving his deputy Menzies Campbell to take temporary charge.

On 14 April Kennedy returned to launch the Liberal Democrats' election manifesto. With a policy content of just over 10,000 words, the tabloid newspaper-styled manifesto entitled 'The Real Alternative' represented a strategic shift from previous elections. The previous election pledge to put 1p on income tax was scrapped in favour of a new 50p top rate of tax for those earning above £100,000. The manifesto launch was overshadowed by Kennedy's blunder over the impact of the party's proposed local income tax. The Liberal Democrats also pledged to replace the council tax with a local income tax. Again this measure was widely viewed as redistributive, aiding pensioners and low-income families whilst penalising middle-class dual-income couples and those owning second homes. Peter Riddell (*The Times*, 15 April 2005) questioned whether this was a wise strategy, as many professionals and managers in Liberal Democrat–Conservative marginals who may support the party over their anti-Iraq war stance were likely to be hit hardest from the Liberal Democrats' local income tax proposals.

During the first two weeks of the campaign, key policies were promoted including free long-term care for the elderly and the abolition of university tuition fees both of which the party had already introduced in Scotland whilst in coalition with Labour. As in 2001, the party's commitment to the euro subject to a referendum was included within the manifesto document. A likely vote-loser in tight Liberal Democrat–Conservative contests across the South of England, particularly the South West, it was barely mentioned.

Kennedy's attempts to reassure disillusioned Labour voters that a vote for the Liberal Democrats would not be wasted because more MPs were needed to strengthen the case for proportional representation were also seized upon as a frank admission that an electoral breakthrough was unlikely. As the second week of campaigning ended, there was no visible electoral momentum in the polls.

The second half

The second half of the campaign proved to be more fruitful. Despite further minor hiccups about who were the likely winners and losers under the party's local income tax proposal, Kennedy began to grow in strength, particularly as the election increasingly focused on the war in Iraq and the issue of trust in Tony Blair's leadership. The defection of the old Bennite Labour stalwart Brian Sedgemore provided a further boost to the Liberal Democrat campaign as the party sought to move firmly on the offensive and persuade Labour waverers to back the party. Yet among hesitant Conservative voters, this defection may have confirmed their suspicions that the Liberal Democrats had become the new left-wing party of British politics.

After competent performances in a series of high-profile television interviews, Kennedy was deemed to have performed better than his two leadership opponents on the BBC's *Question Time* leadership special. During the final days of the campaign, Kennedy began to 'show his teeth'. He claimed that Tony Blair would be 'a lame duck Prime Minister' if he won a third term. Kennedy then attacked Howard's negative campaign, accused the Conservatives of flip-flopping on council tax revaluation and the war in Iraq before questioning Howard's suitability to be Prime Minister. As polling day approached Kennedy declared that the Liberal Democrat campaign mood was the best since the 'heady days of 1983'.

Much of the final two weeks of the campaign was focused on their opposition to the war in Iraq. They were somewhat aided by media leaks on the legality of the war which propelled the issue to front-page news. While Howard branded Tony Blair a liar, Kennedy sought to solidify support among disillusioned Labour voters by stressing the party's opposition to the war. In the final week of the campaign, Kennedy reiterated that the Liberal Democrats would not form a coalition with Labour in the event of a hung Parliament or even if Tony Blair was not leader. With the final few polls predicting Liberal Democrat support as high as 23 per cent or 24 per cent, Labour strategists feared that Labour switching could cost them vital seats. Consequently, Blair, Brown and other Cabinet figures began to stress that a protest vote by one in ten Labour voters for the Liberal Democrats could deliver marginal seats to the Conservatives.

The outcome

Overall, the Liberal Democrats secured 22.6 per cent of the national vote, a rise of 3.8 per cent from 2001, and won 62 seats, a net gain of eleven seats on 2001, its highest representation in Westminster for 82 years. The Liberal Democrats increased their vote in 543 of the 625 seats they contested and are now second in 189 seats; 106 of the 356 seats held by Labour and in 83 of those held by the Conservatives. Yet the national picture obscures a great deal of unevenness in the Liberal Democrats' performance.

In 2005, the Liberal Democrats still polled well in their traditional Liberal heartlands on the 'celtic periphery' and the south coast of England. Yet Table 5.1 shows distinct regional variations in the change in the Liberal Democrat share of the vote. While the party achieved its largest above average increases in Scotland and the North of England it performed less well in the South West and South East. Quite simply, the Liberal Democrats did better in Labour's regional heartlands and less well where the Conservatives were predominantly the main opposition.

In 2001, there was evidence that the Liberal Democrats were experiencing something of a 'ceiling' effect in the South West (Denver 2001: 83). Whilst the party remained strongest in this region and won 16 seats, this masked an

Table 5.1   2005 Liberal Democrat performance: overall and by census region

Regions	LD 2005 vote share (%)	% change 01–05	Total seats	Seats gained	Seats lost
Scotland	22.6	+6.0	11	2	0
Wales	18.4	+4.6	4	2	0
Greater London	21.9	+4.4	8	2*	0
Eastern	21.8	+4.3	2	1	0
South East	25.4	+1.7	7	0	2
South West	32.5	+1.3	16	3	2
East Midlands	18.5	+3.1	0	0	0
West Midlands	18.8	+3.9	3	2	1
North	23.0	+6.1	2	1	0
North West	21.4	+4.7	6	2	0
Yorkshire & Humber	20.7	+3.6	3	1	0
Great Britain	22.6	+3.8	62	16	5

* Includes Brent East (although won in a by-election); 625 seats contested by the Liberal Democrats.

underlying trend. Where the main challenger was the Conservatives, the party either maintained 2001 levels of support or saw its share of the vote decline. Against Labour it secured large swings, even improving its share of the vote in relatively safe Labour seats and consistently challenging the Conservatives for second place. However, the net result was the lowest average increase in vote share of all the regions. Evidence of a ceiling effect can also be found in the South East, where generally the Liberal Democrat vote stuttered in contests against the Conservatives, yet rose by a far greater amount in Labour-held seats. By contrast, after recording the lowest Liberal Democrat share of the vote amongst the English regions in 1997, party prospects in the North have been transformed since. Here evidence of local gains and the strategy of securing second place behind Labour in its regional heartlands seemed to be paying off.

Gains and losses

Like the regional shifts, the pattern of gains and losses reflects both the disillusionment with Labour and the modest recovery of the Conservatives since 2001. Of the 16 Liberal Democrat gains, 12 were from Labour (see Table 5.2). The party increased its representation in the West Midlands (victories in Birmingham Yardley and Solihull) and the North West after securing two further gains (Rochdale, Manchester Withington) from Labour. The Liberal Democrats also became the second largest party in Scotland, both in terms of vote and seat share. This suggests that participation in the coalition with Labour in Scotland has aided their electoral credibility with the party seemingly benefiting electorally from popular concessions gained from Labour over tuition fees and free care to the elderly. Both victories in Dunbartonshire East and Inverness, Nairn, Badenoch & Strathspey were at the expense of Labour. The Liberal Democrats defeated two Labour incumbents in the South West (three-way marginal battles in Bristol West and Falmouth & Camborne) and won a similar number of seats from Labour in London. Generally, the Liberal Democrats 'picked off' Labour where it was a close second in 2001, although there were still local variations (Oldham East & Saddleworth, Aberdeen South and Edinburgh South) that bucked the trend. The unevenness in performance is also illustrated by its success in Cambridge, Hornsey & Wood Green and Manchester Withington all with 15 per cent or above swings from Labour. Similarly, while Sarah Teather held on to one of their by-election successes in Brent East, the party lost Leicester South quite comfortably to Labour.

Table 5.2   2005 Liberal Democrat gains

2005 Liberal Democrat gains	Swing 01–05 (%)
Brent East*	30.7 Lab–LD
Manchester Withington	17.3 Lab–LD
Cambridge	15.0 Lab–LD
Hornsey & Wood Green	14.6 Lab–LD
Solihull	10.0 Con–LD
Leeds North West	9.6 Lab–LD
Falmouth & Camborne	9.5 Lab–LD
Birmingham Yardley	8.8 Lab–LD
Cardiff Central	8.7 Lab–LD
Bristol West	8.4 Lab–LD
Rochdale	7.7 Lab–LD
Dunbartonshire East	7.4 Lab–LD
Ceredigion	6.0 PC–LD
Inverness, Nairn, Badenoch & Strathspey	6.0 Lab–LD
Westmorland & Lonsdale	3.5 Con–LD
Taunton	0.7 Con–LD
2005 Liberal Democrat losses	Swing 01–05 (%)
Newbury	5.5 LD–Con
Ludlow	4.1 LD–Con
Devon West & Torridge	3.9 LD–Con
Weston-Super-Mare	2.5 LD–Con
Guildford	0.9 LD–Con

* Liberal Democrats held Brent East after a by-election victory.

Against the Conservatives, the Liberal Democrats found the going much tougher. Despite recapturing Taunton after losing it in 2001, the party's much publicised 'decapitation strategy' of high-profile Conservative Shadow Cabinet figures proved largely unsuccessful. The failure to capture Dorset West, Haltemprice

& Howden and Maidenhead were only offset by the capture of Tim Collins' seat (Westmorland & Lonsdale). Elsewhere, the Liberal Democrats did win Solihull, a reported target that was kept quiet by Liberal Democrat strategists for fear of alerting Conservative national officials. However, the party lost five seats to the Conservatives and failed to win a number of vulnerable Conservative-held seats including Orpington and Eastbourne the scene of famous Liberal by-election successes in the past. Yet once again the picture is uneven. While the Liberal Democrats lost Devon West & Torridge and Weston-Super-Mare, other nearby vulnerable seats such as Somerton & Frome and Devon North were held. The Liberal Democrats also held Cheadle, the most vulnerable seat in 2001, although they lost Newbury to the Conservatives with a 5.5 per cent swing. Local factors ranging from anti-hunt mobilisation to dissatisfaction with Liberal Democrat controlled West Berkshire council were put forward as explanations for David Rendel's demise.

Constituency contests and marginality

Although the Liberal Democrat national vote rose sharply, it is clear that the national picture obscures a great deal of local variation. In part this reflects different patterns of party competition in different areas. Table 5.3 presents Liberal Democrat vote share, average change in vote share and swing by seat types and vulnerability. Quite clearly, the Liberal Democrats performed worse against the Conservatives than Labour. In contests where Liberal Democrats were defending and the Conservatives were the main challengers, their average vote share actually declined. It seems likely that the level of Liberal Democrat support in these seats has reached a ceiling, with the party unable to make further inroads. The party is therefore vulnerable in close contests to any Conservative revival. Similarly, where the Liberal Democrats were the main challengers to the Conservatives, the party gained some support from dissatisfied Labour voters but failed to win over Conservative supporters. Two important points must be made.

First, the Liberal Democrats are continuing to suffer from the inability to squeeze the Labour vote in tight Conservative–Liberal Democrat contests. This seems a particular problem for the party in the South West and to a lesser extent along the south coast of England. In winnable seats such as Bournemouth East, Wells and Wiltshire North, Labour bucked the national trend, recording similar levels of support as four years previously. Indeed, the Labour vote remained solid in Weston-super-Mare, where a larger swing to the Liberal Democrat incumbent could have staved off a Conservative victory. In 15 Conservative seats, which after the 2001 election were vulnerable to the Liberal Democrats, there was a small swing to the Conservatives and a minor fall in Liberal Democrat vote share. The Liberal Democrat performance in non-vulnerable Conservative seats is much better, although a large proportion of the party's vote share stems from disgruntled Labour voters. Even here, the swing from Labour to Liberal Democrat is nowhere near the level where Labour is the incumbent. Put simply, the Liberal Democrats failed to persuade large numbers of Labour voters in vulnerable Conservative seats to tactically shift their support. This may be partly attributable to the success of Labour's (wholly unsubstantiated) campaign message that it would only take one in ten Labour supporters to vote Liberal Democrat to deliver a Conservative government.

Table 5.3   Liberal Democrat performance: mean percentage vote share; mean change in vote share, 2001–05; Lab–LD/Con–LD swing, 2001–05; by seat type, vulnerability/margin

Seat type/margin	Mean 2005 LD % vote share	± 01–05 mean LD % vote share	Lab–Lib Dem swing (%)	Con–Lib Dem swing (%)
Seat type (N)				
LD–Con (44)	46.23	–0.59	+0.26	–0.61
Con–LD (58)	31.01	+0.47	+1.62	–0.47
LD–Lab (7)	49.94	+6.21	+5.01	+3.64
Lab–LD (53)	28.89	+7.67	+7.33	+4.47
Nat–LD (1)	36.53	+9.66	+6.51	+8.36
Con–Lab (105)	19.84	+2.97	+4.55	+0.88
Lab–Con (308)	17.39	+4.72	+5.88	+2.40
Vulnerability to LD (N)				
*Con seats**				
Vulnerable to LD (15)	38.24	–0.48	+1.06	–1.36
Non-vulnerable (148)	22.35	+2.34	+3.75	+0.58
*Lab seats***				
Vulnerable to LD (13)	36.39	+7.16	+6.01	+4.17
Non-vulnerable (389)	18.04	+5.13	+6.02	+2.66
*LD held****				
Marginal (19)	44.17	+1.61	+2.05	+0.65
Safe (32)	48.26	–0.41	+0.24	–0.43

* Con seats: vulnerable to Liberal Democrats 0–9.9 per cent; non-vulnerable 10 per cent+; should be 149 but Staffordshire South is not included.
** Lab Seats: vulnerable to Liberal Democrats 0–19.9 per cent; non-vulnerable 20 per cent+.
*** LD held: marginal 0–9.9 per cent; safe 10 per cent+.

Second, Russell et al. (2002: 219) claimed that 'the radical repositioning of Liberal Democrat policy in 2001 could have put distance between the traditional base of liberal voters and the party'. Given this, it seems increasingly likely that the radical centre left appearance of the 2005 Liberal Democrats may have further contributed to some electors returning to the Conservative fold. For instance, Sue Doughty, former Lib Dem MP in Guildford, who lost her seat to Conservatives, claimed that the party's local income tax plans scared off middle-income earners.

Similarly, it is conceivable that the party alienated potential Liberal Democrat voters in Conservative–Liberal Democrat contests with its proposals to raise the top rate of tax. More likely is that the 'left of Labour' label among middle-income groups in Southern seats stuck, and that the Conservatives may have tapped into concerns (immigration and asylum, and so on) which the Liberal Democrats simply didn't face up to.

Whilst making further inroads into already rock-bottom Conservative support proved difficult, the tide was moving in a more favourable direction against Labour. The Liberal Democrats performed best in contests where Labour was either the main challenger or the incumbent. The swing from Labour to Liberal Democrat was largest where the Liberal Democrats were challenging Labour, a reflection of the several gains achieved at Labour's expense and the success of the Liberal Democrats' long-term strategy of building support in Labour heartlands. Not surprisingly, the party strengthened its position in vulnerable Labour seats, aided not only by a substantial swing from Labour but also from the Conservatives, indicating a new willingness of erstwhile Conservative supporters to tactically switch to the Liberal Democrats. However, with an average vote share of around 18 per cent in non-vulnerable Labour seats, it is clear that the party still remains too far behind in the majority of Labour seats to substantially benefit from any collapse in the Labour vote.

Despite five losses to the Conservatives, Liberal Democrat average vote change increased by 1.6 per cent in marginal constituencies where they held the seat in 2001. This was mainly due to large swings from Labour in seats such as Norfolk North and Bristol West. The Liberal Democrat vote marginally declined in its safe seats suggesting that the party may have reached its peak with little scope to make much further progress.

Incumbency

Whilst the party improved its performance in seats held before 1997, the Liberal Democrats suffered a reversal in seats that the party won in 1997 and 2001 (Table 5.4). In 1997, the Liberal Democrats had gained seats at the expense of the Conservatives. Four years later, support increased most in those seats where they first made an electoral breakthrough in 1997. Russell and Fieldhouse (2005) claimed that electoral credibility was the most likely explanation. Voters are more likely to support the Liberal Democrats if they feel they can win; winning the constituency at the previous election constitutes firm proof that the Liberal Democrats have become a credible option (Russell et al. 2002: 219). Yet the party's 2001 targeting strategy may also have been an important factor. Then, seats won in 1997 were targeted to stem any Conservative revival. The result was that small majorities in Lewes, Torbay, Kingston & Surbiton and elsewhere became relatively safe. In 2005, these seats did not receive the same level of party support. This resulted in uneven results as some seats saw large swings to the

Conservatives. Liberal Democrat majorities in Torbay and Kingston & Surbiton were halved, while other Liberal Democrat seats such as Lewes and Winchester saw more minor reductions in the Liberal Democrat majorities.

Table 5.4   Liberal Democrat performance and historical base, incumbency (seats) and new candidates

Historical base & incumbency	Mean % LD vote share 2005	Mean % LD vote share ± 01–05	Seats held	Gains	Losses	Total seats
Pre-1997 seats (16)	47.45	+1.42	16	–	0	16
Post-1997 seats (35)	46.41	–0.15	30	–	5	30
First-time inc (8)	46.56	+2.57	6	–	2	6
Other LD incumbents (37)	47.39	+0.67	35	–	2	35
LD new (6)	42.98	–4.64	5	–	1	5
All LD seats (51)	46.74	+0.34	46	–	5	46
All non-LD seats (574)	20.09	+4.30	–	16	–	16

Note: 625 seats in total – excludes the Speaker's seat (Glasgow North East), Staffordshire South (by-election) and Wyre Forest (Liberal Democrats did not stand).

On the face of it, the Liberal Democrats benefited from a first time incumbency effect. However, whilst incumbents in Cheadle, Dorset Mid & North Poole and Norfolk North substantially increased their majorities, aided in no small part by a collapse in the Labour vote through tactical switching, the Conservatives won two seats (Guildford and Ludlow) from the Liberal Democrats and narrowly failed to win Romsey. The Liberal Democrats selected six new candidates to stand in seats where they were the incumbent party. Not only did they lose Devon West & Torridge to the Conservatives, but their average vote share since 2001 declined by –4.64 per cent. Across all Liberal Democrat-held seats, party performance did slightly improve, although it is clear that they are already running at an extremely high water mark. The real story occurred in non-Liberal Democrat seats where the party increased its average vote share since 2001 by 4.30 per cent.

Local platforms for success

Previous research has shown that the party tends to be more successful in areas where it has achieved local election success (Russell and Fieldhouse 2005; Cutts forthcoming). After achieving credibility locally, the Liberal Democrats then use their strong local base as a stepping stone for parliamentary success. To take account of this, Table 5.5 reveals how well the Liberal Democrats did in areas where they had achieved local success between 2002 and 2004. Notably, they polled best where they had more representation locally; indeed half of their parliamentary seats are where the Liberal Democrats are at least the equal largest force on the local council. It also paid dividends in terms of seats, with the party increasing its number of seats from 26 to 32 where it held more that 40 per cent of local council seats.

Table 5.5   2005 Liberal Democrat performance and the local context: percentage of Liberal Democrat seats on the council, 2002–04

% LD seats on Council (2002–04)	Mean 2005 LD % vote share	Mean % LD vote share ± 01–05	Seats won	Gains	Lab–LD swing (%)	Con–LD swing (%)
0–19.9 (324)	17.1	+3.96	5	2	+5.16	+1.73
20–39.9 (184)	25.2	+4.21	25	8	+4.92	+2.12
40+ (120)	31.7	+3.66	32	6	+4.23	+1.87

Note: 625 seats in total – excludes the Speaker's seat (Glasgow North East), Staffordshire South (by-election) and Wyre Forest (Liberal Democrats did not stand).

In terms of change in vote share, the Liberal Democrats benefited from Labour dissatisfaction in Labour's heartlands, and the swing was larger where they had fewer local council representatives. They saw their largest average increase in vote share from 2001 in constituencies where the party had 20–39.9 per cent of seats on the council. With eight seats gained, it seems likely that the long-term strategy of building local representation in Labour heartlands is starting to bear fruit at the parliamentary level. Two prominent examples are Manchester Withington and Leeds North West, where the party has improved its local electoral performance since embarking on the developmental strategy post 1997.

Understanding unevenness: the impact of socio-demographics

Russell and Fieldhouse (2005) point out there is no clear social base of support for the Liberal Democrats, an observation supported in 2005 by MORI data which show that in no one social class did the party win more than 30 per cent of the vote (the highest being the ABs at 29 per cent). However, unlike in previous elections, when success was largely based on targeting strategy and the local government base, in 2005, other specific factors, linked to socio-demographics, were widely believed to influence the Liberal Democrats' electoral prospects.

During the election campaign, the Liberal Democrats promoted their anti-war stance and stressed their opposition to tuition fees. The party hoped that by appealing to Muslim voters and students it could make a number of gains in Labour seats. Table 5.6 shows that Liberal Democrat average vote share increased by nearly 9 per cent from 2001 in the 39 seats with the highest Muslim population. This was largely at the expense of Labour, although there is evidence of Conservatives tactically switching to the Liberal Democrats in a few seats. However, the evidence is far from clear cut. The Liberal Democrats only won Brent East and Rochdale of the 39 most populated Muslim seats and lost Leicester

South which contained a higher Muslim population than the two they won. Despite Labour worries in Blackburn and Ilford South, the Liberal Democrats hardly made a significant impact. In the two most populated Muslim seats (Birmingham Sparkbrook & Small Heath and Bethnal Green & Bow) the Liberal Democrats, despite fielding Muslim candidates, were brushed aside by Respect. However, there were some notable increases in support (Holborn & St Pancras, Bradford North and Birmingham Ladywood) although the Liberal Democrats were starting from such a low base that it was almost inevitable that they would come up short. Four gains were achieved in seats where the Muslim population varied between 5 per cent and 9.9 per cent, although there are similar examples of little progress in other seats. The party also failed to get any Muslim candidates elected, despite strong performances in Birmingham Ladywood and Manchester Gorton. Elsewhere, Muslim Liberal Democrat candidates did generally improve the party's performance (Bradford West, Pendle and Sheffield Central) but failed to achieve anything like the large swings some expected.

Table 5.6 Liberal Democrat performance in Muslim seats: mean percentage vote share; mean change in vote share, 2001–05; Lab–LD/Con–LD swing 2001–05 (England and Wales)

Muslim population (%)	Mean 2005 % LD vote share	Mean % LD vote share ± 01–05	Lab–LD swing (%)	Con–LD swing (%)	Lib Dem gains
0–4.9 (466)	22.29	+3.04	+4.20	+1.27	8
5–9.9 (62)	21.59	+5.95	+7.04	+3.01	4
10+ (39)	21.88	+8.90	+9.81	+5.40	2

Note: 567 constituencies out of 569 for England and Wales: excludes Staffordshire South (by-election) and Wyre Forest (Liberal Democrats did not stand). Two seats won in Scotland: Inverness, Nairn, Badenoch & Strathspey and Dunbartonshire East (no available data).

In sum, the impact of the Muslim vote was always likely to be marginal. Many of the seats with large Muslim populations were simply out of reach, and even where they were not, the Liberal Democrats could not bank on the entire Muslim electorate moving en bloc. Furthermore, there is growing evidence that Muslims like other black and minority ethnic (BME) groups have lower registration levels than whites and that Muslim participation rates are around the same level as whites but lower than other Asian groups such as Hindus or Sikhs (Fieldhouse et al. 2005). When you also consider the level of loyalty to Labour within key Muslim groups and associations, particularly among the elders within the community, it was always unlikely that the Muslim vote would reap the Liberal Democrats huge rewards. Whilst it may have made the difference in

Rochdale and perhaps Brent East, the overall effect in terms of seats gained was probably negligible.

Table 5.7   Liberal Democrat performance in full-time student seats: mean percentage vote share; mean change in vote share, 2001–05; Lab–LD/Con–LD swing, 2001–05 (England and Wales)

Student population (%)	Mean 2005 % LD vote share	Mean % LD vote share ± 01–05	Lab–LD swing (%)	Con–LD swing (%)	Lib Dem gains
0–4.9 (188)	20.91	+2.03	+3.54	+0.72	0
5–9.9 (300)	21.84	+4.08	+5.00	+1.88	7
10–14.9 (50)	23.86	+5.41	+7.18	+2.77	1
15+ (29)	31.12	+8.78	+8.60	+5.16	6

Note: 567 constituencies out of 569 for England and Wales: excludes Staffordshire South (by-election) and Wyre Forest (Liberal Democrats did not stand). Two seats won in Scotland: Inverness, Nairn, Badenoch & Strathspey (not known); Dunbartonshire East (not known).

By contrast, the Liberal Democrats' ability to attract the student vote requires closer inspection. First, Table 5.7 shows that the Liberal Democrats secured their highest average vote share and increase since 2001 in constituencies with more than 15 per cent full-time students. These seats also saw large swings away from both Labour and the Conservatives culminating in six Liberal Democrat gains. These gains included Bristol West, Cambridge, Cardiff Central, Ceredigion, Leeds North West and Manchester Withington, all of which contain or are in the near vicinity of major universities. The party also held Sheffield Hallam (20.4 per cent students), a prominent location for students. Similarly, the Liberal Democrats narrowly failed to win Oxford East and strongly challenged Labour in Newcastle upon Tyne Central and the City of Durham. Significantly, many of these university seats contain not only students but also large numbers of academic staff and young professionals with degrees.

Table 5.8 highlights this. The Liberal Democrats performed well in seats with the largest number of people with degrees, increasing their vote share by 6.4 per cent since 2001 and achieving large swings from both parties, particularly Labour. Indeed, 31 of the 48 most educated seats also contain 10 per cent or more students. More interestingly, Cambridge, Manchester Withington, Ceredigion and Leeds North West and Hornsey & Wood Green feature prominently, adding fuel to the suspicion that a combination of educated, young professionals and full-time students precipitated a Liberal Democrat surge in these seats. This could also account for strong performances in the City of Durham and Oxford East, although anomalies such as Loughborough and Canterbury do exist. The Liberal Democrats also lost Leicester South and failed to achieve large-scale swings in Liverpool Riverside and Exeter. In these university seats, the Liberal Democrats simply did not have the other key ingredient of a strong parliamentary base to mount an effective challenge.

Table 5.8 Liberal Democrat performance in the most-educated seats: mean percentage vote share; mean change in vote share, 2001–05; Lab–LD/Con–LD swing, 2001–05 (England and Wales)

Student population (%)	Mean 2005 % LD vote share	Mean % LD vote share ± 01–05	Lab–LD swing (%)	Con–LD swing (%)	Lib Dem gains
0–7.5 (285)	20.33	+3.49	+4.86	+1.61	3
7.5–9.9 (235)	23.10	+3.55	+4.56	+1.51	4
10+ (48)	28.55	+6.42	+6.76	+3.72	7

Note: 567 constituencies out of 569 for England and Wales: excludes Staffordshire South (by-election) and Wyre Forest (Liberal Democrats did not stand). Two seats won in Scotland: Inverness, Nairn, Badenoch & Strathspey (not known); Dunbartonshire East (not known).

Conclusion

Despite their winning more seats than any Liberal party since 1923, the election of 2005 was fundamentally disappointing for the party. With the electorate increasingly disillusioned with Labour and uninspired by an ineffective Conservative opposition, the Liberal Democrats had arguably their best opportunity of a major breakthrough, but it did not materialise. The single most significant reason this is so is the electoral system. Polling 22 per cent of the votes, the Liberal Democrats won only 9.9 per cent of seats in Parliament. According to 'Make Votes Count',[2] for every million who voted Labour they secured 37 MPs, for every million who voted Conservative they achieved 22 MPs, and for every million who voted Liberal Democrat they secured only ten MPs.

However, there were many positives to come out of the election for the Liberal Democrats. They proved themselves the only challengers to Labour in the big cities, particularly Manchester, Leeds, Birmingham, Cardiff (where the Conservatives have none). Regionally they moved into second place to Labour in the North East and Scotland, and remain second to the Conservatives in the South East and the South West.

However the result was characterised by unevenness. Whilst they made gains they did not dare hope for, they also failed in areas they might realistically have expected to win. Whilst they continued to build incrementally where they enjoyed electoral credibility – established through historical tradition and strong local government performance – their gains were largely attributable to other local factors such as opposition to the war in Iraq (for example, Rochdale), and in areas with high proportions of students and degree holders (such as Bristol West, Cambridge, and surprisingly Manchester Withington). However, is it unlikely that factors such as the war in Iraq or tuition up fees will be as salient at the next election – if not then the Liberal Democrats may find it difficult to hold on to these seats.

Despite the unevenness one clear pattern did emerge. The Liberal Democrats were gaining vote share and seats at the expense of Labour, not the Tories. Given the changing tide of electoral support since 2001, especially the declining Labour share of the vote, and the impact of the war in Iraq, this was hardly surprising. In contrast the Conservative share of the vote was perhaps as low as it could be expected to go in 2001, and if anything the Liberal Democrats performed well to hold off the Conservative challenge as well as they did. However, those changes leave them a huge dilemma for the next election. Do they continue to focus their efforts on eliminating the Tories as the effective opposition, or do they hope to cash in on growing disillusionment with Labour? In reality they have to do both if they are to hold on to their existing seats and make any further gains. Table 5.9 illustrates the nature of the battleground for the party going into the next election. It shows that although they increased their number of second places to 189 (from 111) many of these are relatively safe. Only twelve seats would be gained on a 5 per cent swing from both their main competitors and only 25 on a 10 per cent swing. Notably, unlike the situation going into 2005 when most of their targets were Conservative-held, these are relatively equally Conservative and Labour seats. In the seats they hold, however, their main opponents are disproportionately Conservatives, making them vulnerable to a Conservative revival.

Table 5.9   Post-2005 Liberal Democrat electoral prospects: margin by seat type (subject to redistricting)

Seat types	Very marginal (0–4.9%)	Marginal (5–9.9%)	Fairly safe (10%)
LD hold (62)	14	16	32
Lib Dem–Con (43)	9	8	26
Lib Dem–Lab (18)	4	8	6
LD–Other (1)	1	–	–
LD Second Place (189)	12	13	164
Lab–Lib Dem (106)	5	5	96
Con–Lib Dem (83)	7	8	68

Note: 625 seats in total – excludes the Speaker's seat (Glasgow North East), Staffordshire South (by-election) and Wyre Forest (Liberal democrats did not stand).

So where do the Liberal Democrats go from here? One option is to move to the right and further embrace market principles, individual choice and responsibility. The attraction of this approach is that it may make them more resistant to a Conservative revival especially in the nine seats that are vulnerable to Conservative swings of 5 per cent and under. However, the downside of this approach is that it may precipitate large-scale defections to Labour, especially amongst highly educated, public sector supporters. Furthermore, given the low share of the vote won by the Conservatives in 2005, a swing from the Liberal Democrats to the Conservatives is likely, regardless of a shift to the right.

A second approach is to appeal to the left-of-centre vote by promoting their radical credentials. This would entail selling the party as more radical than Labour on socio-economic issues, whilst continuing to promote a distinctive position on civil liberties, the environment and foreign policy. This would help the party to protect narrow gains from Labour achieved in 2005. However, the scope for advance is limited, the Liberal Democrats being behind Labour by 10 per cent or below in only ten seats and they are more than 15 per cent behind Labour in 87 seats. They would therefore need many more surprise results like Cambridge and Manchester Withington to make any substantial gains against Labour.

The more likely and pragmatic solution is to follow the middle way, and attempt to appeal to disaffected Labour and Conservative supporters by promoting an image that is 'neither left nor right', but at the same time distinctive (Russell and Fieldhouse 2005). As the Liberal Democrat chief executive told us: 'any strategy that is based on winning votes just from the Conservatives or Labour is doomed to failure – we cannot get where we want to be without having any strategy that has got to win from both (Conservatives and Labour)'.

However, for this strategy to pay dividends the Liberal Democrats must hope that a third-term Labour government becomes increasingly unpopular and that there is no Tory revival. Even if this proves to be the case, under the current electoral system the best the party might expect is consolidating its existing seats, and making further incremental gains based on local factors, as it has done in the past.

So was 2005 a good election for the Liberal Democrats? Following the election Charles Kennedy claimed 'the era of three party politics right across the UK is now with us'. While Kennedy found reasons to be optimistic, other officials claimed that 'obviously we need to raise our game'. Recognition, perhaps, that on balance the election result was more of an opportunity lost than a major breakthrough.

Notes

1. The Liberal Democrats won 17 seats in Scotland and six seats in Wales. The party gained one seat at the London Assembly elections, increasing their overall representation to five.
2. <www.makemyvotecount.org.uk>.

References

Cutts, D. (forthcoming) 'Continuous campaigning and electoral outcomes: the Liberal Democrats in Bath', *Political Geography*.

Denver, D. (2001) 'The Liberal Democrat campaign', in P. Norris (ed.) *Britain Votes 2001*, Oxford: Oxford University Press.

Fieldhouse, E., Cutts, D., Purdam, K. and Steel, D. (2005) 'Voter engagement in British South Asian communities at the 2001 general election'. Paper to the Annual Conference of the Political Studies Association, University of Leeds.

Russell, A. and Fieldhouse, E. (2005) *Neither Left Nor Right? The Liberal Democrats and the Electorate*, Manchester: Manchester University Press.

Russell, A., Fieldhouse, E. and I. MacAllister (2002) 'Two steps forward, one step back? The Liberal Democrats' 2001 general election performance in perspective', *Representation*, 38(3).

Manchester Withington

One of the most sensational election results was in Manchester Withington, where a 17.3 per cent swing saw the Liberal Democrats overturn Labour's 11,524 majority. Many within the constituency felt the result might be close. The Liberal Democrats worked exceptionally hard during the campaign, leafleting almost daily towards its conclusion, whilst Labour canvassers acknowledged that the party was struggling to hold its vote.

There was controversy before the campaign began. The Liberal Democrats replaced their 2001 candidate in 2005, Yasmin Zalzala, having viewed her as not up to the task. Zalzala stood as an independent in 2005, denouncing 'opportunist hypocrites' and the 'white majority of bullyboys' in the party (*South Manchester Reporter*, 21 April 2005). However, she achieved a derisory vote share.

Manchester Withington is home to a sizeable number of students, young professionals, particularly in the public sector, and academics. Owner-occupation is below 50 per cent and the private rented sector is much larger than normal at 26 per cent. Although many Withington voters are instinctively Labour-leaning, a set of national and local issues gave the Liberal Democrats particular appeal in this contest.

In some respects, the Labour candidate was 'hung out to dry' by the party leadership, on these issues. Indeed, the sitting MP since 1987, Keith Bradley, conceded privately on the day prior to the election to supporters that he thought he might lose.

Bradley had opposed the Iraq war without a second UN resolution; he supported the extension of the Metrolink light railway system through South Manchester, promised years earlier by a Labour government which had failed to deliver. A Labour manifesto promise to support a rail line already supposed to be nearing completion impressed few. The Labour MP had also been adversely affected by changes in the status of Withington Hospital. Whilst the Liberal Democrats' claim of a threat to services at Christie Hospital was dismissed as scaremongering, it nonetheless impacted upon the campaign. Bradley had voted in favour of university top-up fees, a move unlikely to endear him or his party to many first-time voters, or many of their parents.

The ousting of the Labour MP brought an immediate backlash in the local press, the *South Manchester Reporter* (13 May 2005) carrying letters lambasting students for 'contributing nothing' to the area, whilst 'trendy lefties' were also attacked for the loss of a 'good, hardworking MP'. An alternative reading was that a healthy fusion of national and local concerns had produced change. Either way, the Liberal Democrats' gain confirmed their advance in major northern cities, the party having also captured seats on Manchester City Council in recent years.

Meanwhile, the problems of the Conservatives in northern cities were highlighted. Manchester Withington, once a seat with an older, less transient middle-class suburban population of owner-occupiers, was held by the Conservatives until 1987. Since then, the party has done progressively worse and their candidate, oddly, like Labour's, also a K. Bradley, suffered a 5 per cent fall in vote share.

Result		%
Leech, J. (LD)	15,872	42.4
Bradley, K. (Lab)	15,205	40.6
Bradley, K. (Con)	3,919	10.5
Candeland, B. (Green)	1,595	4.3
Guttfreund-Walmsley, R. (UKIP)	424	1.1
Benett, I. (Independent)	243	0.6
Zalzala, Y. (Independent)	153	0.4
Reed, R. (Their Party)	47	0.1
LD gain from Lab		
LD majority	667	1.8
Swing: Lab to LD		17.3

Turnout: 55.3%

Southport

As with Crosby, the neighbouring constituency down the Merseyside coast, Southport represented a seat indicative of Conservative problems. Here, the contest was between the Conservatives and the Liberal Democrats in a seat held by the Conservatives post-war until 1987, when the Liberal Democrats captured the constituency. The Conservatives recaptured the seat in 1992, before the Liberal Democrats' Ronnie Fearn regained it in 1997, a success repeated by the current Liberal Democrat MP, John Pugh, in 2001.

Defending a majority of only 3,007, with a swing of only 3.5 per cent needed for the seat to fall to the Conservatives, the Liberal Democrats approached the campaign with some trepidation over a Conservative revival. Charles Kennedy and Michael Howard both visited the town, emphasising its marginal status. Perhaps surprisingly in an area of high owner occupation, relatively elderly population and only slightly above-average housing prices, Pugh placed 'affordable housing' at the centre of his campaign (*Southport Visiter*, 8 April 2005).

The other Liberal Democrat policies highlighted by Pugh, including more police and the abolition of the council tax, were obvious vote-winners. The abolition of university tuition fees was also likely to play well among first time voters. Although modest in numbers, a majority of 18–21-year-olds in Southport go on to higher education in what is an affluent town. Pugh could also rely upon his track record as a diligent MP. Recent local controversies, perhaps the most serious being the removal of some hospital maternity services out of the town, were blamed upon the Labour government. His Conservative opponent, although having the advantage of being local, had not previously fought the seat.

A combination of these factors allowed the Liberal Democrats to hold the seat with surprising ease, enjoying a swing *from* the Conservatives of 1 per cent and adding 1,000 to the Liberal Democrat vote. Although the seat remains marginal, it may slowly be heading towards the status of Liberal Democrat 'natural' seat. In the South, the Conservatives proved capable of taking back a similar type of coastal resort, Weston-super-Mare. In the North, the Liberal Democrat position was consolidated.

Result		%
Pugh, J. (LD)	19,093	46.4
Bigley, M. (Con)	15,255	37.0
Brant, M. (Lab)	5,277	12.8
Durrance, T. (UKIP)	749	1.8
Givens, B. (Your Party)	589	1.4
Forster, H. (Veritas)	238	0.6
Lib Dem hold		
Lib Dem majority	3,838	9.3
Swing: Con to Lib Dem		1.0

Turnout: 60.6%

6
The Candidate: Tony Wright

Tony Wright

The election ...

What a curious election this was. Everything about it seemed odd. There was the fact that the date had been known for so long, effectively if not officially, that its formal announcement came as relief rather than surprise. It was like having a fixed-term Parliament. Then there was the fact of a Prime Minister who had already announced that he would be retiring, if re-elected, before another election. It was like having a fixed-term Prime Minister. Nothing about this election seemed quite normal, which is doubtless why so many people found it difficult to know what was really going on.

The feeling was compounded, as a candidate, by the fact that you inhabit your own little electoral bubble, in Cannock Chase in my case, and have little idea what is happening in the larger battle. I did not see a single party election broadcast, nor read any of the acres of newspaper commentary. I caught the news on the radio, cocked an ear for what the polls seemed to be saying, but quickly abandoned Radio 4 for the tranquillity of Radio 3 once the political talking heads came on. The tons of email that arrived daily from party HQ remained happily unread, along with the manifesto on which I was supposedly fighting the election. There was simply too much else to do – another leaflet to get out, another telephone call to be made – and the last thing I wanted to do when I got home each night was to immerse myself in yet more election stuff. A bath was far more inviting.

So when people asked, as they regularly did, 'How is it going then?', my truthful if unsatisfactory answer was invariably 'I have absolutely no idea.' It depended on the last person I spoke to, or whether the mums (and few dads) at the school gate took our proffered leaflets with a friendly smile or rejected them with an unfriendly scowl. A pensioner or parent who said 'I've never been so well off because of what Labour has done for us' could lift my spirits for a whole day, until someone could make them plunge again by saying something like 'I'll

91

never vote Labour again while Tony Blair is leader' or – more depressing – 'You lot are all the same.' It was all very confusing, and made it genuinely difficult to work out what kind of election this was.

The truth, I think, is that it was the election that nobody really wanted to have – not the politicians, not the media, and certainly not the electorate. It had been going on in a phoney form for so long that most people just wanted it to be over when it finally came. The general assumption was that Labour would win, with uncertainty only about the size of the majority. The electorate might not have wild enthusiasm for the government after eight years, but at the same time there was no widespread desire to have a different one. Kick it, perhaps; kick it out, no. This was not a 'time for a change' election, which is why many voters would have preferred the government simply to carry on without the inconvenience of having to go out and vote for it. It was an election to get over.

It was also an election in which it seemed sensible to hang on to nurse for fear of getting something worse. This is where the economy was decisive. The fact that the Conservatives did not even attempt to mount a serious attack on the government's economic record made it a remarkable election in itself; while the memory of the Conservatives' own economic record in government was invoked by Labour in just the way, and with the same effect, as the Conservatives had regularly invoked the memory of Labour's 'winter of discontent' a generation earlier. The danger for Labour was that the electorate might have started to take a benign economic environment for granted – plentiful jobs, rising living standards, low inflation and mortgage rates – and so might assume that this would continue under any government, thus diminishing the risk in voting for somebody else. Labour naturally responded to this danger by talking up the risk.

There was the further sense that only Labour really looked like a government, with a serious governing programme. The Conservatives seemed only to have assembled a clutch of populist slogans, with the rest of its programme depending on heroic assumptions about cutting government 'waste', while the Liberal Democrats did not even pretend to be an alternative government. This did not necessarily mean that the election was in the bag though. The Conservative slogans were cleverly targeted on the nerve ends of public anxiety, and the Liberal Democrats energetically offered themselves as the repository for voters who wanted to give Tony Blair a bloody nose for Iraq. How these cross-currents would play out, in particular constituencies and in aggregate, gave a feeling of uncertainty to an election that otherwise seemed flat and predictable.

Viewed from my little bubble, in what is seen (though never by me) as a 'safe' Labour seat, these uncertainties could only be glimpsed. There seemed to be Conservative billboards everywhere, with their appalling slogans about uncontrolled immigration and released prisoners attacking our daughters, and no Labour ones to be seen. What *were* people thinking about what the Conservatives were thinking? I knew that the anti-immigrant rhetoric would strike a chord with some of my constituents (in a white working-class West Midlands seat), because they regularly told me what they thought about immigrants and asylum seekers, but the question was whether their general dislike and distrust of the Conservatives would trump any liking for what they were saying.

It was difficult to judge, just as it was difficult to judge how the relentless media attention to Iraq would play in a constituency like mine without a *Guardian*-reading class agonising about who might deserve its carefully calibrated tactical vote. A far greater concern for me centred on the tragic case of a six-year-old girl in my constituency who had recently had both her hands and feet amputated as a result of contracting meningitis and its complications. She was the only story locally, as a fund was raised to help her, and a regular item on regional television news. As the election was called, it was announced that she now also had MRSA. The Conservative slogans had been adroitly chosen, and in this case I simply did not know what the electoral fallout might be.

I did realise that Michael Howard's 'liar' charge against Tony Blair might have been a serious blunder, as well as plumbing new depths in British election campaigning, when a well-mannered meeting for candidates in my constituency organised by the local churches (now, sadly, the only kind of public meeting in most constituencies) erupted into hissing when one of my opponents tried to deploy it. I voted against the Iraq war, believing it would do more harm than good, but the charge against Tony Blair is not that he lied (he did not) but that he believed so passionately in the rightness of what he was doing that he paid insufficient attention to the difficulties and doubts. Michael Howard's support for the war (even if he had known there were no weapons of mass destruction, and even if he had been told it was illegal) made his 'liar' charge against Tony Blair seem contemptible and the worst kind of opportunism.

These were the kind of echoes from the larger campaign that I picked up in my constituency, but they were not much to go on. Issues appeared and disappeared, but seemed to leave little lasting mark on the campaign. The final collapse of MG Rover as the election started might have been expected to bring major political consequences in the West Midlands, yet did not seem to. My constituency has a thousand workers producing car parts, but now nearly all for Toyota, Nissan and other foreign manufacturers, which helps to explain why the impact of the Rover collapse was much more muted in the region than it would once have been. There were moments when an issue seemed to threaten to intervene decisively in the campaign the conviction of an asylum seeker for killing a policeman, the leaked legal advice on Iraq – but it never quite happened, despite the desperate media desire that it should.

As the election ground on, I assumed that the core Tory vote would have hardened, that the Liberal Democrats would have stacked up the anti-war protest vote, and that the consequence of these two factors was that Labour's majority would be severely cut. The question, especially in seats like mine, was whether the traditional Labour vote would hold, or turn out in sufficient numbers, and whether enough of those who had come over to Labour in 1997 and 2001 would stay with the party now. I expected to see my 2001 majority of 10,704 (26 per cent) sharply pruned on a low turnout (in 2001 we had one of the worst drops in turnout in the whole country) and a much diminished Labour majority overall. In the event my majority was not much down on 2001, to 9,227, on a turnout only slightly below the national average, and Labour's reduced majority was still very comfortable by pre-Blair standards. The party had secured its historic third term. The election campaign had come and gone but the electorate seemed to have made its mind up long before it started, and nothing much had happened to change it.

... and after

The results were hardly in before some of the usual suspects among my parliamentary colleagues were telling the media that Tony Blair should step down and hand over to Gordon Brown. This might seem a perverse verdict on a leader who had just achieved what no previous Labour leader had done. It also made the first meeting of the Parliamentary Labour Party, in the week after the election, a turbulent and highly charged occasion, as the malcontents were verbally beaten up in a robust demonstration of support for the Prime Minister. The loudest applause came when Tony Blair observed (with a dig at Roy Hattersley) that, having served loyally in the past through three election defeats, it was surely not too much to expect support through three election victories. He promised (and demanded) that there would be an orderly and dignified leadership succession.

What was most striking about this meeting though was not just Tony Blair's barnstorming performance, clearly that of someone planning a legacy not preparing an exit, but his strategic overview of the political landscape following the election. He confessed (as he often did) that he had not come from the traditional wing of the Labour movement, but his relentless mission had been to make it occupy the middle ground of British politics. This was why it had just won its third consecutive election victory and why it was imperative for the party to stay firmly on the ground it had occupied (as it would do while he was its leader, and as the election manifesto had promised). This was also why the Conservatives were in continuing disarray. Here was a leader already writing his entry in the history books, and with good cause.

The 2005 result had secured Tony Blair's electoral legacy, but had it also secured his (and New Labour's) wider legacy? This was much more difficult to say with any certainty. Certainly New Labour seemed to have changed the terms of political trade in Britain towards its view of an active state using the proceeds of economic growth to redistribute income and opportunity and invest in public services, while at the same time maintaining its broad electoral coalition by eschewing rises in income tax and other measures likely to alienate middle-class voters and colonising issues (such as crime and disorder) that were once the hallmark of the right. So effectively had Labour staked out this territory as the new consensus that in the 2005 election the Conservatives were anxious to show, by the modesty of their tax proposals and their commitment to match Labour's spending on the key public services, that they also accepted that this was indeed the territory (rather than the small state/low tax one they might prefer) on which elections now had to be fought.

In this sense the prospectus on which the New Labour project had been founded – that it was possible to combine economic efficiency with social justice in a viable political and electoral strategy – could claim to be vindicated. Yet it is still too premature to claim more than this. It would be tempting, but foolish, to conclude from the 2005 election that Britain was an irrevocably social democratic country. It is much more sensible to conclude simply that New Labour has won three elections. This does make it a party of government, perhaps even the 'natural' party of government, in a way that was often aspired to in the past but never achieved. However, it still has to be tested in a less benign economic environment, while the Blairite reform programme for public services – on which New Labour's domestic legacy will in large part be judged – is still very much work in progress.

In ideological terms, the election left some interesting questions hanging in the air. Was this the last hurrah of Blairism, after which the Labour Party would revert to its old ideological ways? Those expecting this to happen under Gordon Brown will almost certainly be disappointed, while there is now a whole new New Labour generation in key positions. What ideological direction will the Conservatives now take? During the election a united ideological front was more or less maintained (despite Howard Flight's leaked suicide speech about the party's long-term tax and spending intentions), but after three election defeats it will be difficult for the party to avoid some fundamental ideological choices. As for the Liberal Democrats, the election results will make it more difficult for the party to evade the question of whether its direction of travel is leftwards or rightwards.

What was striking about the election was the narrowness of the policy territory on which it was fought, a reflection of the age's muted ideological antagonisms. So Labour had to seek to expose the 'real' intentions of the Conservatives in order to suggest seismic differences behind the modest areas of actual disagreement, while the Conservatives had to engage in hyperbolic personal attacks and scare tactics as a substitute for radical policy alternatives. The result was that many significant issues – from Europe to climate change – went wholly undiscussed and there was a collective terror of saying anything that any body of electors might find disagreeable.

The outcome of the election raised questions for all the parties, and for the political system itself. Labour's reduced parliamentary majority suggested that politics might be returning, at last, to something like normal after the one-sidedness produced by two consecutive landslides. Yet it was not normal. Labour's share of the vote would have produced electoral humiliation a generation earlier. The Conservatives' modest advance in seats took the party nowhere in terms of vote share, and its failure to recapture any seats in the big cities outside London showed just how far the party still had to go if it was ever to win a majority again. It left the party marooned between the 'one more heave' tendency and those who thought that what was needed was a 'Clause 4 moment' similar to the Blairite reinvention of the Labour Party. The Liberal Democrats had advanced in both seats and vote share, but had not secured the kind of breakthrough that the particular circumstances of the election had seemed to promise.

Still, it was destined to make the House of Commons a rather more interesting place, as crushing automatic majorities had to be replaced by a process of winning support, above all on the Labour benches. Some thought (and hoped) it would mean a field day for dissidents; others that it would strengthen collective discipline. It might mean that Tony Blair would have to learn to trim, except that his trimming faculties were not well developed and he showed no sign of wanting to develop them any further. In reality, Labour's comfortable majority provided it with a solid buffer against serious parliamentary trouble, but it was no longer so commanding that it sapped all the independence and energy out of Parliament itself. Insofar as the election made Parliament (and Cabinet) matter a little more again, its outcome was to be welcomed.

It would be further welcome if we heard rather less about trust (or its absence), the dispiriting leitmotif not only of the election but of a long period beforehand. If Iraq provided its immediate focus, it was deliberately widened to frame a more general indictment. The problem with this style of politics is that it seems to offer short-term advantage but at the cost of a corrosive denigration of public life itself. A culture of distrust is fostered in a polity which in fact has some claim to be regarded as one of the most corruption-free in the world and where a tradition of public service is carefully nurtured and protected. We are in danger of talking ourselves into an early civic grave. It is much to be hoped that the 2005 election, in all its unpleasantness, will come to be seen as the moment when the danger was both recognised and attended to.

One consequence of not attending to it was seen in the fact that four out of ten electors turned their back on the election altogether. Not quite as dire as 2001, helped by the boosted postal voting, but miserable by historic standards. When all the necessary allowances and caveats have been made – the blurring of traditional ideological divisions, the widespread assumption that the outcome was known beforehand – it is nevertheless difficult to resist the conclusion that a process of civic erosion is taking place in Britain and that this election is further evidence of it. Some will dispute this, arguing that the non-participants are those who were actively making a political point, but this was not my experience. Voting is no longer seen as a civic responsibility by large numbers of people in Britain, and politicians no longer feel able to tell them that it is.

It is likely that the 2005 election will herald a period of renewed attention to the repair and reform of Britain's political and electoral institutions. There will be proposals for compulsory voting, for votes at 16, weekend elections, more postal voting (Electoral Commission permitting), and much else besides. Some of these proposals will be sensible; others will not. There is always a temptation to seek solutions to problems in quick institutional fixes. In particular, the issue of electoral reform will make another of its periodic outings, fuelled by the ability of a party in 2005 to win a substantial Commons majority on scarcely more than a third of the votes cast. The Jenkins Report will be dusted down, further reviews undertaken, more promised. The Conservatives will be urged by some to embrace electoral reform as a shortcut back to power. Labour may flirt with the alternative vote, as will the Liberal Democrats, but whether flirtation will eventually lead to consummation is uncertain.

Whatever the eventual outcome, the argument about electoral reform now needs to be engaged. Traditionally Britain has traded representativeness for governing capacity and clear accountability, but the terms of the trade-off clearly require revisiting after the 2005 election. There is also the question of whether an increasingly variegated electorate, less attached to party, can be corralled into the electoral disciplines of catch-all parties in an adversarial simple plurality system. One reason why a range of important issues and positions were neglected during the election was that they were squeezed out by the imperatives of electoral competition among parties vying for the same narrow political territory.

This is not by itself an argument for changing the electoral system (which will anyway be decided by calculations of party advantage), but it is an argument for having the argument. All systems have advantages and disadvantages, but they also have to take account of the altered circumstances in which they operate. Britain can have rather more confidence in undertaking such a review as a result of its experience of initiating major constitutional reform since 1997, including an assortment of voting systems for different institutions. There is still much unfinished constitutional business, not least in relation to the second chamber, but new business too. This includes the debilitating effect of a political culture of unbridled centralism, sharply reflected in the 2005 election by the total neglect of the fact that elections to county councils were taking place on the same day. We know that Britain will have a new Prime Minister by the time of the next election, but it may also have started to become a different kind of political system.

7

The Election in Scotland[1]

James Mitchell

In his acceptance speech on being returned as Scotland's only Conservative MP, David Mundell sought to find succour in another dreadful night for the Scottish Tories. Mundell pointed out that the Tories had gained their first representative in the Scottish Borders in 40 years and their first South Lanarkshire seat in almost half a century. His spin hid significant truths about the 2005 election, a contest in which the electoral problems of the Conservatives were again confirmed. The plight of the Conservatives was one feature of an intriguing election, one in which the Scottish National Party (SNP), led again by Alex Salmond, attempted to prove their ability to win Westminster seats, Labour attempted to defend altered constituencies and the Liberal Democrats were hopeful of benefiting from UK-wide concerns such as the Iraq war, allied to a progressive record within the Scottish Executive.

The impact of boundary changes

Much pre-election discussion centred upon the impact of boundary changes. The size and shape of Scottish constituencies had changed dramatically during the previous Parliament. Under the provisions of the devolution legislation, Scotland's representation in the Commons was cut from 72 to 59 at this election resulting in very different boundaries and, for the most part, larger constituencies. What had previously been the Labour–Conservative marginal of Dumfries, held by the Tories until 1997, now reached eastwards into the Borders and northwards into Lanarkshire to create Dumfriesshire, Clydesdale and Tweeddale, 'perhaps the oddest element of the new political map' (Fraser 2005). Devolution had another impact on the British general election. Mundell was a Member of the Scottish Parliament (MSP) who had used his base as a List Member for a region covering the South of Scotland to challenge for a seat at Westminster. The issues he and other candidates across the parties throughout Scotland had raised included devolved and retained matters. Post-devolution politics in Scotland had not resulted in clear boundaries between Westminster and the Scottish Parliament as some simplistic commentaries suggested. What can now be seen clearly is that the parties, electorate and media have no intention of distinguishing between devolved and retained matters in election campaigns even where such a distinction could be made.

Comparisons with the 2001 election were even more difficult than with previous boundary changes given the scale of the change. The convention that Scotland should have at least 71 MPs had been abandoned and the electoral map of Scotland with it. In the previous Parliament, Scottish constituencies averaged 55,000 electors compared with 70,000 in England. The removal of this difference affected all but three constituencies and in two of these the Boundary Commission had decided to change their names even if not the seats' boundaries. In two others there had been minor changes to boundaries with substantial changes in the remaining 54.

Skilful calculations of 'notional' results using previous election results superimposed on the new electoral map of Scotland had resulted in widely accepted figures (Denver et al. 2004).[2] Under these calculations, Labour would have won ten fewer seats in Scotland in 2001 if the 2005 boundaries had been in place, the Tories would not even have won the single seat they won four years before, and the Liberal Democrats and SNP would have been down one each (see Table 7.1).

Table 7.1 Votes and seats (notional and actual) in the 2001 and 2005 Westminster elections in Scotland

	2001 seats	*2001 notional seats*	*2001 % vote*	*2005 seats*	*2005 % vote*
Lab	55	45	43.3	40	38.9
Lib Dem	10	9	16.4	11	22.6
SNP	5	4	20.1	6	17.7
Con	1	0	15.6	1	15.8
Other	1*	1*	4.6	1	5.0

* Speaker.

One of the first battles in the 2005 contest, therefore, concerned which were the main contenders in each constituency. Establishing first mover advantage would allow the party that can convincingly claim to be the main challenger to the sitting party a distinct advantage over its rivals. This is particularly significant with a promiscuous electorate willing to shift allegiances in order to challenge a sitting member. According to the notional results, the SNP were in second place to Labour in 29 seats, the Liberal Democrats in nine and the Conservatives in seven. The problem for the SNP was that it was less than 10 per cent behind

Labour in only three seats (Dundee East, Ochil and South Perthshire and Na h-Eileanan an Iar) and indeed was 22.5 per cent behind Labour in its next most hopeful Labour seat. The Liberal Democrats also were lying under 10 per cent behind Labour in three seats (Inverness, Nairn, Badenoch and Strathspey; Dunbartonshire East; and Aberdeen South) and in Edinburgh South were 13.9 per cent behind while in the highly marginal Dumfries and Galloway constituency the Tories were breathing down Labour's neck and the Tories were 12.1 per cent behind Labour in Dumfriesshire, Clydesdale and Tweeddale (DCT) on the 2001 notional results. In eight seats there was less than 15 per cent separating the first three parties.

The battle to secure nomination in safe seats amongst existing MPs began in earnest as soon as the Boundaries Commission for Scotland had produced its proposals in February 2002. This was most pressing inside the Labour Party which held most seats. Ultimately, the consequence was that more sitting MPs either chose to stand down or failed to secure a nomination in a winnable seat than at any previous election. Twelve Scottish Labour MPs stood down or were forced out before polling day. Three had battled unsuccessfully to secure a seat: Irene Adams in Renfrewshire, Malcolm Savidge in Aberdeen and Jimmy Wray in Glasgow, while others simply retired or chose to stand aside. Helen Liddell had been in the invidious position of facing the possibility of having to fight John Reid, her Cabinet colleague, for a seat, but opted to become UK High Commissioner for Australia after the election, assuming Labour was returned. Others were expected to end up in the Lords.

The Liberal Democrats had faced the prospect of a battle in the Borders between Sir Archy Kirkwood and Michael Moore, Kirkwood's former research assistant who had entered Parliament for the neighbouring seat. In the event, Kirkwood stood aside for the younger, more ambitious man and later entered the Lords. The SNP notional number of seats was also down one but the electoral geography meant that Annabel Ewing had little alternative than to fight the Labour marginal seat of Ochil and South Perthshire. The selectorate can be more important in determining who will serve as elected representatives than the electorate.

Amongst those retiring was Tam Dalyell, Father of the House, who had entered Parliament aged 29 in a by-election in 1962. One of his parting comments was typical of the maverick old Etonian and former chairman of Cambridge University Conservative club whose Labour constituency included his family's baronial home. When asked to name the worst of the eight Premiers he had confronted over his parliamentary career, he replied Tony Blair. Having spent years inveighing against devolution and warning that devolution and nationalism was mainly supported by women who 'tend to be more emotional about their politics than men' (Dalyell 1977: 224) his departure was a reminder of how much had changed in Scottish politics in the half century he had been in the Commons.

Another maverick amongst Labour's contingent who was to disappear from Scottish politics, but remain in the Commons, was George Galloway. Galloway had always faced a difficult contest for a nomination for a seat in Glasgow but his expulsion from Labour finally removed him from the scene. His interests had long focused on foreign affairs and he had happily allowed his opposite number in the Scottish Parliament to take the lead on local Glasgow constituency matters. Having built a political career in Scotland, first in the hothouse of local Labour politics in Dundee where he had first developed an interest in Middle East politics, he had chaired the Scottish party, been a prominent figure on the nationalist wing of Scottish Labour before taking Glasgow Hillhead from Roy Jenkins in 1987. His interest and involvement in the Scottish dimension had waned. Less colourful but still significant figures also bowed out. George Foulkes, former junior Minister, stood down, but was given a seat in the Lords and was set to have a new career as chairman of Hearts football club. Brian Wilson, anti-devolution Labour Minister and one of the party's few leading figures to have had a serious interest in the Highlands and Islands, chose to stand down at the relatively young age of 56. He too looked set to take up a career on the board of a football club but, with that ecumenicalism that gives Scottish Labour its electoral success, for Celtic. Scottish politics in the House of Commons was set to be duller after 2005.

Amongst Members of the Scottish Parliament, three Conservatives decided to try for a Commons seat, but only Mundell succeeded, although Ben Wallace, a former Tory MSP who stood down from Holyrood in 2003, was elected in Lancaster. Only the Conservatives have seen the Scottish Parliament as a possible stepping stone to Westminster, although there remains the possibility that one or two of those defeated in 2005 may appear as candidates for Holyrood in 2007. The Greens and SSP also chose to contest seats though both knew they stood little chance of winning. Tommy Sheridan had been removed as Scottish Socialist Party (SSP) leader in a party putsch and replaced by Colin Fox, who lacks both Sheridan's charisma and strategic thinking. The party contested 58 seats, declining to stand in East Kilbride, Strathaven and Lesmahagow. The SSP obtained an average 2 per cent of the vote, with their best result in Glasgow South West with 5.4 per cent. The SSP saved deposits in only two seats and only in Orkney and Shetland did the party's share of the vote rise, by a mere 1 per cent. The more canny Greens contested only 19 seats winning 3.5 per cent on average with their best performance in Glasgow North with 7.7 per cent. The most notable independent candidate was Rose Gentle who stood against Adam Ingram, the Armed Forces minister. Mrs Gentle's son had been killed in the Iraq war and she fought the election on a 'Troops Out' platform, winning 3.2 per cent of the vote and coming sixth.

Multilevel elections

The most significant event of the long campaign leading up to the 2005 election was the election of the Scottish Parliament in 2003. The 2003 Scottish parliamentary election was a more Scottish affair than the British general elections had been, although many retained matters intruded into the campaign. Iraq had featured in the 2003 election despite the Scottish Parliament's lack of remit in foreign affairs. That election had seen Labour and the SNP suffer setbacks: Labour lost six seats leaving it with 50; the SNP lost eight leaving it with 27. The Conservatives and Liberal Democrats remained on 18 and 17 respectively with the 'Others' making headway. The Greens won seven seats, the SSP six, and independents claimed four. The rise of the 'Others' was in large measure a result of the electoral system and it was never likely that this result would be repeated in Scotland in the UK general election.

New party leaderships; new political contexts

Since devolution there has been much speculation as to the nature of the relationship between elections to the House of Commons and the devolved bodies. In the first devolved elections in 1999, both the SNP and Plaid Cymru in Wales had done much better than in the previous UK general election fuelling predictions that the devolved elections had provided a springboard for the nationalist parties to advance at the next devolved elections and possibly also at the following elections to the House of Commons. In the event, the SNP suffered a setback in the 2001 UK general election when it was unable to capitalise on its advance two years before. Speculation that the 1999 election might have been a highpoint and that predictions made by George Robertson, former Scottish Labour leader, that devolution would kill off the nationalists, were resurrected. At the 2003 Scottish parliamentary elections, when the SNP fell back though holding comfortably onto its second place, speculation intensified. This focused particularly on the leadership of John Swinney who had taken over as leader from Alex Salmond in 2000. Swinney's timing had been unfortunate. Salmond had taken the SNP from fourth place in number of Scottish seats and third place in seats when he was first elected leader in 1990 to second place in seats and votes in the Scottish Parliament and had been the central figure in the 1997 devolution referendum campaign. In standing down after ten years, he could justifiably claim to have advanced his party and ensured that a Scottish Parliament had come into being. Like John Major following Margaret Thatcher, John Swinney would live in his predecessor's shadow even though in his case he had the unstinting backing of his predecessor.

Not only had there been a change in the leadership of the SNP. The leadership of Scottish Labour had changed since 2001. Donald Dewar's death had brought

Henry McLeish to leadership and office of First Minister for Scotland. McLeish had kept a low profile in the 2001 UK general election. But his leadership proved no more happy than his opposite number in the SNP. After a bizarre episode involving accusations of mishandling finances on a constituency office, McLeish was forced to stand down in November 2001 and was replaced, without an election, by party apparatchik Jack McConnell. Relations between Labour MSPs and MPs had not been good and there had been suggestions that Labour in the Scottish Parliament had done little to assist the re-election of Scottish Labour MPs at that year's general election. In an effort to improve relations, one of McConnell's first initiatives was to visit the Commons one month after becoming leader to address his party's contingent of Scottish MPs. It was not only relations with fellow members at Westminster that proved difficult for McConnell. On becoming First Minister he had sacked most of the Labour ministers in his predecessor's cabinet. The only ministers who remained in post who had served under Donald Dewar a year before were the two Liberal Democrat members of the coalition and Wendy Alexander. McConnell's 'Night of the Long Knives', as it was dubbed by the media, was unsparing and ensured that he had many enemies behind him. By May 2002, Wendy Alexander, who had been given a massive ministerial portfolio as Minister for Enterprise, Transport and Lifelong Learning had also resigned.

The Liberal Democrats had been more successful than any of the established parties in using devolution as a springboard to further success. Coming from fourth place in 1997 in share of the vote and with a disparate bunch of local heroes as MPs, the Liberal Democrats have been in coalition with Labour in Edinburgh since 1999. The party had quietly gained footholds in local government which acted as bridges to challenge for Westminster seats over many elections. Seats had been won in the Highlands and Borders and Fife mainly at the expense of the Conservatives. They had not presented much of a threat to Labour, allowing reasonably comfortable relations to develop between the two parties prior to devolution and in coalition after 1999. A further coalition deal had been struck after the 2003 Scottish elections, again providing the party with both status and prominence. Jim Wallace had the added status of being Deputy First Minister and had twice stood in briefly as Acting First Minister. With some justification, the Scottish Liberal Democrats claimed credit for two of the flagship policies of devolution – both middle-class populist measures which had initially had little support within the Labour Party. 'Free' care for the elderly and 'abolition' of tuition fees had been part of the first flush of devolutionary excitement when parliamentarians had set out to be different in policy terms from the rest of Britain. It was rare for a senior Liberal Democrat to fail to make mention of these policies in the succeeding years, to the extent that these Scottish Liberal Democrat 'successes' became part of the party's British narrative. While Labour leaders in London seemed reluctant to champion their colleagues' achievements in Edinburgh, there was never any such hesitation from the Liberal Democrats' British leadership who, of course, included Charles Kennedy and Menzies Campbell, prominent Scottish MPs. Relations between the Scottish and London elements of the two coalition partners could not have been more different: the Liberal Democrats appeared seamlessly together while Labour's Scottish leadership appeared distant yet simultaneously linked to Labour's London leadership. Instead of Rhodri Morgan's exaggerated 'clear red water' rhetoric in Wales, Scotland's First Minister emphasised 'partnership' despite some significant differences between what the Scottish Parliament has been doing compared with London. Unusually, the Scottish Liberal Democrats had managed to gain credit for the apparent successes of the coalition despite being the minor party in the coalition. Older party members still remembered the days of the Lib-Lab Pact in the late 1970s when David Steel had taken the party into an agreement with Jim Callaghan's minority Labour government at Westminster only to gain nothing of substance. That experience has not been repeated in the Edinburgh coalition.

The Conservatives in the Scottish Parliament have been deeply divided since 1999. When one List MSP, who had been highly critical of the leadership of Scottish leader David McLetchie, stood down in August 2001 he was replaced by Murdo Fraser. Under the operation of the electoral system, by-elections only occur when constituencies become vacant while list vacancies are filled by whoever is next in line on the list. Fraser proved even more bothersome to McLetchie having a more significant base within the party, an alternative programme and leadership ambitions. Fraser became the name associated with a more radical programme which emphasised fiscal autonomy and separating the Scottish party from that south of the border. These proposals emerged again in response to the results of the 2005 election. Simultaneously, Peter Duncan, the Tories' only Scottish MP elected in 2001, eventually became Shadow Scottish Secretary and Scottish party chairman but his duties as an MP meant that he failed to register north of the border beyond his constituency.

The campaign

Labour's strategy, as in most recent election campaigns in Scotland, was defensive. With 45 notional seats, it had little alternative. It stood little chance of making gains especially given that the party was on the defensive across Britain. It would have been sensational had Labour ended up with more Scottish seats against this backdrop. This meant targeting resources in key seats and frequent visits from prominent figures to these areas. The party avoided making any predictions. The Tories targeted a number of seats and privately were hoping to win between two and three seats. Resources poured into seats such as Dumfriesshire, Clydesdale and Tweeddale, Dumfries and Galloway and Angus. There was little that was distinctively Scottish about the Conservatives' campaign, with the familiar themes of immigration and law and order from the election in England being repeated north of the border. One problem was that Peter Duncan, sole Tory MP, was unable to do much for his party being tied up fighting to win a seat for himself. Although he had high visibility through television appearances, his performances were plodding. The absence of any significant, charismatic figure personifying and projecting the Conservatives' Scottish message was notable.

The SNP strategy was radically different from anything in the past. The blunderbuss approach with limited targeting, at least as compared with other parties had dominated previous SNP election strategy. The contrast between Alex Salmond's first election as party leader in 1992 with 2005, the first under the Salmond II leadership, was stark. In 1992, the SNP had gone for broke and pushed up its share of the vote by 7.5 per cent, but failed to win one additional seat and had lost the Govan constituency won in a by-election in 1989. In 2005, targeting was concentrated on a small number of seats. Salmond had predicted that his party would win 'between six and fifty-nine seats' (*Scotsman*, 16 April 2005). In sections of the media, this prediction was thought to have been unwise (MacWhirter 2005) with a haul of six seats seen to be an 'ambitious target' and a 'risky strategy' (*Scotsman*, 16 April 2005). The party leadership cared less about the overall share of the vote than in winning more seats, a strategy that unusually won the backing of some of Salmond's long-term critics including former party leader Gordon Wilson. Those constituencies which were not targeted were left to their own devices, much to the chagrin of activists in places like Glasgow.

The Liberal Democrats, the supremos when it comes to targeting, moved in the opposite direction and while not quite adopting an old-style SNP approach made wilder predictions than normal. Publicly hoping to take five seats, though privately expecting fewer, they managed expectations less well. Having taken all the Scottish Conservative seats possible in previous elections, they had to concentrate their efforts on Labour seats. This created tensions inside the coalition in Edinburgh exacerbated by Liberal Democrat claims to be the architects of populist policies of the Executive whilst managing to stand aloof from the difficulties and criticisms of the Executive's health and economic policy records.

Labour's message was simple and no different from the past. It was a two horse race and a vote for anyone other than Labour would let Michael Howard into Downing Street. From the outset of the campaign through to the *Daily Record*'s pre-election warning, this mantra was repeated by Labour: 'There are three ways you can get a Conservative government: vote Tory, vote for another opposition party – like the Nats or LibDems – or stay at home' (*Daily Record*, 5 May 2005). Labour had difficulties during the campaign. The Scottish Labour manifesto launch two days after the launch of the English manifesto was marred by problems that recurred in the campaign. Journalists noted the different promises that were made north and south of border as well as the different record which Labour at Westminster was defending compared with that of the Scottish Executive. Even sympathetic journalists referred to Jack McConnell's 'gaffe' when it was conceded that hospital waiting lists could be twice as long in Scotland as in England (*Herald*, 15 April 2005). Less sympathetic papers referred to the 'damage limitation exercise' following 'confusion and controversy' (*Scotsman*, 15 April 2005). If, as reported, the intention had been to focus on the economy and the harmony between London and Edinburgh, then the launch had the opposite effect, raising questions as to why Scotland appeared to lag behind England despite larger sums of public money going into the health service north of the border. Both McConnell and Alistair Darling, Shadow Scottish Secretary, appeared at the Scottish launch, provoking unnamed Labour figures to question whether the First Minister ought to have been present. However, Labour's blushes were partly saved by the fact that this happened on the same day that Charles Kennedy proved to have little understanding of his party's flagship policy on a local income tax. Labour were to suffer a similar fate when, later in the campaign, the Prime Minister promised to cut crime in England by 15 per cent while more general commitments were made in Scotland (*Scotsman*, 22 April 2005). This raises the question as to why these matters were in Labour's Scottish manifesto at all. It might have been argued that these were devolved matters and beyond the scope of this election. However, it was recognised across the parties that this did not mean that parties could ignore key concerns of voters. Constitutional-legal distinctions disappeared in the real world of public policy and elections.

One matter that had a clear Westminster focus was defence but it also had a particular Scottish dimension. One of the most prominent campaign groups to attempt to enter the election was the Save the Regiments campaign. The campaign leaders announced their intention of standing in two constituencies – those of Gordon Brown and Adam Ingram, junior Defence Minister – and that they would endorse opposition parties in nine Labour-held seats. In the event, only three of these seats were lost and it is far from clear whether the Save the Regiments intervention made much of a difference. Ironically, the campaign ended up endorsing Rose Gentle, the anti-war candidate who also had the support of the SSP against Ingram (*Herald*, 15 April 2005).

Assessing the results

Without doubt, Scottish politics had become multi-party by the 1999 Scottish elections and no party could claim to dominate as in the past. Nonetheless, the myth of Labour's dominance continues to have a hold on the imagination. Iain MacWhirter, BBC journalist and print columnist, commented during the campaign that 'Scots will vote for anything wearing a red rosette' (MacWhirter 2005). That may appear so in the number of seats won by Labour, but is not true when share of the vote is assessed. The 2005 election confirmed the multi-party nature of Scottish politics. Labour's position as the largest party is secured in large measure because no other party has managed to secure its position as the real alternative. Despite the losses suffered by Labour, the result underlines the lack of a clear single alternative and this divided opposition may continue to work to Labour's advantage. The Liberal Democrats are now the second party in number of seats and share of the vote for Westminster but still lie behind the SNP in both for the Scottish Parliament.

While the Liberal Democrat Party substantially increased its share of the Scottish vote by 6.3 per cent, it won only two more seats. In only four seats did its vote go down and was up by over 5 per cent in 38 seats and over 10 per cent in nine seats. The problem was that some of the most dramatic increases in its share of the vote occurred in seats it already held, including three seats in the Highlands. After 2005, it found itself in second place to Labour in 15 seats. The party did well in university seats with high proportions of middle-class voters. Its care for elderly and tuition fees policies appear to have created a positive message amongst better-off sections of the community. Notably, the party failed to advance where it was defending a seat against the Tories, though probably because it had mopped up most of the potential votes in these areas already. The amalgam of Liberal Democrat voters included disaffected Labour voters and those who in the past might have voted Conservative. In Scotland at this election it was the Liberal Democrat Party which had turned triangulation into an electoral strategy most successfully by appealing across the old left–right divide.

The SNP, by contrast, saw its vote fall overall by 2.5 per cent and rise in only ten seats, but enough to give them the same increase in number of seats as the Liberal Democrats. Additionally, the SNP can still claim to be the main challenger to Labour finding itself in second place in 18 seats. The main weakness from these elections for the future of the SNP was the downside of vigorous targeting. One failure of targeting was in Dumfries and Galloway where the party failed to secure first mover advantage. The SNP vote fell by more than in any other seat helping Labour to take the constituency. Similarly, the SNP's failure to secure first mover advantage in Inverness, Nairn, Badenoch and Strathspey (part of which is held by the SNP in Holyrood) ensured that it slipped back. The SNP has fallen behind badly in large parts of Scotland where it needs to build up support. Having left the local activists to their own devices in Glasgow meant leaving it to the amateurs with the consequence that the Liberal Democrats, a party with barely an organisation across much of the city but gaining from a higher media profile at UK level, is in second place in four seats and the SNP in two (the Speaker's seat is excluded though the SNP alone of the main parties contested the seat) and with almost 34,000 votes compared with the SNP's 27,000 (excluding the 5,000 the SNP won against the Speaker). Although Glasgow now has only seven seats, it remains a symbolically significant prize. No party is ever likely to be a serious challenger to Labour without advancing in the city.

The Conservatives saw their share of the vote go up by 0.2 per cent across Scotland with a gain of one seat on none in the 2001 notional results. The share of the vote was up in 27 seats but down in 32 and up by 3 per cent or more in only five seats. Its vote went down in the target seat of Angus despite considerable efforts, though the effort in Dumfriesshire, Clydesdale and Tweeddale was rewarded by an increase of 11.4 per cent. They are now the second party in 16 seats (seven Labour; five Liberal Democrat and four SNP). However, they are within striking distance in a number of other seats. The party fared well in the Borders and may emerge strongly there in future elections, challenging the Liberal Democrats. Table 7.2 provides a breakdown of second places for each party.

Table 7.2   Second places in the 2005 Westminster election in Scotland

Labour-held seats	(40)	Liberal Democrat seats	(11)
SNP	18	Labour	6
Lib Dem	15	Conservative	5
Conservative	7	Others	0
SNP seats	(6)	Conservative seat	(1)
Conservatives	4	Labour	1
Labour	2		
Lib Dem	0		
Speaker	(1)		1 (contested only by
SNP			SNP of main parties)

Liberal Democrats are quick to point out that they lie within 20 per cent of Labour in eight seats compared with only three where the SNP is in that position. However, there are now ten marginals, assuming these to be seats where a swing of 5 per cent or under is required to win. Five of these are Labour seats with the Liberal Democrats challenging in three (Aberdeen South; Edinburgh North and Leith; Edinburgh South); one under challenge from the Tories (Dumfries and Galloway); and one SNP (Ochil and South Perthshire). Two are SNP-held seats: one under challenge from Labour (Dundee East) and the others from the Tories (Perth and North Perthshire); two Liberal Democrat seats are both under challenge from Labour (East Dunbartonshire and Inverness, Nairn, Badenoch and Strathspey); and where Labour is the challenger in Tory-held DCT. In other words, the key battleground at the next UK general election will involve five seats in which Labour and the Liberal Democrats will go head-to-head.

It was little surprise, therefore, that in the immediate aftermath of the election relations between the coalition partners in Edinburgh became more strained. Prior to 1999 when the coalition came into being, there were few constituencies in which these parties confronted each other, but that is no longer the case. Of course, a very different picture emerges when looking at the Scottish parliamentary elections. Nonetheless, the likelihood of more intense competition between the Liberal Democrats and both Labour and the Conservatives at Westminster combined with these Scottish results ensure that the long campaign for the elections to the Scottish Parliament, which began the morning after the recent UK general election, will see strains in relations within the coalition.

Scotland compared with rest of UK

In at least one respect there was little difference between Scotland and Britain/UK. Turnout was up by under 3 per cent to 60.6 per cent in Scotland compared with an increase of just over 2 per cent across the UK at 61.5 per cent. The striking difference between Scotland and the rest of Britain was the extremely low level of support for the Conservatives north of the border. Even in Wales, the Tories won a higher share of the vote and more seats than in Scotland, and in England the Tories outpolled Labour. Labour's share of the vote in Scotland lay between the higher level attained in Wales and that in England, although Scottish Labour saw a smaller decline than in either England or Wales while the Liberal Democrat vote in Scotland and England was almost the same, although its increase was greatest in Scotland. The SNP sustained a larger decrease in its share of the vote than its sister party in Wales but managed to increase its number of seats while Plaid Cymru lost a seat. The overall picture suggested the possibility of a growing territorialisation of British politics as the Conservatives appear to be more and more an English party.

Conclusion

The future of Scottish politics may, as ever, be determined more by events in England than home-grown matters. The Conservative temptation to play the English card, dabbled in by William Hague when he was leader, will be great. Just as its opponents unashamedly played the Scottish card during the long years of Conservative government, the opportunity now available for Conservatives to insist that policies introduced in England have been foisted on them by the peripheries will be tempered by the fact that Labour still has an overall majority of 44 seats in England. Nonetheless, backbench rebellions may resurrect the West Lothian Question, so forcefully articulated by Tam Dalyell. Though Dalyell has left the House, it is likely that the question named after his constituency may begin to be raised seriously for the first time since devolution. However, this will present challenges to the new leader of the Conservatives. It will not make it any easier to win back seats in Scotland. If disagreements and divisions are any indicator of an election's result then the leaking of an internal report and subsequent resignation of its author as deputy chairman of the Conservative Party is an indication that the Conservatives were the big losers in Scotland. While each of the other parties can take some comfort in the results, it is the Tories who remain lost as to what they should do to recover even to the level of support they had in the Thatcher era.

What has become clear is that devolution has had an impact on Westminster elections, but not as some might have expected. The constitutional-legal policy distinction which suggests that each level would have responsibility for discrete policy areas does not happen in public policy practice. Big decisions on health and education, for example, are determined by the funding available and that is decided in London. Not only is the devolved-retained powers distinction blurred in public policy terms, but it is all but indistinct in electoral politics. Parties, the media and the electorate make little effort to distinguish between matters that are devolved and retained especially in Westminster elections. This is a closer reflection of public policy realities than constitutional-legal distinctions. Britain's multilevel elections are, to borrow a phrase from the comparative federalism literature, more marbled, perhaps even garbled, than layered.

Devolution has provided the Liberal Democrats with a platform, but now presents that party with a challenge. Jim Wallace announced he was standing down as leader in the Scottish Parliament and Deputy First Minister shortly after the election. He could claim to be going on a high. His successor will have to grapple with how the party balances being in coalition with Labour while now Scotland's second party in votes and seats in Westminster elections and in opposition to Labour. The party has proved itself in winning Conservative seats. The challenge in Scotland, even more than elsewhere in Britain, will be to pick away at Labour seats. The SNP came out of the election jubilant at having returned the Western Isles and Dundee East, albeit the latter with different boundaries, after losing these seats to Labour in 1987. These were the first Labour seats the party had gained in a general election since 1974. The strategy of vigorous targeting had worked, but had its cost with the SNP losing its status as Scotland's second party, held only in terms of votes and never in seats in Westminster elections, to the Liberal Democrats. However, the targeting strategy which might work for Westminster would not be appropriate for the Scottish Parliamentary elections in which the Additional Member System operates. While vigorous targeting might win constituency seats it would damage the party's prospects on the list where the SNP gains most of its seats. Over the next two years, the SNP will have to regain the initiative and develop a different strategy. Labour remains in power and the largest party, but is suffering a gradual decline. Its posture has been defensive for many elections now as it has seen its vote challenged first from the SNP and now the Liberal Democrats. One of the party's greatest challenges over the next two years will be how to cope if the party in London, entering its third Parliament, becomes unpopular in two years' time and this rubs off on

Scottish Labour. Tam Dalyell had warned his Scottish Labour colleagues pre-devolution that the first elections to the Scottish Parliament would take place midway through the first Labour government when, he maintained, all parties suffer a bout of unpopularity. In the event, Dalyell had not taken account of the extended honeymoon enjoyed by New Labour which served his party well in the 1999 Scottish elections. Whether the West Lothian Question finally raises its head and whether Dalyell's warning of the consequences of mid-term unpopularity for Labour at Holyrood may in part depend on whether Gordon Brown becomes Prime Minister in succession to Tony Blair. If that happens, it may encourage the emergence of the West Lothian Question, but simultaneously help the party in the short term in Scotland. What seems certain is that the implications of devolution on British elections is complex and are only beginning to be seen.

Notes

1. I would like to thank Dr Nicola McEwen for comments on an earlier draft.
2. There were, inevitably, some challenges to the notional calculations. The notional calculations which were deemed least reliable according to all parties were those in south-west Scotland. The view of the main parties was that the Conservatives were stronger in Dumfriesshire, Clydesdale and Tweeddale than in Dumfries and Galloway, though it was accepted that the calculations had been based on consistent measurements. This is significant as the results in these seats proved amongst the most notable in terms of swings.

References

Dalyell, T. (1977) *Devolution: The End of Britain?* London: Jonathan Cape.

Denver, D., Rallings, C., and M. Thrasher (2004) *Media Guide to the New Scottish Westminster Parliamentary Constituencies*, Plymouth: Local Government, Chronicle Elections Centre.

Fraser, D. (2005) 'Prospective MPs to clash on new-look battleground after cut in Scottish seats', *Herald*, 6 April.

MacWhirter, I. (2005) 'The Truth is, Scots will vote for anything wearing a red rosette', *Sunday Herald*, 24 April.

Dundee East

Dundee East was a 'must-win' seat for the SNP if it was to emerge as a credible Westminster force after the 2005 election. Labour had held Dundee East since 1987, when it captured the seat from the former SNP leader Gordon Wilson. However, boundary changes favoured the SNP in the 2005 contest. The towns of Monifeith and Carnoustie, formerly located in SNP-held Angus, had been incorporated into the constituency, whilst some more Labour-leaning parts had been transferred. Given this, Labour performed creditably in keeping the swing to the SNP to a mere 1 per cent.

The defending Labour MP, Iain Luke, acknowledged that 'some people are unhappy with Tony Blair', notably on the issue of trust, preferring instead to emphasise his local record of achievement (*Guardian*, 13 April 2005). Like many of his colleagues, Luke played up the 'Scottish Labour' side of the party, rather than its Blairite New Labour component.

Given that the SNP leader had been one of the most vociferous opponents of the Iraq war, in a crowded field, it was obvious that this would form part of the SNP's campaign. However, it was on the more local issue of the future of Scottish regiments on which the SNP's candidate, Stewart Hosie, campaigned strongest. The merging of regiments, including the Black Watch, which recruited on Tayside, provided a big campaigning issue for the party, which stressed that whilst Scottish soldiers lost lives in an 'illegal' war, a 'London Labour' government closed Scottish regiments.

As Vice-Convenor of the SNP since 2003 and previously its national secretary, Hosie was one of the SNP's most prominent candidates. He succeeded in raising the SNP's vote by 1,000, yielding a narrow victory over Labour, whose vote proved solid, virtually unchanged from 2001. The Conservatives' problems in Scotland were emphasised by falls in their actual and percentage shares of the vote.

Result		%
Hosie, S. (SNP)	14,708	37.2
Luke, I. (Lab)	14,325	36.2
Bustin, C. (Con)	5,061	12.8
Sneddon, C. (LD)	4,498	11.4
Duke, H. (SSP)	537	1.4
Low, D. (UKIP)	292	0.7
Allison, D. (Ind)	119	0.3
SNP gain from Lab		
SNP majority	383	1.0
Swing: Lab to SNP		1.1

Turnout: 62.4%

8
Wales: The Second Post-Devolution General Election

Jonathan Bradbury

Party fortunes in general elections in Wales have long been distinctive from broader UK-wide patterns. Labour has been dominant in both attaining a strong lead in vote share and winning a majority of constituencies since the inter-war period. The party system is further differentiated by Plaid Cymru (Party of Wales), the ethno-regionalist party that emerged in the 1960s. The Liberal Democrats have also looked upon Wales as a key source of support, particularly in rural areas. In contrast to their English performance the Conservatives perform poorly, and even during the hey-day of Mrs Thatcher in 1983 won only 14 out of 38 seats. In 1997 Welsh distinctiveness was defined even more sharply by Labour dominance, as the party won a majority of votes cast and 34 of the 40 seats. Plaid Cymru and the Liberal Democrats picked up the scraps, and Wales became a 'Tory-free zone'. In 2001 Labour's vote share was reduced and Plaid Cymru's saw a significant rise. Nevertheless, the two parties simply exchanged Ynys Mon and Carmarthen East. In 2005 the interest lay in seeing whether such heightened Labour dominance could still withstand the rigours of office.

Since 1999 Welsh politics has been made more complicated by devolution. The first elections to the Welsh Assembly were held in 1999, using a mixed-member electoral system of 40 constituency seats on the same boundaries as for Westminster, with 20 top-up regional list seats. Labour was returned as the largest party but with a much- reduced share of the vote compared to UK elections and Plaid Cymru had their best ever election result. The second elections in 2003 saw Labour marginally improve their vote share and formed a government with a majority of one. However, both Labour's vote share and constituency haul were still below their performance in UK elections. While Plaid Cymru was disappointed by its fall in vote share and loss of seats, it still performed at a level not seen before 1999. The Conservatives enjoyed a small revival and the Liberal Democrats flatlined. Over the two elections, such results created interest in the emergence of differential voting in Wales in the UK and Welsh electoral contexts, and whether this might be related to different types of UK and Welsh-related issue voting (Trystan et al. 2003; Wyn Jones and Scully 2003).

It is of equal importance to examine the parties' election strategies and how they may have influenced the results. It should again be noted that devolution has complicated the task of how parties derive their strategies given that major UK-wide election issues like education and health are extensively devolved responsibilities in Wales, each of the parties has separate UK and Welsh Assembly leaders and, for assembly election purposes, the parties have developed more Welsh-focused campaigning. This has raised the question as to whether general elections become events which are demarcated – respectful of a separate devolved political terrain; devolution-blind – in which devolution is largely ignored; or devolution-sensitive in embracing Assembly-related approaches and political controversies that may help party interests specifically in Wales. The first post-devolution general election campaign in Wales was largely notable for the more effective strategy pursued by Labour compared to all of its opponents and its largely devolution-blind character (Mitchell and Bradbury 2002). The question four years on was whether such characteristics would be repeated.

The chapter duly examines, first, the 2005 election and party fortunes in the context of both recent general election and Assembly election results. It also considers some other key features of political participation and representation. It then examines the parties during the 2005 general election, assessing approaches to policy debate, leadership and campaigning. The conclusion addresses how the results in 2005 raise questions about future party fortunes at both Assembly and UK levels.

Election results and party fortunes

In 2005, the main story of the election was that the Labour Party finally did indeed see some erosion of the impressive electoral fortress that had been built up in 1997 and 2001 (see Table 8.1). Labour's vote share fell by 5.9 per cent and the party lost five seats. Three of these were marginal seats that they lost to the Conservative Party. The most marginal of these, Monmouth, was captured by the incumbent Conservative Assembly Member (AM) David Davies, with a 4,527 majority. The other two, Clwyd West and Preseli Pembrokeshire, were turned from being Labour marginals to Conservative marginals with majorities of a few hundred votes. The fourth loss was that of Cardiff Central to the Liberal Democrats. Like Monmouth, Labour was defending a wafer-thin majority and the defeat was not unexpected given the Liberal Democrats' capture of the seat with a large majority in the 2003 Assembly elections. In contrast, the fifth defeat was a huge shock to the party. In Blaenau Gwent, Labour's safest seat in Wales, Peter Law, the Labour AM, ran as an independent against the official Labour candidate in protest at her selection on the basis of an all-women shortlist. A Labour majority of over 19,000 was replaced by one for Peter Law of over 9,000. Overall, there was a swing from Labour to the Conservatives in 18 constituencies and from Labour to the Liberal Democrats in a further nine.

Table 8.1   UK general elections in Wales, 1997–2005

	Con	Lab	Lib Dem	Plaid Cymru	Others
1997					
Vote share	19.6%	54.7%	12.4%	9.9%	3.4%
Seats	0	34	2	4	0
2001					
Vote share	21.0%	48.6%	13.8%	14.3%	2.3%
Seats	0	34	2	4	0
2005					
Vote share	21.4%	42.7%	18.4%	12.6%	4.9%
Seats	3	29	4	3	1

Turnout: 1997: 73.6%; 2001: 60.6%; 2005: 62.4%.

Plaid Cymru, however, were also losers in the election, seeing their vote share drop by 1.7 per cent, with the accompanying loss of one seat. While the party increased its majority in three of the four seats it held in 2001, in the fourth – Ceredigion – a seemingly safe seat was lost to the Liberal Democrats by 219 votes. This was a major setback in the party's West Wales heartland. The party also fell back in the areas in which they might have hoped to improve their position if not take seats. In Ynys Mon, a North Wales seat where Plaid Cymru had the biggest hopes of taking a Labour seat, the Labour MP increased his majority. Of a further six seats in South Wales where Plaid Cymru were the principal, if somewhat distant, competitor against Labour, five also saw a swing from Plaid Cymru to Labour.

In contrast, in different ways the Liberal Democrats and the Conservative Party emerged with improved positions. The Liberal Democrats increased their vote share by 4.6 per cent and took two additional seats, one each from Labour and Plaid Cymru. With four seats the Liberal Democrats now became Wales' second party in terms of representation at the UK level. At the same time, the Conservative Party made important breakthroughs. While only slightly improving their vote share from 2001, the party targeted its efforts well and won the three seats from Labour already noted. In the battle between the two parties in rural Wales the Liberal Democrats came off the better, increasing its majorities over the Conservatives in both Montgomeryshire and the previously marginal Brecon and Radnorshire. The Liberal Democrats also had much to be pleased about in their results in Newport East, Swansea West and Swansea East where the party achieved in each case a swing from Labour of over 9 per cent.

In certain respects the result appeared to seriously question the strength of Labour dominance in Wales. The party's vote share had dropped by 12 per cent since 1997, but even more significantly one has to go back to 1983, when the party polled 37.5 per cent of the vote, to find Labour otherwise polling less than 45 per cent of the vote. Such a result suggests the increasing long-term vulnerability of the Labour vote in Wales in the context of being a party in office. However, in terms of their share of the seats Labour simply slipped back to their position in the 1992 election when they won 27 out of 38 seats on 49.5 per cent of the vote. In terms of number of seats held, Labour merely lost the heightened dominance achieved in 1997 and 2001, and in winning 29 out of 40 seats returned to party fortunes more regularly experienced prior to that, now on a much reduced vote share of 42.7 per cent. Labour retained all of their safe seats in North and South Wales. With the exception of Blaenau Gwent, Labour lost four seats that were more commonly held by the Conservative Party prior to 1997, one of which – Cardiff Central – was unusual for seeing the Liberal Democrats emerge instead of the Conservatives to capture it in 2005. Even then Labour retained a number of seats that had in the past been Conservative, notably the Vale of Glamorgan, Cardiff North and Conwy. Consequently, it is only on the outer edges of their fortress that Labour lost seats. Continued success in winning specific contests under a simple plurality electoral system through an efficient distribution of their vote outweighed the broader problem of decline in overall vote share.

The other part of the story of Labour's continued dominance, albeit diminished and despite a historically low share of the vote, may be found in the performance of the other parties. The lack historically of a concerted Conservative challenge to Labour in Wales has not been compensated by something similar from either Plaid Cymru or the Liberal Democrats. Plaid's result in 2005 was their second best ever general election result and that of the Liberal Democrats was their best since 1983. Nevertheless, the non-Labour vote remained deeply fragmented in Wales, allowing Labour dominance under the simple plurality voting system to be sustained with even greater disproportionality than is the case in England. Labour won 74 per cent of the seats on 42 per cent of the vote.

When one considers the 2005 general election result in the context of multilevel electoral politics the election is also noteworthy for indicating some convergence rather than further divergence in vote share for the major parties between general elections and National Assembly elections. The Labour Party's share of the vote in 2005 was remarkably similar to the party's constituency performance in the 2003 National Assembly election (see Tables 8.1 and 8.2). Equally, but for the self-inflicted defeat in Blaenau Gwent they would have won the same number of seats. Just Preseli Pembrokeshire and Clwyd West are seats where they have the Assembly seat but not the Westminster one, and Ynys Mon and Wrexham are ones where they have the Westminster seat but not the Assembly one. Wrexham is a special case, where Labour had committed an earlier self-inflicted wound in 2001 when a deselected Labour member won the seat as an independent. In the other three seats, though, the margins of victory or defeat at either level of election are small. Conservative vote share in constituency elections between the 2003 Assembly and 2005 general election is also very similar.

Such results do not necessarily suggest that differential voting is no longer a key distinctive feature of Welsh politics. The 2005 result showed that there remained a big difference in the fortunes at the two levels of election between Plaid Cymru and the Liberal Democrats. Plaid Cymru have a vote share nearly three-quarters higher in the Assembly context, and the Liberal Democrats one significantly better in the Westminster context. Equally, survey research may uncover that there were differences between actual voting behaviour in the 2005 general election and intended voting behaviour in an Assembly election had it been held on the same day. It may also uncover different motives behind parties' votes in 2003 and 2005. There will almost certainly be cause for future variation in voting behaviour. Currently, however, the two major state-wide parties, Labour and the Conservatives, have a fairly stable vote irrespective of the level of government concerned. Theories of differential and multilevel voting have a stiff evidential challenge.

Table 8.2   Elections to the National Assembly for Wales, 1999–2003

	Con	*Lab*	*Lib Dem*	*Plaid Cymru*	*Others*
1999					
Constit vote share	15.8%	37.6%	13.5%	28.4%	4.7%
Constit seats	1	27	3	9	0
Regional vote share	16.5%	35.4%	12.5%	30.5%	5.1%
Regional list seats	8	1	3	8	0
Total	9	28	6	17	0
2003					
Constit vote share	19.9%	40.0%	14.1%	21.2%	4.7%
Constit seats	1	30	3	5	1
Regional vote share	19.2%	36.6%	12.7%	19.7%	11.9%
Regional list seats	10	0	3	7	0
Total	11	30	6	12	1

Turnout: 1999: 46.0%; 2003: 38.2%.

When one turns to other features of political participation and representation the election results suggest both continuity and change. Turnout in Wales was as usual slightly above the UK average, at 62.4 per cent. Generally, however, the concerns over voter disengagement from the electoral process across the UK were shared in Wales. Swansea East, the constituency with the lowest turnout in 1997 and 2001, repeated the trick with a turnout this time of just 52.4 per cent. The issue of postal votes on demand was a major concern both of electoral registration officers and the parties, but, in contrast to other parts of the UK, concerns over postal ballots were confined simply to differences in electoral registration officer resources and practices. There were no allegations of postal ballot fraud. Voter participation in the election also stuck principally to support for the four main parties, with the major exception of Peter Law's independent candidature in Blaenau Gwent. UKIP and the Greens polled only just over 20,000 (1.5 per cent) and 7,000 (0.5 per cent) respectively. The Forward Wales Party, led by ex-Labour MPs John Marek and Ron Davies, mustered only just over 3,000 votes across Wales.

The candidates that electors returned to office exhibited more change. There was a 25 per cent turnover in MPs from 2001, with six of the ten leaving the House of Commons through retirement. Gone were former ministers Win Griffiths and Alan Howarth, as well as the widely respected former chair of the Foreign Affairs Select Committee, Donald Anderson. A key aspect of the renewal of blood was a step towards greater descriptive female representation. The number of women MPs doubled from four to eight, representing now 20 per cent of Wales' MPs. This achievement was almost entirely due to Labour's all-women shortlist selection policy in a number of safe seats, although the Liberal Democrats also boosted their female representation with their victory in Cardiff Central. Undoubtedly, in these respects the face of Welsh politics is beginning to change but the underlying characteristic of electoral involvement and patterns of representation remained that of continuity.

Parties and the election campaign

The election campaign unsurprisingly was largely a story of the Labour Party against the rest. Labour had some success in repeating the reasonable coherence of its 2001 campaign. Again the party presented a dual Welsh leadership of the Secretary of State for Wales, Peter Hain, and Labour's First Minister in the Assembly, Rhodri Morgan. This projected an image of party unity and sought to suggest the advantages to Wales of partnership between Labour administrations at the UK and Welsh levels. They sought to present a positive message based on successes in economic management and investment in public services. However, Labour was subjected to far higher levels of criticism than had been the case in 2001 and generally failed to control the news agenda. The party spent most of the campaign on the defensive.

The opposition parties launched six key angles of attack. Only three were entirely matters of Westminster determination. The key issue here was that of the decision to go to war in Iraq, a decision that the Liberal Democrats and Plaid Cymru opposed. Plaid Cymru had attempted to emphasise their position on the war by leading a campaign to have Tony Blair impeached over the decision. As in the rest of the UK, the issue of the Labour government's decision to go to war in Iraq dominated debate in Wales between 25 and 28 April, just as postal voters received their ballots and a week or so before polling day for everyone else. The other two key issues were the Conservatives' criticism of Labour over immigration and asylum policy and in more local contexts over Labour's banning of hunting foxes with hounds.

A fourth issue – that of variable top-up tuition fees for university students – had been legislated for at Westminster, but the decision on whether it would be introduced now lay with the Assembly. A fifth issue was effectively out of the control of Westminster MPs altogether, namely the record of the National Health Service in Wales. The Labour-led administrations in the Assembly had repeatedly failed to hit targets over cutting waiting times or waiting lists since 1999 and there was a strong perception of Labour's investment in health care expenditure not being matched with judicious usage. All the opposition parties in Wales sought to attack Labour over its Assembly health record.

Finally, Plaid Cymru opened up a specific attack on Labour for failing to clarify in detail its plans for extending the powers of the Assembly following the publication of the Richard Report in 2004. This was a matter that ultimately would have to be legislated for at Westminster, but UK Labour policy would be influenced by Labour policy at the Assembly level. This was linked to an attack on Labour's ability to secure further European Union funding for Wales, with the implicit suggestion of Wales' greater purchase if the Assembly had enhanced status.

The Conservative and Liberal Democrat alternative policies on the first five of these issues followed lines familiar in the UK-wide election campaign. On the sixth issue the Liberal Democrats had an official policy of being pro-federal and therefore supported more powers for the Assembly. The Conservatives had a policy of offering a referendum on change with several options, including abolition of the Assembly, no change in its powers as well as an expansion to primary legislative powers. In taking this line the Conservatives sought to maximise its support in Wales on an issue where they could not afford to alienate grassroots supporters who remained sceptical of devolution, but at the same time wished to reach out to other potential floating voters.

Plaid Cymru were distinctive for seeking to outflank Labour with an avowedly more socialist platform. They campaigned on a policy of 50 per cent tax for people earning over £50,000, new investment in post-industrial South Wales to create a city of the valleys, and further expansion of public services based on state intervention without any significant role for the private sector (Plaid Cymru 2005). The party underlined its distinctive nationalist position by pushing Labour on its constitutional plans, but its core aim was to emphasise its socialist platform. It was hoped that whilst sustaining its core supporters this would again expand its appeal to voters not specifically motivated by nationalism, in particular former Labour voters who wished to protest against the party.

How did Labour fare in defending itself against these attacks? On the central issue of the Iraq war, Hain proved to be a consistent and articulate defender of government policy, the result of which was probably only not to make the government look any worse to those critical of the policy. On other key issues, Labour largely adopted an approach of deflecting controversy by flagging up recent initiatives, playing for time or rhetorical attacks on the other parties. Health strategy reflected a combination of all three tactics. Prior to the election the party had sought to neutralise opposition on health service waiting times. In January 2005, after much grumbling from Labour MPs, Jane Hutt had been reshuffled from her position as Assembly Health Minister to that of Assembly Business Minister after nearly six years. Her replacement, Brian Gibbons, himself a former GP, set about a revision of policy on reducing waiting times and set new targets. During the campaign, the first new waiting time figures were released and Hain and Morgan were able to claim some improvement in performance to go along with the record of investment. Such initiatives, it was claimed, would reap even greater dividends over time. Morgan's specific interventions in the campaign also focused partly on health policy. He criticised the Conservative Party for exaggerating the number of MRSA cases contracted in Welsh hospitals. More bluntly he accused Michael Howard, the Conservative Leader, of refusing to address the scientific evidence on MRSA, instead 'hiding behind the death of his mother-in-law' from the condition. For this he was roundly condemned by Conservative candidates (*Western Mail*, 4 May 2005).

On top-up tuition fees whilst Labour defended the basic principle of the legislation, Hain stressed that how it might be implemented was an Assembly responsibility. The Rees Report on options for the Assembly was delayed until after the election. Morgan intervened on issues of constitutional reform and European funding, both of which related to his responsibilities. On the constitutional question, Morgan and Hain retorted that Labour would not produce a White Paper until later in 2005, but that the party had already committed itself to an expansion of Assembly powers. Whether that should be on the basis of primary legislative powers or expanded secondary legislative powers would be a matter for debate, but if it was to be the former there would be a further referendum. This position sustained Labour as a pro-devolution party whilst more importantly sidelining the constitutional question as an election issue to be one that deserved separate debate and public consultation. This repeated Labour's successful quarantining of the 'national question' in 1997 when the creation of an Assembly was first raised and Labour promised a separate debate and referendum. On European funding Morgan was typically dismissive of what he saw as Plaid Cymru scaremongering, saying of Plaid Cymru suggestions of Labour's inability to secure what Wales deserved as 'not so much a storm in a teacup as a zephyr in a thimble' (*Western Mail*, 4 May 2005).

Labour's campaign literature in Wales was the same as in England. Ultimately the central focus was the strategy of stopping the Tories from getting in by the back door. Given the fragmented nature of Labour's opposition in Wales, there were parts of the country where this was an irrelevant strategy. However, in practice, the Conservatives did indeed prove to be Labour's principal challenger in marginal seats and the campaign literature may well have helped Labour retain potential switchers and in sustaining turnout in these seats. In this respect, a key seat of interest was Cardiff North, one of the wealthiest constituencies in Wales and one that the Conservatives should have won if they were to form a government. Here Labour were nevertheless helped by the high number of resident civil servants who feared more job cuts under a future Conservative government than a Labour one (*Western Mail*, 28 April 2005). The strategy of scaring voters with the threat of a Conservative government was thought to be influential in stemming the flow of potential Labour protest voters either to non-participation or a vote for the Liberal Democrats.

Undeniably, Labour experienced self-inflicted problems as a result of its decision to hold all-women shortlists in a number of seats where the Labour MP was retiring. The most high-profile cost of this policy was borne in Blaenau Gwent, where Labour chose Maggie Jones, a trade union official and NEC member, as its candidate to succeed Llew Smith. Peter Law, Labour's AM for the constituency, led a Constituency Party rebellion, claiming that such central direction it was an insult to a local organisation that had previously selected great left-wing MPs such as Aneurin Bevan and Michael Foot. Law threatened to stand as an independent, but withdrew on discovering that he had a brain tumour that required hospital treatment. Miraculously he made a rapid recovery and decided to stand, and with the support of a number of leading Constituency Party activists who also automatically brought their party membership into question, he mounted the campaign that took him to victory. Blaenau Gwent was visited by Michael Foot, David Blunkett and Peter Hain. Gordon Brown also leant his personal backing to Maggie Jones but to no avail. Different but related problems were experienced in Preseli Pembrokeshire, where the Conservatives, who fielded a male candidate with local family connections, were able to exploit resentments that Labour's candidate, chosen from an all-women shortlist, was an MPs' researcher whose family home was in Worcester and had been similarly 'parachuted' into the constituency.

From a perspective of championing women's representation in Wales Labour could be worthy recipients of some sympathy. In addition, all was not as it seemed in Blaenau Gwent. The background to Peter Law's candidature was one of his immense resentment at his sacking by Rhodri Morgan from the National Assembly Cabinet in 2000 to make way for a Liberal Democrat minister as part of the 2000–03 Labour–Liberal Democrat partnership government. Despite the claimed advantages to governmental stability and the electoral dividend that Labour achieved in the 2003 Assembly elections, Law became a persistent and vocal critic of Morgan, offering himself as a leadership contender against the First Minister. His detachment from all party colleagues was made clear by the fact that he received no supporters. Critics within Welsh Labour viewed Law as a perfect example of Old Labour, not the party of principled socialism, but the party of parochial power networks. His claims of standing on the principled basis of party democracy and socialist principles were thus viewed with some scepticism. This said, charges of Labour Party centralism stick rather more firmly when it is acknowledged that the all-women shortlist that the constituency party had to choose from in selecting Maggie Jones contained no clearly left-wing candidate.

In turn, how effective were the other parties in playing their hands against Labour? The picture was mixed. First, the election had strong echoes of the 2001 campaign in that Labour's reasonable coherence was contrasted with Plaid Cymru's ineptness. The party had a fairly rousing start to the campaign. The campaign launch, in which leading party members wore Welsh rugby shirts to suggest the party as a Welsh team seeking to emulate the Six Nations triumph, received a lot of media coverage. Similarly, the manifesto launch at the Wales botanical gardens was well publicised. During the campaign, the death of former party president, Gwynfor Evans, had the effect of making respect for the nationalist cause a matter of cross-party rhetoric for several days. On the other hand, the party had no coherent leadership during the campaign, failed to communicate its policies effectively and committed basic campaigning mistakes.

The party in effect had three leaders: Dafydd Iwan, the folk singer elected as party president in 2001; Elfyn Llwyd, the party's parliamentary leader in the House of Commons; and Ieuan Wyn Jones, the party's leader in the Assembly, who had resigned under pressure as party president in 2001. Of these Lloyd technically fronted Plaid Cymru's campaign, but because the Welsh media's political coverage is so Assembly-focused he was little known to the Welsh public. Wyn Jones very much took a back seat in the campaign, and Iwan's appearances were problematic given that he was not standing in the election and because his presidency had been won on a ticket of emphasising Plaid Cymru as a pro-independence party. Leadership was thus either largely invisible or cut across attempts to reach out to voters beyond the party's core supporters. As a result, the party's policies were not communicated to the electorate with any coherence. To top all of this, the party took its existing four seats too much for granted. Buoyed by an opinion poll that suggested they were ahead in Ynys Mon, Plaid Cymru poured resources into that constituency in a vain attempt to win, meanwhile allowing strong campaigning by the Liberal Democrats in Ceredigion to outflank them.

The Conservatives had some similar problems. They too had three leadership figures: Michael Howard; Shadow Welsh Secretary, Bill Wiggins, an MP sitting for an English constituency; and Nick Bourne, the Welsh Assembly group leader. They also had three different policies on the constitutional future of the Welsh Assembly. While they all agreed on the policy of offering a multi-option referendum, Bourne was an advocate of primary legislative powers, Wiggins wanted to abolish the Assembly, and Howard said he had no opinion and that it was up to the people of Wales. It could also be said that the Conservative campaign literature in being, like Labour's, centralised, hampered Welsh campaigning. In Wales it would have been much more helpful for party leaflets to emphasise Labour's problems about hospital waiting times, but instead they focused on the UK-wide theme of MRSA.

However, such difficulties proved much less important for the Conservatives than for Plaid Cymru. Coverage of Conservative viewpoints in the UK media, which dominates media consumption in Wales, was extensive and in the UK context the focus on Michael Howard managed to sustain a projection of clear leadership and a coherent presentation of policy priorities. A relevant factor to the success of local campaigning was that the Conservatives were the only party whose representatives elected to the Welsh Assembly sought to gain a seat at Westminster. This made success in Monmouth, where David Davies was the popular constituency AM, virtually assured. A former Conservative List AM was the successful candidate in Clwyd West. Equally, opposition to the ban on fox hunting was a theme that the party could successfully tap into in both Monmouth and Preseli Pembrokeshire. On this basis, whilst not making much impact on their vote share, the Conservative Party was able to organise its vote to better results.

Clearly, the party that went on to achieve most in the election was the Liberal Democrats. Their campaign strategy was the most coherent in a Welsh context. Again, the Liberal Democrats potentially had three leadership figures, but significantly Lembit Opik as the leader of the Welsh Liberal Democrats in the House of Commons had achieved a high media profile. He was able to appear as a plausible and articulate lieutenant to Charles Kennedy in leading the campaign in Wales. The policy position of the Liberal Democrats was also effective. Analysis of the Liberal Democrat performance in southern England suggests that the party's position to the left of the Labour Party hampered the party in competing with the Conservative Party, their main opponent in most of their target seats. In Wales, however, the Conservatives were not the main opposition. The left-of-centre policy position helped them in competition with Labour and Plaid Cymru, who, of course, prior to the election, held all other constituency seats. Equally, the policies on Iraq and student top-up fees helped the Liberal Democrats in contesting elections in the main urban and university seats. Finally, the party's reputation for vigorous local campaigning helped harness the vote not only in winning the key target seat of Cardiff Central but also Ceredigion.

Consequently, overall, one may come to a mixed evaluation of party performance in the election campaign. Labour made the best of a bad job. Faced with the prospect of conducting the campaign on the defensive the party sustained coherent leadership and deployed a number of strategies to diffuse criticism, while seeking to maximise turnout. The Blaenau Gwent episode was a self-inflicted wound, where arguably laudable intentions were poorly implemented. Plaid Cymru significantly underperformed in all aspects of their election campaign. The Conservatives had a mixed performance but were much more effective than in 2001. In particular local campaigning in target constituencies was effectively deployed to exploit Labour weaknesses. Of all the parties the Liberal Democrats' election strategy appeared the best tailored for making gains. The central issues in their campaign, the Iraq war and university tuition fees, maximised their chances in Wales.

In terms of the impact of devolution on the nature of the election campaign compared to England, there are three key points to emphasise. First, it would be hard to make any case that the parties assumed demarcation of electoral arenas between those which might be discussed in a general election and those which should feature in a Welsh Assembly election. All issues were potentially open to party campaigning, whether they were devolved or not. Second, the 2005 general election campaign was in a number of respects much more devolution-sensitive than the 2001 general election. This was readily apparent in the parties' manifestos. While in 2001 all of the UK parties had released Welsh versions, this time policy differences between UK and Welsh level manifestos were much more apparent. This was particularly true in the case of the Labour Party. For example, while UK and Welsh manifestos sought to promote the party's achievements in public services, the UK version embraced a language of competition and choice whilst the Welsh Labour version was built around a language of universal state provision (Labour Party 2005). Equally, when parties sought to attack Labour they made little distinction between campaigning on issues that were solely Westminster-related, primarily a matter for the Assembly, such as health policy, or issues that were of concern to both Westminster and the Assembly. Labour in turn openly displayed their policy differences between UK and Welsh levels when required to respond.

Finally, however, while parties sought to be devolution-sensitive in these ways, it is questionable whether these conversations between parties, played out in the Welsh media, really penetrated the wider Welsh public. Indeed, differences between a party's UK and Welsh manifesto were not the subject media debate. The electorate instead received most of their information from a UK media and state-wide party campaigning tools that as we have seen were largely written off a UK-based template. Labour, the Conservatives and the Liberal Democrats in Wales were all forced to follow the campaign themes being pushed by their party leaderships on a UK-wide basis, and often on a detailed basis set by English rather than Welsh concerns. The Conservative emphasis on MRSA as a key health concern in Wales, rather than Labour's performance on health waiting times in the Assembly, is a striking example. Plaid Cymru in particular felt that in a post-devolution context UK media coverage as it related to Wales struggled to adapt. Plaid Cymru felt marginalised in that coverage, which can be taken as a reflection of the broader marginalisation of the debate of specifically Welsh concerns and policy debates that have been drawn into sharper focus since devolution. Consequently, despite some developments, the conduct of the 2005 general election in Wales remained to a large extent a devolution-blind event.

Conclusion

The 2005 election in Wales held substantial interest for analysts of electoral politics and election campaigning. The importance of the election could also be felt in relation to the future conduct of politics in Wales. This was immediately evident in relation to Welsh Assembly politics, Peter Law's candidature and election as an independent in Blaenau Gwent ensuring his departure from the Labour Party. In remaining as an Assembly Member as well as an MP, Law's defection cut the size of the Labour group in the National Assembly to 29 out of 60 members. As a result Rhodri Morgan faced the prospect of running a minority Labour administration through to the next Assembly elections in 2007. This period was also likely to be a testing one. The block grant largesse dispensed to the Assembly during its early years could be undermined by tougher public expenditure decisions at Westminster. At the same time the pressure on Labour to deliver on key health policy targets would be intensified. Labour would also come under increasing scrutiny over the success of their great reform project of the same term, namely the abolition of key quangos, such as the Welsh Development Agency, and the incorporation of their work within Assembly departments. Finally, Labour was due to publish a White Paper on the reform of the constitution and powers of the National Assembly, an issue that would cause considerable controversy.

Minority government was also likely to face a rejuvenated opposition in the Assembly. Prior to the election, Assembly Conservative leader, Nick Bourne, had taken the lead in advocating more all-party co-operation to stand up to the Labour administration in Cardiff Bay (Bourne 2005). Following the election, the Welsh Conservative Group in the Assembly exploited Labour's new weakness by proposing a resolution, two days ahead of the Rees Report, that top-up fees should not be introduced in Wales. Labour's 29 votes were beaten by the 30 votes of the combined opposition, including Peter Law, who defiantly insisted on remaining an AM as well as an MP, demonstrating that Bourne's proposal could be turned into practice. On all of the problematic issues raised above a continued Labour minority administration faced potential defeats, and lurking round the corner was also the possibility that the Assembly could pass a motion of no confidence in the First Minister, Rhodri Morgan, just as it had formerly threatened to do in the case of Alun Michael, Morgan's predecessor, a threat which precipitated his resignation in February 2000. In addition, the most public post mortem after the election was held in Plaid Cymru, where it was recognised that the party in its leadership and campaigning had simply failed to adapt to and capitalise on its historic performance in the 1999 Assembly elections. The deep depression felt after a succession of perceived missed electoral opportunities had the potential to create pressures for quite radical surgery to improve their performance in opposition.

In the Assembly elections in 2007 that will follow this potentially turbulent period in Welsh politics, Labour will confront the issue of whether the 29 seats they currently hold in the Assembly represent a platform or a ceiling. Taking a bullish approach Labour may be confident about defending all of the seats that they currently hold and, if reasserting party loyalty in both Wrexham and Blaenau Gwent, at least take their tally up to 31 seats. They may also be hopeful of a larger regional list vote in Mid and West Wales securing their one realistic chance of a list seat. This would re-establish Labour's majority. On the other hand, the Conservatives will be hopeful of building on their Westminster triumphs in Clwyd West and Preseli Pembrokeshire by taking the seats in the Assembly as well. They will also target again Cardiff North, where a Conservative list AM has now stood as a constituency candidate in both the Westminster and the Assembly elections and attained increasing visibility. Equally, the Liberal Democrats are likely to target Swansea West, a seat that has large numbers of students and middle-class professionals and could provide fertile territory for a Labour protest vote. A potentially rejuvenated Plaid Cymru could compete again with Labour outside its West and North Wales heartland. If Labour lost any seats the still large disproportionality of Labour's constituency representation in the Assembly would most likely mean that Labour would not get any compensatory list seats. Labour would remain the largest party but find the achievement of an actual majority increasingly difficult.

Of course, the Assembly offers much greater opportunities for the other parties in Wales because of its proportional element. The general election of 2009/2010 would return us to the question of how successfully Labour might sustain even a conventional electoral dominance in Wales after over a decade in power at Westminster under a simple plurality system. Here the political soothsayers are caught between assessing the potential impact of two different influences that are already apparent. On the one hand, Labour has already dealt with the succession and renewal issue through Tony Blair's advertised departure before the next general election. The election of Gordon Brown as Labour leader could work very well in Wales in reviving support among core Labour voters whilst also through his track record as Chancellor sustaining New Labour supporters as well. The Labour fortress under such circumstances might hold. On the other hand, Labour's vote share has gone down in two successive elections and the opposition parties would expect that Labour's position would worsen the longer it stayed in power. Defeats in specific constituencies in 2007 and prominent Conservative AMs standing for Westminster seat may also have local effects. Even a Gordon Brown leadership may not staunch concerns about gradual fractures within Labour party solidarity that the Blaenau Gwent episode revealed, and which may have played through in assembly politics between 2005 and 2009/10.

These issues point to the overriding change in the character of politics in Wales. The parties now live with a cycle in which there are major elections every two years. No matter how devolution-blind state-wide party campaigns are in a general election, it is clear that the results in one set of elections have knock-on consequences for politics and campaigning in the next, from Assembly to Westminster elections and back again. Adaptation to electoral politics in Wales after devolution has seen Labour hold on to their dominance at the UK level and mostly at the Welsh level. Nevertheless, Labour has been weakened by the experience and the other parties have had more opportunities. Beyond the current continuities lies much uncertainty.

References

Bourne, N. (2005) 'Welsh Conservatism: A Chance to Shine', Welsh Governance Centre St David's Day Lecture, March

Labour Party (2005) *Britain: Forward Not Back*, London and Cardiff: Labour Party.

Mitchell, J. and Bradbury, J. (2002) 'Scotland and Wales: the first post-devolution general election', in A. Geddes and J. Tonge (eds) *Labour's Second Landslide: The British General Election 2001*, Manchester: Manchester University Press.

Plaid Cymru (2005) *We Can Build a Better Wales*, Cardiff: Plaid Cymru.

Trystan, D., Scully, R. and Wyn Jones, R. (2003) 'Explaining the "quiet earthquake" voting behaviour in the first election to the National Assembly for Wales', *Electoral Studies*, 22(4): 635–50.

Wyn Jones, R. and Scully, R. (2003) 'Coming home to Labour? The 2003 Welsh Assembly Election', *Regional and Federal Studies*, 13(3): 125–32.

Monmouth

Monmouth might be regarded as one of very few naturally Conservative Welsh seats. A border constituency sometimes regarded as a semi-English seat, it has never possessed strong labourist or nationalist tradition. With a Labour majority of only 384 from the 2001 election in essentially a straight Labour–Conservative fight, the seat was highly likely to change hands in 2005. Nonetheless, the large size of the swing to the Conservative candidate, the Deputy Leader of the Welsh Conservative Party, David Davies, may have surprised. The Conservatives gained nearly 3,000 votes, despite turnout rising only slightly from the very healthy 2001 figure of 71.5 per cent.

The Conservatives played down lingering scepticism over the value of devolution, even though Monmouth, the most infertile constituency for Plaid Cymru, had been one of the areas most sceptical over the creation of the Welsh Assembly. In terms of local issues, hunting, which failed to become a significant national election issue, did feature here, with the Countryside Alliance making the ousting of the anti-hunting Labour incumbent, Huw Edwards, its top target. Rather than engage in potentially counter-productive large demonstrations, the Alliance decided to assist in the removal of marginal pro-hunting MPs by assisting pro-hunting MPs in their conventional electoral activity. Two local hunts joined the Conservatives' campaign in Monmouth, although, nationally, the Conservative Party was disinclined to make hunting an issue, given its limited salience, outside certain localities.

Result		%
Davies, D. (Con)	21,396	46.9
Edwards, H. (Lab)	16,869	37.0
Hobson, P. (LD)	5,862	12.8
Clark, J. (PC)	993	2.1
Bufton, J. (UKIP)	543	1.2
Con gain from Lab		
Con majority	4,527	9.9
Swing: Lab to Con		5.4

Turnout: 72.4%

9

Northern Ireland: Meltdown of the Moderates or the Redistribution of Moderation?

Jonathan Tonge

The Westminster election in Northern Ireland proved a dramatic affair, in which the realignment of unionist and nationalist politics neared completion. The relatively moderate and ostensibly pro-Good Friday Agreement (GFA) Ulster Unionist Party (UUP), for so long the dominant force within unionism, was eclipsed by the Reverend Ian Paisley's anti-GFA Democratic Unionist Party (DUP). With the UUP leader, David Trimble, losing in Upper Bann, the UUP holding only a solitary constituency and the DUP winning seats, the triumph of Paisleyism appeared complete. The peace and political processes part-brokered by the UUP yielded the demise of the party once seen as the embodiment of unionism, an electoral obliteration which had gathered pace with each election since the 1998 GFA.

Intra-nationalist competition was equally evident, but the outcome was less startling. The election confirmed the growth of Sinn Fein, which gained one seat at the expense of the Social Democratic and Labour Party (SDLP) despite controversies surrounding activities of the Irish Republican Army (IRA), some of its members having been implicated in recent murders, robberies and other criminality before being 'stood down' after the election. Amid Sinn Fein's continued expansion, reports of the imminent death of the SDLP nonetheless proved premature, as the party gained a previously unionist seat and held two of the three seats it had been predicted by some to lose to its nationalist rival.

The shift towards the supposedly more hardline unionism of the DUP and the tougher nationalism of Sinn Fein begs the question of whether the devolved power sharing and cross-border political institutions established under the GFA, suspended since October 2002, will be restored. Two of the three main pro-Agreement parties are in retreat. Amid a general lack of confidence in the GFA within the Unionist community, the DUP has crushed the UUP. Sinn Fein's triumphs ensure that any restoration of devolution requires a far-reaching deal between the supposed extremes of Northern Ireland politics. Electoral polarisation has been accompanied by the 'Balkanisation' of society, with increased residential segregation of the unionist and nationalist communities in a form of benign apartheid.

A more upbeat prognosis suggests that the province's ethnic bloc party system requires single-party representation within each bloc if a consociational deal like the GFA is to succeed. Since 1998, political progress has been impaired by intra-unionist rivalry, allegations of IRA activity and the slow pace of decommissioning of paramilitary weapons. During the election campaign, the Taioseach, Bertie Ahern, acknowledged in respect of the IRA that 'there still is training, there still is recruiting and ... there still is the crossover into criminal activity' (*Daily Ireland*, 21 April 2005). However, the 2005 election result offered the prospect of the removal of impediments, leaving a single party speaking for unionism and facilitating the IRA's exit from the stage.

The results

The election confirmed the trend of rising DUP and Sinn Fein support, in actual terms and relative to their in-bloc party rival, evident since the 1998 GFA, indicated in Table 9.1 and Figures 9.1 and 9.2 below. The 2005 election replicated the 2004 European election in producing a DUP vote share almost twice that garnered by the UUP.

Table 9.1   Party vote shares in Northern Ireland elections, 1997–2005

Election	First-preference party vote share (%)			
	DUP	UUP	SF	SDLP
Pre GFA				
1997 Westminster	13.6	32.7	16.1	24.1
1997 Council	15.6	27.9	16.9	20.7
Post GFA				
1998 Assembly	18.1	21.3	17.6	22.0
1999 European	28.4	17.6	17.4	28.2
2001 Westminster	22.5	26.8	21.7	21.0
2001 Council	21.4	22.9	20.7	19.4
2003 Assembly	25.7	22.7	23.5	17.0
2004 European	31.9	16.5	26.3	15.9
2005 Westminster	33.7	17.7	24.3	17.5
2005 Council	29.6	18.0	23.2	17.4

A breakdown by votes and seats of the 2005 contest illuminates the new dominance of the DUP (Table 9.2). The overall shares of the vote held by unionists and nationalists were virtually unchanged from the 2001 Westminster election, at 51.4 per cent and 41.8 per cent respectively.

Table 9.2 Votes and seats in the 2005 Westminster election in Northern Ireland

| | Votes | | | Seats | | | |
	Actual	% share	% change	Actual	Gains	Losses	Net
DUP	241,856	33.7	+11.2	9	4	0	+4
SF	174,530	24.3	+2.6	5	1	0	+1
SDLP	125,626	17.5	–3.5	3	1	1	0
UUP	127,314	17.7	–9.1	1	0	5	–5

Whilst the overall swing from the UUP to the DUP of 10.1 per cent was exaggerated by the entry of Paisley's party into constituencies where it previously allowed the UUP a free run, the trend was nonetheless stark. The once dominant UUP was reduced to the status of Northern Ireland's fourth party in terms of Westminster representation. The swing from the SDLP to Sinn Fein was much

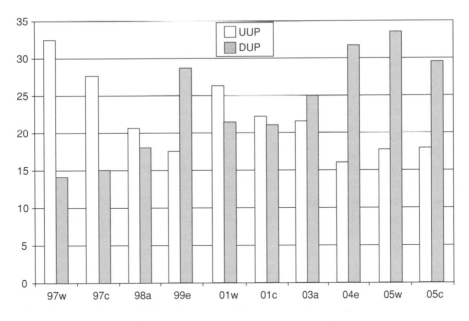

Figure 9.1 UUP–DUP electoral rivalry, 1997–2005 (% vote share)

Key:
97w 1997 Westminster election
97c 1997 Council election
98a 1998 Assembly election
99e 1999 European election
01w 2001 Westminster election

01c 2001 Council election
03a 2003 Assembly election
04e 2004 European election
05w 2005 Westminster election
05c 2005 Council election

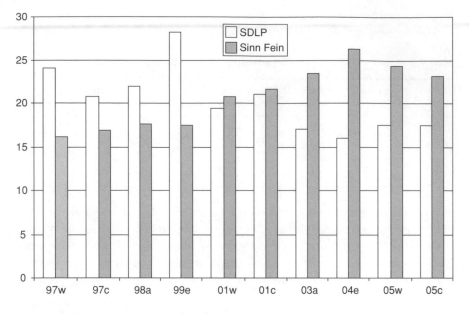

Figure 9.2 SDLP–Sinn Fein electoral rivalry, 1997–2005 (% vote share)

Key:

97w	1997 Westminster election	01c	2001 Council election
97c	1997 Council election	03a	2003 Assembly election
98a	1998 Assembly election	04e	2004 European election
99e	1999 European election	05w	2005 Westminster election
01w	2001 Westminster election	05c	2005 Council election

more modest at 3.1 per cent, but continued a trend evident since the GFA. For the SDLP, the results indicated a slowing in decline relative to Sinn Fein, but did not indicate a reversal of declining fortunes.

Broken down by Westminster constituency and seat changeovers, the desperate plight of the UUP is clearly indicated (Table 9.3). Constituencies regarded as safe UUP seats prior to the GFA, such as South Antrim, were taken comfortably by the DUP. The UUP's Lady Sylvia Hermon held predominantly middle-class North Down. In other unionist areas, however, with the exception of liberal South Belfast, the DUP's move from overly militant loyalism to new respectability (whilst still offering a stouter unionism) found appeal among middle-class Protestants who had eschewed the party in previous decades.

The UUP was disadvantaged by the impact of the first-past-the-post system, retained exclusively for Westminster elections. The UUP could hardly cry foul; for years the 'winner takes all' system had favoured the party as the DUP's respectable second places counted for little, or led to Paisley's party vacating the territory in the knowledge that being runner-up to the UUP would be worthless. The

Table 9.3 2005 Westminster election results by constituency in Northern Ireland

Constituency	DUP	% share UUP	SDLP	SF	% Swing (in bloc)	% Turnout
East Antrim	49.6	26.6	5.3	2.6	11.7 UUP–DUP	54.5 (–4.6)
East Belfast*	49.1	30.1	2.7	3.3	0.1 DUP–UUP	58.0 (–5.0)
East Londonderry	42.9	21.1	17.1	16.1	8.5 UUP–DUP	60.3 (–5.9)
Fermanagh & S. Tyrone	28.8	18.2	14.8	38.2	12.4 **	72.6 (–5.4)
Foyle	14.4	2.4	46.3	33.2	5.3 SDLP–SF	65.9 (–3.0)
Lagan Valley*	54.7	21.5	7.5	6.1	38.1 UUP–DUP***	60.2 (–3.0)
Mid Ulster	23.5	10.7	17.4	47.6	2.0 SF–SDLP	72.5 (–8.8)
Newry & Armagh	18.4	13.9	25.2	41.4	11.3 SDLP–SF	70.0 (–6.8)
North Antrim	54.8	14.5	12.2	15.7	5.7 UUP–DUP	61.7 (–4.4)
North Belfast	45.6	7.1	16.2	28.6	4.8 UUP–DUP	57.8 (–9.4)
North Down*	35.1	50.4	3.1	0.6	20.3 UUP–DUP	54.0 (–4.8)
South Antrim	38.2	29.1	12.4	11.6	5.7 UUP–DUP	56.7 (–5.8)
South Belfast	28.4	22.7	32.3	9.0	0.2 SF–SDLP	60.8 (–3.1)
South Down	18.3	9.9	25.8	44.7	3.8 SDLP–SF	65.4 (–5.4)
Strangford*	56.5	21.3	2.6	3.9	16.4 UUP–DUP	53.6 (–6.3)
Upper Bann	37.6	25.5	21.0	13.0	8.1 UUP–DUP	61.2 (–9.1)
West Belfast	10.6	2.3	14.6	70.5	4.4 SDLP–SF	64.2 (–4.5)
West Tyrone****	17.8	6.9	17.8	38.9	15.6 SF–IND	72.1 (–7.8)

Seats changing hands

DUP gains (all from UUP)	SF gain (from SDLP)	SDLP gain (from UUP)
East Antrim	Newry & Armagh	South Belfast
Lagan Valley		
South Antrim		
Upper Bann		

* The Alliance Party came third in East Belfast (12.2 per cent), Lagan Valley (10.1 per cent), North Down (7.6 per cent) and Strangford (9.0 per cent).
** DUP did not stand in Fermanagh & South Tyrone in 2001, thus 'swing' meaningless.
*** The DUP candidate, Jeffrey Donaldson, was elected as a UUP candidate in 2001, which partly explains the extraordinary swing.
**** An Independent candidate came second in West Tyrone with 27.4 per cent of the vote.

realignment of votes now exaggerates *DUP* hegemony. Almost 18 per cent of the vote yielded one seat for the UUP, whereas one-third of the vote netted half of the seats for the DUP. In contrast, nationalist seat shares were broadly proportional. The Westminster elections continue to offer a much more disproportional outcome than all the PR-STV (proportional representation – single transferable vote) contests held in Northern Ireland, except for European contests, where, in the four-party–three-seat system, there is one major loser, presently the SDLP, but possibly the UUP in future.

Similar trends within unionism and nationalism were evident in the council elections held on the same day. The UUP trailed the DUP (by 67) and Sinn Fein (by 11) in respect of council seats, suffering a swing of 6.7 per cent to the DUP. There was a swing of 2 per cent from the SDLP to Sinn Fein. With 182 council seats and 29.6 per cent of first-preference votes, the DUP emerged as the strongest party in local government, followed by Sinn Fein with 23.2 per cent of the vote and 126 seats. The UUP, hitherto the leading party, was relegated to third place with only 18 per cent of the vote and 115 seats, its worst ever performance, whilst the SDLP obtained 17.4 per cent of the vote and won 101 seats.

The disastrous UUP result led to the immediate resignation of David Trimble as party leader. Trimble urged the DUP 'that when negotiating with Sinn Fein make sure everything you get is nailed down because they can't be trusted to live up to their commitments' (*Observer*, 8 May 2005). The comment appeared merely to vindicate the verdict offered – on the day the GFA was reached – by Jeffrey Donaldson, the UUP negotiator who quit Trimble's team in protest at the ambiguities of the deal and later joined the DUP. Donaldson argued that the lack of clarity within the deal would prove costly for the UUP and would destabilise the agreement, a prescient view.

Within nationalism, there were overblown expectations that Sinn Fein might end the SDLP's Westminster representation. This always appeared unlikely, given the size of the SDLP's majorities in Foyle, where the SDLP leader, Mark Durkan, inherited the legacy of the popular former leader, John Hume, and in South Down. The one realistic Sinn Fein target, Newry and Armagh, was gained on a sizeable swing. Elsewhere, the swing to Sinn Fein was more modest, but all of its seats now appear safe, even though, until the 1997 election, the party held only two Westminster seats.

Sinn Fein has displayed a capacity to mobilise young voters and former non-voters (McAllister 2004). Its erosion of the SDLP's middle-class Catholic vote was likely to be slowed in the 2005 contest, given controversies over continuing IRA activity outlined in the campaign discussion below, most notably the killing of the Belfast Catholic, Robert McCartney, in January 2005. Sinn Fein's vote share fell in five constituencies and there was even a swing to the SDLP in South Belfast. Overall, however, the growth of Sinn Fein continued.

A discernible trend is towards voter disengagement. Turnout in the Westminster contest fell by 5.5 per cent, dropping in all constituencies, and dropped by 5 per cent in the local elections, continuing a trend evident throughout the decade. There is a positive relationship between votes for nationalist parties (Sinn Fein's at 0.78 (significant at $p<.01$) is stronger than the SDLP's, at 0.48 ($p<.05$). However, there is a negative relationship between votes for unionist parties and turnout (for the UUP, –0.61, for the DUP –0.70, both significant at $p<.01$). The general rule was that the higher the unionist share of the vote, the lower the turnout.

As violence has faded and the peace process embedded, the accompanying stalemate in the political process may have created an increasing sense of disillusionment, particularly amongst the unionist electorate which has perceived the process of one of concessions to nationalists. At 68 per cent, turnout in the eight nationalist-held constituencies remains appreciably higher than in those held by unionists, at 57 per cent. Indeed the differential widens if South Belfast, where a natural unionist majority was turned into a nationalist majority through unionist electoral rivalry, is excluded from the nationalist turnout figure. Clearly, nationalists in Northern Ireland remain more exercised by the electoral process and the possibilities engendered by the GFA than unionists. The falls in turnout did not vary according to which bloc held the seat, dropping by 5.8 per cent in unionist constituencies and by 5.6 per cent in those held by nationalists.

Elections in Northern Ireland remain sectarian headcounts; what matters is the breakdown of votes within the blocs. Figures 9.3 and 9.4 demonstrate how the *aggregate* size of the unionist and nationalist bloc vote could be predicted very accurately from 2001 census data on the percentage of Protestants and Catholics within each constituency.

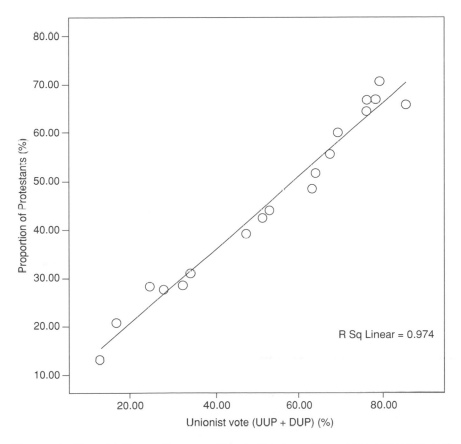

Figure 9.3 Unionist bloc voting according to the percentage of Protestants in each constituency in the 2005 Westminster election in Northern Ireland

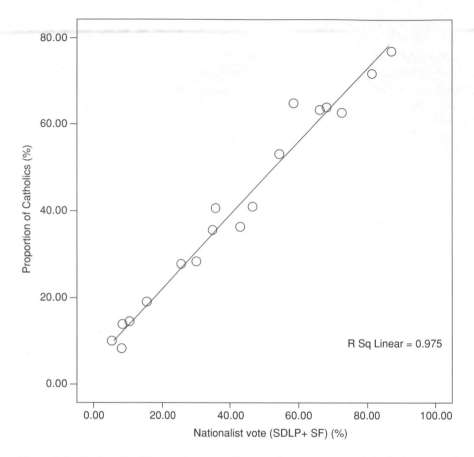

Figure 9.4 Nationalist bloc voting according to the percentage of Catholics in each constituency in the 2005 Westminster election in Northern Ireland

There are few outliers from the line of best fit, in what is palpably an extremely strong relationship between percentage bloc vote size and the percentage of the population holding a particular religious affiliation. Obviously first-past-the-post single vote elections discourage voting outside the ethnic bloc, whereas PR-STV affords the opportunity for cross-community lower-preference vote transfers. Nonetheless, the above figures indicate the continuing ultra-strong relationship between religion and voting in Northern Ireland. Within the blocs, it is the UUP and SDLP votes which deviate much more than those of the DUP and Sinn Fein from those which could be expected given the religious composition of individual constituencies.

The general political context

The election was held amid political stalemate. Following the collapse of the devolved Executive and Assembly in autumn 2002, amid unproven allegations of an IRA spy ring at Stormont, direct rule from Westminster had returned indefinitely, although few saw this as a long-term proposition. The DUP, newly ascendant after the delayed elections to the suspended Assembly in November 2003, promised to get rid of the GFA. However, in autumn 2004, the party appeared prepared to do a deal with Sinn Fein, now the largest party within nationalism, which would restore devolved institutions. Since the signing of the GFA, however, the issue of IRA weapons decommissioning had dogged political progress and it was little surprise that wrangling over the modalities of the process thwarted an accommodation.

Contrary to popular myth, the GFA did not require the IRA, or any other paramilitary group, to decommission its weapons. The deal merely required political parties to exert maximum pressure upon paramilitary organisations to achieve decommissioning, an expectation rather than an outcome. Given Sinn Fein's 'special relationship' with the IRA, it was nonetheless unsurprising that the party came under acute pressure to achieve the decommissioning of the IRA's arsenal.

As political institutions oscillated between suspension and semi-functional status, the IRA, under political and moral pressure, engaged in three acts of decommissioning between 2001 and 2003. The IRA regarded decommissioning as a likely part of the peace process, but was insistent that its timetabling and operation were to be determined by the IRA, in conjunction with the International Commission on Decommissioning (ICD), headed by General John de Chastelain, rather than by unionists. Unlike many others, the IRA engaged in a literal, rather than aspirational, reading of the GFA on this issue. However, the three acts of IRA decommissioning were shrouded in such secrecy, barely lifted by a brief report on each occasion by de Chastelain, that they further undermined confidence in the process. Dissatisfaction with the lack of transparency of the IRA's third act of decommissioning led to the UUP's rejection of re-entry into government with Sinn Fein. This refusal led to the British government's decision to call fresh Assembly elections for autumn 2003, a contest which ended the UUP's leading position within unionism.

Despite these problems, a deal appeared possible in autumn 2004, as the DUP and Sinn Fein appeared set to conclude an accord. This involved the IRA disposing of its weapons, witnessed by General de Chastelain and clergy from the Protestant and Catholic Churches. The deal collapsed, ostensibly when the DUP demanded photographic evidence of decommissioning, following Ian Paisley's insistence that the IRA wear 'sackcloth and ashes'. Within weeks, new controversies emerged. Firstly, the IRA was blamed by the Chief Constable of Northern Ireland for the £26 million robbery of the Northern Bank in Belfast, the largest such robbery ever undertaken in Britain and Ireland. As with the 'spy ring' at Stormont allegations in 2002, the Chief Constable proved quicker at blaming the IRA than apprehending the culprits, but few doubted republican involvement in the robbery. Secondly, the murder of Robert McCartney by IRA members in Belfast produced a high-profile campaign for justice by the sisters of the murder victim, which spread beyond the hitherto pro-IRA area of Short Strand in Belfast to the US administration and the European Parliament.

Despite continuing political problems, successive Northern Ireland Life and Times Surveys indicated a desire for devolved power-sharing among the population. Against this, the GFA lacked backing from the Unionist population. Only 57 per cent of Protestants supported the deal in the 1998 referendum; five years later backing had fallen to one-third (Hayes and McAllister 2001; Dowds, Hayes and McAllister 2004). Protestants were not opposed to power-sharing *per se*, but resented much of the GFA non-constitutional agenda, in particular, the release of paramilitary prisoners and the changes to policing, including the replacement of the Royal Ulster Constabulary by the Police Service of Northern Ireland and the introduction of 50–50 Catholic–non-Catholic recruitment.

Devolution was hardly an unqualified success between 1999 and 2002, yielding power-broking and power division, rather than genuine power-sharing. Ministries were chosen by political parties according to the D'Hondt formula, based upon Assembly strength. These departments tended to become party fiefdoms and the Executive was never a collective and rarely a genuine coalition (Wilford 2001; Tonge 2005). Devoid of a system of government and opposition, it appeared impossible to hold the Executive to account. Although Assembly committees worked well, establishing a modicum of cross-party co-operation, none of the other institutions performed in the consensual manner envisaged under the GFA.

The campaign within unionism

The unionist campaign followed predictable lines, the DUP selling itself as the voice of strong unionism and the UUP marketing itself as the party that had achieved results for unionism, indicated by a more peaceful Northern Ireland. Strong intra-Unionist rivalry has been persistent since the birth of the DUP in 1971, but the GFA provided the first clear faultline along which enmities could develop since the previous power-sharing experiment in 1974. The DUP criticised the 'pushover unionism' of the UUP, arguing that the political process had been a series of concessions to nationalists. The DUP's pitch to voters stressed the need to elect robust unionist representatives, given Sinn Fein would emerge as the larger nationalist party.

The UUP claimed (legitimately) that it had helped secure the Union via the GFA, a deal whose core principle was that of consent, that is, Northern Ireland would remain part of the United Kingdom for so long as the majority of its citizens so desired. Moreover, it was unclear how the DUP could reverse some of the changes of the GFA. As David Trimble had sardonically remarked after the 2003 Assembly elections, unionists would await with interest the DUP's plans for the returning of paramilitary prisoners to jail and the re-establishment of the Royal Ulster Constabulary.

Arguments over what had happened between 1998 and 2002, and whether the changes were beneficial, dominated the contest within unionism, at the expense of ideas on the way forward. In terms of future plans, the DUP appeared more hostile to the devolution of policing and security, claiming that the UUP was still desirous of such a transfer of powers and would accept a Sinn Fein Minister of Policing and Justice. Moreover, the DUP insisted that the decommissioning of IRA weapons had to be 'timetabled, verifiable and transparent' (Democratic Unionist Party, 2005: 10). This was important in placing the modalities of decommissioning beyond the private concord of the IRA and the ICD and into the public domain.

The UUP's campaign was designed to portray itself, firstly, as the party that 'delivered', and secondly, as unionism's acceptable face, compared to a DUP which had occasionally flirted with extra-constitutionalism. In terms of delivery, the UUP's manifesto insisted that it had 'forced republicans to sign up to democracy and disarmament' (Ulster Unionist Party 2005: 1). The GFA remained the framework within which political parties would have to negotiate. However, the UUP's plea for voters not to be 'DUPed' fell on an unreceptive audience. The debate on the IRA's 'signing up' to decommissioning had moved on to delivery rather than republican statements of intention. In terms of the debate on 'nice versus nasty' unionists, the UUP offered some historical truths, given the DUP leader's brief flirtations with paramilitary-linked organisations, but the DUP had always condemned violence and striven to be 'respectable'. Moreover, there was little contemporary mileage in such a campaign and few unionists saw the DUP's robust loyalism, seen as necessary post-GFA, as beyond the pale. In any case, semi-constitutionalism has been a feature of unionism since its inception in the nineteenth century.

The UUP's tactics were criticised internally, one of its ousted MPs, David Burnside, complaining in a leaked memorandum that the slogan that 'decent people vote UUP' was 'puerile and amateurish' (BBC Northern Ireland, *Spotlight*, 10 May 2005). Indeed the UUP's campaign was tainted with snobbery, harking back to the age of its dominance, when the DUP was seen as a dubious fusion of working-class loyalists and rural fundamentalists, whereas the UUP represented ordinary Protestants. Indeed Trimble's resignation speech referred to the dominance of Paisley's Free Presbyterian Church within the DUP, although recent evidence suggests a (slight) downgrading of the religiously conservative approach of the party, in favour of pragmatism (Southern 2005).

Beyond the rhetoric, there was little substantive difference in policy between the two parties. The UUP claimed the DUP's attitude to North–South co-operation had caught up with reality, highlighting a 'secret meeting' between the DUP leadership and business leaders in the Irish Republic at the start of the campaign (*Newsletter*, 23 April 2005). The DUP was far less sanguine than the UUP on progress during the peace process and remained sceptical of republican commitments. This wariness appeared to be lauded by Trimble in his resignation speech after the election, when he warned the new Secretary of State that he must insist that Sinn Fein disbands its 'private army', even though, as UUP leader, he had entered government with republicans bereft of any such undertaking (*The Times*, 10 May 2005).

In a move scarcely cognisant of the electoral mood, the UUP raised the prospect of a voluntary Executive coalition between it and the SDLP after the election. Attempting to appear more hardline than the DUP, the UUP declared that 'we do not intend to re-enter an Executive that includes Sinn Fein' (Ulster Unionist Party 2005: 1). The pledge raised the obvious question among Unionist voters of why the party had entered government with Sinn Fein with the IRA still armed and with Sinn Fein not having asked the IRA to stand down. Against this, the UUP could point to the DUP's apparent willingness to do a deal with Sinn Fein in December 2004, a position defended by the DUP on the grounds that it had demanded transparent decommissioning as a precursor.

As the UUP attempted to shore up its core vote, it was deserted by its traditional allies in the Protestant Orange Order. In March 2005, the Order announced that it was ending its increasingly contentious, century-old, alliance with the UUP. The Order had opposed the GFA and been critical of the UUP leadership ever since, its delegates on the Ulster Unionist Council particularly critical of the GFA and David Trimble's leadership of the party (Tonge and Evans 2001; Kaufmann and Patterson 2004). The separation of unionism and orangeism offered the prospect of the UUP articulating a rational, secular case for the Union, but the 2005 election was not the time for a dilution of appeals to Protestant Britishness.

Throughout the campaign it remained unclear whether the DUP would 'do business' with Sinn Fein, assuming that the IRA stood down. Ian Paisley referred to the 'forlorn hope that Sinn Fein can be sanitised' (*News Letter*, 20 April 2005). The DUP Deputy Leader, Peter Robinson, declared that 'it could well take a generation before the republican movement divests itself of the criminality endemic within it', indicating that direct rule might have to continue (BBC Northern Ireland, *Hearts and Minds*, 14 April 2005). Clearly a period of 'decontamination' was to be required even after the processes of IRA disbandment and decommissioning were completed, indicating that a restoration of devolution was not imminent.

The nationalist campaign

The nationalist campaign was dominated by two features. Firstly, Sinn Fein called for the IRA to embrace 'peaceful and democratic methods', with the surprising inference that the IRA was presently anti-democratic, not a criticism evident previously from the republican leadership. The second question was the extent of the widely predicted SDLP meltdown, which, unwisely, given the large SDLP majority in Foyle and the legacy bequeathed by former SDLP leader John Hume, led to one bookmaker making party leader Mark Durkan an odds-on shot to lose his seat.

The call from Gerry Adams for the IRA to abandon its 'armed struggle' came because 'alternatives were now available'. Adams' missive to the IRA was not one requiring a stamp. His subsequent declaration that the IRA had begun the process of debate yielded a sharp exchange on BBC2's *Newsnight* (28 April) between Jeremy Paxman and Martin McGuinness along the lines of 'How could Adams possibly know?'

Predictably, Adams' 'plea' for the IRA to stand down was denounced as an election gimmick by opponents. Whilst the timing of Adams' plea was indeed opportunistic, the criticism overlooked the extent to which removal of the IRA was the logical outworking of the long-term Adams' project. The IRA's value had been in dismantling the old 'Orange state' of Unionist one-party government in Northern Ireland from 1921 until 1972. Following this, its actions may have helped eradicate discrimination against Catholics in Northern Ireland, but in recent years the IRA had no obvious role. Its inability to force British withdrawal and a united Ireland, via a war of attrition in which 3,600 eventually died, was evident by the 1980s. Adams began the search for political alternatives, through a series of private initiatives aimed at securing a formula for Irish self-determination which might not necessarily lead to British withdrawal from Northern Ireland (Moloney 2002). These initiatives came into the public domain with the Sinn Fein–SDLP discussions of the late 1980s and early 1990s and the broadening of 'pan-nationalism' to include various Fianna Fail governments in the Irish Republic, abetted by a sympathetic US administration (English 2003; Murray and Tonge 2005).

The Adams endgame in the move towards exclusively peaceful republican methods would leave the movement considerably short of the united Ireland for which the IRA fought, but could place Sinn Fein in coalition government North and South of the border. This requires continued Sinn Fein electoral growth in the Irish Republic, hitherto inhibited by the IRA. Moreover, nationalists in Northern Ireland support a united Ireland, but not militant republicanism. According to one survey, only 2.1 per cent of Sinn Fein supporters said they could not live with the Union under any circumstance (Bric and Coakley 2004).

The peace process has lifted the ceiling on Sinn Fein's support and the party has been particularly successful in attracting the backing of young voters and in mobilising previous non-voters (McAllister 2004). For such voters, there was no memory of the IRA's campaign of the 1970s, when violence was at its peak, whilst the party had the attraction of purporting to act as the stouter defender of nationalist interests within a post-GFA polity. Sinn Fein's entry towards constitutional politics did split republicans, in 1986 and, more seriously, in 1997, when the Real IRA, which killed 29 civilians at Omagh, was formed. Nonetheless, the campaigns of ultras have been ineffective and Sinn Fein has confirmed its dominance within the republican movement (Tonge 2004). The IRA's campaign of the 1990s, which devastated parts of London and Manchester, placed Sinn Fein in a fair negotiating position at the time of the GFA, but the party preferred to concentrate upon issues that would reassure its base that this was an acceptable deal. The all-Ireland dimension of the GFA was therefore modest, Sinn Fein concentrating upon the release of IRA prisoners, policing reforms and an 'equality agenda'. The price was entry to a Northern Ireland Assembly under British jurisdiction. Further concessions and full implementation of the GFA could be achieved via a protracted process of IRA weapons decommissioning, before the inevitable reappraisal of Sinn Fein's relationship with the IRA (Feeney 2002).

Clearly the extension of the decommissioning process could not be indefinite. The triumph of the DUP in the 2003 Assembly elections, the allegations one year later of IRA involvement in the Northern Bank robbery and the McCartney killing, increased the pressure upon the IRA to disband as a functioning organisation. The McCartney murder added considerably to the demands for the IRA to go away. Sinn Fein attempted to minimise potential electoral damage, inviting the McCartney sisters to its ard-fheis (party conference) in March 2005 and suspending twelve party members. For the party leadership, however, the community protests, whilst an obvious threat, offered an opportunity for Sinn Fein to call for the IRA to go into a 'new mode'. The Provisional IRA had not acted against British rule in Northern Ireland since 1997 and was bereft of purpose, the party with which it was associated having accepted that it would work within a British political system to try and achieve constitutional and political change.

Sinn Fein's campaign stressed the party's republican credentials, notwithstanding the political somersaults performed by the party over the previous decade. Since its re-entry into electoral politics in the early 1980s, it has been a party possessing a republican core fused with tactical flexibility (Maillot 2005). According to the 2004 Northern Ireland Life and Times Survey, only 15 per cent of Catholics desire the retention of Northern Ireland's place in the United Kingdom. As such, Sinn Fein's promotion of its 'united Ireland agenda' was rational; indeed it was imitated by the SDLP, which stressed its support for Irish unity. Sinn Fein called upon the Irish government to publish a green paper setting out its strategy for a united Ireland, with a minister appointed to oversee this. Meanwhile, the party called for Northern Ireland's MPs to be allowed to participate in the Irish parliament.

Recognising the potential unpopularity of calls for the exclusion of Sinn Fein from the Executive, the SDLP ruled this out as an option, although the party leader, Mark Durkan, claimed that 'destination progress' could not be reached by a DUP–Sinn Fein triumph (*Irish Independent*, 18 April 2005). The SDLP concentrated upon calls for a return to the GFA, whilst also attempting to tackle visible symptoms of grassroots sectarianism by calling for a ban on 'all sectarian flags' (Social Democratic and Labour Party 2005). The party's campaign was supported by a visit from the Irish government minister, Michael McDowell, an intervention denounced by the Sinn Fein leadership, criticism itself derided as a partitionist approach to the election by the SDLP (*Irish News*, 18 April 2005). McDowell's claim that 'it is consensus politics – not census politics – that will deliver a united Ireland' appeared at odds with the SDLP leader Mark Durkan's insistence that unionists would have to accept a united Ireland if there was a majority of one in favour in Northern Ireland (*Irish World*, 22 April 2005).

There was little substantive disagreement between Sinn Fein and the SDLP, both looking 'very like other left of centre political parties in Europe' (Harvey 2005: 5). Sinn Fein continued to offer a more territorial-leaning approach to Irish unity, compared to the SDLP's agreed Ireland, but the republican emphasis upon a distinctive Irish nation state continues to diminish, the party having switched from an anti-EU stance until the late 1990s to now supporting the extension of the euro from the Irish Republic to the North as a means of Irish unification.

Sinn Fein stressed the need to implement the 'equality agenda' associated with the GFA, including the eradication of unemployment differentials between Catholics and Protestants, strengthening of the Equality and Human Rights Commissions, continuing changes in justice and policing, further investigations into security force collusion with loyalists and greater funding of the Irish language (Sinn Fein 2005). Sinn Fein called for 'demilitarisation' pointing out that there were more British troops stationed in Northern Ireland than Iraq, despite the removal of half of the army bases.

The SDLP, equally keen to promote the 'equality agenda', criticised Sinn Fein and the DUP for attempting to change key aspects of the GFA in their ill-fated 'deal' of December 2004. Indeed that pact would have removed the joint election of First and Deputy First Ministers and provided new vetoes on ministerial choices for the big two parties. The SDLP criticised the way the proposed Sinn Fein and DUP accord 'fails to offer a single extra North/South body or area of cooperation' (Social Democratic and Labour Party 2005: 3). However, Stand Two of the original GFA, supported by the SDLP, also failed to provide any dynamic in this respect. The SDLP argued that the GFA's protections should continue in a united Ireland, although given that Northern institutions might be superfluous in a unitary state, the value of this guarantee was unclear. The party also claimed that 'only the SDLP can persuade a majority in the North in favour of unity', which would represent a major advance on its ability to persuade fewer than one in five voters to vote for the SDLP (Social Democratic and Labour Party 2005: 4).

Political futures

There are three main intellectual schools of opinion on the way forward. Supporters of the consociational approach inherent in the GFA believe it to be a realistic attempt to manage Northern Ireland's political difficulties (McGarry and O'Leary 2004). They argue that the political framework of the GFA has produced incentives for moderation within the former 'extremes' of Sinn Fein and the DUP. The GFA acknowledges the existence of competitive ethnic blocs and attempts to manage difference peacefully, with a devolved, power-sharing framework. Given the absence of consensus for alternatives, the consociational ideas of power-sharing, mutual veto, proportionality in government and community autonomy (although such autonomy barely featured in the deal) continue to offer a means of conflict management in a divided society. For consociationalists, the acknowledgement of difference is a necessary precursor for the management of division. Recent election results may assist the implementation of a consociational settlement. The emergence of unrivalled leaders of ethnic blocs, Paisley and Adams and the movement to a single-party bloc system may allow a deal to be done. The DUP and Sinn Fein may be insulated from electoral problems in clinching a political agreement, a luxury that was never afforded to the UUP leadership. A pragmatic wing of the DUP is emerging and may begin to flourish if Paisley steps down as leader.

Critics of the conflict management approach of the GFA argue for a deeper process of conflict resolution. They argue for societal transformation and the addressing of key issues such as sectarianism, about which the GFA says nothing (Dixon 2001; Taylor 2001; Wilford 2001). The societal transformation approach is sceptical of the rigid ethnic bloc designations associated with the GFA, in which members of the Northern Ireland Assembly are required to designate as 'unionist', 'nationalist' or, uncommonly, 'other'. The societal transformation approach argues for greater effort in eradicating the unionist versus nationalist faultline, rather than its recognition and legitimation, which merely consolidates division and assists the growth of strong defenders of unionism and nationalism. The peace and political processes, on this reading, are seen as failures in terms of enhancing mutual understanding and tackling sectarianism (Peatling 2004). The logical conclusion of transformationist arguments is that devolved power-sharing ought to be built from below, rather than through the top-down implementation. Given the lack of power of local councils, where limited sharing of roles takes place and the limited impact of community initiatives, the means of building reconciliation from below are not always apparent, not least because most social institutions replicate communal division (Coulter 1999).

A third approach questions whether the political faultline which gives rise to sectarianism can be eradicated in a polity constructed on sectarian head-counting (Tonge 2005). This approach suggests that a shift towards joint authority by the

British and Irish governments might be required to incentivise devolved power-sharing for unionists otherwise content with the default position of direct rule. Moreover, joint authority might be a useful means of circumventing a border of dubious local geopolitical logic and could reflect the island-wide desires of the population (which remain, overall, for Irish unity) more accurately than the single-option referenda on an agreement which has proved difficult to implement.

The election confirmed the demise of the parties traditionally associated with moderation, ending any lingering aspirations of a coalition of the broad centre, embracing the UUP, SDLP and cross-community Alliance Party. The result instead offered the prospect of a coalition of the hitherto centrifugal forces of Sinn Fein and the DUP. Neither faced the risk of being outflanked by hardliners within their community. Republican dissidents, based within the Continuity and Real IRAs and their political associates, had barely offered a paramilitary threat since the Omagh bombing of 1998, when 29 were killed. The DUP enjoyed a hegemonic position within unionism. As such, the key impediments to a power-sharing deal were the Provisional IRA – soon to be removed – and political will, perhaps the stronger barrier.

The IRA's departure leaves one final obstacle to Sinn Fein's entry to devolved power-sharing. The party's backing for the Police Service of Northern Ireland will require the approval of a special party conference. Given earlier approval of a political deal well short of a united Ireland and entry to a Northern Ireland Assembly within the United Kingdom, this ought not to present undue difficulty for the party leadership.

The SDLP's reprieve in the 2005 election might prove only temporary if Sinn Fein displays an unambiguous commitment to constitutionalism. The party lost ground to Sinn Fein in all constituencies except South Belfast, where it was helped by local factors and unionist rivalry in capturing a seat. The deeper problems for the SDLP of an ageing membership and erratic organisation were not resolved. Most fundamentally, however, the SDLP lacks Sinn Fein's structural advantages. Whilst Sinn Fein can continue to grow as an all-Ireland party, the SDLP is confined to Northern Ireland and thus appears to be a party of narrow northern nationalism devoid of wider links. To overcome this, the party could do a deal with one of the major parties in the South. Under a licensing arrangement, the SDLP could operate as Fianna Fail North (the most sensible choice) but there would be opposition within both parties. Without change, however, the SDLP will continue to be seen as a green Catholic nationalist Six County party, unable to collect many votes from unionists and overlooked by northern nationalists who prefer a green Catholic nationalist 32 county party in the form of Sinn Fein.

Within unionism, the situation for the UUP appears potentially terminal, notwithstanding the party's continuing sizeable council and membership bases.

Whilst the UUP could claim credit for the GFA, the 2005 and preceding elections were contests based upon the issues of trust, implementation and delivery. The chaotic nature of devolution in the early post-GFA years meant that many Unionists switched allegiance to a united party which might deliver the deal and would not place faith in republicans.

Conclusion

For those still clinging to the political framework offered by the GFA, the reordering of electoral politics confirmed by the 2005 election was not necessarily a disaster. It was claimed that 'it would be wrong to interpret the swing to the DUP as wholesale rejection of the Good Friday Agreement' (*Belfast Telegraph*, 10 May 2005). The demise of the traditionally more moderate parties of the UUP and SDLP would lead to a relocation of moderation within Sinn Fein and the DUP. Whilst the British government was now less rabid in its insistence that the GFA was the 'only show in town', it remained the framework within which it hoped that Adams and Paisley – or Paisley's successor – would 'do business' on behalf of their respective ethnic blocs. Shorn of damaging intra-unionist bloc rivalry, a renegotiated GFA might thrive as the DUP moved from its former 'oppositionist' status and accepted the need to work in a soulless marriage (although these often end in divorce) in government with a Sinn Fein party no longer burdened by association with the IRA. The two parties already work together, albeit imperfectly, on local councils.

A less sanguine take on the election was that it confirmed that devolved power-sharing does not work in Northern Ireland, a dysfunctional polity which has never functioned as a viable democracy. Its previous incarnation in 1974, after the Sunningdale Agreement, lasted five months and led to the demise of the UUP leader, Brian Faulkner. Trimble lasted longer, but met the same fate, denounced as a 'Lundy' (traitor) by a majority within his community. This more cautious interpretation suggests a lack of appetite within unionism for sharing power with nationalists and a tacit acceptance of direct rule from Westminster, with the DUP hopeful, if over-optimistic, of bringing greater accountability to governance by ministerial decree from the fifth Secretary of State in seven years, Peter Hain. Whilst the Westminster rule scenario is less acceptable to nationalists, they hope that direct rule might have a green tinge, nudging towards joint authority and thus the clamour for devolution is not tumultuous.

The British government appeared likely to continue direct rule over an acquiescent electorate, whilst never abandoning the prospect of devolution, a desirable, but non-essential, component of its Northern Ireland policy. Meanwhile, a gradual extension of voter disinterest seems probable, as the old constitutional question which fired political hostility fades in salience. Indeed it is difficult to dissent from Aughey's (2005: 175) view that 'people in Northern Ireland appeared to be comfortable with the knowledge that things had just got worse (political polarization) [as] a consequence of their realization that things had also got better (there was little likelihood of a return to terrorist violence)'. For Northern Ireland, the maintenance of a benign sectarian apartheid, accompanied by the spread of apathy, represented some form of progress, albeit curious, compared to previous decades of political violence.

References

Aughey, A. (2005) *Beyond the Belfast Agreement*, London: Routledge.
Bric, M. and Coakley, J. (2004) 'The roots of militant politics in Ireland', in M. Bric and J. Coakley (eds) *From Political Violence to Negotiated Settlement: The Winding Path to Peace in Twentieth Century Ireland*, Dublin: UCD Press.
Coulter, C. (1999) *Contemporary Northern Irish Society*, London: Pluto Press.
Democratic Unionist Party (2005) *Leadership that's Working: Democratic Unionist Party Election Manifesto 2005*, Belfast: DUP.
Dixon, P. (2001) *Northern Ireland: The Politics of War and Peace*, Basingstoke: Palgrave Macmillan.
Dowds, L., Hayes, B. and McAllister, I. (2004) 'The erosion of consent? Protestant disillusionment with the 1998 Northern Ireland Agreement'. Paper presented to the Elections, Public Opinion and Parties Annual Conference, Nuffield College, University of Oxford, September.
English, R. (2003) *Armed Struggle: The History of the IRA*, London: Macmillan.
Feeney, B. (2002) *Sinn Fein: A Hundred Turbulent Years*, Dublin: O'Brien.
Harvey, C. (2005) 'Nationalism: a good cause', *Fortnight*, 435: 5.
Hayes, B. and McAllister, I. (2001) 'Who voted for peace? Public support for the 1998 Northern Ireland Agreement', *Irish Political Studies*, 11: 61–82.
Kaufmann, E. and Patterson, H. (2004) 'Orange traditionalists or Orange sceptics? The complex social base of pro-Agreement unionism'. Paper presented to the Devolution and Unionism conference, University of Ulster, May.
McAllister, I. (2004) 'The armalite and ballot box. Sinn Fein's electoral strategy in Northern Ireland', *Electoral Studies*, 21(1): 123–42.
McGarry, J. and O'Leary, B. (2004) *The Northern Ireland Conflict: Consociational Engagements*, Oxford: Oxford University Press.
Maillot, A. (2005) *New Sinn Fein*, London: Routledge.
Moloney, E. (2002) *A Secret History of the IRA*, London: Penguin.
Murray, G. and Tonge, J. (2005) *Sinn Fein and the SDLP: From Alienation to Participation*, Dublin: O'Brien.
Peatling, G. (2004) *The Failure of the Northern Ireland Peace Process*, Dublin: Irish Academic Press.
Sinn Fein (2005) *Parliamentary and Council Election Manifesto 2005*, Belfast: Sinn Fein.
Social Democratic and Labour Party (2005) *A Better Way to a Better Ireland: SDLP Election Manifesto 2005*, Belfast: SDLP.
Southern, N. (2005) 'Ian Paisley and evangelical Democratic Unionists: an analysis of the role of evangelical Protestantism within the Democratic Unionist Party', *Irish Political Studies*, 20(2): 127–45.

Taylor, R. (2001) 'Northern Ireland: consociation or social transformation?' in, J. McGarry (ed.) *Northern Ireland and the Divided World*, Oxford: Oxford University Press.

Tonge. J. (2004) 'They haven't gone away you know. Irish Republican "dissidents" and "armed struggle"', *Terrorism and Political Violence*, 16(3): 671–93.

Tonge, J. (2005) *The New Northern Irish Politics?* Basingtoke: Palgrave Macmillan.

Tonge, J. and Evans, J. (2001) 'Faultlines in unionism: division and dissent within the Ulster Unionist Council', *Irish Political Studies*, 16: 111–32.

Ulster Unionist Party (2005) *The People for the Union. Election Manifesto 2005*, Belfast: UUP.

Wilford, R. (ed.) (2001) *Aspects of the Belfast Agreement*, Oxford: Oxford University Press.

Upper Bann

The most dramatic defeat of the entire election occurred in Upper Bann. MP for Upper Bann since 1990, UUP leader since 1995 and Nobel Peace Prize winner in 1998, David Trimble lost his seat in the surge in Unionist support towards the DUP. He resigned the party leadership within 24 hours of the result.

As the *Irish Independent* (7 May 2005) put it, this time there was 'no escape for political Houdini'. That Trimble had proved himself a survivor on previous occasions, negotiating a dozen difficult votes within his party on support for the Good Friday Agreement and overcoming two leadership challenges, fuelled some optimism that he might again triumph against the odds. Instead, the bookmakers' assessment that Trimble would lose (his DUP rival, David Simpson, was quoted at long odds-on) proved correct.

Trimble's campaign highlighted a more peaceful Northern Ireland and the economic progress evident in the province. The DUP campaigned against the UUP's 'pushover unionism', arguing that Trimble had been naive in entering government with Sinn Fein without the IRA having disarmed. Although violence in Northern Ireland had lessened, the DUP was entrusted by the Unionist electorate as the custodian of its interests in the future. Protestant support for the Good Friday Agreement had subsided, although if the DUP desired the restoration of devolved power-sharing it was likely to be organised within its framework. Meanwhile, the DUP celebrated a famous coup, its leader, the Reverend Ian Paisley, arriving at Trimble's count to celebrate the first removal of a party leader by his electorate at a general election since Ramsey McDonald's demise in the 1930s.

In his resignation speech, Trimble blamed the British Prime Minister ('the man and woman in the street ... no longer trusts Tony Blair'); the Irish government ('talked robustly about it [IRA activity] and yet did nothing about it') and republicans for failing to deliver (*Observer*, 8 May 2005). Ultimately, however, it was his community that had delivered the knockout blow. Like the previous Unionist exponent of devolved power-sharing, Brian Faulkner, David Trimble found international plaudits count for little when set against the demands of the Unionist electoral bloc.

Result		%
Simpson, D. (DUP)	16,679	37.5
Trimble, D. (UUP)	11,381	25.6
O'Dowd, J. (SF)	9,305	21.0
Kelly, D. (SDLP)	5,747	12.9
Castle, A. (Alliance)	955	2.2
French, T. (Workers)	355	0.8
DUP gain from the UUP		
DUP majority	5,298	11.9
Swing: UUP to DUP		8.0

Turnout: 61.4%

10
Feminising British Politics: Sex and Gender in the Election[1]

Sarah Childs

The 2005 Parliament does not look very different from the 2001 one, nor for that matter the 1997 one. To be sure there is a welcome increase in the number of women present: women now constitute an unprecedented 128 of the 646 MPs, up from 118 in 2001. But this increase constitutes nothing like a significant, or sufficient, presence: women MPs constitute a mere 19.8 per cent of all members. In comparative terms the UK ranks 41st, below, inter alia, Rwanda (in first place), the Nordic countries, the Netherlands, Spain, Argentina, South Africa and Germany. Closer to home, it compares unfavourably to the Scottish Parliament (42 per cent) and the National Assembly for Wales (50 per cent).

The number of women MPs elected in 2005, as well as their distribution between the parties, reinforce conclusions drawn from previous elections, not least the 1997 general election and the 1999 elections to the devolved institutions, that British political parties are institutionally sexist (Shepherd-Robinson and Lovenduski 2002: 1). The parties may say they want to increase the number of women MPs. They may also provide women with training and support. But the Conservatives' net gain of three women MPs and Labour's success in increasing its number of women MPs despite losing seats in 2005, suggests that only when the parties employ positive discrimination will significant moves towards the equalisation of women and men in Parliament be achieved.

However important the equalisation in the numbers of women in our political institutions is, it is nonetheless only one dimension of the feminisation of politics. The feminisation of politics also refers to the transformation of politics, as women's concerns and perspectives move towards the centre of the political agenda (Lovenduski 2005: 12). With all parties keen in 2005 to win women's votes (Mortimore 2005) and a Labour government keen to campaign on its domestic record, women were promised a feminised election campaign: out with the Westminster-village focus, male-dominated press conferences and macho verbal jousting; and in with a feminised style of politics and a focus on the work/life balance, support for families (tax credits, maternity/paternity pay and child care) the health service and education (*New Statesman*, 9 May 2005).

Yet the election swiftly became a presidential contest between the male party leaders, which in turn degenerated into negative campaigning and name-calling. Women politicians were conspicuous by their absence: the Tories' most high-profile (but sidelined under Howard) woman MP, Theresa May, spent most of her election defending her head from the Liberal Democrats' decapitation strategy; while the Liberal Democrats, because they had so few women MPs, were forced to rely upon their elder stateswoman, Baroness Shirley Williams. With greater numbers, Labour's women MPs and ministers should have been more visible. But other than the Education Secretary, Ruth Kelly, and belatedly, the Secretary of State for Trade and Industry, Patricia Hewitt, women were rarely seen on the national stage. Instead, we learnt more about the leaders' wives – the contents of Sandra Howard's make-up bag (*Evening Standard*) and hair travails (via her blog on the party's website), Cherie and Tony's sex life (in the *Sun*) and baby Kennedy than we did about what women politicians and their parties might want to do for women.

The usual male suspects similarly dominated the media's coverage. On TV and radio, Jeremy Paxman and John Humphrys and, on election night itself, the Dimbleby brothers shared the BBC and ITV's election spoils. Women broadcasters were relegated to the sidelines: in the BBC election night coverage, literally to the upper deck of the studio, just as in 2001. In the tabloid press, the coverage was true to form. There were football metaphors – a picture of Blair and Brown in football shirts had the headline, 'Come on you Reds' (*Sun*, 5 May 2005); wartime analogies, to the battle of El Alamein (*Guardian*, 3 May 2005), while the *Sun* used topless Page Three models to encourage voting, with the headline 'Nip out to vote!' – at the 2001 election the models had, at least, been wearing bikinis.

This chapter subjects the 2005 general election to a gender audit in order to capture the feminised nature of British politics. First, it documents and accounts for the election of the record 128 women MPs to Parliament. In particular, it evaluates the parties' efforts to increase the numbers of women elected and examines the effect of Labour's positive discrimination measures. It then addresses the gendered nature of party competition at the 2005 election by providing a feminist reading of the main parties' election manifestos and reflecting on the wider election campaign. The final section briefly explores the likelihood of a more feminised politics in the new Parliament by considering the difference women in politics make.

Political recruitment: still the twelfth man?[2]

The 2005 headline figure of 128 women MPs – up ten from 2001 – hides a complex story. On the one hand, it signals a welcome return to a rise in the number and percentage of women MPs elected to the House of Commons, reversing the first decline in more than a generation witnessed in 2001. On the other hand, it hides the continuing importance of Labour's electoral fortunes: it is true that the Conservative Party has seen a continued, albeit small, increase in the number of women MPs, from 13 to 14 in 2001 and 17 in 2005. (See Table 10.1.) Similarly, and on much smaller numbers, the Liberal Democrats doubled their representation from five to ten this time. Yet these changes do not represent a significant inter-party rebalancing: Labour remains the party with the highest number (98) *and* percentage of women MPs. Women constitute 27.5 per cent of the Parliamentary Labour Party (PLP), 16.1 per cent of Liberal Democrat MPs and only 8.6 per cent of Conservative MPs. The comparative figures for 2001 were 23.1 per cent, 9.6 per cent and 8.4 per cent respectively. Furthermore, only the Labour Party selected and elected the same percentage of women. So despite the fact that Labour had a net loss of 47 seats at the 2005 general election, it managed to increase the percentage of women in the PLP. In contrast, the Conservative Party pretty much stood still, while the Liberal Democrat gains – significant for intra-party sex balance – remain small in absolute terms.

Table 10.1　Women elected in British general elections, 1979–2005

Year	Lab	Con	Lib	Others	Total	% MPs
1979	11	8	0	0	19	3.0
1983	10	13	0	0	23	3.5
1987	21	17	2	1	41	6.3
1992	37	20	2	1	60	9.2
1997	101	13	3	3	120	18.2
2001	95	14	5	4	118	17.9
2005	98*	17	10	3	128	19.8**

* 　This figure includes Sylvia Heal, First Deputy Chairman of Ways and Means.
** 　This figure does not include the constituency of South Staffordshire where the election was suspended due to the death of the Liberal Democrat candidate.

Systemic factors are not significant inhibitors of women's political recruitment in the UK; women do not face legal barriers to their election, although the majoritarian electoral system is less favourable than proportional ones (Norris and Lovenduski 1995). The outcome of the selection process – in the UK, the responsibility of political parties – is normally understood as reflecting the supply of those wishing to pursue a political career and the demands of selectors who choose candidates on the basis of their preferences and perceptions of abilities, qualifications and perceived electorability (Lovenduski 1997; Shepherd-Robinson and Lovenduski 2002). In the UK supply-side factors have reduced in their explanatory value over time and party demand is now regarded as the key to increasing women's representation; during the selection process, direct discrimination (where gender-discriminatory questions are posed) and indirect discrimination (where ideas of what constitutes a good MP count against women) have been found to come into play (Vallance 1979: 48; Lovenduski and Norris 1989: 546–7; Shepherd-Robinson and Lovenduski 2002: 11–12, 24–5; Norris and Lovenduski 1989: 94).

There are three strategies to increase the numbers of women MPs: equality rhetoric, equality promotion and equality guarantees (Lovenduski 2005). All were in place in 2005. Each of the party leaders *said* they wanted more women in Parliament; all of the main political parties undertook equality promotion measures: training, mentoring, and in some parties, money, were provided to help women prospective candidates get to the starting line. This time too, equality guarantees were permitted under the Sex Discrimination (Election Candidates) Act 2002 (Childs 2002; 2003). In 2005 all the main parties selected more women than in 2001 (see Table 10.2).

Table 10.2   Women candidates for the main parties, 1992–2005

	Conservative	Labour	Liberal Democrat
1992	63	138	143
1997	69	157	140
2001	92	146	135
2005	118	166	142

Source: P. Norris and J. Lovenduski (1995) and *The British Parliamentary Constituency Database, 1992–2005*.

Eschewing equality guarantees, the Conservatives went into the selection process confident that their revised procedures, in particular a new 'objective' test for six skills (communication, intellectual skills, relating to people, leadership and motivation, resilience, and drive and conviction), along with the introduction of innovative selection mechanisms in some seats (open and closed primaries – where the selectorate extends beyond members of local associations, and the City Seats Initiative (CSI) where teams of candidates campaign city-wide) would prove particularly effective in selecting greater numbers of women candidates. This was, indeed, the case: 16 of the 30 city seats selected women and equal numbers of the eight primaries selected male and female candidates. None of these women were, however, elected. To put it crudely, too many Conservative women candidates were selected for unwinnable seats.

In contrast, the return of ten women Liberal Democrat MPs looks, at least initially, to prove the party's own all-women shortlist (AWS) sceptics right: in their absence the party doubled its representation. Yet there was a sex quota operating at the shortlisting stage: subject to there being a sufficient number of applicants of each sex, shortlists of three or four had to include at least one member of each sex, and shortlists of five or six had to include at least two. It is possible that this rule caused local parties to both consider and select greater numbers of women candidates in winnable seats. However, three of the returned Liberal Democrat women MPs were arguably unexpected gains – Solihull, Falmouth and Cambourne, and Hornsey and Wood Green[3] and it will not be until the next election before it is clear whether the party's successes in 2005 are indicative of a wider acceptance of the selection of women candidates in Liberal Democrat-held and winnable seats. Labour's successes also put Liberal Democrat gains into perspective.

Nine sitting Labour women MPs were defeated at the election out of a total of 47 losses, with Oona King the most high profile. In Bethnal Green and Bow, George Galloway overturned her 10,000 plus majority on an anti-Iraq war platform.[4] Nonetheless, the re-adoption of AWS by Labour prevented a fall in the number and percentage of women MPs in the face of a swing against it. Importantly, and because they were not expecting to win any new seats, sitting Labour MPs were asked to inform the party of their intention not to contest the 2005 election before December 2002. If too few of these constituencies volunteered to use an AWS the NEC would impose them in at least 50 per cent of these early retirement seats. 'Late' retirements would be automatically declared AWS except in special circumstances. At the election 23 of the 30 women selected on AWS were returned to Parliament. This means that just over half of *all* Labour's women MPs in the current Parliament were elected on the basis of AWS, either in 1997 or 2005.

In addition to their undoubted success, there are two key stories about Labour's AWS in 2005. The first is the failure of Maggie Jones to win the safe seat of Blaenau Gwent; the second is the failure of any black or minority ethnic women to be selected via AWS. Blaenau Gwent saw a swing of 49 per cent to the ex-Labour Assembly Member, Peter Law, who stood on an explicit anti-AWS ticket, overturning a 19,000 majority: 'This is what you get', he said, 'when you don't listen to people' (*Guardian*, 6 May 2005). While Welsh hostility to equality guarantees was evident in 1997 and 1999, and another Welsh AWS seat (Preseli) was lost in 2005, there was little evidence of wider anti-AWS sentiment. The enormity of Law's swing suggests that there was probably something more than a simple anti-AWS factor at work in Blaenau Gwent. While it might have been expected that local members would transfer their vote to Law, it is less convincing that thousands of Labour voters were conscious of, and sufficiently troubled by, AWS to do the same. It is likely that wider anti-New Labour feelings, as well as a perception that Maggie Jones was an outsider and had been imposed by the party hierarchy, were also factors. John Prescott's retort to a local reporter that he was 'amateur' and should 'bugger off', arguably did not help either.

The behaviour of the Blaenau Gwent constituency party also suggests an attempt to subvert the AWS policy. Law and his supporters claim that they 'thought they had had an assurance that an AWS would not be imposed' *because* the sitting MP announced his intention to retire before December 2002, whereas the rules makes clear that 50 per cent of early retirements would be so designated (*Telegraph*, 7 May 2005). Furthermore, though local members criticised AWS for creating an 'earldom' for Maggie Jones (*Telegraph*, 5 May 2005), 'many in the constituency believed' that Peter Law had 'earned the right to stand' (*Mirror*, 6 May 2005).

The experience of Dawn Butler – unsuccessful in West Ham (AWS) but successful in the open, but, by default, all black shortlist for Brent South – highlights the difficulty black and minority ethnic (BME) women faced in getting selected on AWS. This difficulty might reflect the party's informal decision to locate AWS predominantly in constituencies without significant BME populations, suggesting a lack of local supply – although this was definitely not the case in West Ham. But it also looks like a question of party demand, with BME women facing selectorate discrimination. A black, female, West Ham party member claims that black and Asian male councillors had 'sabotaged' Butler's campaign (*Guardian*, 25 February 2005). With the defeat of Oona King, Labour is left again with only two black women MPs: Dawn Butler and Diane Abbott.

In the aftermath of the election, the Labour Party will revisit the issue of its selection procedures, although at this stage, it seems that their commitment to positive action has not been shaken.[5] If past form is also an indicator it is likely that Labour's women MPs would also come out publicly to defend AWS. Supporters of AWS should also consider whether it is time for hybrid 'women and BME shortlists' to ensure greater numbers of women, both white and BME, as well as BME male MPs (*Guardian*, 23 February 2005; *Guardian*, 25 February 2005).

A feminist reading of the manifestos

Comparing the three main political parties' 2005 party manifestos is complicated by the different formats they took. Labour's 112-page book presented detailed accounts of Labour's second term and its proposals for a third term, and took more than an hour to read. In contrast the Conservatives' A4 28-page brochure-style manifesto had eight pages devoted to large print, handwritten, single statements, while on other pages there were numerous colour photographs. It took less than 20 minutes to read. Different again, the Liberal Democrats' manifesto repeated its 2001 format – a tabloid-size newspaper with detailed policy statements accompanied by the respective party spokespeople's photos, profiles and views. It took some 40 minutes to read. Both the Liberal Democrats and Labour produced manifestos for women, downloadable from their websites, although neither were much more extensive or detailed than their full manifestos.

The Fawcett Society's 'Make your Mark. Use your Vote!' guide[6] identified key questions that women should ask of the political parties, and formed the basis of this reading of the manifestos:

- What will you do to close the pay gap between women and men?
- How will you provide affordable childcare for all? How will you support mothers and fathers who want to stay at home with children?
- How will you make employment more flexible so that women and men can be equal partners at work and at home?
- Will you introduce state pensions that recognise the value of caring for family?
- How will you reward unpaid carers for the important work they do?
- How will you tackle violence against women and ensure victims get justice and support? How will you ensure that women offenders are given sentences that fit their crimes and help the wider community?
- How will you reform our education system to ensure that girls and women fulfil their true academic and professional potential?
- What will you do to help the poorest women in our society escape poverty?
- How will you provide effective health services for women's specific needs?
- How will you ensure women feel safe on public transport? How will you tackle bogus minicab drivers who target women?
- How is your party ensuring women reach the top in business and public life?
- How will your policies help women in other countries who are suffering because of war, disaster and violence?

It is clear that many of these questions are simply not addressed by all of the party manifestos, as Table 10.3 shows.

With the least comprehensive of the three manifestos, the Conservative Party trail in third place with their coverage of gender equality concerns. In his foreword Michael Howard states that 'to be treated equally is a birthright, and that discrimination is wrong'. And he goes on to state that a Conservative government will govern in the interests of everyone in our society – 'black or white, young or old, straight or gay, rural or urban, rich or poor'. Unfortunately, women seem to be missing. Women are addressed in terms of the party's maternity and child care provision – with women having a choice of receiving maternity leave over six or nine months and receiving financial support for familial as well as formal child care, although there is little specific detail. Women are also depicted as victims of crime – a series of photographs show a woman having her handbag snatched – and as matrons being brought back to 'deliver clean and infection-free wards'. Beyond this, though, there is very little. Indeed, the party's discussion of education policy includes a commitment to 'root out political correctness', a use of language that might suggest the party is hostile towards feminist analysis of educational provision.

Table 10.3   Analysis of manifesto policy commitments

	Labour	Conservative	Lib Dem
Maternity leave/pay	Nine months maternity leave by 2007 (worth extra £1,400) One year maternity leave by end of 2005 Parliament Consultation on option of shared parental leave	Flexible maternity pay – either nine or six months	Raise maternity pay from £102 to £170 for first six months
Equal pay	Take further action to narrow the pay and promotion gap The Women and Work Commission will report to the PM 'later this year'		
Equal opportunities	Introduce duty on public bodies to promote quality of opportunity between women and men Establish Commission on Equality and Human Rights Single Equality Act		Single Equality Act
Domestic violence	Expand specialist courts and specialist advocates		
Health	Faster test results for cervical smears Choice over where/how women have their babies/pain relief Every woman to be supported by a personal midwife		End age discrimination that prevents older women from receiving routine breast cancer screening
Pensions	2nd Pensions Commission Report due autumn 2005 that 'must address the disadvantages faced by women'		Citizen's pension (for over-75s) based on residency rather than National Insurance contributions
Child care	By 2010, 3,500 Sure Start Centres Increased rights to free part-time nursery provision (rising to 20 hours in longer term) Tax credit for nannies/au pairs Consultation on extending rights to flexible working for older parents	Families receiving working tax credit will receive up to £50 per week for under-fives child care, including familial child care	
Politics	All-women shortlists		Proportional representation to better reflect 'diversity'
Sexuality	Committed to improving the rights/opportunities of gays and lesbians		Equality Act will ensure fairness for same sex couples in pension arrangements

Note: This table was drawn up independently of the Fawcett Society, whose analysis included additional material (<www.fawcett.org.uk>).

Women were more central to the Liberal Democrats' manifesto, particularly older women. Kennedy's foreword addresses women's pensions explicitly: 'it's time we redressed the scandalous discrimination against women in the state pension system'. Their citizen's pension would, in contrast, 'provide women who have spent their time caring for children and elderly parents a pension in their own right'.

The party's mini-manifesto for women presents a list of the 'top five' Liberal Democrat policies for women:

1. Maternity income guarantee
2. Citizen's pension
3. Abolition of tuition fees
4. Free personal care for the elderly
5. Child care

In this document the gendered impact of policies, using a distinctly feminist language of discrimination/equality, is more explicitly stated. For example, a link is made between women's unequal pay and the cost of university tuition and top-up fees – 'unequal pay makes student debt harder on women, with female graduates earning on average 15 percent less than their male counterparts at the age of 24'. The discussion of pensions emphasises that two-thirds of the 2.2 million poor pensioners are women. It also emphasises that those who would benefit most from free personal care would be women, and claims that the party would 'take immediate steps to alert women' who paid the reduced 'married women's national insurance rate' and allow women to pay back NI contributions. Similarly, there is recognition of the gendered patterns of poverty and employment – with many women working part-time, for low wages, and as homeworkers. These insights provide the basis upon which the party intends to tackle discrimination in the workplace, through providing: a maternity income guarantee; a comprehensive Equality Act; a requirement of certain (unspecified) employers to address equal opportunities/equal pay issues; an extension of 'appropriate' (again, unspecified) workplace protection to homeworkers; the establishment of an annual review of the minimum wage; a voluntary code against inadvertent discrimination drawn up by CBI, FSB, TUC; and the encouragement of good practice through the publication of employers' diversity strategies and measures.

In respect of women's reproductive health, the Liberal Democrats are committed to ensuring that all contraceptive options are available in all GP surgeries; providing free condoms in GPs surgeries and other sexual health services; and improving access to emergency contraception. Regarding crime, the party again recognises the gendered nature of crime – by noting women's greater fear of crime – and suggests that their policy of more police will reduce this fear. There is, notably, no discussion of domestic violence or rape.

The Liberal Democrats' manifesto feminist rating relative to the other main parties is impressive. But another reading of the Liberal Democrats' main manifesto reveals one of the party's historic problems; its lack of women MPs. In contrast to the prominence of the party's shadow spokesmen (with photographs and accompanying statements mostly in the same place on each page) there are only two photographs of current women MPs. And both Sandra Gidley and Sue Doughty are given smaller space and are less formally presented. They are also, along with Baroness Shirley Williams, on the same double-page spread.

Labour's general appeal to women in the 2005 election was unquestionably on the basis of its package of policies related to 'hard-working families'. These included: family tax credits, Sure Start, Child Trust Funds, the expansion of child care provision, and the reduction of child poverty. Looking more closely at the party's record for women (something which their manifesto format allowed), the manifesto emphasised the extension of maternity leave from 14 to 26 weeks and the 'doubling' of maternity pay; stressed how its pension credit had particularly benefited women; highlighted parents' right to request flexible working arrangements; the 'tailored help' for lone parents; and the various child care policies that they claim have improved the work/life balance. They also, in bold print, state that the Conservatives opposed their improvements in maternity and paternity pay and the introduction of flexible working rights. The manifesto also stresses legislative changes that advance lesbian women's opportunities and rights, namely, civil partnerships, the repeal of Section 28 and reform of sexual offences legislation.

Labour's discussion of maternity, paternity and parental leave, while quite detailed, is not accompanied by specific and guaranteed commitments: there is much talk of consultation and aims. Furthermore, the party acknowledges that there is a 'need to balance the needs of parents and carers, with those of employers, especially small businesses' – suggesting that the party's intentions may be constrained, for example, by limiting regulations to only certain kinds of employers. The right to request flexible working is, in the same vein, not the same as a right to flexible working; a goal or target is not a guarantee.

The party's 'What is Labour Doing for ... Women?' web page repeats many of the same points made in the main manifesto. There is a little more detail on the impact of the minimum wage on women and in respect of the 'most radical overhaul' of domestic violence legislation. But the material is not a detailed supplement. It also makes reference to women's multiple roles – as mothers, pensioners, students, workers, taxpayers, patients, victims of crime, mortgage payers and the majority of those working in and using our public services. Nonetheless, the Labour Party's literature overall has a tendency to equate women with motherhood.

The substance of the election campaign: so it wasn't about women after all ...

Each of the three main parties took their campaigns to women through the placement of interviews and articles in women's magazines, newspapers, on daytime television and on the radio. In these forums women's concerns were addressed at some length: on the BBC's *Woman's Hour*, for example, each of the main party leaders was asked about their views on gender roles, women's work/life balance, and the representation of women in Parliament. Abortion threatened to turn into a general election issue, although when the campaign proper took over, questions of personality/trust, immigration and asylum, and Iraq dominated.

The furore over abortion was sparked by Michael Howard's announcement in *Cosmopolitan* magazine (April) that he supported a reduction in the legal limit from 24 weeks to 20 weeks.[7] Claiming that the current legislation was 'tantamount' to 'abortion on demand',[8] he also claimed (erroneously) to have voted for a reduction to 22 weeks (BBC News online, 20 March 2005; *Guardian*, 18 May 2005; <www.revolts.co.uk>). In the same *Cosmopolitan* article, Blair made it clear that 'however much' he 'might personally dislike the idea of abortion' he had no plans to change the law. Charles Kennedy, who had voted for 22 weeks in 1990, said he did not 'know' what he would 'do now'.[9] In the following days, first Cardinal Cormac Murphy-O'Conner and then the Archbishop of Canterbury, along with numerous anti-abortionists, weighed into the fray.

In this maelstrom both Howard and Blair quickly agreed that abortion should not be an election issue. Labour women MPs Tessa Jowell and Harriet Harman made their views clear: 'polling day is not a referendum on particular moral issues' (*New Statesman*, 4 April 2005); a re-elected labour government would not allow an early vote (*Guardian*, 31 March 2005). The public too were unimpressed. A YouGov poll found that almost 60 per cent do not see abortion as an appropriate subject for debate between parties (Cowley 2005a). Pro-choice commentators were similarly adamant: 'this is certainly not a subject for politicians to toss into the brutally knee-jerk arena of pre-election vote-grabbing' (Hester Lacey, *New Statesman*, 4 April 2005). By this stage it already was: the *Daily Mail* went into overdrive with a front page, two-thirds full with the headline: 'ABORTION BECOMES ISSUE IN ELECTION' (*Daily Mail*, 15 March 2005). Inside, another three pages were devoted to the issue. Anti-abortionists acclaimed the survival rates of babies born at 20, 22 and 24 weeks,[10] emphasised the rising number of abortions[11] and suggested that women use late abortion as a contraceptive and for lifestyle reasons: 'Perhaps she feels it would interfere with her career or social life. Perhaps she's fallen out with the father. Perhaps she's worried about the effect on her figure', wrote Amanda Platell (*Daily Mail*, 15 March 2005). In contrast, pro-choice commentators reiterated that, rather than being available 'on demand', abortion is permitted only with the agreement of two doctors if the mental or physical health of the mother could be endangered by continuing with the pregnancy' (*Sunday Times*, 20 March 2005; *New Statesman*, 4 April 2005).

There is an argument that abortion is a party issue already and *should* be an election issue (Cowley 2005a). When voting on the current legislation in 1990, Parliament divided along party lines: two-thirds of Labour MPs compared with just 5 per cent of Conservative MPs voted for the current time limit of 24 weeks; while 64 per cent of Conservative but only 15 per cent of Labour MPs supported 22 weeks (Cowley 2005a). Newspaper coverage is similarly pro and anti in line with the paper's party political persuasion. Treated historically as an issue of conscience, only the Respect party committed itself to defend a woman's right to choose in its manifesto, contra George Galloway's public position in Bethnal Green (*Observer*, 17 April 2005). Howard's comments on abortion led him to be accused of using abortion as a 'dog whistle issue' (*Guardian*, 18 March 2005; *Independent on Sunday*, 24 April 2005; *Sunday Mirror*, 27 March 2005).[12] Or, as Zoe Williams put it: 'it's merely a signalling device, a way of expressing disapproval to appease conservative opinion' (*Guardian*, 15 March 2005). Indeed, David Davis MP (and leadership frontrunner) was quick to state that Mr Howard had been 'signalling' that a Conservative government would allow a parliamentary vote on the issue (BBC News online, 21 March 2005; *Guardian*, 31 March 2005).

The campaign style: more handbags, fewer bayonets?[13]

The Labour's Party's first big pre-election campaign launch was an all-male affair: Milburn, Brown and Prescott in a 'sub-Reservoir Dogs' stroll across a parking lot. It seemed that the party had failed to learn the lessons from the 2001 campaign when it was rebuked by women journalists – Gordon Brown memorably answered a question about women despite being flanked by women MPs. Women journalists again called for Labour to bring women to the forefront of its campaign (*Guardian*, 9 February 2005). These reports also revealed a perception amongst the party's campaign strategists that some of Labour's high-profile women MPs were 'too posh' and that the election campaign was about 'more than child care' (*Observer*, 6 February 2005; *Guardian*, 22 February 2005). Senior women MPs, such as Harriet Harman, Patricia Hewitt and Joan Ruddock, as well as the PLP 'women's committee' made their views clear to the leadership.

The launch of the Labour manifesto itself did see Patricia Hewitt and Ruth Kelly (who was felt to possess a 'classless air') prominent in the front row of the two-row stage set. Tony Blair was also 'doughnutted' (encircled), by Margaret Beckett and Tessa Jowell. Yet in the national campaign women MPs were rarely seen, or when present, they were, in Jackie Ashley's terms, like 'a nice bunch of flowers on the kitchen table – decorative, calming and silent'. Patricia Hewitt arguably had the highest profile. She was, for example, brought out to defend the Attorney General on Channel 4 News (28 April 2005), an opportunity she also used to mention women's concerns about trust and politics.

This is not to say that efforts were not made by male MPs, including the Prime Minister and Gordon Brown, to connect with women voters. This election, 'Worcester Woman' was replaced by 'Sandwich Mothers' – women who had both children and parents to care for. Labour produced a magazine, *Family Matters*, in the style of a woman's weekly magazine and participated (along with the other leaders) in interviews in various women's magazines (*Cosmopolitan*, *Glamour* and *Vogue*, for example). The front page of the *Daily Mirror* (15 April 2005) had a photograph of Blair with his arms around the shoulders of two female journalists accompanied with the headline 'Can He Turn Women On?', while on the inside pages he detailed the party's position on women's concerns. Such efforts often met the derision of Labour's critics (*Daily Mail*, 16 April 2005), not least for patronising women voters (*Daily Mail*, 28 April 2005). But if, as Jowell states, the aim is to connect with women who are currently disconnected with politics, then alternative approaches should be made (*New Statesman*, 4 April 2005; *Guardian*, 9 February 2005).

Labour's women were, as a group, determined to campaign for women. Discussions had begun more than a year prior to the election in the PLP women's committee and both Blair and Milburn attended meetings of that group. Issues of concern to women that the MPs felt should be in the manifesto were identified; they also stressed the importance of women's presence in the campaign, as well as the need to go out and meet women. There was also a 'women's strategy group' chaired first by Ruth Kelly and then by Jacqui Smith. One campaign, that received little media coverage (other than by women journalists – Jackie Ashley in the *Guardian* and Rosemary Bennett in *The Times* – and on the party's website), was the 'women's bus'. A 'slightly old white minibus', funded by the party and filled with women MPs, women ministers (including Cabinet ministers Hewitt and Jowell) and trade unionists visited more than 30 constituencies (*Guardian*, 28 April 2005). One MP felt it produced 'stunning' reactions from women, and was convinced that it had encouraged women to vote: connections between what happened in government and women's lives were much better made, she claimed, when she talked with young women in marketplaces, in playgrounds and outside school gates. To the derision of her critics, Harriet Harman was interviewed in her home by *Hello* magazine (*Sunday Times*, 8 May 2005).

The Conservative Party also engaged in 'women's campaigning', although with few high-profile women MPs they relied more heavily on the leader's wife. Sandra Howard was said to be the 'ace in his pack' (*Glamour*, April 2005), just as Ffion Hague had been William's. Sandra Howard spent half her days with her husband and half the time visiting constituencies with women candidates (*Daily Mail*, 21 April 2005). Michael Howard also engaged in some astute 'doughnutting' of his own. At one event in East London (Channel 4 News, 2 May 2005) he was surrounded completely by women, including one Asian and one black woman.

Substantively representing women in the 2005 Parliament

Caveats about the difficulty of proving the causal relationship between women's descriptive and substantive representation aside (Childs 2004), it definitely looks as though women's concerns and perspectives were, if not at the *heart* of the 2001–05 Parliament, closer than before – Iraq notwithstanding. The potential for women MPs to make a feminised difference has long been established, not least because of attitudinal differences between women and men representatives (Lovenduski 1997: 719; Norris and Lovenduski 1989; 1995; Lovenduski and Norris 2003). Analyses of Labour's women MPs in the 1997 and 2001 Parliaments have also demonstrated behavioural differences where women have feminised not only the political agenda through the articulation of women's concerns and perspectives (Childs and Withey 2004; Bird 2004), but also legislation. The passage of the Sex Discrimination (Election Candidates) Act (Childs 2002) and the reduction of VAT on sanitary products constitute two such cases (Childs and Withey, forthcoming).

Analysing the three main parties' policies put forward for the 2005 election – in their manifesto and policy documents, if not their key campaigning issues – similarly reveals a more feminised political terrain. Issues such as maternity leave, flexible working, a national child care strategy, citizens pensions and the work/life balance, are concerns over which the parties now compete (*Guardian*, 4 March 2005; *Guardian*, 1 March 2005).[14] As Polly Toynbee argues, the Conservative Party's manifesto commitments to child care are 'one more symbol of how far Labour has shunted the ideological tectonic plates' (*Guardian*, 30 March 2005). The Conservative moderniser Damian Green MP made a retrospective recognition of this, just after the election: 'if we dismiss childcare or the work/life balance as soft issues then we dismiss the main concerns of millions of people, especially women' (*Guardian*, 7 May 2005).

The increased salience of such issues did not simply fall out of the sky. Rather, it reflects the concerns and actions of Labour women MPs and ministers over many years, as well as the support of sympathetic male colleagues who have been persuaded by gendered analysis (Toynbee and Walker 2005). Illustrative examples include: Tessa Jowell's work on Sure Start; Patricia Hewitt's efforts to extend maternity and paternity rights, rights to flexible working and to achieve equal pay; Margaret Hodge and Harriet Harman's championing of child care, and Harriet Harman's work on domestic violence.[15]

In the new Parliament, all of these women are members of the government. The six Cabinet ministers are: Hilary Armstrong, Chief Whip; Margaret Beckett, Environment, Food and Rural Affairs; Patricia Hewitt, Health; Tessa Jowell, Culture,

Media and Sport; Ruth Kelly, Education and Skills; and Lady Amos, Leader of the House of Lords. At the lower levels of government there are another 26 women MPs and peers.[16] Most Departments of State have women ministers, although the Cabinet Office, the Ministry of Defence, the Foreign and Commonwealth Office, the Department for International Development, the Northern Ireland Office and the Law Officers' Department are male bastions. Moreover, and in a return to form, the Minister for Women (Parliamentary Under-Secretary), Meg Munn, is not to be paid, just like her predecessor in 1997, Joan Ruddock (*Guardian*, 16 May 2005; Childs 2004: 166). To announce this in the same week that the Department of Trade and Industry announced new statistics on the gender pay gap seemed politically inept, in extremis.

Conclusion

The 2005 general election was ultimately dominated by the political parties' male leadership; women MPs were largely absent. The issues that dominated the election were trust, asylum and immigration, and Iraq; little time was spent contesting the work/life balance, maternity/paternity leave and pay or child care. The parties' national campaigns, as well as the mainstream media, were similarly male-dominated and macho. Howard repeatedly engaged in name-calling, while Blair, according to the masochism strategy, invited the general public to harangue him. The *Daily Mail* may have called on voters to give Blair 'a bloody nose',[17] but the example, par excellence, was Alpha-male Jeremy Paxman subjecting Kennedy, Howard and Blair to a 30-minute grilling on primetime BBC TV.

In contrast, women's concerns remained marginal and very much the province of women journalists. Nonetheless, these issues are becoming part of the mainstream political agenda, not least because of their impact on Britain's economic performance. They are also likely to become more central to party competition because of the pro-Labour gender gap in women's voting (Campbell and Lovenduski 2005). Despite extensive and rightly criticised (Zoe Williams, *New Statesman*, 4 April 2005; *Guardian*, 22 February 2005), talk of 'betrayed lovers' and the 'seven-year itch', women did not desert Labour (Mortimore 2005: 80): 38 per cent of women voted Labour compared to 34 per cent of men; 32 per cent of women voted Conservative compared to 34 per cent of men and 22 per cent of women voted Liberal Democrat compared to 23 per cent of men (*Observer*, 8 May 2005). It seems that women were persuaded by the government's record on the domestic agenda, not least its family policies, and were left unimpressed by the Conservative campaign (*Guardian*, 7 May 2005).[18]

With women MPs constituting less than 20 per cent of the House of Commons, the 2005 Parliament remains an overwhelmingly male (and white) space. Despite all the main parties being committed to increasing the numbers of women MPs, aspirant women candidates find themselves at the mercy of party selectorates who, in the absence of an artificially created demand, continue to show a preference for the male body. Without cross-party use of equality guarantees – only the Labour Party took up the new opportunities provided by the Sex Discrimination (Election Candidates) Act 2002 and reintroduced AWS – it was always going to be hard for there to be a significant improvement in the numbers of women elected at an election that would see a swing away from the only party that was using them. Any losses of women MPs on Labour's side would need to have been filled by the Conservatives and the Liberal Democrats. In this sense, it could have been a lot worse: Labour's 98 returned women MPs represents an important defence of the gains made in 1997.

In the future, long-held and in some cases heartfelt opposition to equality guarantees may need to be reconsidered. They may not be 'fair'; they may grate against liberal principles; they may, as critics claim, cast aspersions on the merit of the women elected; but one thing can not be denied, AWS – measures that *guarantee* women's election – work, and work quickly. The sunset clause which causes the provisions of the 2002 Act 'to expire at the end of 2015' unless Parliament passes a statutory instrument suggests that supporters of equality guarantees in all parties need to act soon (May 2004; Childs 2003). They will also need to address the failure of all parties to select (via AWS or not), and get elected, a more diverse group of women MPs.

Notes

1. This chapter draws on research undertaken with Joni Lovenduski and Rosie Campbell, as part of the British Representation Study 2005, funded by Nuffield (SGS/01180/G).
2. Source: Conservative Central Office official. For a full description of party selection processes see Childs et al. (2005).
3. Personal communication from E. Fieldhouse and D. Cutts.
4. The others were: Melanie Johnson, Linda Perham, Helen Clark, Barbara Roche, Candy Atherton, Anne Campbell, Valerie Davey and Lorna Fitzsimmons.
5. Source: two Labour Party officials.
6. Available at <www.fawcett.org.uk>.
7. See also *Glamour* (April 2005).
8. The *Mail on Sunday* (1 May 2005) argued on the basis of the time limit that British abortion laws are 'among the most liberal in Europe'.
9. Rob Williams states. 'I don't know' is not an answer and its certainly not one you would dare to give to any other question' (*Guardian*, 15 March 2005).
10. The *Express* (2 May 2005) claims that babies born at 24 weeks have 40 per cent chance of living, although the *Sunday Times* (17 April 2005) says that many of these will 'develop disabilities'. *The Times* (23 April 2005) suggests that 'hardly any babies born before 24 weeks leave hospital'.
11. In 2003 there were 181,582 abortions, a rise of 3.2 per cent from 2002 and 15 per cent since 1993 (*Daily Mail*, 16 May 2005).

12. The *Guardian* and *The Times* (27 April 2005) reported that Mark Textor, an associate of Lynton Crosby, the Conservatives' election guru, had paid £34,000 in damages to an Australian female Labour candidate when telephone canvassers had suggested that she supported abortion at 36 weeks.
13. Mary Riddell, *New Statesman* (4 April 2005).
14. Senior male political editors attended related press conferences (*Guardian*, 1 March 2005).
15. This list should not be taken as exhaustive.
16. Just two women, Caroline Spelman and Theresa May, are amongst the 22-member Conservative frontbench.
17. Cherie Blair was reported to have called on voters to 'Give George Galloway a bloody nose' (*Times*, 13 April 2005).
18. Comprehensive analysis awaits the publication of the British Election Study (BES) 2005, University of Essex.

References

Bird, K. (2004) 'Disrupting the sex/gender dichotomy? "Masculine" women and "feminine" men in the British House of Commons'. Unpublished paper presented to the Women and Politics, Annual Conference, University of Bristol, February.
Campbell, R. and Lovenduski, J. (2005), 'Winning women's votes? The incremental track to equality', *Parliamentary Affairs*, forthcoming.
Childs, S. (2002) 'Conceptions of representation and the passage of the Sex Discrimination (Election Candidates) Bill', *Journal of Legislative Studies*, 8(3): 90–108.
Childs, S. (2003) 'The Sex Discrimination (Election Candidates) Act and its Implications', *Representation*, 39(2): 83–92.
Childs, S. (2004) *New Labour's Women MPs*, London: Routledge.
Childs, S., Campbell, R. and Lovenduski, J. (2005) 'Delivering diversity'. Paper presented at Network of European Women's Rights Conference, University of Birmingham, July.
Childs, S. and Withey, J. (2004) 'Women representatives acting for women: sex and the signing of Early Day Motions in the 1997 British Parliament', *Political Studies*, 52: 552–64.
Childs, S. and Withey, J. (forthcoming) 'A simple case of feminist cause and feminist effect? Reducing the VAT on sanitary products', *Parliamentary Affairs*.
Cowley, P. (2005a) 'Why it *should* be an election issue', *New Statesman*, 28 March.
Cowley, P. (2005b) 'What's two weeks between friends?' <www.revolts.co.uk>.
Criddle, B. (2002) 'MPs and candidates', in D. Butler and D. Kavanagh (eds) *The British General Election of 2001*, Basingstoke: Palgrave Macmillan, 2002, pp. 182–207.
Lovenduski, J. (1997) 'Gender politics: a breakthrough for women?', *Parliamentary Affairs*, 50(4): 708–19.
Lovenduski, J. (2005) *Feminizing Politics*, Cambridge: Polity Press.
Lovenduski, J. and Norris, P. (1989) 'Selecting women candidates: obstacles to the feminisation of the House of Commons', *European Journal of Political Research*, 17: 533–62.
May, T. (2004) Women in the House: the continuing challenge', *Parliamentary Affairs*, 57(4): 844–51.
Mortimore, R. (2005) 'Opinion polls since 2001', in S. Henig and L. Bason (eds) *Politicos Guide to the General Election*, London: Politicos.

Norris, P. and Lovenduski, J. (1989) 'Women candidates for Parliament: transforming the agenda?', *British Journal of Political Science*, 19(1): 106–15.

Norris, P. and Lovenduski, J. (1995) *Political Recruitment*, Cambridge: Cambridge University Press.

Shepherd-Robinson, L. and Lovenduski, J. (2002) *Women and Candidate Selection*, London: Fawcett Society.

Toynbee, P. and Walker, D. (2005) *Better or Worse? Has Labour Delivered?* London: Bloomsbury.

Vallance, E. (1979) *Women in the House*, London: Athlone Press.

Blaenau Gwent

Perhaps the most remarkable result of the entire election occurred in Blaenau Gwent in South Wales. The fifth safest seat in Britain and former electoral base of Labour luminaries such as Michael Foot and Aneurin Bevan, changed hands. The independent candidate, Peter Law, converted a Labour majority of 19,000 into a personal majority of over 9,000.

A Labour Party member for over 40 years and local member of the Welsh Assembly, Law stood as an independent in protest against Labour's decision to have an all-women shortlist for its candidate for the seat. Law believed he should have been adopted to fight the seat, rather than the London lawyer, Maggie Jones.

Amid mounting concern over the impact of the imposition of the gender-based shortlist, Labour sent John Prescott to campaign in a seat it normally takes for granted. Prescott's visit proved controversial, as he rounded on a local reporter, describing him as an 'amateur' whereas Prescott was a 'national politician'.

Law's campaign hit more serious difficulties when he temporarily withdrew his candidature after being diagnosed with a brain tumour, which required a six-hour operation. He decided to resume campaigning only two weeks before polling day, backed by some local Labour Party members. By polling day, he was odds-on favourite with local bookmakers to achieve a result ending seemingly perpetual Labour dominance in the seat.

Result		%
Law, P. (Ind Law)	20,505	58.2
Jones, M. (Lab)	11,384	32.3
Thomas, B. (LD)	1,511	4.3
Price, J. (PC)	843	2.4
Lee, P. (Con)	816	2.3
Osborne, P. (UKIP)	192	0.5
Ind Law gain from Lab		
Ind Law majority	9,121	25.9

Turnout: 66.1%

Guildford

Guildford has been a hard-fought constituency at the last three general elections. Despite their national unpopularity, the Conservatives held a seat long-regarded as 'true blue' fairly easily in 1997, with a 5,000 majority. That made the Liberal Democrat gain in 2001 all the more surprising and their claim on the seat proved temporary. Although their sitting MP, Sue Doughty, endured a smaller swing against her than several other Liberal Democrats defending seats against Conservatives in the South, this affluent commuter-belt seat was always going to be difficult to defend. At the previous election, Guildford had become the first Surrey constituency to elect a non-Conservative MP for 40 years.

Unusually, all three main parties fielded a woman candidate in what was a far from genteel campaign. A website featured spoof coverage of the Conservative campaign, with pictures of Anne Milton (the party candidate) picking up litter under the headline 'taking action on the environment' (*Sunday Times*, 1 May 2005). The Liberal Democrat complained that Milton was 'not local' (*The Times*, 18 April 2005) scarcely convincing given that she hailed from nearby Reigate.

An important local issue was the concentration of housing in the area. The Liberal Democrats blamed the Conservative County Council for allowing 5,000 more homes to be built since the previous election; the Conservatives blamed regional and government planning bodies. National issues ought to have worked in the Liberal Democrats' favour; Guildford contains the largest concentration of students of any town in England and opposition to tuition fees and the Iraq war should have helped the Liberal Democrats, particularly as they could expect to have been the repository of the 1,500 fall in Labour's vote. This of course presumes that Surrey University students are substantially to the left of Guildford's ordinary voters. In the event, the town reverted to Conservative type, ending its brief flirtation with the Liberal Democrats.

Result		%
Milton, A. (Con)	22,595	43.8
Doughty, S. (LD)	22,248	43.1
Landies, K. (Lab)	5,054	9.8
Pletts, J. (Green)	811	1.6
Haslam, M. (UKIP)	645	1.3
Morris, J. (Peace and Progress)	166	0.3
Lavin, V. (Independent)	112	0.2
Con gain from LD		
Con majority	347	0.7
Swing: LD to Con		0.9

Turnout: 68.3%

11
Campaign Finance

Justin Fisher

The 2005 general election represented the end of the first full electoral cycle since the introduction of the Political Parties, Elections & Referendums Act (PPERA). Passed at the end of the 1999–2000 session, it came into force four months before the 2001 election. And, whilst its introduction went relatively smoothly (Fisher 2001), the subsequent period presented some challenges to the new Act, both in terms of unforeseen circumstances and seemingly an element of strategic learning by the main political parties. In this chapter, there is an analysis of both long- and short-term trends in party finance in the period leading up to the election, as well as both patterns in income and expenditure during the campaign itself.

Long-term trends in income and expenditure[1]

The period following Labour's election in 1997 represents something of a new era in British party finance – Labour has become the wealthy party.[2] As Figures 11.1 and 11.2 illustrate, since 1997, Labour has consistently generated more income than the Conservatives.[3] Indeed, as Figure 11.2 shows, Labour central income has on occasions been around twice that of the Conservatives. This is as a result of the clear trend observable in Figure 11.1, namely that in real terms, Conservative income has remained relatively constant, whilst Labour's has been steadily increasing. For all parties, there have been the income peaks associated with general elections (Fisher 2000). However, post-1997, Labour's troughs have been significantly higher than its previous peaks. Indeed, if we look at the 'smoothed' time series (Figure 11.3), the trend is even more apparent.

A second trend has been the rise in income for the Liberal Democrats. Whilst still dwarfed in relative terms by the two larger parties, income has shown a steady rise since the formation of the new party, buoyed no doubt by continuing electoral advances. Indeed, comparing the party's income in 1994 with 2003 (both two years after an election), it has increased in real terms by 280 per cent. Of course, any increase from a low base may appear exaggerated. Nevertheless,

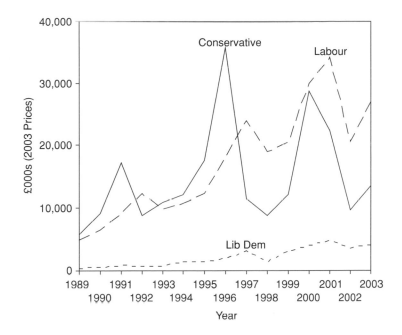

Figure 11.1 Central party income, 1989–2003

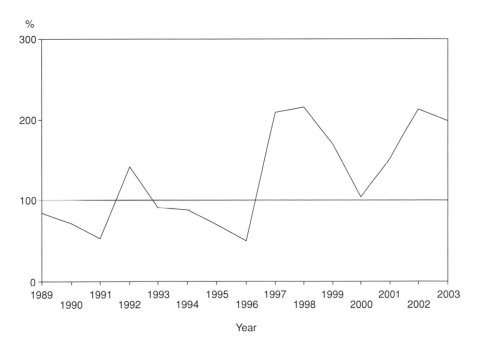

Figure 11.2 Labour income as a percentage of Conservative income, 1989–2003

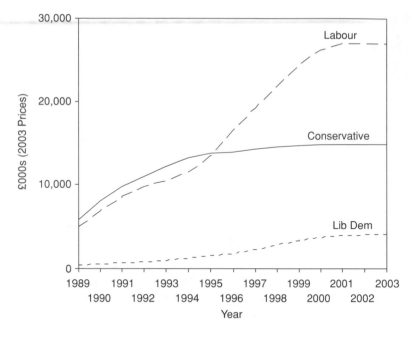

Figure 11.3   Central party income (smoothed), 1989–2003

the trend in Liberal Democrat income is clearly one of steady increase. For all that, however, the party's income in 2003 represented just 15 per cent of that of Labour and 30 per cent of the Conservatives.

Not surprisingly, similar patterns are apparent in terms of central party expenditure (see Figures 11.4 and 11.5). Since 1997, Labour has consistently out-spent the Conservatives. And, once again, whilst the parties' spending reflects the general election cycle, Labour's has increased steadily whilst that of the Conservatives has remained relatively constant. Indeed, in 2003, Conservative expenditure amounted to only two-thirds of that of Labour. Liberal Democrat expenditure has also increased. Comparing 1994 with 2003 once again, we can see an increase of 273 per cent in Liberal Democrat expenditure. Nevertheless, the gap between the Liberal Democrats and the other main parties remains significant. Expenditure in 2003 represented 25 per cent of that spent by the Conservatives and 16 per cent of that of Labour.

Finally, it is clear that older patterns of expenditure in relation to income are apparent (Fisher 2000). Dating back to the early 1970s, Labour's levels of expenditure have generally been in line with its levels of income (see Figure 11.6). Where expenditure has significantly exceeded income, this has been a reflection of the general election cycle. The Liberal Democrats, too (with the exception of 1992), have generally maintained their expenditure within the

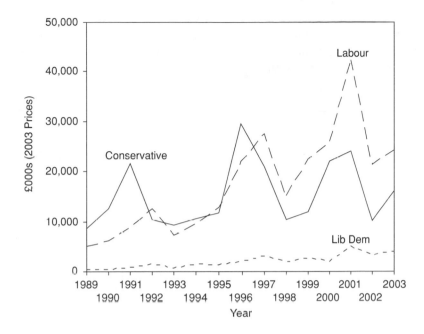

Figure 11.4   Central party expenditure, 1989–2003

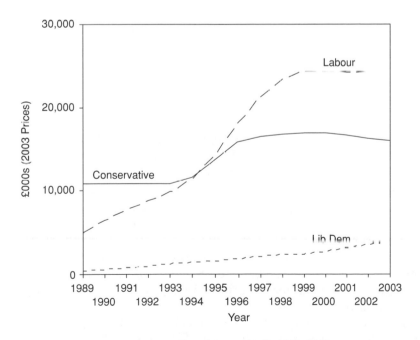

Figure 11.5   Central party expenditure (smoothed), 1989–2003

limits of their income. In the case of the Conservatives, however, the pattern of more significant fluctuation remains, albeit perhaps being less stark than in previous years. In 2003, the party spent 17 per cent more than its income in that year – the highest figure since 1997.

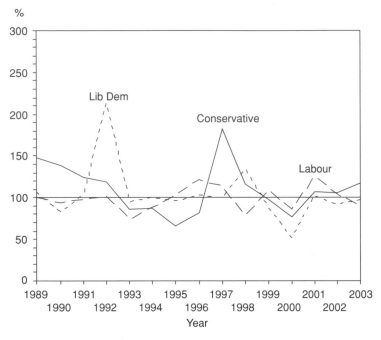

Figure 11.6   Expenditure as a percentage of income, 1989–2003

Party donations, 2001–05

Labour's financial advantage, not surprisingly, has been a result in part of its ability to attract donations. As a result of the PPERA, donations over £1,000 are declared every quarter,[4] and as Figure 11.7 shows, Labour received the largest sums in almost every period. However, both other main parties also received a significant boost in the run-up to the 2005 election. Conservative income had been rising steadily since 2003 – a process seemingly triggered by the change of leadership (Fisher 2004). In the case of the Liberal Democrats, however, the party's coffers were significantly swelled by four donations totalling over £2.4 million from one source (5th Avenue Partners Ltd), together with a further £275,000 donated by Carrousel Capital Ltd and £250,000 from previous donors, the Joseph Rowntree Reform Trust Ltd.

In terms of sources, Labour was the principal recipient of sums received from individuals until after the fall of Iain Duncan Smith (Figure 11.8), though

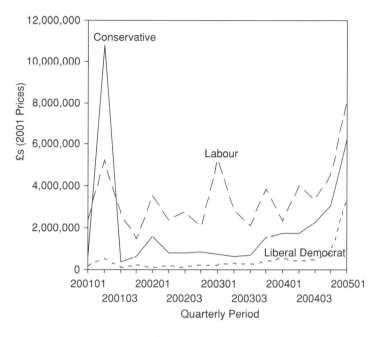

Figure 11.7   Registered cash donations, 2001–05

both the Conservatives and the Liberal Democrats received more in number over the whole period. This was reflected by the fact that the mean individual donation to Labour was generally higher than for the other parties, and in some quarters by a significant margin. In terms of corporate donations, the Conservatives continued to be the main beneficiaries. They received more than the other parties in every quarter bar one. Indeed, in the final quarter before the campaign (Quarter 1, 2005), they received 98 donations compared with Labour's 38 and the Liberal Democrats' 23. As with individual donations, an upward trend began when Michael Howard became leader. This larger number of corporate donations was reflected in the sums received. The Conservatives received most in corporate donations throughout the period 2001–05, with the exception of the final quarter, when the Liberal Democrats had such a welcome financial boost (see above). For all that, however, around two-thirds of Labour's 'donations' came from trade unions.

Finally, it is worth noting the additional value of 'donations in kind', or 'non-cash' donations. As Figure 11.9 shows, the value of these on occasions was substantial, with the Conservatives being the principal beneficiaries. However, when the value of these is added to cash donations, it remains the case that Labour consistently received most in donations over the period 2001–05.

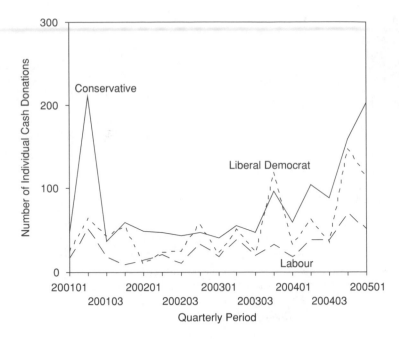

Figure 11.8   Number of 'individual' donations, 2001–05

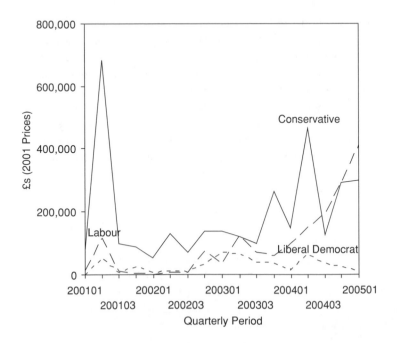

Figure 11.9   Value of non-cash donations, 2001–05

Election period donations

During the election period itself, donations are declared weekly. Table 11.1 illustrates donations received over the five weeks of the campaign. A number of patterns emerge. Firstly, in keeping with other donations made over the period 2001–05, Labour received most. As in 2001 the Liberal Democrats were some distance behind, though unlike 2001, this would have been easily offset by the party's significant donations in the period immediately before the campaign. Secondly, after a stuttering beginning, when Conservative donations were more than double those of Labour (reflecting perhaps, early Conservative optimism), the income from donations to Labour was relatively steady. By way of contrast, after receiving more in donations than Labour in the first two weeks of the campaign, the Conservatives saw their donations decline rapidly thereafter; so much so that the Liberal Democrats received more in the final week of the campaign. However, by this time, the Conservatives had raised sufficient income to fight the campaign. Thirdly, both Labour and the Liberal Democrats received significantly more in donations than in the same period at the 2001 election. Notwithstanding the reductive effects of inflation, Labour received around £1 million more than in 2001, whilst the Liberal Democrats received four times as much. Moreover, as the analysis of the 2001 figures shows, Conservative campaign donations were highly skewed by a last-minute donation of £5 million (Fisher 2001). If we discount that sum, the Conservatives roughly doubled the amount they received in donations during the 2005 campaign.

Table 11.1   Declared cash donations, 5 April–5 May 2005

£s	Con	Lab	Lib Dem	UKIP	Respect	SNP	SSP
Week 1	362,500	165,927	10,000	20,000	20,000	–	–
Week 2	1,018,500	791,307	32,000	25,000	–	–	–
Week 3	475,064	526,251	25,000	–	–	–	–
Week 4	148,500	361,000	5,000	–	–	–	9,000
Week 5	80,000	790,894	125,000	–	–	25,000	–
Total	2,084,564	2,635,379	197,500	45,000	20,000	25,000	9,000

Source: Electoral Commission.

The sources of donations broadly reflected the trend observed in the 2001 campaign (Fisher 2001). Individual donations were very significant for both main parties, with the Conservatives again being most successful in this respect (Table 11.2). Secondly, whilst Labour was again successful in securing some corporate donations, the Conservatives were, as in 2001, the main beneficiaries. Indeed, whilst Labour received 29 per cent of that of the Conservatives' 2001 corporate donations, in 2005, it was only 16 per cent. In the case of Unincorporated

Associations, a similar pattern emerged. The Conservatives were again the main beneficiaries, and in 2005 the sum they received (£231,380) was far more than in 2001 (£36,000). Thirdly, as in 2001, Labour received most in donations from trade unions – in both years over 50 per cent of campaign donations came from this source. Coupled with the Conservatives' relative success with corporate donations, this may signal a return to more traditional demarcation in terms of sources of institutional funds to the two main parties. By way of contrast, donations to the Liberal Democrats during the campaign were rather different than in 2001. During the previous campaign, the Liberal Democrats received no corporate donations. In 2005, not only did they increase the sums received from individuals by about a third, they also managed to secure £125,000 in corporate donations during the campaign – twice the amount received by Labour.

Table 11.2   Sources of declared cash donations, 5 April–5 May 2005

£s	Con	Lab	Lib Dem
Individuals	1,418,700	1,089,644	67,000
Companies	452,484	70,679	125,000
Unincorporated Associations	231,380	10,000	5,500
Trade Unions	–	1,465,056	–

Source: Electoral Commission.

In terms of non-cash donations, there was something of a reversal of fortunes compared with 2001. Then, the Conservatives received around £400,000 in the campaign period, and Labour nothing (Fisher 2001). This time, it was Labour who was the main beneficiary, further enhancing the party's financial advantage (see Table 11.3). Labour's non-cash donations came principally from three sources: Philip Gould Associates contributed £18,000 worth of polling and focus group research, TBWA Ltd (an advertising company) contributed nearly £60,000 in staff time, and Lord Sushathatha Bhattacharrya, who contributed cars to the value of £139,822. In terms of other parties, the sums received by the Liberal Democrats were slightly higher than in 2001, whilst UKIP received less than a tenth of the non-cash donations it had enjoyed four years previously.

Table 11.3   Declared non-cash donations, 5 April–5 May 2005

Value (£s)	Non-cash donations	Total donations (cash plus non-cash)
Con	29,420	2,113,984
Lab	219,950	2,855,329
Lib Dem	15,000	212,500
UKIP	50,981	95,981

Source: Electoral Commission.

Adaptation to the new legislation and strategic learning

The 2001 election represented a challenge for the parties, the Electoral Commission and the new legislation. It was the first test of how parties would adapt to the new regulatory environment. In fact, the evidence from 2001 suggested that the parties adapted very well (Fisher 2001). In addition, the legislation came through unscathed, with no problematic loopholes identified. Whilst 2005 represented the first full electoral cycle of PPERA and indeed, the Electoral Commission, all actors had now had the experience of several other elections in-between, including major ones in Scotland and Wales and the UK-wide European elections. The result was that whilst the legislation remained intact, new challenges were emerging, demonstrating first the potential need for additional legislation, and secondly, that the parties were not only adapting well to the legislation, they were also arguably engaging in strategic learning.

In the first instance, questions about the probity of party donations refused to go away. PPERA introduced a degree of transparency into party donations that had not previously existed. However, far from transparency eliminating concerns about party finance, a series of problems clearly remained. Firstly, both main parties continued to receive substantial donations – one of the concerns, which prompted legislation in the first place. Concerns about donations well in excess of £1 million prior to the legislation even coming into force, prompted the chair of the Electoral Commission to suggest that the question of donation caps might be re-examined in the future (Fisher 2001). This duly occurred, with the Electoral Commission conducting an inquiry into this and other aspects of party finance in 2004. Concerns also remained that preferential treatment had been given to donors. Four such episodes occurred in close succession during 2002 relating to Labour (Fisher 2002). The Conservatives, too, experienced such questions (Fisher 2004). In particular, the prominence of a major donor in debates about the party's leader in 2003 appeared to suggest that financial gifts lead to political influence.

The regular appearance of these episodes prompted some to call for further state funding – the expectation being that this would prevent such episodes. At the time of the original report by the Neill Committee in 1998, both the main parties concurred with the report's view that the time for state funding had not yet come. However, as a result of these episodes (and one suspects, the difficult financial situation that parties have found themselves in following the both general and devolved elections) both main parties now endorse an increase in the limited state funding.

This appears to demonstrate strategic learning by the parties based in the new values engendered by reform. Limited increases in state funding were originally introduced in recognition of the argument that parties were struggling to fulfil their principal functions. Yet whilst the tradition of voluntarism in party finance remains, it is arguable that the recognition of the importance of parties (explicit in the Neill Committee Report which prompted the reforms) and the acknowledgement that the state can play an enhanced role in party finance has made it more acceptable for both parties to argue for enhanced provision. Whilst neither the Conservatives nor Labour argued for comprehensive funding in the Electoral Commission's 2004 review, both agreed that an extension to cover some aspects of parties' work was desirable. In effect, all parties have now united around a theme of modest increases in state funding to facilitate particular party functions. This consensus did not exist prior to the extension of state funding post-Neill. Moreover, both Labour and the Conservatives have also resisted calls to place caps on individual donations, noting that the success of actors like the Committee on Standards in Public Life and the Electoral Commission has been in part built on promoting reforms, which have cross-party support.

In the build-up to the 2005 campaign, the Conservatives and the Liberal Democrats appeared to demonstrate further strategic learning associated with the new legislation. First, it emerged that in the run-up to the election, the Conservatives had been in receipt of a number of loans in excess of £1 million (*The Times*, 21 April 2005). In some ways, this was nothing new – the party had for some years relied on loans from individual backers as well as some wealthy constituency associations. However, what marked out these loans was that the terms upon which these loans were made – no declaration was required, unless the loan was subsequently turned into a donation. This is potentially significant since the transparency requirements of PPERA ensure that donations are made public shortly after the donation is received. However, by making loans, the lenders and the party could avoid declaration. And even if the loan was made into a donation and subsequently declared, the political 'moment' would have passed. It should be stressed that neither the Conservatives, nor the lenders were doing anything that contravened PPERA. However, a senior Conservative source was quoted as saying: 'The loans are entirely legitimate and within the letter of the law, but I concede that we may be criticised for breaching the spirit of the legislation.' And, reflecting this, the chair of the Electoral Commission declared that given that the thrust of PPERA was to generate transparency, that the position of commercial loans would be reviewed after the election (*The Times*, 21 April 2005).

In the case of the Liberal Democrats, the party received substantial donations in the first quarter of 2005, preceding the weekly declarations during the campaign itself. Of particular note, were the donations in excess of £2.4 million from 5th Avenue Partners Ltd, a company whose registered address is in London. Again, no breach of the law had occurred. However, the donations were criticised as the benefactor through whose company the donations were made, was actually resident in Majorca. Overseas donations were banned by PPERA. However, according to *The Times*, the company had only been bought a year previously, had yet to file accounts and used a law firm as its registered address (*The Times*, 25 May 2005). In effect, it was argued that the company had been bought 'off the shelf' and enabled individual donations to be made anonymously.

Overall then, whilst the spirit of the legislation continued to be upheld, it did suggest that parties were adapting well to the new regulatory environment and on occasions, arguably exploiting small loopholes. It should be stressed that this loophole-seeking was neither extensive nor especially serious. However, these examples do demonstrate that the efficiency and durability of any reform will be subject, to an extent, to strategic learning by actors.

Expenditure during the 2005 campaign

At the time of writing, parties have yet to declare the break down of their election spending to the Electoral Commission. Nevertheless, where data are available, broad patterns clearly emerge in terms of principal areas of campaign expenditure.

Labour strategy

In 2001, Labour ran a much more 'inclusive' campaign. There was still a focus on target seats, but that focus was less clinically observed than in 1997. 2005 represented a return to a more focused approach. Labour's overall strategy was to translate its national message into a local context, and to promote local achievements to key voters in target seats. A significant amount of the party's campaign and the techniques employed was focused on the 100–111 target seats identified by the party. For example, billboards, which featured so strongly in the 2001 campaign, were now positioned mainly in target areas. Whilst some posters appeared in Labour heartland areas, most were in or around the key battleground constituencies. Secondly, the bulk of the tours undertaken by key party personnel were focused on the target seats. Some missed out on the grounds of geographical difficulty – there was no visit to Inverness or Ynys Mon, for example. However, the route of tours was designed to generate coverage in the regional press.

Where campaign spending was especially focused on target seats was in the area of direct communication. A huge effort was put into contacting key voters in target seats – mainly those designated as 'weak Labour' or those who had voted Labour in 2001, but were considering changing their vote. Underlying this voter contact strategy was the Mosaic database, which was combined with Labour's own records of voter identification. And, for the first time, commercial purchasing data were also added. This database was then used for a highly targeted round of direct mail and telephone contact. Indeed, the whole process was synchronised so that one form of contact would follow another. Direct mail and the bulk of the personal phone calls came from the party's National Communication Centre, situated this time in Gosforth – previously the call centre was in North Shields.

Not only that, whilst in 2001 the phone bank began operations in the January of that year, this time telephone voter identification began in January 2004, with direct mail commencing two months after. And, as in 2001, paid staff were used to make the calls, this being permissible as voter identification is considered to be qualitatively different from canvassing.

What was particularly innovative was the additional use of automated telephone calls. Whilst the party considered there to be a hierarchy of voter contact in terms of efficiency, with automated calls being less effective than human ones, it estimated that automated calls generated a response rate which was ten times greater than that achieved by direct mail. Not only therefore was this technique cheaper, but it generated much more in the way of voter identification, achieving a contact rate of 35 per cent. Notwithstanding, direct mail continued to play a key role in the party's campaign strategy. The difference this time was that direct mail was locally focused to a greater degree than was previously the case.

A further innovation was a development from the 2001 campaign. Then, some 300,000 videos were distributed to key voters in 60 target seats. The video featured a common national message followed by a local one featuring the constituency's MP (Fisher 2001). This time, reflecting technological change, the medium was DVD. Once again, key voters (weak Labour and 'not sures') in 60 target constituencies received a DVD from Labour. As in 2001, costs were shared between the local and central parties. The new medium offered rather more than the videos. All viewers would see a presentation based upon their constituency. Then, there would be a menu with a number of additional features – four additional local stories, a national message presented by Tony Blair, and a Labour Party election broadcast, which focused on the economy. It also included a feedback mechanism to allow the party to evaluate how much of the DVD was viewed. By all accounts, many voters watched the whole thing.

In only two areas did Labour's campaign strategy not focus strongly upon its target seats. Firstly, electronic communications (emails and texts) were sent to supporters irrespective of their geographical location. Since spamming is not permitted, the party's e-campaigns unit simply used these media to try and boost turnout amongst its existing support, suggesting once again that electronic campaigning has some way to go before it becomes as important in campaign terms as it is in some other democracies. Secondly, in a departure from 2001, Labour spent some funds on advertising in national newspapers. In 2001, the party took the view that national newspaper advertising was neither cost-effective nor necessary as most of the press was supporting Labour anyway. In 2005, the picture was rather different. Not only was the election race seemingly closer, the press had become far less enthusiastic about the party. Labour took the view therefore that national advertisements were worthwhile to counter some of its poor press. Nevertheless, the party's regional newspaper advertising was as important and, in keeping with the rest of the campaign strategy, was focused in areas with a preponderance of target seats.

Conservative strategy

Like Labour, the Conservative's campaign was focused very strongly on its 180 target seats. It was based on floating voters who might be 'Conservative minded'. By its own admission, the party was ruthless in centring its attention on these seats. Most of the party's energy (and campaign expenditure) was aimed at floating voters in these constituencies. It used a number of campaign techniques in an attempt to achieve this goal. Firstly, in a change from 2001, the party made extensive use of billboard advertising, though in sum, the party probably spent a little less on this medium than it had at the last election on account of early and more efficient purchasing. Like Labour, billboards were mainly positioned in target areas or in busy 'travel to work' locations where target voters would see them. However, as with 2001, the party also made use of 'virtual' billboards. The 'Wipe the Smile Off His Face' campaign was only shown on a limited number of billboards, but as in 2001, an electronic version was sent to news companies, which significantly increased the coverage.

A second area of expenditure and again one that was different from 2001 was an increased use of polling and focus group data. In target seats, daily tracking polls were taken looking at key issues and candidate recognition. Focus groups were also conducted in these seats to check how messages were being received. These were used to 'tweak' messages where necessary, rather than set any campaigning agenda. The party had used fewer polls in 2001, but the decision to use more this time was in part a function of there being fewer polls in the national press, and in part because of the belief that those published in the press were of limited use anyway.

Perhaps the main strategy pursued by the Conservatives was individual voter contact, of which most was spent on direct mail. Using the party's 'Voter Vault', key voters were identified and sent up to eight direct mailings – four times during the short campaign and four times beforehand. In addition, the party used telephone voter identification to a greater degree than in 2001. In effect, this began soon after the 2001 election and this time the party employed people rather than relied wholly on volunteers to make the calls. The start date may appear very early, but of course the party needed to catch up with Labour in this respect, having done less telephone canvassing previously. Like Labour, the Conservatives also made some use of automated calling. It was tried on the grounds of efficiency but unlike Labour, was viewed as having only mixed value.

To complement these strategies, the Conservatives also engaged in newspaper and cinema advertising, focusing on areas containing target seats. Cinemas featured the 'Wipe the Smile Off His Face' campaign, whilst regional advertising attempted to localise the national message, where possible. For example, adverts dealing with MRSA would feature statistics from local hospitals. Different messages would also be stressed in different areas. Like Labour, however, the Conservatives also heralded some return to national newspaper advertising, though the reasons were somewhat different. National advertisements were used as part of a 'teaser' campaign. They appeared mainly at weekends in an attempt to set the news agenda and were then followed by more targeted direct mail and regional advertising. Indeed, so important was the regional advertising that combined with the targeted billboards, it represented the second largest item of party campaign expenditure.

Finally, like Labour the Conservatives concluded that at present, electronic campaigning was of limited use. Emails were principally sent to existing supporters – and whilst some included games, they were not viewed as techniques that would move voters. In sum, the Conservative campaign was well funded, but took place mainly in its target seats. Leadership tours were based mainly in these seats and safe Conservative or hopeless seats were largely bypassed.

Liberal Democrat strategy

The Liberal Democrats went into the 2005 election better funded than ever. The party spent an estimated £5–6 million this time compared with around £2.5 million in 2001. Whilst the new income was of course welcome, it arrived too late to invest in the kinds of infrastructure which the other parties had. This meant that unlike Labour and the Conservatives, the Liberal Democrats could not engage in direct voter contact to anything like the same extent. This meant, as in 2001, little or no direct mail or telephone voter identification. Most money was spent on Charles Kennedy's leadership tour, which visited two Liberal Democrat target seats every day. And, the additional income meant that for the first time, the party could make extensive use of billboards as well as advertising in both national and regional newspapers. In 2001, the party had used 'poster vans' rather than fixed sites in an attempt to generate local and regional news. Moreover, the party had not had the resources to advertise even in the regional press other than to promote party rallies.

Beyond these forms of expenditure, the main election costs for the Liberal Democrats were staffing ones (out in the 'field' and in the communications team), the costs of making party election broadcasts and party literature. All in all, the Liberal Democrats' campaign therefore demonstrated both similarities and differences with those of the other main parties. All three campaigns were targeted up to a point. But what made the Conservative and Labour campaigns so different was that their greater resources made it possible to target voters within those key seats as well. In sum, the Liberal Democrats' comparative lack of resources continued to drive the strategic direction of its campaigning.

Conclusion

In some ways, 2005 represented 'more of the same'. Labour was again the wealthy party; the Liberal Democrats were again in relative terms, the party with far less money. Secondly, Labour was again seemingly the most advanced in its campaign techniques. Whilst the Conservatives are catching up fast, Labour's heavy use of direct voter contact, including automated calls, localised national messages and DVDs kept it ahead of the other parties. Thirdly, the Liberal Democrats were again unable to utilise these direct voter contact techniques because while more wealthy than before, the money was not there when they needed it.

However, 2005 also represented some significant changes. The first difficulties with the new legislation appeared to emerge. Whilst the spirit of compliance still dominated, some episodes suggested that a review of aspects of the legislation might be in order. In terms of campaigning, all parties' activities were ruthlessly targeted. Indeed in some ways, the idea of a 'national' campaign by any of them seemed wide of the mark. For all three parties, expenditure was tightly focused on their target seats. Given that each party enjoyed at least some success at the election, this is unlikely to change. Secondly, election campaigning again took a step forward. The widespread use of automated calling and increasing sophistication in both the Labour and Conservative techniques for contacting voters was clearly evident. Thirdly, the collapse in national newspaper advertising witnessed in 2001 was seemingly a blip. All parties used this medium. Critically, however, all parties also took the view that regional advertising was as important, if not more so. In sum, the demarcation between local and national campaign expenditure became ever more blurred, suggesting perhaps that the differentiation between these two categories of expenditure should be re-examined.

Notes

1. The source for all data in the figures and tables is the Electoral Commission and party accounts.
2. At the time of writing, full accounts are only available up to the end of 2003.
3. Exact year-on-year comparisons on total income and expenditure between the Conservative Party and Labour are complicated by two factors. Firstly, prior to 2002, Labour and Conservative accounting year-ends differed – Labour's was 31 December, the Conservatives' 31 March. As in previous studies, the Conservatives' 'year' was designated as the one in which most months occurred (that is, 1996/97 was classified as 1996). Under the PPERA, parties are required to submit accounts with an identical year-end of 31 December. As an adjustment, therefore, the 2002 figure for the Conservatives includes only the nine months to 31 December 2002.
4. These totals include smaller donations to local constituency parties as well as to the parties' head offices.

References

Fisher, J. (2000) 'Economic evaluation or electoral necessity? Evaluating the system of voluntary income to political parties', *British Journal of Politics & International Relations*, 2(2): 179–204.

Fisher, J. (2001) 'Campaign finance: elections under new rules', *Parliamentary Affairs: Britain Votes 2001*, 54(4): 689–700.

Fisher, J. (2002) 'Next step: state funding for the parties?', *Political Quarterly*, 73(4): 392–9.

Fisher, J. (2004) 'Money matters: the financing of the Conservative Party', Political Quarterly, 75(4): 405–10.

Westmorland and Lonsdale

The supposed 'decapitation' strategy of the Liberal Democrats was to some extent a media invention. The Liberal Democrats were far more concerned with aggregate seat gains. Moreover, the party recognised that it would be difficult to achieve 'big-name' Conservative (possibly an oxymoron) scalps in the South of England, given the likelihood of some improvement in Conservative fortunes.

The Liberal Democrats proved equally incapable of claiming major prizes in some northern seats, the successful Conservative defence of Haltemprice and Howden by David Davis offering one obvious example. The main impact of the 'decapitation' strategy, insofar as it existed, was to 'ground' Conservative Shadow Cabinet members in their constituencies, increasing the impression that the Conservative campaign was leader-dominated.

However, one important Conservative scalp was claimed by the Liberal Democrats. In Westmorland and Londsdale, their candidate, Tim Farron, unseated Tim Collins, the Shadow Education Secretary and former Vice-Chairman of the Conservative Party. Although the seat lay thirteenth on the Liberal Democrats' national target list, Collins had not anticipated defeat. He had held the seat in 2001, restricting the swing to the Liberal Democrats to a modest 1.2 per cent, at a time when the foot-and-mouth crisis engendered hostility to the Labour government (the Labour vote halved). Collins had bet with the Liberal Democrat peer, Lord Razzall, that he would hold the seat. In 2005, Collins reportedly offered to raise the bet to £2,500, Razzall declining on the grounds that 'He will need the money when he is made redundant' (*The Times*, 22 April 2005).

Given that the Liberal Democrats needed to almost treble their 2001 swing, Collins' confidence was perhaps understandable, but the decision to spend time on the national election at the expense of a difficult local fight was a disastrous miscalculation. Collins was later to criticise the messages emanating from the national campaign as overly negative. The local campaign was unusual in that the tradition of mass poster displays was maintained, unlike in most other parts of the country, and the turnout was high. Farron's appeal to homebuyers disenchanted with high prices struck a chord. The Liberal Democrat pledged to increase taxes on second homes, a well-received pledge in an area where one in six homes are of this type. Farron's local agenda deprived the Conservatives of the seat for the first time since 1910.

Result		%
Farron, T. (Lib Dem)	22,569	45.5
Collins, T. (Con)	22,302	44.9
Reardon, J. (Lab)	3,796	7.7
Gibson, R. (UKIP)	660	1.3
Kemp, A. (Ind)	309	0.6
LD gain from Con		
LD majority	267	0.6
Swing: Con to LD		3.6

Turnout: 71.6%

12
The Internet, E-Democracy and the Election: Virtually Irrelevant?

Stephen Ward

> Wherever we look it is clear that Internet tools like email, websites and chat are going to be central to this election. It will happen at every level and goes far beyond the national campaign run by the national parties.
>
> (Bill Thompson, BBC online, 11 April 2005)

The first Internet election (again)?

The 2005 election was the third national campaign to be fought online and like the previous two (1997 and 2001), it was dubbed the first Internet election by some commentators. As with the 2001 campaign, expectations in the run-up to the election were fairly high with suggestions that ICTs (information communication technologies), such as the Internet and email, might be influential in producing new campaigning techniques, increasing public engagement and even influencing the results. Such optimism was prompted by both technological and political developments. By 2004 more than half the adult UK population had access to the Internet. Most UK political parties had run online campaigns for a decade and new technologies were now well entrenched into party communication strategies. Perhaps more importantly, though, the high profile attention generated by net campaigning in the US presidential elections, heightened expectations about the potential role of new ICTs. Yet the reality, at the end of the campaign, was that the Internet again proved to be a marginal battleground for the parties and of interest to a minority of the UK public. This chapter therefore examines why the Internet continues to remain marginal to UK electioneering and why expectations of a so-called net election were never likely to be realised. In doing so, it concentrates on the potential of the net in three areas: campaigning style, party competition and public engagement. It examines the official party campaigns online and the alternative campaigns run by net activists, whilst also assessing the public's involvement in the online election. It argues that whilst the Internet itself may have remained at the margins, it does not mean that ICTs are of no consequence in political campaigning. They may be helping to accelerate long-term trends already present in UK politics before the arrival of the Internet.

Electoral campaigning online

The rapid growth of the Internet and other new ICTs since the mid 1990s has provoked considerable debate about their political implications. In terms of parties and election campaigns interest has centred on three areas: campaigning style – assessing how far the net will change the way parties campaign; party competition online – looking at the extent to which the Internet can facilitate new or fringe campaigns; and public engagement – analysing how far the net can help ignite public interest in elections.

Current debate on political campaigning suggests that parties are moving into a post-modern era of stylised packaging and sharp marketing techniques, where their efforts are focused on discovering what the voter wants and shaping and targeting their policies (products) to meet these demands (Norris 2000; Bowers-Brown 2003). This marks a significant shift from the modern campaign era, which centred on parties bringing their message to the people via the electronic media, especially television. It has been suggested that new media technologies might contribute to such a shift by driving changes in the following areas of campaigning:

- *Increasing substance?* The Internet presents conflicting possibilities for the relationship between style and substance in campaigning. The high volume and speed of information transmission possible via the Internet means that it has the potential to offer more substantive basis for campaigning than traditional forms of media. Parties may use their sites primarily as information vehicles to provide voters with policy based material. Alternatively, however, parties may be tempted to exploit the emerging combinations of audio-visual and graphical features of the web plus its unmediated nature to provide more images, gimmicks and soundbites to attract and retain visitors.
- *Increasing narrowcasting?* The increasing ability to gather information on voters means that parties have greater opportunities to target certain groups of voters and even to individualise or personalise campaign messages. This narrowcasting approach allows parties to direct their appeal to segments of the electorate, such as younger voters, who are often the most computer literate, but least likely to vote or engage in traditional political activity.
- *Increasing interactivity?* From a party perspective, the interactive potential of ICTs offers parties a low cost and very direct means of seeking immediate

feedback from voters on policy and campaign tactics. Technologies also present the opportunities for parties to form ongoing relationships with voters to both mobilise and retain supporters. Online surveys, online dialogue sessions between voters and politicians, along with blogs[1] could all be used in this respect.

- *Increasing decentralisation?* The television era has been seen as supporting an increased centralisation of campaign control around party headquarters, a focus on national messages and party leaders. Arguably, the growth of new media campaigning might challenge such centralisation by heralding a return to more localised campaigning and fragmentation of the national campaigns since it provides candidates and local parties with a relatively low cost platform for their own message (Norris 2000).

Party competition online

It is not simply a matter of *facilitating* changes in electioneering. Some commentators have raised the possibly of new ICTs actually *shaping* party competition. The past 20 years have seen the emergence of a range of fringe parties, from the extreme right to the Greens, as well as strong challenges from independents and single-issue campaigners. It has been suggested that new ICTs might further increase electoral volatility and the willingness of voters to look beyond the traditional Parliamentary Parties. Whilst election campaigns in the old media are dominated by information and personnel from the major parties, the new media theoretically could erode some of this dominance and help smaller parties or fringe candidates level the campaign communication field (Rash 1997). This equalisation argument rests largely on two factors: firstly, the net and other technologies have the potential to increase the volume and quality of information that minor parties and candidates can distribute to voters compared with the other media. By contrast to the traditional media, the decentralised aspect of the net, its huge bandwidth capacity and the minimal running costs arguably means that anyone can author a reasonably sophisticated website. Secondly, in theory, the Internet can help equalise access to all parties and thus exposure to party views for voters because it allows for greater user control of information. Internet users can access party sites independently of external editorial control. Unlike the traditional media where news is often collated and distributed from a central point to a largely passive audience, the Internet allows the user to choose from an increasingly vast array of news sources, which they voluntarily seek out.

Critics have, however, countered this equalisation thesis, arguing that increasingly over time the net is coming to resemble the traditional political battlegrounds, with mainstream political parties dominating the new media just as they do the old. This idea of the normalisation of cyberspace has increasingly gained ground. For example, Margolis and Resnick (2000) argue that far from being cost-free, sophisticated online campaigns require considerable resources that only the major parties can produce. Moreover, the mainstream actors' dominance of the traditional media gives them a considerable advantage in advertising their online presence and consequently driving traffic to their sites.

Public participation and involvement online

In order to fully understand whether parties' online campaigns facilitate wider change, one needs to examine public involvement in, and engagement with, such campaigns. At one level, it has been argued that new technologies could lower the costs of electoral participation. Activities such as information gathering, contacting politicians or joining parties, are potentially far easier and quicker (Bonchek 1995). Those who find it difficult to attend public events and meetings can participate online from their own homes. Furthermore, as we have noted above, it has been suggested that ICTs could be a more attractive communication tool for younger people. However, others have suggested that the Internet is unlikely to make much difference and may, indeed, widen the participation gaps (Norris 2000; 2001). Firstly, access to the technology is still restricted and those without access tend to be the very people who are already disengaged from the political process. Secondly, technology may provide the means but does not necessarily provide the motive to participate in electoral politics.

Beyond simply widening the numbers involved in electoral politics, the Internet could also extend participatory activity and deepen the quality of the participatory experience. The speed, the level of information and the interactive and networking possibilities supported by new ICTs could help participants supplement and extend their range of participatory experiences. So rather than simply being passive spectators in the electoral process, new technologies raise the possibility of voters shaping their own information sources and moving beyond the parties' and news organisations' agendas. Sceptics have argued, however, that new ICTs are unlikely to add much to political engagement and are doubtful that technologies can produce meaningful political deliberation. They see ICT communication as a largely solitary push-button experience (Street 1997; Barber et al. 1997). The large amounts of information available online may simply lead the public to become overloaded and disengaged or select only a narrow range of online information sources, which merely reinforce their own prejudices (Sunstein 2001).

The development of online electioneering in the UK

The vast majority of UK political parties developed their web presence between 1994 and 1996 in preparation for the 1997 election. Although all the main parties had websites and ran email campaigns in 1997, the web was, at this stage, still an experimental tool for parties and seen as quirkily interesting but of little real importance. This was highlighted by the fact that Labour's website was run by relatively junior staff outside the main communications department (Ward and Gibson 1998). The audience for online campaigns in 1997 was minuscule. Less than 100,000 people visited Labour's site in 1997, but e-campaigning soon increased in importance. The main parties invested in dedicated e-campaign teams and integrated web campaigning into the mainstream of party communications. Nevertheless, even in 2001 the web was still being used mainly as a supplementary communication tool aimed at mobilising sympathisers, or opinion formers such as journalists (Coleman 2001b).

In terms of the development of web content UK parties/candidates have been relatively circumspect about online electioneering. In the first five years of their development, party sites were often criticised for their poor quality. Yet it is evident that from the late 1990s there was an increasing focus on professionalisation and website design, with efforts to reduce the text based nature of the sites, although the party sites remained content heavy (Gibson et al. 2003). One consistent criticism has been the lack of interactivity and personalisation in party campaigns. None of the mainstream party sites have allowed public discussion on their sites and much of the communication remains based on the broadcast model – top-down from party to public. Whilst parties have tried limited experiments with interactivity or message targeting – for example, Labour's widely derided 'RU UP 4 IT' youth site in the 2001 campaign – they have tended to remain cautious about such possibilities, fearing a fragmentation of key campaign themes and the risk of confusing voters with different messages to different groups (Jackson 2001). Similarly, until recently, we had not seen much development of decentralised local based web campaigning in the UK. At the last election, few candidates bothered to use new media tools actively and those that did remained very much wedded to delivering the national party message (Ward and Gibson 2003).

In relation to party competition online, the consensus so far has been that there is limited evidence of equalisation. Certainly, in previous UK elections, there has been no indication that the Internet delivers votes for any particular party and in any case it would be difficult to demonstrate any such link (Gibson et al. 2003). Studies do suggest, however, that the main parties, especially the big three, maintain an advantage in terms of the sophistication and visibility of their sites. This is especially pronounced at election time where mainstream parties have significantly more staff and financial resources (Ward et al. 2003). Nevertheless, any normalisation process does not seem to be inevitable or inexorable. Smaller parties can close the gap between election times when their major counterparts tend to leave their sites to stagnate. Moreover, some smaller parties, notably the Greens and the BNP, have maintained reasonably sophisticated e-campaigns and have claimed that they derive useful benefits from the Internet and email in terms of organisation and recruitment. Both the Greens and the far right have more incentives than most to use new media technologies, although for different reasons. For the Greens, their target audience tends to be amongst those groups which use the Internet heavily – the young, urban, middle class, students and environmental activists. For parties like the BNP, the semi-covert nature of their organisation means that emails are a useful means of communication and organisation. The far right are particularly enthusiastic about using the net as a means of circumnavigating the restrictions (as they see it) of the traditional 'liberal' media. Additionally, as Copsey (2003) has argued in relation to the BNP, a professional website can also convey the appearance of legitimacy and make the party seem larger than is actually the case.

From a bottom-up perspective there has been very limited empirical evidence about public use of the web and involvement in political campaigns. Numbers accessing political organisational sites tend to be small. Recent surveys suggested that around 5–8 per cent of the British public have accessed party sites and around 2–3 per cent local party websites or those of MPs (Lusoli et al. 2005). In the 2001 election, news sites were the most popular online destination, a pattern that has held firm throughout the past five years (Coleman 2001a). A recent survey indicated that around one-quarter of the public gathered news online, particularly from BBC online. Government sites, partly because of their service and information functions, are also significantly more popular than those of political parties or other political organisations (Lusoli et al. 2005).

The profile of those engaged in political activity online has also remained fairly constant. The web tends, not surprisingly, to attract the middle class, urban, well educated population and, more particularly, those that are already politically active and engaged, although some survey work has detected a small widening effect. Research conducted after the 2001 election, indicated a possible small but intriguing mobilisation effect amongst some younger people (Gibson et al. 2006). Similarly, studies of party activists indicate that they are increasingly using the technologies to supplement and extend their offline activities (Lusoli and Ward 2004).

Whilst the first decade of web use in the UK led to a backlash against the more speculative optimism about ICTs in the political world, in the run-up to the 2005 election, several factors raised expectation that ICTs would perhaps play a more prominent role. By 2004, a majority of the British electorate had used the Internet and those regularly using the net had almost doubled since the last election.[2] Furthermore, the rapid increase in broadband, with its enhanced online capabilities and the massive increase in mobile phone technology suggested that there would be a greater demand for online activity around the election. More specifically, the past couple of years had also seen the growth of the net as marketing tool. In particular, commentators highlighted the growing success of so-called virals (online films, games and cartoons) which spread rapidly via email, prompting suggestions that parties might usefully develop subtle viral campaigns so that the messages do not appear to come directly from the parties themselves. The other major development in cyberspace from a political campaign perspective was the rapid development of blogs. By 2003–04 a nascent and expanding blogsphere was in place in the UK, attracting the attention of some politicians, including seven blogging Westminster MPs.[3] Prior to the campaign, Iain Duncan Smith, the former Conservative leader, not previously known for his technophile views, proclaimed the potential importance of blogs for the political right, suggesting that 'the Internet's level playing field gives Conservatives opportunities that the mainstream media has denied them'. Duncan Smith even went on to claim:

> the Internet could do more to change the level of political engagement than all the breast beating of introspective politicians and commentators. A 21st century political revolution is now only a few mouse clicks away. (*Guardian*, 19 February 2005)

What arguably prompted most of this interest, particularly amongst the parties, was online campaigning in the 2004 US presidential campaign. As usual, the major parties sent staff to monitor the Bush and Kerry campaigns. However, it was Howard Dean's primary campaign which captured the imagination of net activists and journalists. His innovative use of blogs and online meet-up mechanisms to build supporter networks, along with his ability to raise funds from small scale donators renewed interest in the interactive possibilities of campaigning. Indeed, in the aftermath of the failed Dean campaign it was clear that some parties had been looking to learn lessons. At their 2004 conference, the Conservatives launched an online recruitment tool, 'Conservatives Direct', aimed at recruiting online activists and volunteers and focusing initially on marginal seats.

The official online campaign: parties and candidates in cyberspace

At first glance, the 2005 party online campaigns appeared to be a continuation of existing practice with few radical departures. Hence the standard party website comprised the well established pattern of: news and policy, including audio-video clips of party broadcasts and campaign speeches; about us – basic aims, organisational structure and key people; how to get involved – volunteering joining and donating online; get in touch/keep in touch – email contacts and campaign diaries. In general, the party sites all followed similar basic formats and much the same basic structure as they had at the previous election, despite many having undergone overhauls in design prior to the election. There was little sense of a separate cyberspace campaign or much that was different from the traditional media. Similarly, party e-news facilities via email reinforced this controlled integrated approach, with most parties (the Ulster Unionist Party, the Greens, and the Liberal Democrats in particular) simply repeating their key news releases and guiding one to the party website, although the Conservatives' e-news tried a broader approach with appeals for funds and use of video clips.

Superficially, the party websites appeared to adopt a something for everyone style but underlying this was a more subtle two-pronged approach. Firstly, there was headline news, soundbites, party slogans, online billboards and advertising hooks to join, support or volunteer seemingly aimed at the casual surfer, a voter who generally spends no more than a couple of minutes on a site. These were particularly prominent on lead and home pages and were designed to reinforce the key messages of the party. The big three parties regularly altered their home pages to make sure they reflected their key issue of the day. Secondly, underlying this political marketing style approach was more in-depth policy, news and organisational information aimed primarily at a more specialist (journalists, researchers) or more partisan audience (members, activists and potential sympathisers). Whilst parties are hoping to get their message to the public unmediated via the web, they are equally trying to set the media agenda by providing stories for journalists to pick up. It is clear, however, that parties generally believe their core audience to be their members, activists and sympathisers and that the primary task of websites and email is to draw in volunteers, galvanise existing supporters and to provide the means with which to educate and arm party workers. As a Labour Party spokesman admitted: 'to be honest and realistic about it, the key use of it is to rally the converted' (*Washington Post*, 4 May 2005). Similarly, Mark Pack, the Liberal Democrats' e-campaigns manager, commented: 'its greatest importance to us is internal organisation and mobilising helpers/supporters who will then influence the floating voter' (*Revolution*, 9 May 2005).

Although the websites of the parties were all fairly similar in general content the levels of sophistication were clearly different. For the most part, the smaller parliamentary parties and parties, such as the Greens and the BNP, have sites that are professional in appearance. Where minor parties cannot compete is in terms of the add-on extras of e-marketing, some of the audio-visual elements, the scale and depth of information and the frequency of updating. When one moves to fringe parties that are entirely reliant on volunteers, then it is clear that they cannot hope to compete with the bigger players. For example, the Pensioners Party <www.pensionersparty.org> offered a muddle of broken links, ill designed fonts and information 'coming soon' that never arrived. Many of the very small parties managed to update their sites only infrequently. The Liberal Party <www.liberal.org.uk> and the Socialist Labour Party <www.socialist-labour-party.org.uk>, for instance, barely appeared to update their sites during the campaign. Such sites effectively become static cyberbrochures rather than active communication tools. Nevertheless, fringe parties are still keen to proclaim the benefits of the net. The Senior Citizens Party, for instance, has part of its site dedicated to a tele-democracy campaign and argues:

The great thing about the Internet is that it empowers individuals and groups to communicate and join together to achieve common aims. Seniors International has been founded to help all seniors to gain access to the Internet both to improve their quality of life, and to enable them to make their voice heard much more effectively. <www.seniorsinternational.net>

Developing trends?

Within this general pattern of continuity in web campaigning three trends give an indication of the general direction of party online campaigns: e-marketing, targeting and databases, and interactivity, blogging and diaries.

E-marketing

Coleman (2001a) noted the emergence of e-marketing approaches on the party sites in the 2001 election campaign, a trend developed further in this campaign. It was noticeable that more parties used the websites for branding and also made increasing use of audio-visual possibilities of the new media. Besides offering the usual party broadcasts on their websites, Labour produced video diaries of the campaigns and the Liberal Democrats experimented with podcasting. The main parties also all offered SMS services. Many parties also offered posters, banners and screensavers to download which, whilst not new, were more prominent than 2001. The Liberal Democrats invested in online banner ads on the *Independent* and *Guardian* newspaper sites to try to drive traffic to their site and encourage donations. In a nod to the viral phenomenon, the Conservatives produced an online game which encouraged voters to wipe the smile off Tony Blair's face. The Liberal Democrats and the Greens allowed visitors to circulate semi-humorous email postcards.

Targeting and databases

Connected to the e-marketing approach was the continued development of database targeting to identify key groups and individuals and gather opinion and instant feedback on key issues. Whilst databases have been around since the 1980s, the Internet and email are helping add to them. The 2005 online campaign seemed heavily geared towards gathering information especially in marginal constituencies. Whilst all the main parties use databases, perhaps the most interesting development in 2005 was the Conservatives' use of Voter Vault database software borrowed from the successful Bush campaign. This moves the focus from ward level to individual level targeting. Using consumer classification data, which categorises 23 million households, supplemented by local party information and telephone canvassing the party could then identify potential conservative and swing voters allegedly more accurately than ever before (*Brand Republic*, 21 April 2005).

As a supplement to this, parties devoted effort on their sites to gathering email and postcode addresses. Hence on Labour's site one could ask for personalised policy information, sign up for e-news, and sign online petitions, all of which demanded postcodes, email addresses and in certain cases some additional personal data. This information gathering exercise is in part about creating integrated and more efficient campaigning. IT produces more precision in identifying key target groups, who can then be contacted using largely traditional campaign methods, such as direct mail drops, and door knocking in marginal constituencies. Some have suggested that the development of the high-tech option is a response to the falling level of local activism in the two main parties (Dorling et al. 2002). Where once parties could blanket areas with local activists, with fewer volunteers parties are now forced to be more selective and precise about such activities. Undoubtedly, new technologies are accelerating a trend towards campaigning being focused on smaller and smaller numbers of target voters in key marginal constituencies.

Interactivity, blogging and diaries

In previous campaigns the lack of interactivity on party sites has been heavily criticised. However, increasingly, party websites have included more interactive elements. But as we have seen, the type of interactivity on offer is with the website (games, downloading e-campaign material, email news) rather than dialogue with the parties or politicians. Some of the smaller parties had discussion fora but these were often hidden and rarely well used. The SDLP youth pages <www.sdlp.ie/party/youth.shtm> had the discussion area, but this was very much at arm's length from the main party campaign.

The new element in 2005 was the emergence of so-called campaign blogs, suggesting a greater level of interactivity. At least seven parties ran blogs during the campaign including all three main parties, the SNP and a number of fringe parties like Veritas. Whilst some were described as blogs, they were in reality diaries. In only one case (the Liberal Democrats) could visitors respond with comments. They were not, therefore, encouraging dialogue between parties and voters. Nor for the most part were they written by politicians. Labour's campaign diaries were in the names of Blair and Prescott, who ironically both admit to being technophobes, but were put together by party workers. The Liberal Democrats' blog was written by campaign workers on their battle bus. In general, party blogs were largely anodyne accounts of the campaign, supposedly giving an inside view but offering little by the way of real insights and verging on propaganda about how well the campaign was progressing. It was difficult to see what either party or voters might have gained from the experience. Arguably, the most engaging and apparently authentic was Michael Howard's wife Sandra's campaign diary. The diary managed to generate press interest, although the stories focused mainly on Mrs Howard's hairstyle rather than the issues of the day.

It is not surprising that parties are reluctant to open up their online campaigns in such a way. Offering open spaces for comments or dialogue on websites is problematic. Since it offers opponents the opportunity to ask awkward questions or simply post abuse. The small English Democrats Party <www.englishdemocrats. org.uk> was forced to remove the comment facility from its blog during the campaign because of misuse. Whilst blogs are useful for campaigning, they are not necessarily appropriate for electioneering in a party environment. If blogging is partly about creating transparency, openness and authenticity, then starting one during an election campaign is unlikely to deliver when parties are more than ever concerned to control the party message.

Subnational campaigning online: candidates and local parties[4]

The 2005 election saw a significant increase in the number of candidate and local party sites. In total there were around 1,300 candidate websites, equating to 37 per cent of the total number of candidates, although around 7 per cent of these sites either lacked election content or were invalid URLs. There were also distinct differences between the parties. Conservatives led the way, a reversal from the last election, with 68 per cent of constituencies covered by local party or candidate sites. They were followed by the Greens, although their sites focused on the local party or constituencies rather than candidates. Labour and Liberal Democrats had a similar local presence with around 43 per cent and 45 per cent candidate coverage respectively. Aside from the Greens, though, it is clear that few of the other smaller parties could compete online. Even parties running a large number of candidates, such as UKIP, had only a handful online. Others, such as the BNP, had no candidate websites whatsoever. In part, this is not simply a question of financial resources as many fringe parties simply lack a local branch infrastructure. Moreover, the UK electoral system provides little incentive for smaller parties to create candidate sites or devote resources beyond a national site when they have virtually no chance of success.

The basic pattern of website presence is not unexpected. There was greater activity in marginal seats, particularly amongst the main contenders in those seats. Safe Labour constituencies were, by contrast, the least likely to have any web activity. This website electoral geography is also underpinned by the level of access to the net in certain constituencies – those where access to the Internet and broadband is low are unlikely to have seen much cyberspace activity. There was also an incumbency factor at work, with sitting MPs more likely to have developed a web presence than their challengers.

The patterns of web competition provide only a partial story. Although there has been a clear development of the web locally this does not necessarily support a decentralisation thesis. This is for two reasons. Firstly, there are still a large number of sites which are really no more than cyberbrochures or leaflets, that is, they are static sites with limited information – usually a biography, contact numbers and some key issue themes. They are in no way active campaign tools, since they were not updated during the course of the campaign. Secondly, there has been a significant growth of party templates, especially amongst Conservative and Liberal Democrat parties. These are sites with the same basic format and containing some of the same nationally determined content. For example, a large number of the main party sites now carry a news feed direct from the national party site. By contrast, Labour's relatively well established 'web-in-a-box' template increased only marginally at this election. Consequently, a significant number of local Conservative Party websites carried identical information with limited local content. Even where templates were not used, websites tend to mirror the national party line. Again, there was little in the way of interactivity, although blogs entered the local websphere. There were around 60 candidate blogs, although few of these had any developed dialogue between voters and candidates.

Despite the prevalence of templates, there were the beginnings of candidates tentatively developing more individualised campaigns or targeting groups within their constituencies. Some Labour candidates and incumbents in marginals were keen to distance themselves from Blair and highlight their opposition to the war in Iraq or top-up fees.[5] Students, perhaps because of their high levels of access to the net, were targeted online by Liberal Democrat candidates. Not only was there more web activity in seats with large student populations but Liberal Democrat candidates gave prominence to the top-up fees issue on their site and highlighted their links to student groups.[6]

Overall, though, it is questionable whether websites in particular are any more than marginal campaign tools. Interviews with sitting MPs in the run-up to the 2005 election highlighted three issues: Firstly, the continued belief in the traditional tools of local campaigns canvassing, door-knocking and leafleting and generally pressing the flesh and being seen, were what voters wanted. Secondly, websites and email don't reach the voters you necessarily want to mobilise, such as the relatively uncommitted and the less politically interested. Thirdly, email and localised databases are beginning to be valued much more than websites as electoral tools. Hence a small but growing number of MPs are starting to manage their postbags electronically and to develop email newsletters, allowing them to build more regular contact with constituents and send more personalised messages to them. Yet as Richard Allan, former MP and techno-enthusiast, has argued, it is difficult to see what additional benefits are to be gained from local online campaigning in the UK other than organisational efficiency:

> the impact on the elector of a nicely printed letter landing on their doormat is far greater than that for any email the party might send. Direct contact on the doorstep or via telephone is much more effective than any form of net interactivity. And glossy leaflets with photos of candidates that are pushed

at the elector beat websites for putting a message across. In other words, we do not do much net campaigning because it is second best to the political campaign tools we have at our disposal.[7]

The unofficial election online: blogs, vote-swapping and satire

An alternative election campaign was also occurring in cyberspace, one which was more interesting and less predictable than the controlled party environment. A plethora of websites were active around the election. Some of these were well established, others emerged rapidly during the campaign. The 2005 election saw a large increase in the amount of information available about the election, the parties and the issues. Indeed, the quantity of information was potentially overwhelming. Much of the expansion can be attributed to the rise of the blogging phenomenon. Broadly, three types of site can be identified. informational resources, alternative campaigns, and satire/humour sites.

Informational resource websites

These were sites that aimed at providing information largely on a non-partisan basis about the election, issues, and candidates. All the traditional media, television channels and broadsheet newspapers had online election sites, the two largest being *BBC Online* and the *Guardian*. Although clearly these sites are an extension of their traditional coverage, they provide additional depth to issues and stories carried on TV news or in the newspaper. The sites also provide a wealth of information about the parties and the candidates that is often not readily available elsewhere. The Channel 4 website provided a factcheck facility designed to monitor party claims. Moreover, many mainstream media sites allow their visitors opportunities to interact through discussion forums, blogs and online soapboxes. Several, including the BBC, Channel 4 and the *Guardian*, also carried blogs and diaries from a range of candidates.

Besides the traditional media there was also a variety of groups and networks operating purely online who aimed to provide the public with information not readily available elsewhere from the parties or government or to interpret official information into a more easily understandable format. Sites such as <www.theyworkforyou.org> and <www.publicwhip.org.uk> have provided evidence of MPs' voting records for the past couple of years. One new development was the emergence of voter compass sites where voters can answer questions related to policy issues to find out to which party they are most closely aligned. One such site, <www.whoshouldyouvotefor.com>, claimed it attracted more than 200,000 hits in its first week (*The Scotsman*, 19 April 2005).

Alternative campaign sites

These were sites with a partisan purpose and aimed at influencing the way people voted, trying to persuade people not to vote for particular candidates or parties or, in one case, allowing people space to explain why they were not going to vote (<www.notapathetic.com>). One important group of sites here was those encouraging vote-swapping. The vote-trading idea originated in the 2000 US presidential campaign but was declared illegal in the courts. However, the idea quickly spread to the UK in 2001, drawing on the growing trend towards tactical voting. The basic premise of such sites is that they act as virtual clearing houses that pair up voters in marginal constituencies. So a Liberal Democrat supporter might vote Labour in return for their Labour-supporting pair voting Liberal Democrat in another constituency in order to keep the Conservative out. In 2001, it was suggested that vote-trading sites may have influenced results in two constituencies – Cheadle and Dorset South – leading to the defeat of two sitting Conservative MPs (Coleman 2001a). In 2005, the two most prominent voting-trading sites from 2001 <www.tacticalvoter.net> and Billy Bragg's <www.votedorset.net> returned, along with a range of others. The majority continued to aim at the Conservatives, supporting Labour or Liberal Democrat candidates in marginal constituencies.

The new development in 2005 was the emergence of several sites targeting Labour MPs who had supported the war in Iraq, such as <www.whodowevotefornow.com>, <www.libdemthistime.co.uk> or <www.backingblair.com>. Tactical voting websites gained considerable press coverage and several predictions that they might influence results in a number of seats. Their actual impact in 2005 is difficult if not impossible to measure. The numbers of vote-swappers are relatively small, no more than a few thousand, although it does not require huge numbers to affect results in some constituencies. Certainly, the anti-Conservative campaigns to unseat Oliver Letwin and David Davis appeared to have failed partly because tactical voting had passed its peak. Nor are such sites necessarily engaging new voters. As Jason Buckley, creator of TacticalVoter.net, has stated: 'most vote traders are politically aware individuals with clear party allegiances – often with a history of political activism' (*Guardian*, 28 April 2005). Nevertheless, such sites may have a longer-term impact through renewed support for electoral reform, since, as Coleman (2001a) notes, such sites are essentially attempts at DIY proportional representation. Within days of the election some of the vote trading sites had morphed into campaigns for PR.

The Backing Blair campaign highlighted a number of new developments in these types of campaign. Firstly, it aimed at targeting Labour MPs who had supported the war with the intent of reducing Labour's majority significantly in order to force Blair to resign. It also offered assistance to anti-war independents such as Craig Murray, who challenged Jack Straw by promoting his blog site. Secondly, it did not simply facilitate or encourage tactical voting, but was a fairly sophisticated online campaign created and supported by leading UK bloggers. As well as offering the usual e-campaign tools such as anti-Blair marketing material, it was also designed to link up supporters trying to force the Iraq issue up the political agenda. The site contained a meet-up facility to try and stimulate the formation of local networks, but this was not used extensively. Whilst Backing Blair may have had limited direct impact it does indicate a possible prototype e-campaign for the future. A relatively sophisticated campaign was put together in weeks by volunteer activists at a relatively small cost and achieved some media coverage. It is quite possible that in the future leading political figures could find themselves increasingly targeted in this way by the blogging and activist community.

Satire and humour

Aided by the growth of blogging and the increasing popularity of virals, 2005 saw an explosion of sites dedicated to extracting humour from the election campaign. Several sites such as <www.gbjab.com> seemed to draw on the US presidential campaign, where games and online humour satire proved hugely popular. Broadly, there were three types of election humour sites. Firstly, there were those with a non-partisan political purpose aimed at engaging people's interest in the election and getting people to vote. The successful Spin On site <www.spinon.co.uk> was reinvented from 2001 offering a range of games such as 'the uncredibles', 'weapons of mass destruction hunt' and 'Gordon Brown changing rooms'. Underlying Spin On's humour was a serious effort to engage people's interest through such material. Secondly, partisan sites used humour or satire as a political weapon to ridicule particular campaigns or politicians, for instance, through spoof blogs such as <www.michaelhowardmp.co.uk>. One popular type of site invited visitors to either alter or deface campaign posters both on and offline, for example, <www.toryscum.com>. Thirdly, there were sites that had no particular political message (except perhaps that politicians are all the same), and had no interest in whether one voted. They were aimed simply at creating satire and humour. The long-standing <www.punchaceleb.com> saw all major party leaders appear in their list of celebrities people wanted to punch, with Blair topping the poll ahead of the ever-popular footballer Craig Bellamy.

The public response to online campaigning

In the UK there has been little detailed evidence about the public's online political behaviour and the parties themselves rarely reveal much in the way of their own website data. However, two indicators have emerged about public involvement with the online campaign and the effectiveness of party campaigns – web traffic data and public opinion survey evidence.

Web traffic data

In this election, Internet monitoring firm Hitwise tracked visits to party sites throughout the campaign. One clear trend in traffic for all parties is how far it is driven by offline events. Hence the biggest surges in traffic correspond in particular to their manifesto launches. Overall, although traffic was comparatively small, patterns suggest the Conservatives had the most hits and the biggest share of the party traffic, although their lead over Labour and the Liberal Democrats fell considerably during the course of the campaign. The Liberal Democrats appear to be the biggest winners on this measure, increasing their share of website traffic from 19 per cent to 27 per cent by election day and being the subject of the most Internet searches. One explanation, of course, is the increased publicity gained during the election period, indicating how far new media traffic is driven by publicity in the traditional media. Some minor parties scored relatively well. The Greens, especially, in keeping with their technophile support, achieved 7 per cent of Internet party traffic by election day, indicating that, although the web is not a level playing field, for some minor parties it is a valuable means of publicity, more so than for large mainstream parties.[8]

Public opinion evidence[9]

Public opinion data reveal that interest in online politics is still a minority although growing hobby. Around 28 per cent of those with access had been online to look for election information and news and another 8 per cent came across election information unintentionally. However, only a small number, around 3 per cent, used the net regularly and as their major information source. Mainly, the net acted as a supplementary news gathering tool. Over half those who went online for election information visited the BBC site. The vast majority of the public still rely on the traditional news media for their political information and even party literature is a more effective means of reaching the bulk of the public directly than the new media. As for the party campaigns online, only around 3 per cent of people with access had visited a party website and 1 per cent had visited candidate sites during the election. Similarly, small numbers had received email from parties (4 per cent) or candidates (1 per cent) during the campaign and the only type of election activity which registered significant numbers was online humour or games about the election. For the most part, people with access to the net did not use online sources for two main reasons: either they had little interest in the election (33 per cent) or they felt they received enough information from the traditional media (24 per cent), which was easier to use anyway.

As with previous surveys in this area, it is mostly younger male educated and Internet-literate citizens who went online for electoral information: 18–24-year-olds are twice as likely than others to have used the Internet in relation to the election and 25–34-year-olds were the most likely to have used the Internet for 'a lot' of their election information. Strikingly, students were the category most likely to have used the Internet; one in two student respondents claimed to have used the net for electoral information. Hence the net does seem to appeal to some groups that traditionally are harder to mobilise in elections. Nevertheless, overall, the opinion data highlight the problems of Internet campaigns from a party perspective – that people are difficult to reach online unless they have a pre-existing interest in politics and where this is the case the party message has probably already got through via other sources. The sites, if not preaching to the converted, are preaching to the politically active and engaged. This may lead to a further problem for those concerned about participation. The net is undoubtedly an excellent tool for the small minority of the highly politically engaged public. It is also useful as an organisational tool for activists and for the party hierarchy, but its effectiveness as a general communication tool with the bulk of the electorate is still marginal.

Conclusions and future directions: marginal but not irrelevant?

It is tempting to declare that the Internet was largely irrelevant to the UK election. It was mainly a supplementary campaign tool; it did not shift votes or alter the results to any noticeable extent; nor did it do much to engage public interest outside the existing political junkies. However, looking for such direct impacts was always likely to be a futile task – the Internet, like television or radio, does not shift votes by itself. Moreover, it is a mistake to believe that the US Internet experience could be replicated here. The UK political system in its current state is always likely to minimise the Internet's usefulness as a campaign tool. Net campaigns work better in a more personalised format, where candidates are building organisations sometimes almost from scratch and have to campaign nationally over vast distances. The UK with its party-centred system means that well entrenched organisational machines are already in place. Moreover, constituency campaigning in relatively concentrated small geographic areas means that the old techniques of door knocking and face-to-face contact are still more valuable for parties.

What ICTs are doing, however, is accelerating pre-existing campaign trends in electoral politics. Certainly, ICTs and technology are being used to produce more targeted campaigning seemingly aimed at an ever decreasing number of key swing voters. Equally, the party campaigns were very much in line with political marketing approaches that have emerged offline. In terms of the equalisation–normalisation debate, it is fairly clear that the net does not as yet produce any direct benefits in votes for minor parties. However, the growth in the number of parties and candidates in recent elections may be further facilitated by technology since the net and email reduce the basic start-up costs of running a campaign and can network disparate supporters. In other words, the net allows minority parties to survive, but not necessarily thrive. It allows more parties to play the game but doesn't necessarily make them equal (Ward et al. 2003). Whilst technology may allow increased pluralism, the electoral system, party finances and the media system all act as a check.

In terms of public engagement, neither of the two online election campaigns (official or alternative) described here really spoke to, or penetrated, the consciousness of many voters, although the numbers using the net for information is growing, mainly as people visit traditional news outlets online. The party online campaigns largely replayed the offline campaigns, but focused more extensively on mobilising the politically active and sympathetic. The alternative campaign spoke to those politically interested, but often disaffected from party politics, but neither the official nor unofficial campaigns really moved beyond the usual suspects. Certainly, there is more information available to the public than ever before and those that use the net can make themselves more informed. There is more transparency, discussion and scrutiny, yet it seems likely that this may further increase participation and knowledge gaps amongst the electorate, where the educated and already politically engaged will derive the most benefit.

It is interesting that in the aftermath of the campaign, technology in the form of e-voting has again been held up as a panacea for turnout, despite all the evidence to the contrary, not least the government's local election trials. E-voting may produce a short term boost, but is unlikely to change the underlying problems of the electoral system or public perceptions about politics. What this election and others illustrate is that people are engaged through the issues and politics not because of the technology. The Internet can be an excellent informational and organisational tool, but if the campaign is dull and the parties and candidates seen as irrelevant and unrepresentative, then slick websites and fancy gadgets will not alter people's perception about the value of voting.

Notes

1. A blog is a diary which allows readers to post comments in response to entries.
2. Recent surveys indicate 52–60 per cent of the UK population has access to the Internet.
3. In March 2005 these were: four Labour MPs – Austin Mitchell, Clive Soley, Tom Watson, Sean Woodward; two Liberal Democrats – Richard Allan and Sandra Gidley; and Conservative Boris Johnson. Soley and Allan retired at the election whilst the others were all re-elected.
4. The author is grateful to Wainer Lusoli for collating the information in this section.
5. See, for example, Judith Blake's site <www.20six.co.uk/leedsnwblog>, the defeated Labour candidate in Leeds North West.
6. See, for example, Stephen Williams' site <www.stephenwilliams.org.uk>, Liberal Democrat candidate in Bristol West.
7. <www.voxpolitics.com/weblog/archives/2005-04.html>, accessed 29 April 2005.
8. Figures obtained from press releases supplied by Hitwise.
9. The figures in this section are drawn from a stratified, representative NOP poll of 1,937 voters, conducted 12–17 May 2005, commissioned by the author.

206   *Britain Decides*

References

Barber, B., Mattson, K. and J. Peterson (1997) *The State of Electronically Enhanced Democracy: A Survey of the Internet*, New Brunswick, NJ: Walt Whitman Center for Culture and Politics of Democracy.

Bonchek, M. (1995) 'Grassroots in cyberspace: Using computer networks to facilitate political participation'. Paper presented to the 53rd Annual Meeting of the Midwest Political Science Association, 6 April, Chicago.

Bowers-Brown, J. (2003) 'A marriage made in cyberspace? Political marketing and British party websites', in R. Gibson, P. Nixon and S. Ward (eds) *Net Gain? Political Parties and the Internet*, London: Routledge, pp. 98–119.

Coleman, S. (2001a) 'Online campaigning', *Parliamentary Affairs*, 54(3), 679–88.

Coleman, S. (2001b) *2001: Cyber Space Odyssey*, London: Hansard Society.

Copsey, N. (2003) 'Extremism on the net: the far right and the value of the internet', in R. Gibson, P. Nixon and S. Ward (eds) *Net Gain? Political Parties and the Internet*, London: Routledge, pp. 218–33.

Dorling, D., Eyre, H., Johnston, R. and C. Pattie (2002) 'A good place to bury bad news? Hiding the detail in the geography on the Labour Party's website', *Political Quarterly*, 73(4): 476–92.

Gibson, R., Lusoli, W. and S. Ward (2006) 'Online participation in the UK: testing a contextualised model of internet effects', *British Journal of Politics and International Relations*, 8(1), (forthcoming).

Gibson, R., Margolis, M., Resnick, D. and S. Ward (2003) 'Election Campaigning on the WWW in the US and UK: a comparative analysis', *Party Politics*, 9(1): 47–76.

Jackson, J. (2001) 'View from the parties: the Conservatives', in S. Coleman (ed.) *2001: Cyber Space Odyssey*, London: Hansard Society.

Lusoli, W., Ward, S. and R. Gibson (2005) 'Reconnecting politics? Parliament, the public and the internet'. Paper presented to the Political Studies Association Conference, University of Leeds, 6 April.

Lusoli, W. and S. Ward (2004) 'Digital rank and file: activists' perceptions and use of the internet', *British Journal of Politics and International Relations*, 7(4), 453–70.

Margolis, M. and D. Resnick (2000) *Politics as Usual: The Cyberspace Revolution*, Thousand Oaks, CA: Sage.

Norris, P. (2000) *A Virtuous Circle*, Cambridge: Cambridge University Press.

Norris, P. (2001) *Digital Divide*, Cambridge: Cambridge University Press.

Rash, W. (1997) *Politics on the Nets: Wiring the Political Process*, New York: Freeman.

Street, J. (1997) 'Citizenship and mass communication', *Contemporary Political Studies, Vol. 1*, Belfast: Political Studies Association, pp. 502–10.

Sunstein, C. (2001) *Republic.com*, Princeton, NJ: Princeton University Press.

Ward, S. and R. Gibson (1998) 'The first internet election? UK political parties and campaigning in cyberspace', in I. Crewe, B. Gosschalk and J. Bartle (eds) *Political Communications: Why Labour Won the General Election of 1997*, London: Frank Cass, pp. 93–112.

Ward, S. and R. Gibson (2003) 'Online and on-message? Candidate websites in the 2001 general election', *British Journal of Politics and International Relations*, 5(2): 188–205.

Ward, S., Gibson, R. and P. Nixon (2003) 'Political parties and the internet: an overview', in R. Gibson, P. Nixon and S. Ward (eds) *Net Gain? Political Parties and the Internet*, London: Routledge, pp. 11–38.

Solihull

The result in Solihull emphasised the continuing problems of the Conservative Party. Whilst the party enjoyed a revival in the South and South East, the upsurge in fortunes petered in the Midlands. Few anticipated the loss of Solihull to the Liberal Democrats, on a remarkable 10 per cent swing.

The Conservatives failed to gain any urban seats in the Midlands, despite holding potential targets including nearby Edgbaston, although they did perform much better in rural areas. Solihull appeared a rare entity, a safe Conservative urban seat. An affluent part of the West Midlands, a prosperous seat on the fringe of Birmingham with a middle-class population, high owner-occupation, high-performing schools and low unemployment, it did not feature on the Liberal Democrats' target list, the party having beaten Labour by only 200 votes in 2001, to come a distant runner-up. The Midlands could not be described pre-2005 as an area of Liberal Democrat strength.

Yet the Conservatives' contender, John Taylor, who had held this seat without discomfort since 1983 and who had enjoyed a fractional swing from the Liberal Democrats at the 2001 election, saw his majority disappear. The Conservative campaign was lacklustre and lacking in focus, whereas the Liberal Democrats' promise to replace council tax, allied to the addressing of local grievances and the energetic campaign of Lorely Burt played well with the local electorate (Wyre Forest, not too far away and held by an Independent, offered a useful reminder of the importance of a local focus). The Liberal Democrats also appeared to benefit from tactical voting from Labour supporters keen to unseat the Conservative incumbent. Labour's vote fell by 10 per cent, whilst the Liberal Democrats' share soared by 14 per cent.

Result		%
Burt, L. (LD)	20,896	39.9
Taylor, J. (Con)	20,617	39.4
Vaughan, R. (Lab)	8,058	15.4
Carr, D. (BNP)	1,752	3.4
Moore, A. (UKIP)	990	1.9
LD gain from Con		
LD majority	279	0.5

Turnout: 67.2%

13
Election Unspun?
Mediation of the Campaign

David Deacon and Dominic Wring

Culture Secretary Tessa Jowell spoke for many politicians when she complained that the 2005 general election was really about two distinct campaigns. The combatants in the second, less obvious, case were not the two main rival parties, but the candidates fighting to secure support and the journalists seeking to report their efforts. Jowell adhered to a widespread view that there were distinctive 'air' and 'ground' wars taking place and that the latter was an arguably more critical dimension in an election that had long been interpreted as an effort to encourage people just to vote following the marked fallout in participation last time. Politicians' and journalists' combined efforts to get public attention and even their endorsements would be challenged in various ways. The most obvious one was the multitude of rival stories that vied for the news agenda including major happenings like the death, burial and selection of a new Pope as well as the long expected marriage between the Prince of Wales and his partner Camilla Parker-Bowles. Allied to this, dramatic events such as the announcement of the impending collapse of MG Rover and the vicious, seemingly unprovoked attack on a young mother also deflected attention from politics and elections. Arguably though it was the combined dominance of celebrity and lifestyle culture, particularly but not exclusively in the popular redtop newspapers, that underlined that the election and those fighting it would have to fight even harder to be seen and heard in a favourable light. It is then perhaps not surprising that one of the most effective media-driven political interventions during the last Parliament was from the television chef Jamie Oliver's Channel 4-sponsored crusade to change the poor quality of food served to the nation's schoolchildren. Such populist interventions and their celebrity-style informality would also be a marked feature of the 2005 campaign.

The 'phoney' war

Since at least 1992 and on some occasions before then, British general elections have been preceded by a 'phoney' or pre-election in which major politicians have come to increasingly rely on image consultants, spin doctors and other presentational experts to promote their case. The degree to which this is happening has led many to argue politics is in the grip of a permanent campaign but whilst this may have been the case in the first Labour term, the Iraq invasion seriously hampered attempts by the government to manage the news agenda during the second (Wring 2005). Iraq harmed Tony Blair's public image and brought into question his trustworthiness on this and a whole range of issues. In approaching the 2005 campaign Blair and his strategists attempted to seize back the initiative by launching a so-called 'masochism' strategy that centred on him appearing in a variety of broadcast formats in an attempt to win back the confidence of those voters he had previously alienated. The Prime Minister did so in the knowledge his incumbency and media abilities appeared to give him a distinct advantage over his rivals Charles Kennedy and more especially Michael Howard.

The most significant event of the pre-campaign involved the three main party leaders as guests on their own individual day of Channel 5 programming. Although the appearances were not part of the formal election they were transmitted in February during a period potentially crucial for many millions of people making their decisions on how to vote. This factor was no doubt important in encouraging Tony Blair and his opponents to answer questions on special editions of the channel's topical audience-participation mid-morning *Wright Stuff* programme and an early evening debate presented by Kirsty Young. The later format led to sustained and robust questioning, primarily because the interrogation was restricted to half a dozen or so invited members of the public challenging the leaders who were able to explore, over the course of a few minutes, a topical issue of special relevance to them. Blair, for instance, was closely cross-examined by a nurse who demanded whether he would work in the health service doing unpleasant but vital duties for comparatively poor pay. The directness of the questioner and her fellow female guests was picked up by the national press, but also noteworthy were the searching interventions from male participants on Iraq, tuition fees and education. Ultimately, though, the impact of these largely well-executed interviews was overshadowed by the intervention of a woman heckler who tackled Blair with a specific complaint about the treatment of her son. The case, though picked up and used by the Conservatives, arguably reinforced Blair's message that he was prepared to listen to irate voters. Yet like much of the debate in the subsequent election, the more substantive exchanges between voters and politicians that had taken place on Channel 5 during the day were neglected in favour of reporting an unexpected event with a charismatic protagonist, compelling human interest dimension and/or good pictures.

The Prime Minister aided by an uncharacteristically low-profile Alastair Campbell and David Hill, Campbell's successor at Downing Street, exploited his incumbency to an almost unprecedented degree in other ways. Aside from the masochism strategy Blair was a guest in a series of the less formal programmes he had long cultivated but which he now appeared on in a far more compressed space of time prior to his announcement of the election. These included a debate with an invited audience of young people on the popular Channel 4 Sunday lunchtime strand *T4* in January before which a film of presenter June Sarpong shadowing the Prime Minister for a day was broadcast. Media commentators were cynical about Blair's intent but some viewers were evidently impressed by the party leader's candour as one first time elector later acknowledged when she admitted to supporting Labour on the strength of his 'fantastic' performance (*Guardian*, 21 April 2005). Blair followed this with guest appearances on the GMTV breakfast show and Channel 4's *Richard and Judy* in an effort designed to particularly appeal to the concerns and issues of so-called 'school-gate mums' and their 'hard-working families', key target audiences identified by pollsters and who both played a significant part in developing Labour's approach to this campaign. The Prime Minister even agreed to be the celebrity guest on the Channel 4 programme's 'You Say We Pay' interlude where he attempted to win a cash prize for a caller.

The Prime Minister's inability to answer many of the questions in the game show element of the *Richard and Judy* programme demonstrated the potentially embarrassing consequences of his strategy, specifically that he was not as in touch with popular culture as he made out. Nevertheless his preparedness to court the kinds of mass audiences who increasingly avoided traditional current affairs programming led him to accept the invite to feature on ITV1's popular *Saturday Night Takeaway* where presenters Little Ant and Dec interviewed him in Downing Street in a discussion in which the junior protagonists made fun of him. This and the other appearances broke new ground and it would have been unthinkable for a serving Prime Minister to have contemplated allowing this particular form of access a generation ago for fear of the adverse public reaction. Now the response was likely to be more journalistic cynicism, but this was ultimately of marginal importance to a politician when set against the opportunity to reach millions of undecided voters. Labour strategists also reasoned this kind of self-promotion played to strengths Blair's main rival Michael Howard did not possess. Howard responded with a photo opportunity alongside his extended family and his wife made a number of interventions during the ensuing campaign, notably as a solo if less than animated guest of the ITV1 lunchtime talk show *Loose Women*. In 2001 her predecessor Ffion Hague had been curiously muted and rarely seen anywhere but by her husband's side. By contrast Cherie Booth played a more formal part of the Labour campaign by making a speech, although the intervention against the anti-war Respect coalition attracted less mainstream comment than it might have done if she had attacked the Conservatives in the same way. Charles Kennedy and his wife Sarah received considerably more coverage following the arrival of their new baby son Donald during the opening stages of the campaign. The self-conscious appearance of so many family members in this way offered a strikingly domesticated image in sharp contrast to the momentous events that had preceded the campaign and the bitterness of an election that was about to unfold.

Broadcasting

In sharp contrast to 2001, Blair made a relatively low-key announcement of the election date and immediately embarked on a helicopter trip to his party's most marginal seat in Dorset where he was greeted by the kind of photogenic crowd of invited supporters that would dominate most of his visits around the country. The only journalists who regularly made up his entourage came from the BBC, ITN, Sky and the Press Association because space was restricted to what were deemed to be the most important news media. Consequently a marked feature of the campaign was the way other excluded correspondents made a point of reporting their travels round Britain by helicopter, car, motor home, scooter or even motorcycle sidecar in pursuit of Blair, other leading figures and floating voters. By doing this the politicians and media were endorsing an increasingly popular view that they needed to go beyond the confines of Westminster to reach out to the public and, more especially, those who had abstained in the previous general election.

Party strategists increasingly recognised the importance of developing a rapport with local rather than just national media as a means of reaching voters as regional journalists were perceived as being more interested in the substantive issues and in touch with their audiences. Furthermore, the lack of previous contact between local media and central government was likely to make for a more meaningful dialogue devoid of the cynicism or even sycophancy characteristic of the Westminster lobby. The controlled if somewhat suddenly announced regional visits to seats by different politicians meant there were relatively few meaningful encounters between electors and the elected. There were, however, some altercations between Michael Howard, John Prescott, Charles Kennedy and assorted hecklers, protesters and determined journalists like BBC2 *Newsnight*'s Michael Crick and ITV1's Nick Robinson. Tony Blair avoided most of this courtesy of a very obvious security cordon and his party's carefully planned invitation-only 'events', one of which did liven up when a Labour activist's daughter from Yorkshire accused Blair over his record in what had hitherto been another mundane visit.

The preponderance of public relations' 'pseudo events' involving staged encounters between politicians and their most loyal followers had a notable impact on other aspects of the campaign coverage. Protests from hecklers and cynical journalists aside, the relatively formulaic reporting of a succession of visits and soundbite driven speeches was a recurrent feature of news bulletins. By contrast the major live set-piece debates hosted by the broadcasters involving the leaders during the latter stages of the campaign enabled members of the public to directly vent their frustrations. ITV1's *Ask the Leader* devoted separate editions to each of the main party leaders as well as the nationalist allies from Scotland and Wales. The session with Michael Howard involved a particularly tense exchange over the perceived centrality of immigration to the Conservative case and the charge that it was promoting racism. The equivalent BBC *Question Time* debate took the form of a single programme in which all three main leaders appeared in separate half-hour slots. Blair was booed but Charles Kennedy appeared to come out of the encounter the least scathed, and seemed more at ease with his public interrogators than in his meeting with the feared BBC broadcaster Jeremy Paxman in the latter's series of televised interviews with each prime ministerial candidate.[1] Several commentators wrongly acclaimed the *Question Time* debate's apparent novelty (the same format had been used as early as 1983) as the next best thing to the much-lobbied-for live debate between the leaders. Despite assorted journalists' demands for such a broadcast contest it is likely to be some time before a Prime Minister concedes to being directly cross-examined by his main opponents.

Most radio coverage of the general election was provided by the BBC. Local, regional and national stations all approached the campaign with a clear focus on their audiences' interests or, in some cases, the limits of their patience. Radio 4 catered for the more politically engaged with its flagship morning programme *Today* featuring in-depth analysis and characteristically direct questioning of leading politicians from presenter John Humphrys and his colleagues. Similarly, the station's other main news coverage and features like *Any Questions* debate also devoted themselves to the election. There was, however, one significant change from recent campaigns with the downgrading of *Election Call*, traditionally an agenda-setting morning co-production with either BBC1 or BBC2 but which was now not simultaneously broadcast with either of them. Furthermore, the audience phone-in programme was relegated to a slot after Radio 4's *World at One* and its loss of prominence confirmed when the Prime Minister declined to make a traditional appearance on its last edition. Blair also failed to play his intended part alongside his political rivals in *UK Leaders Live*, an independent radio network debate simultaneously broadcast across a range of affiliates.

Conscious of its demographic reach to younger people, Blair was more accommodating of Radio 1's question-and-answer session than he had been with other stations. Radio 1's innovative *Newsbeat* programme also carefully tailored its reporting of the campaign and provided additional information on a special website. Older audiences were also catered for with Jeremy Vine's show as it toured round the country providing the main focal point for Radio 2 coverage. The talk-based Radio 5 Live inevitably devoted airtime to the election and the opinions of politicians and others including the actor and 'official' Labour supporter Kevin Whately who called up the programme to make his case like any other member of the public. However, the most unexpected intervention of this kind came prior to the formal campaign and involved Tony Blair making a surprise appearance on presenter Jono Coleman's final broadcast for London's Heart FM radio. A dumbfounded Coleman responded to the Prime Minister's praise by suggesting he was in fact impersonator Jon Culshaw; Blair's attempts to confirm his identity made it a surreal exchange.

If the politicians were given ample opportunity by broadcasters to promote themselves, these news media also attempted to assert their own agendas. For instance, BBC's *The Politics Show* and presenter Andrew Neil's other strands together with BBC2's *Newsnight* and its Saturday special tried to offer their own particular take on events. Similarly, concern with voter engagement led to the creation of ITV1's *Ballot Box Jury* and its interviews with floating voters whilst *Newsnight*'s Student House performed a similar function, providing insights into how a largely undecided group of young people made up their minds over the course of the campaign. Sky News did this by concentrating on public concerns in the key marginal constituency of Darwen and Rossendale in Lancashire. Likeminded features formed the basis of the regional coverage provided by the BBC and ITV local news media, and if this was not enough election watchers could also follow the campaign on the round-the-clock BBC News 24, BBC Parliament, ITV, Sky and CNN news channels, some of which provided live broadcasts of the party's morning press conferences.

The rise of and debate over spin encouraged media inquisitiveness and interrogations of the various parties' well rehearsed claims; Channel 4 News, 'Factcheck', ITV1 News, 'Unspun' and other broadcast features consciously applied a technique popularised in American reporting of politics to subject candidates' statements, claims and the facts they based them on to expert scrutiny. 'Body language' specialists also appeared on at least three of the terrestrial networks to hold forth on what politicians' gestures could tell us about them and their motives. One appeared in a Channel 4 series of 'Election Unspun' documentaries that also offered compelling insights into matters that were in danger of being neglected by the mainstream campaign. To this end BBC3 offered a quirky film about the history of heckling and had two trainees attempting but failing to unnerve various politicians at live events. They did, however, manage to aggravate the Conservative press office. Elsewhere BBC1's *Panorama* continued with its hard-hitting series of programmes on different social policies which, though not explicitly linked to the election, were nevertheless of great relevance.

Table 13.1 lists the top ten themes covered by all national news media during the formal campaign (4 April–6 May 2005). The dominant topic was the election process, a hybrid that covers the reporting of public opinion polls, party strategies, publicity initiatives and related themes. This is by no means a new phenomenon but it is noteworthy that the attention given the subject was even greater than in the last election when media and opposition criticism of 'spin' had become a recurrent feature of political debate. Here a particular concern was the apparent rise of voter disaffection and how this might be analysed and better understood. The second most prominent theme was impropriety, a theme analogous to sleaze, which appeared in 1997, and politicians' conduct (principally John Prescott punching a protester) in 2001. Here the emphasis was on allegations relating to new rules that had encouraged a great increase in postal voting. Significantly, a timely and highly critical statement by Richard Mawrey, the judge presiding over a fraud case in Birmingham involving Labour victors in the 2004 local elections, intensified criticisms of the government. The *Daily Mail* was particularly vehement in attacking ministers and claimed the scale of postal balloting amounted to a 'corruption of democracy itself'.

Table 13.1 The issue agenda: top 10 themes in national media coverage

Theme	2001	Prominence (%)	2005	Prominence (%)
1	Electoral process	39	Electoral process	44
2	Europe	9	Political impropriety	8
3	Health	6	Iraq	8
4	Politicians' conduct	6	Asylum and immigration	7
5	Taxation	6	Taxation	5
6	Crime	4	Health	4
7	Education	4	Crime	4
8	Public services	4	Economy	4
9	Social security	3	Education	3
10	Other	19	Other	13

Sources: Loughborough University Communication Research Centre; *Guardian*, 2 May 2005.

Whilst the postal fraud issue seemed to favour the Conservatives' agenda, the third theme, 'Iraq', reinforced that of the Liberal Democrats. Although not a major aspect of the earlier stages of the campaign, the invasion became a key debating point later on with the leak and then publication of the controversial memo by Attorney General Lord Goldsmith on the legality of Blair's support for the US government's military action in the absence of UN sanction. Goldsmith's words were scrutinised and, more importantly, the wider issue revisited at arguably the most inopportune moment for Labour. The Prime Minister once again had his personal integrity called into question by Michael Howard who labelled him a 'liar' and Charles Kennedy who once again criticised Blair's judgement. Where Iraq partly dominated the final full week of the campaign, the next-placed item, asylum and immigration, had been more of an issue during the preceding fortnight. Media attention to the topic had been sustained by newspaper coverage of the issue going back some years and, more particularly, a controversial *Express* series of lead stories midway through the last Parliament. The central claims that the government was failing to control immigration and that the asylum system was in chaos were given renewed impetus by the Conservatives' own focus on an issue where the party enjoyed one of its few substantial leads in the polls over Labour. The conviction of illegal migrant Kamel Bourgass for the killing of a police officer gave the government's media and political critics another prime opportunity to raise the issue.

It was a telling feature of the election how few substantive policy issues arose and even where 'bread and butter' topics of major interest to voters were discussed, these debates tended to focus on particular case stories such as the outbreak of the hospital superbug, MRSA, or the case of a frustrated patient waiting for an operation to the detriment of wider discussion about other important aspects of NHS provision. Similarly, Europe was marginalised as an issue as were other critical areas of public policy such as transport, Northern Ireland and housing.

Newspapers

Whilst British broadcasting and satellite remains heavily regulated by statute to guard against party political and other biased reporting, the so-called 'free press' are able to editorialise and slant news to suit their own varied perspectives. Audiences realise this and consistently place television and radio above the print media as a reliable source of information. This has not, however, prevented certain newspaper proprietors, editors and journalists from expressing forthright opinions, especially during election campaigns. Yet the agenda-setting 'Tory press' of the 1980s is no more and there has been a notable pattern of dealignment in recent years whereby titles have been more likely to publish criticisms of their favoured politicians or, perhaps more importantly, articles sympathetic towards or even written by those whose views they oppose. Labour, or more particularly its leader, benefited from this trend in the 1990s and the personal focus on him rather than the party gave rise to the 'Tony press' (Wring 2002; Deacon and Wring 2002). Table 13.2 shows the declared political support of the press in the 2001 and 2005 elections.

Rupert Murdoch was a leading protagonist in creating the 'Tony press'. His decision to switch the support of bestselling *Sun* and its *News of the World* sister paper from Conservative to Labour became a major media talking point during the 1997 general election given the way these titles had mercilessly lambasted

Table 13.2   Declarations of national newspapers, 2001 and 2005

	2001		2005	
Daily press		*Circulation (m)*		*Circulation (m)*
Guardian	Labour	0.40	Labour	0.34
Independent	Anti-Cons	0.23	Lib Dem	0.23
The Times	Labour	0.71	Labour	0.65
Telegraph	Conservative	1.02	Conservative	0.87
Financial Times	Labour	0.49	Labour	0.38
Daily Express	Labour	0.96	Conservative	0.87
Daily Mail	Anti-Labour	2.40	Conservative	2.30
Sun	Labour	3.45	Labour	3.26
Mirror	Labour	2.79	Labour	2.29
Star	Labour	0.60	No preference	0.85
Sunday press				
Observer	Labour	0.45	Labour	0.42
Independent on Sunday	Anti Labour Landslide	0.25	Lib Dem	0.18
Sunday Times	Labour	1.37	Conservative	1.35
Sunday Telegraph	Conservative	0.79	Conservative	0.65
Mail on Sunday	Conservative	2.33	Anti-Labour	2.37
Sunday Express	Labour	0.90	Conservative	0.84
Sunday Mirror	Labour	1.87	Labour	1.53
News of the World	Labour	3.90	Labour	3.64
People	Labour	1.37	Labour	0.94
Star on Sunday	n/a	n/a	No preference	0.46

Source: Audit Bureau of Circulation.

Blair's party before then. The endorsement was viewed as a pre-emptive act by Murdoch to protect his UK business interests from future government scrutiny. During the run-up to the 2005 election there was speculation as to whether the proprietor might order the *Sun* to switch its support from Labour, with the paper even arguing 'our mind has yet to be made up' near the beginning of the campaign, although it was unequivocal about the Liberal Democrats whom it dismissed as a 'pathetic shambles'. Ultimately the likelihood of another Blair victory made the possibility of partisan change remote and the paper's prevarication limited any impact on the result it might have had.

When the *Sun* finally declared for Labour, it released red smoke from an office roof in a stunt resembling the recent announcement of the new Pope. The front-page editorial 'One Last Chance' and other comments such as 'Blair still has a big job to do until his place in history is guaranteed' underlined the conditionality of its support for the government. There were also warnings that perennial *Sun* concerns such as crime, immigration and welfare needed to be addressed, although the fiercely pro-war paper also mounted a strong defence of Blair after challenges to his trustworthiness in a debate over Iraq that intensified towards the end of the campaign. Just prior to polling day the *Sun* also managed to include an interview with 'Tony and Cherie' in which the couple were asked highly personal questions under the suggestive headline 'Why Size Matters'.

Overall, the *Sun*, like a number of redtops and its *News of the World* sister, downplayed much of the election and preferred to lead on the type of celebrity-driven items it felt were of more interest to its youthful readership. There were even attempts to combine the two stories with the launch of a 'Get out and vote' campaign featuring various personalities including Americans like Britney Spears. The paper also emblazoned some of its election coverage with three models in states of undress to represent the parties in a feature that had dominated the limited campaign reporting in the rival *Star* in 2001. The similarity is instructive because the latter newspaper is the only national title to have noticeably gained in circulation terms since then; the *Star* is also the publication in Table 13.2 that had the least to say about the general election, an acknowledgement perhaps of the fact that a majority of its largely pro-Labour audience had not voted in 2001 and would not in 2005. Significantly and uniquely, the *Star* was the only national newspaper to express no clear preference for or against any party.

Though owned by the same company as the *Star*, the *Express* titles offered a very clear message to their readers to endorse the Conservatives. The daily had been particularly vociferous in attacking Labour for having, in its view, neglected to take firmer action against illegal asylum seekers. This was to be expected given the paper had retracted its support and returned to its traditional pro-Conservative position in 2004 following the accession of Michael Howard to the leadership. Ideological consistency, clearer leadership and commercial success made the paper's mid-market rival the *Daily Mail* a more formidable political force. It, too, pursued Labour on many issues, but also made specific criticisms of Blair's own perceived failings as a leader. The *Mail* came out with a more emphatic statement in support of Howard than in 2001 when it had focused its entire editorial on attacking the government. Interestingly, the slightly more liberal *Mail on Sunday* did the reverse by changing its pro-Conservative stance to one that remained stridently anti-Labour, but also acknowledged the Liberal Democrats as a party worthy of support.

The other most politically consistent newspaper is the *Mirror* which, for many years, was the only popular title to support Labour. Former editor Piers Morgan's fierce denunciation of the Iraq invasion weakened the paper's standing within Downing Street and further deteriorated a relationship that had already been strained by the Prime Minister's courting of its bitter *Sun* rival with exclusive stories and favours (Morgan 2005). Morgan's departure improved the situation and, motivated by a concern that it needed to mobilise the overwhelmingly pro-Labour *Mirror* readership, Blair wrote a handwritten appeal for publication in the paper, declaring: 'Only you can make sure Britain keeps going forward with Labour rather than back with the Tories.' Successive editorials, features and stories responded in kind by making the case for a third term alongside items on the Conservative threat. The polling day edition underlined the message with a graphic front-page portrayal of Michael Howard as a vanquished vampire under the headline 'Vote Labour – there is too much at stake'. The *Sunday Mirror* and *People* followed a similar though less engaged editorial line, mindful of the former's editor Tina Weaver's view that front-page political stories 'are nigh on commercial suicide – unless we're looking at the shenanigans of cabinet ministers' (*Observer*, 24 April 2005).

Like the *Mirror*, the *Guardian* and latterly the *Independent* had been repositories of anti-Tory sentiments during the 1980s and had thus consolidated their reputations among left-of-centre readers. Their criticism of government did not, however, desist once Labour got elected and there were often tense exchanges over various issues, notably Iraq. Ministers often singled out the *Guardian*, the most popular newspaper with their party members, for particular criticism for the way it opposed many new initiatives. Yet the newspaper once again endorsed the government in spite of the fiercely divergent opinions on the election expressed in its guest columns and letters' pages: denunciations of Blair were matched by an offer from journalist Polly Toynbee to send nose pegs to reluctant Labour voters in the hope of persuading them to the polls. Furthermore, several front-page stories published during the campaign framed issues in a way that promoted the government's position. Sunday sister the *Observer* did likewise but there was no rapprochement between the *Independent* titles and a party they had both briefly endorsed in 1997. Motivated by a firmly anti-war position, both newspapers gave media representation to the upsurge in public sympathy for the Liberal Democrats. The *Independent* betrayed its sentiments by devoting considerable coverage to the defection of former Labour MP Brian Sedgemore to the party and portrayed it as 'a signal moment' and symptomatic of a wider electoral trend apparent in the polls and confirmed on election day.

There was some speculation that the *Telegraph* newspapers might soften their attitudes or even support the government following their group's acquisition by the Barclay brothers. Various restructuring plans and editorial changes did not, however, result in a notable shift of political emphasis and both titles not only continued with their criticisms of Blair and his party but were some of the Conservative leadership's more fervent supporters. The *Telegraph*'s traditional centre-right rival *The Times* continued with its position of supporting the government, having closely aligned itself with Blair's controversial foreign policy decisions, notably over Iraq. It was an agenda shared by all of proprietor Rupert Murdoch's newspapers worldwide. Interestingly an article by Murdoch's economist Irwin Stelzer shortly before the campaign argued 'Why Brown is Wrong for No. 10' and gave a strong hint that the businessman's patience with the government might not outlast Blair's departure.

The Times finally declared its position on the election by arguing that Labour should remain in office with a reduced majority, more Conservative representation and the defeat of a number of named left-wingers from the government backbenches. By contrast the *Sunday Times*, which has always boasted a different, more strident political if not partisan approach to its sister paper, made successive attempts to embarrass the government with the publication of a leaked memo from Alastair Campbell to his fellow strategists and an even more sensitive civil servant document relating confidential advice authored prior to the invasion of Iraq. The newspaper also made the alarming claims that there were an estimated 500,000 illegal immigrants, approximately 1 per cent of the population, currently in the UK. It was then of little surprise when the *Sunday Times* finally declared for the Conservatives reversing its albeit tepid support for Labour last time.

The Times and Financial Times' support of Labour meant they were the only two papers that voted differently to their audiences' first-choice party, although it is worth noting that both were the only titles to have at least a significant minority of readers (20 per cent or more) voting for each of the three main alternatives (Table 13.3). Even the *Star*'s declaration for no one was technically in line with its nominally pro-Labour followers because it was the only national with a majority of readers who did not vote in the general election, thereby extending a trend begun in 2001. The paper had in the past veered from Labour to Conservative and back again, but its stance, a perhaps still surprisingly rare position for a national newspaper, reflected some understanding of the market for news and that the election did not appear to be a primary or even significant interest for most purchasers. Arguably, the ability of the *Star* to counter the downward trend in circulation was linked to an aggressively celebrity-driven product that consciously emulated and provided a daily equivalent of successful glossy weekly and monthly magazines like *Heat* and *Take a Break*. The *Sun*, by comparison, may be contemplating whether to continue with its relatively highly political and politicised coverage.

Table 13.3 Readership allegiances of national daily newspapers, 2001 and 2005

Daily Press	Lab	Con	LD	Lab–Con (LD)
Result	36 (42)	33 (33)	23 (19)	swing 3.1
Guardian	43 (52)	7 (6)	41 (34)	8 (LD)
Independent	34 (38)	13 (12)	44 (44)	2 (LD)
The Times	27 (28)	38 (40)	28 (26)	1.5 (LD)
Telegraph	13 (16)	65 (64)	17 (14)	2
Financial Times	29 (30)	47 (48)	21 (21)	–
Daily Express	28 (33)	48 (43)	18 (19)	5
Daily Mail	22 (24)	57 (55)	14 (17)	2
Sun	45 (52)	33 (29)	12 (11)	5.5
Mirror	67 (71)	11 (11)	17 (13)	4 (LD)
Star	54 (56)	21 (21)	15 (17)	1

Source: Worcester et al. (2005).

Aside from editorial changes to its news content, the *Sun* may also be contemplating switching its partisan support back to the Conservatives in line with the steady though unspectacular rise in support for the party among its readership in this election. This is not to say the underlying right-wing ideological agenda of the paper is likely to change given it has remained largely in tact since Murdoch first imposed it a quarter of a century ago. The other most noteworthy swing amongst newspaper audiences replicated a wider shift of support to the Liberal Democrats that was contributed to, perhaps significantly in some seats, by the change of allegiance among those who read the titles most associated with Labour. The change among *Mirror* consumers was noticeable but made little difference to the overall pattern of support within the paper's constituency.

Advertising and new media

The major parties enjoy a major advantage in terms of the overall exposure the news media give them when compared with their smaller rivals. This ability to generate publicity is of course a reflection of their electoral status and greater resources in the form of expertise and funding for advertisements. The election was, however, noteworthy for the way the Liberal Democrats were able to mount a major marketing campaign courtesy of £2.4 million from City financier Michael Brown, a huge donation and the largest given to a third party for some time. The grant enabled the party's advertising agency to buy space in newspapers, on billboards and on certain popular websites to promote a core message that challenged the assumption that a vote for them was a wasted one. Other copy focused on key policy issues including health and also featured celebrities who had switched allegiance from Labour, such as Claire Rayner, Anita Roddick and former BBC Director General Greg Dyke. Leader Charles Kennedy, who was regarded as a major asset, appeared in many of the advertisements and also in several of the party election broadcasts, the most memorable of which had a boy representing Tony Blair 'crying wolf' in an attack on the government for having supported the Iraqi invasion based on a mistaken belief that weapons of mass destruction existed.

The Conservatives rehired the services of the Saatchi brothers' agency which was hardly surprising given one of them, Maurice, had previously been appointed Co-Party Chairman alongside the Shadow Cabinet member Liam Fox. Yet for all their experience it was widely believed that the main strategic acumen behind the Tories' campaign came from Lynton Crosby, an Australian political consultant who had played a major role in his native right-wing Liberal Party's successive election victories. The Conservative advertising did, however, resemble earlier Saatchi copy from previous campaigns because of the way the strong by-line 'Are You Thinking What We're Thinking' became one of the few memorable electoral messages. Most of the posters consisted of pointed questions which drew attention to apparent shortcomings of the Labour government, such as its alleged failure to deal with illegal immigration, rising violent crime and dirty hospitals. These advertisements included highly suggestive messages to voters claiming it was not racist to mention asylum or how they would feel if their own daughter was attacked by someone out on a government-backed parole scheme. The party election broadcasts conveyed a similar message, although they were slightly more upbeat. Leader Michael Howard was not widely regarded as a popular figure with the public although he had contributed to a revival in party morale following his election as its leader. Consequently, the presidential style of the campaign encouraged his strategists to devote a broadcast to endorsing Howard with comments from his senior colleagues which thus in a way also promoted the team.

Labour again used the services of the advertising agents TBWA, a firm managed by the high-profile sympathiser Trevor Beattie. The agency's more memorable work did not appear through the usual channels but on the party's website prior to the beginning of the formal campaign. An unflattering image of Michael Howard and his Shadow Chancellor Oliver Letwin as flying pigs was intended as an attack on their economic policies and appeared as one of four possible designs to be used on a site which asked members to vote for their favourite. The copy and another depicting Howard as a manipulative sorcerer-type figure were criticised for their allegedly anti-Semitic overtones given the politicians' Jewish ancestry. Labour denied the charge and quickly removed the offending items from the website, but they achieved the kind of exposure with that message that they never really achieved through their other, more 'official' advertising. The latter focused on promoting the government's role in sustaining economic growth and stability and suggested that a vote for the Conservatives risked this. In addition the affiliated trade union Unison launched its own advertising campaign against Letwin's alleged plans to cut public spending by £35 billion.

Michael Howard appeared in other Labour advertising, most notably a party election broadcast designed to remind voters of his record as minister implicated in some of the Thatcher and Major governments' more controversial measures. This, other party election broadcasts and most of the advertising stressed a contentious belief that the Conservatives might retake office by default, involving the mass abstention or defection to alternatives by Labour voters. The consequences of this were addressed in one broadcast featuring loyal supporters extolling the virtues of the National Health Service and the party's role in its formation. The most striking party election broadcast was, however, carefully directed and edited by Anthony Minghella, the Oscar-winning director of *The English Patient*. Minghella's film centred on the relationship between its two featured protagonists, Tony Blair and Gordon Brown, and attempted to demonstrate that media stories of their allegedly deteriorating relationship were more speculative than based on fact. The broadcast did not convince some of the critics.

Conclusion

The 2005 general election was noteworthy for the understated and in some cases limited coverage many news media organisations gave the campaign. Their approach was motivated by a number of factors, but none more so than a perception, reinforced by the dramatic fall in turnout in 2001, that a significant minority of their audience was not particularly interested in the election. In a highly competitive media market boasting hundreds of rival publications and channels vying for audience attention, producers of campaign-related coverage gave considerable thought as to how they might make their offerings more attractive and interesting to new and existing viewers, readers and listeners. Here there is a clear worry among the more commercially minded that any further loss of consumers could have a significant and detrimental effect on their profitability in terms of advertising revenues. This could lead to even more dramatic changes in coverage in the future, all predicated on a similar assumption, specifically that elections are boring and do not shift product or boost shareholders' profits. It will be interesting to see how certain news media, the *Sun* in particular, attempt to straddle their self-styled roles of being in touch with popular opinion and also leading it. Britain's bestselling daily continues to decline and with it might go its fortunes and influence.

Looking through the television schedules, radio programming and newspaper articles during the 2005 campaign it is striking how compartmentalised the election coverage was into certain pages or time slots and how easily avoidable it all was for many citizens, and especially the growing number with access to new media technologies and who could thus follow any of a myriad of interests. It is notable how in this election strategists tried to bypass the problem by placing their candidates and their family members into the widest range of media possible and in doing so probably spent as much time preparing candidates for appearances on talk shows and other supposedly 'soft' programming as they did for the major set-piece interviews. Allied to this trend another commentator has noted how the parties are responding to audience desertion from the news media by seeking to communicate their case more directly to prospective supporters with 'more sophisticated messages [that] are being highly targeted and taking place out of sight of the mass media' (Fraser 2005). The 2005 general election may be remembered as the campaign when journalists and politicians finally awoke to the realities of living in a diverse, multichannel age. Arguably some of the voters did likewise by turning over or switching off.

Note

1. Philip Cowley, a fellow contributor to this volume, was present at the studio debate and recognised that Blair suffered a disadvantage appearing last on the programme given the rising temperature in the auditorium caused by the heat of the lighting, not to mention the heightened passions among those present in the audience.

References

Deacon, D. and Wring, D. (2002) 'Partisan dealignment and the British press', in J. Bartle, I. Crewe and B. Gosschalk (eds) *Political Communications: The British General Election of 2001*, London: Frank Cass.

Fraser, D. (2005) 'Election 2005 – the Media Campaign', in S. Herbert et al. (eds) *The UK Election 2005 in Scotland*, Edinburgh: Scottish Parliament Information Centre.

Morgan, P. (2005) *The Insider*, London: Ebury.

Worcester, B., Baines, P. and Mortimore, R. (2005) *Explaining Labour's Landslip*, London: Politicos.

Wring, D. (2002) 'The Tony press', in A. Geddes and J. Tonge (eds) *Labour's Second Landslide: The British General Election 2001*, Manchester: Manchester University Press.

Wring, D. (2005) 'Politics and the Media: the Hutton Inquiry, Public Relations State and Crisis at the BBC', *Parliamentary Affairs* 58 (2), 380–93.

Bolton West

Bolton West is a 'classic' marginal, the sort of seat held by whichever party is in the ascendancy. Except in 1979, when it stayed Labour – but only until 1983 – Bolton West has returned a winner from the governing party at each election since 1964. As a barometer seat, it was always going to be a hard-fought contest, all the more so given the status of the defending MP.

Education Minister Ruth Kelly took the seat for Labour in 1997, on an 11.3 per cent swing, when aged only 29. Tipped for high office, she appeared to be fulfilling her potential. In the 2005 election, Kelly was highlighted by *The Times* (2 May 2005) as a candidate who should be returned by the electorate, the paper declaring: 'A shrewd elector in Bolton might well ask who would be the most credible advocate of their personal and collective interests in the next House of Commons. They should conclude that the able Ms Kelly is a smart bet in this regard.'

Yet Ms Kelly was defending a precarious majority in a seat far from natural Labour territory. Much of the constituency lies outside the town of Bolton and comprises suburban and rural land. Bolton West is comfortably the most affluent of the three Bolton seats, with unemployment at 3.6 per cent and the lowest percentage of unskilled and semi-skilled workers. For much of the 1980s and 1990s, the population had associated its aspirations with the Conservative Party. Having captured the seat, Kelly now faced the task of convincing them that Labour's economic record guaranteed continued prosperity. Labour did not greatly fear a backlash against the war; only 3 per cent of the constituency is Asian (mainly Muslim). Tax and the economy were bigger issues.

Kelly's campaign was marred briefly by an incident in which Fathers4Justice protestors attempted to handcuff her at a meeting. She was rescued by Veritas candidates, surely that party's major contribution to the election. The Conservative and Labour leaders visited the constituency in the final two weeks of the campaign. Blair argued that Conservative education plans for 'pupil passports' would 'strip the state system' (*Manchester Evening News*, 27 April 2005). Howard concentrated upon housing, immigration and reductions in council tax for pensioners.

The Conservative candidate, Philip Allot, could not achieve a coup which would have taken the gloss from Labour's overall victory. The 4.2 per cent swing he achieved was above average, but such is the size of Labour's post-1997 majorities in the North West that the 2005 election was about establishing beachheads for the Conservatives, rather than capturing seats. With her majority reduced to 2,064, Ruth Kelly faces the prospect of several years in Cabinet being accompanied by nagging concerns over the need to nurture a constituency certain to be a close contest next time.

Result		%
Kelly, R. (Lab)	17,239	42.5
Allot, P. (Con)	15,175	37.4
Perkins, T. (LD)	7,241	17.9
Ford, M. (UKIP)	524	1.3
Ford, M. (Veritas)	290	0.7
Griggs, K. (XPP)	74	0.2
Lab hold		
Lab majority	2,064	5.1
Swing: Lab to Con		4.2

Turnout: 63.5%

14

It's Not the Economy Stupid! The Disappearance of the Economy from the 2005 Campaign

Martin J. Smith

It has almost become a law of elections that the crucial issue affecting the outcome is the voters' perception of the economy. From the Sanders et al. (1987) model of the importance of voters' feelings about the economy to Bill Clinton's, 'It's the economy stupid', it is widely recognised that perceptions of economic competence and the state of the economy have a tremendous impact on the final result. Despite the salience of the economy in elections, the 2005 election was curious in terms of economic policy. Unlike most previous elections relatively little attention was paid to the economy during the campaign. According to polls, the economy was one of the key issues of the campaign. The last ICM poll before the election placed the economy second to the health service and equal with law and order, and slightly above education and taxation, as the most important issues for the electorate (ICM 2005). Whilst Labour was clearly regarded as the party with the highest level of economic competence, the irony for Labour was that its success with the economy meant the economy was less of a concern to voters. However, the election campaign was marked by a number of economic indicators which highlighted a fragility to Labour's economic miracle. A curious feature of the campaign was that neither the Conservatives nor the Liberal Democrats exploited Labour's track record on the economy. It is possible that Labour's reputation for economic competence was such that the opposition preferred to confront other aspects of Labour's programme. An alternative explanation is that in terms of economic policy the opposition parties had little different to offer and any sustained criticism of Labour's economic policy may have revealed their own weaknesses. Both the Conservative Party and the Liberal Democrats offered little new in terms of economic policy. In essence, for both parties their economic policy was based on modification of Labour's policy. This chapter will examine Labour's record on the economy before looking at the policies offered by the three main parties and the way that the economy played out in the 2005 campaign.

Labour's economic policy in government

Toynbee and Walker highlight why Labour by 2005 became perceived as so strong on the economy:

> The UK economy had kept growing during the global slowdown after the Internet bubble burst in 2000; indeed shops in the high street and staff at work were hardly aware of the a cycle at all. Growth was combined with the lowest price inflation for three decades, the lowest interest rates for forty years and the highest levels of employment in recorded history. (Toynbee and Walker 2005: 157)

In the 1990s the economy had grown by 1.7 per cent a year, in the new millennium it was 2.7 per cent a year.

It had, however, taken considerable effort on the part of the leadership for Labour to develop a reputation for economic competence. Labour left office in 1979 with its economic credibility in tatters. Unemployment was rising, inflation was high and economic productivity was declining. Political debate was defined by the perception that the British economy was in a permanent decline in relation to most of its international competitors. Following the economic problems of the 1970s, it took nearly 15 years for Labour to re-establish any belief amongst the electorate that it could be trusted with the British economy. The electorate's change of heart was more a consequence of Conservative failure in terms of Britain's expulsion from the European Exchange Rate Mechanism, rather than anything positive on the part of the Labour leadership. Nevertheless, throughout the 1980s and 1990s Labour had been concerned to reposition itself on the economy. It dropped Clause 4 of its constitution which committed Labour to nationalisation, it abandoned commitments to renationalise privatised industries, it moved away from its preferences for economic planning and intervention, and it became increasingly circumspect in terms of its commitments on public expenditure and taxation. The belief within the Labour Party leadership was that Labour's economic failures in government had resulted in Labour's inability to ensure a sustained period in government. The financial power in the City of London and international markets regarded Labour as profligate in spending and too willing to raise taxes, which were seen as disincentives to economic activity. So from 1987 one of the main elements in Labour's economic policy was the need to reassure the markets that they could run the economy. As a consequence, underpinning Labour's policy was a commitment to macro-economic stability.

What this meant was that Labour would aim for low inflation and sound public finances. The party also committed itself to not raising income tax and rejected any return to the public ownership or national economic planning that had existed in the 1970s.

In 1997 the new government attempted to institutionalise its new economic responsibility in three ways:

- In a radical and bold move Gordon Brown, the Chancellor of the Exchequer, announced that he would give independence to the Bank of England. The Bank can now set interest rates according to economic criteria rather than decision being made on political grounds by the Chancellor and/or the Prime Minister (for instance, despite all her free market rhetoric, Margaret Thatcher continually attempted to restrain Nigel Lawson when it came to increasing interest rates because of the impact that she thought it had on the votes of home owners) (Lawson 1992). What happens now is that the Chancellor sets an inflation target and the Bank has to set a rate which it believes is appropriate to achieving the target.
- The government, in order to reassure the markets on public expenditure, committed itself to keeping spending within the plans set by the Conservative government for the first two years of a Labour government.
- Gordon Brown announced his commitment to the 'golden rule': expenditure and income were to balance over the economic cycle and borrowing would only be for investment, and not for current expenditure such as benefits, salaries, and so on.

Labour and public expenditure

Whilst the government did stick to the Conservatives' levels of expenditure in the first two years, it redistributed money within the budget (so, for example, defence spending was cut whilst health expenditure was increased) and after the two year moratorium it increased expenditure significantly (see Table 14.1).

Table 14.1   Real increases in spending in six policy areas (%)

	Long-term trend	April 1979 to March 1997	April 1997 to March 2003	April 2003 to March 2006
Social security	3.7	3.5	1.7	2.0
NHS	3.6	3.0	5.6	7.3
Education	4.0	1.5	4.1	5.8
Defence	0.3	–0.3	–0.5	0.8
Transport	Na	0.5	1.8	4.9
Law and order	Na	4.0	4.8	1.1
GDP	2.4	2.1	2.8	2.8

Source: Emerson et al. (2003).

Table 14.1 illustrates a number of interesting things about public expenditure. The first is that both Labour and Conservative governments have cut expenditure on defence. Indeed, defence spending has declined from 5.6 per cent of GDP in 1963/64 to 2.4 in 2002/03. Second, despite the apparent antipathy of the Conservatives to the public sector and aspects of the welfare state, they increased public expenditure in health, education and social security. However, in both cases they increased at a slower rate than the general trend. Education in particular saw a much smaller growth. Labour on the other hand has increased spending on health and education well above trend. There can be little doubt that Labour has significantly shifted resources towards health and education in the period since 1997. In most cases in the post-war period government expenditure is close to trend. In other words, there has been a steady rise in public expenditure in the post-war period regardless of which party has been in power. However Labour has significantly increased expenditure on health and education above trend (Table 14.2). It is important to point out that expenditure on health in Britain continues to be below that of comparable countries like France, Germany, Italy and the United States.

Table 14.2   Departmental expenditure limits, 2002–06

	2002–03 (£m)	2003–04 (£m)	2004–05 (£m)	2005–06 (£m)	Annual average growth rate (%)
Education and Skills	23,170	25,600	27,750	31,140	7.6
Health	58,000	63,930	70,260	77,250	7.3
Transport	7,660	10,690	11,200	11,640	12.1
Office of the Deputy Prime Minister	6,030	6,730	7,230	7,570	5.2
Home Office	10,680	12,280	12,730	13,530	5.6
Defence	29,330	30,920	31,760	32,780	1.2
Foreign Office	1,350	1,450	1,500	1,590	2.8
International Development	3,370	3,700	3,840	4,590	8.1
Trade and Industry	4,740	5,110	5,130	5,540	2.8
Environment, Food and Rural Affairs	2,520	2,900	2,890	2,940	2.7
Work and Pensions	7,020	7,530	7,800	7,820	1.1
Scotland	18,210	19,720	20,880	22,320	4.4
Total departmental limits*	239,710	263,740	279,820	300,990	5.2

*Columns do not add to totals because some departments have not been included in table.

Source: <www.hm-treasury.gov.uk/spending_review/spend_plancontrol.cfm#Departmental_Expenditure_Limits>.

Whilst Labour has attempted to control and plan public expenditure, Labour's policy on public expenditure has been significantly different to that of the Conservatives:

1. They have made an explicit commitment to increasing public expenditure. It is seen as a good, rather than a bad, thing.
2. They have particularly focused spending on welfare policy and especially education and health.
3. A large amount of the expenditure has gone into increased jobs and pay increases, which has acted as a boost on the economy.
4. The deficit is greater than that allowed under the European Stability Pact and is stretching Gordon Brown's 'golden rule'. The Chancellor redefined the economic cycle after the election.

Whilst Labour leaders have distanced themselves from the Thatcherite agenda on public spending, they have attempted to be closer to the Conservatives on taxation.

Labour and taxation

Government, of course, has to pay for public expenditure and the way that it does this is through taxation. In 2003/04 the government received £9,020 for every adult in Britain and the largest source of this was through income tax (28.5 per cent) (Adam and Shaw 2003). Labour was keen to distance itself from the tax and spend policies that were seen as the core of the Keynesian welfare state. Labour was explicitly committed to not increasing income tax and appears to have abandoned the tax system as a mechanism for redistribution. However, despite the rhetoric Labour did raise extra income through the tax system. The first budget included a £5.2 billion windfall tax on privatised utilities and the taxes on pensions were changed raising a further £5.4 billion. Through abolition of the married couple's allowance and mortgage tax relief and with increased National Insurance, the Chancellor managed to raise extra money without increasing income tax. What is clear is that the tax burden has increased under New Labour, although they have not raised income tax. The Institute of Fiscal Studies (IFS) demonstrates that government receipts through taxation have increased from about 37 per cent of GDP to nearly 41 per cent of GDP (Adam and Shaw 2003: 4) (see Table 14.3). If we take taxation and public expenditure together, the Labour government has increased both spending and taxation. However, because of slower than predicted economic growth, there has been a decline in tax revenues and therefore the Public Spending Borrowing Requirement — the amount the government needs to borrow to meet its commitment is predicted to grow over the coming years.

An important development in recent years has been the introduction of tax credits. Rather than government just using the taxation system to take money from people they have also used it as a mechanism for giving money; in other words it has become part of the welfare system. Since April 2003 there have been two tax credits: the child tax credit and the working tax credit. In the case of the former, families receive credit in the tax for children, which is adjusted according to income. The working tax credit provides support for people with low working incomes. It is a way to encourage people on low incomes to work rather than to claim benefit.

Table 14.3　Sources of government revenue, 2003–04 forecasts

Source of revenue	2003–04 (£bn)	Proportion of total (%)
Income tax	122.1	28.5
National Insurance	74.5	17.4
Value added tax (VAT)	66.6	15.5
Fuel duties	23	5.4
Tobacco duties	8	1.9
Alcohol duties	7.4	1.7
Betting and gaming duties	1.3	0.3
Vehicle excise duty	4.8	1.1
Air passenger duty	0.8	0.2
Landfill tax	0.7	0.2
Insurance premium tax	2.2	0.5
Climate change levy	0.9	0.2
Customs duties and levies	1.9	0.4
Capital gains tax	1.2	0.3
Inheritance tax	2.4	0.6
Stamp duties	7.9	1.8
Corporation tax	30.8	7.2
Petroleum revenue tax	1.5	0.4
Business rates	18.6	4.3
Council tax	18.6	4.3
Other tax and royalties	11.9	2.8
Interests and dividends	4.0	0.9
Gross operating surplus and other receipts	17.2	4.0
Current receipts	428.3	100

Source: Adam and Shaw (2003).

Supply side policy

The other element of economic policy which has been important to government has been improving the supply side of the economy; in other words, attempting to improve the economy's efficiency and productivity. The government has been concerned to encourage investment and to improve the infrastructure, technology and the level of intervention. The government has also tried to reduce the red tape on business and through its taskforce on regulation it has attempted to prevent new controls acting as a disincentive to business. For many commentators the government developed a policy which is pro-business. It is for instance more concerned to reduce restrictions on the labour market than to protect the rights of workers through the acceptance of the EU's working hours directive. In many ways it has followed Conservative policy of allowing business to operate as freely as possible within the market. Indeed, one of the few areas where the Conservatives undertook a sustained attack on Labour's economic policy was over the issue of the level of increased red tape restricting business activity.

Labour has combined both elements of Conservative policy and traditional Labour policy in its economic approach. It has adopted Conservative prudence, the role of the market and the need to balance the budget. It has also promised not to increase income tax. On the other hand it has increased public expenditure and through a range of mechanisms it has increased the tax return to government. Nevertheless, Labour is pro-market and apart from the unusual cases of Railtrack and the Post Office, it is not committed to public ownership or economic intervention.

The economy and the election

The economy is traditionally one of the central elements of an election. In 1992 the Conservatives seemed to successfully undermine Labour's campaign by questioning their policies on tax and their economic competence. In 1997 Labour focused on the debacle of Black Wednesday (the day in September 1992 when Britain was forced out of the European Exchange Rate Mechanism. Following Black Wednesday, the Conservatives lost their reputation for economic competence and have not regained it since). Labour's commitment to limit public expenditure and not to increase income tax made it difficult for the Conservatives to portray Labour as a tax-and-spend party. In 2001 Labour emphasised their economic success, their ability to maintain economic growth and the extra money invested in public services. However, what is interesting about the 2005 election is that the economy played a relatively limited role in the campaign. Labour aimed, and repeatedly tried, to get the economy as the principal theme of the campaign agenda but the other parties were more concerned to focus on other issues such as Iraq, immigration and distrust of the Prime Minister. We can assume that the view amongst the Liberal Democrats and Conservative strategists was that they would lose the economic argument and focus attention on one of Labour's successes. As a consequence they did their best to avoid the issue. Yet there is evidence to suggest that the economy was not such a strong factor for the Labour government as the opposition parties believed, and that there were a number of indicators, both objective and subjective, which suggested that Labour was vulnerable on the economy. Indeed, a case can be made that the opposition's lack of attention to the economy was not necessarily because they believed Labour was vulnerable on other issues, but because they did not have an alternative. Any attempt to criticise Labour would have revealed the absence of any significant alternative and their own inability to deal with the problems of the British economy.

An examination of the policies of the three main parties on economic policy highlights the extent to which Labour currently dominates the economic agenda. Both Conservative and Liberal Democrat policies are a reaction to, rather than a critique of, Labour's economic policy. Labour's manifesto was based on maintaining the fiscal rules on borrowing and keeping debt low. According to the IFS it also seems likely that Labour will meet, or miss marginally, the rule at the end of the cycle in a year's time (Chote et al. 2005). Labour continued its commitment to not increasing income tax and Blair was forced to promise during the campaign that National Insurance would not be increased again to pay for health (which presumably does not rule out it being raised for other things). The commitment to full employment was retained with further supply-side commitments to more training. At the same time Labour renewed its emphasis on a market economy with promises on enterprise and further deregulation. Nevertheless, Labour promised not to privatise the Post Office. Fundamental to economic policy, however, was the commitment to continue to increase public expenditure in the areas of health and education. However, the claim in the manifesto is that much of the future expenditure will come from improvements in public sector efficiency. The Gershon Report, initiated by the Treasury to examine ways of reducing labour and increasing efficiency in government, identified £21 billion of savings which Labour is committed to reinvesting in front-line services.

One of the fascinating features of Labour's presentation of economic policy during the campaign was that it was almost completely national. Much of the debate in economics and political science during recent years, and indeed the Thatcherite critique of Keynesianism, is based on the assumption that economic policy is no longer national and that the decisions governments can make in terms of macro-economic policy are highly constrained. There is an interesting (and from their point of view rational) trend within governments to blame external factors for poor economic performance and difficult economic choices. As Hay points out, globalisation is often referred to by both Blair and Brown as a mechanism to justify why they have to abandon interventionist measures, restrict borrowing and push for a flexible (in other words lightly regulated) labour market (Hay 2003). However, at times of economic success governments are much more likely to take the credit themselves. Indeed, the whole rhetoric of Labour's campaign centred on how they had laid the framework for sustained economic growth. The renationalisation of economic policy perhaps explains the absence of the euro from the election campaign. Labour have moved from a position in 1997 when membership of the European Monetary System seemed relatively likely, to one during the 2005 campaign where both Blair and Brown seemed to remove any chance of membership in the lifetime of the new Parliament. This had the effect of choking off any debate concerning the economy and European integration during the campaign (see Chapter 17).

Conservative economic policy was based on cutting taxes and not continually increasing the level of public expenditure as a proportion of gross domestic product. Despite these claims, they promised to spend the same as Labour on the NHS, education, transport and international development and 'more than Labour on the police, defence and pensions'. Over the next four years they planned to increase public spending by 4 per cent a year compared to Labour's 5 per cent a year. The extra spending was to be paid for by £12 billion a year in efficiency savings. Since the last election, in recognition of the electorate's desire to maintain public services, the Conservatives have transformed themselves from a party that wanted to cut taxes and spending, to one that would spend marginally less than Labour. As a consequence of this new policy, the promises they could make on taxation were severely constrained. They proposed targeted cuts in council tax bills and an increased threshold in stamp duty on house purchases (which as William Keegan pointed out, would merely fuel house inflation). Effectively, the Conservatives were committed to Labour's economic policy but with the intention to return a share of the projected economic growth into tax cuts rather than public spending. However, as the IFS pointed out: 'it is uncertain whether the Conservative's offsetting cuts in public expenditure could be achieved as quickly as the party hopes' (Adam and Brewer 2005).

Liberal Democrat economic policy was uncomplicated. It was based on a commitment to the golden rule, an increase in taxation on those earning over £100,000 a year, and a modest increase in public expenditure. Perhaps the only innovative measure was the proposal for local income tax to replace council tax. This plan led to considerable debate during the election campaign because for a number of two-wage households on relatively modest incomes it would have meant a significant increase in local taxation.

In regards to the economy, the campaign had a slightly surreal air. It was as though the opposition parties were so convinced by Brown's arguments on the economy that not only did they accept his policies, they were also happy to take his word that Labour's record on the economy was unimpeachable. Whilst it is hard to deny the success of Labour's economic record, there is an argument that much of it followed on from the policy laid down in the final years of the Major government. Moreover, the campaign was marked by a number of indicators which seemed to suggest some underlying economic problems.

Sanders et al. (1987) have argued that electoral success depends to a considerable degree on personal economic expectations – people's subjective perceptions of how well the economy is doing. Similarly, it was the shock to the Conservatives' reputation for economic competence in 1992 that was significant for Labour's victory in 1997. Sanders demonstrate that for the Labour government, particularly from 2002, there was a decline in people's perception of personal economic expectations (Sanders 2005). There was also a decline in the belief that Labour was a better manager of the economy than the Conservatives. From 2002, despite Brown's confidence, Labour was beginning to lose its reputation for economic competence and people were increasingly pessimistic about their own economic circumstances.

What is significant is that during the campaign this economic pessimism seemed to be confirmed. The campaign started with the news that the MG Rover car company was to close at Longbridge. The company employed 8,000 people and its closure would have a knock-on effect on thousands of other supply companies and, of course, families and communities. It was a clear indication that Labour's market-led industrial strategy had been unable to prevent the continual decline of Britain's manufacturing base. Throughout Labour's period in office manufacturing had been further disadvantaged by the high value of sterling in the first years in relation to the euro and, more recently, in relation to the dollar. Other major companies such as Kingfisher and Boots issued profits warnings. In the course of the campaign inflation increased to 1.9 per cent (still historically low) and unemployment rose by 11,000 to 828,700. It was also suggested by a number of economic commentators that the government would either have to cut spending or raise taxes in order to meet the golden rule. Voters had faced a number of interest rate rises in the year preceding the election and this seemed to be having an impact on retail sector with the Confederation of British Industry (CBI) revealing a few days before polling that retail sales were the weakest since 1992 (Moore and Elliot 2005). Business activity was down, with indications that manufacturing industry might be slipping into recession, fuel prices were higher and the housing market seemed to have slowed down considerably (Elliot 2005). So whilst voters seemed to be aware of the signs of economic gloom and were changing their behaviour accordingly, the opposition party did not take the opportunity to examine Labour's economic record. Oliver Letwin's approach was to respond to Labour's attack on the Conservatives rather than to analyse Labour's economic record and policies.

What explains this absence of economic debate? Labour's vulnerability on economic policy was glided over because all the parties had the same vulnerabilities. All three parties were committed to the 'golden rule' and 'sustainable investment rule' (Chote et al. 2005) and to limited changes in taxation – the Conservatives' slight cuts and the Liberal Democrats' slight increases. All parties more or less accepted Labour's policy on public expenditure but with the Conservatives making slight cuts and the Liberal Democrats increasing public expenditure slightly more than Labour. The Tories planned a £35 billion cut by 2011–12, but this was a relative cut. They would be spending £35 billion less than Labour plans to spend, but this would still have represented an increase in absolute terms. The Conservatives have moved a long way from the Thatcherite rhetoric of the welfare state as a drain on enterprise. In 2005 the Conservatives were as committed as Labour to an efficient and effective welfare state (see Chapter 4, this volume). There were only minor differences on how economic policy fed into welfare effectiveness. As a leader in the *Guardian* pointed out:

> For a general election in which the economy has been held up as a central theme, it is remarkable how rarely economic policy has been at issue. This is because there are few points of disagreement between the major parties over macroeconomic policy ... What disagreement there is at the margins – as the Institute of Fiscal Studies forecast yesterday, the difference between its projections for Labour and Tory fiscal plans amount to just 0.3% of national output by 2008. (*Guardian*, 22 April 2005)

As the IFS illustrated, all the parties were vulnerable on not meeting the golden rule if the economy failed to grow as fast as projected, or if they failed on their efficiency savings.

Both opposition parties could have easily attacked the Gershon savings (the cuts in the costs of running government recommended by Sir Peter Gershon). Both Conservative and Labour governments had long been committed to improving efficiency but these savings are difficult to find. Often the increases in efficiency are virtual in the sense that they are about moving money and people around rather than making real savings in the cost of government. Labour also could have been criticised for increasing the cost of bureaucracy by significantly increasing the number of public sector workers and now saying that it is going to improve services by cutting them (when presumably the reason for increased public services was to provide better services). Moreover, Toynbee and Walker (2005: 157) point out how Gershon leads Labour to a 'simplistic and utterly misleading distinction between the front line and "back offices"'. However, rather than attack Labour, the Conservatives and Liberal Democrats committed themselves to similar, or greater cuts, and their own spending plans were dependent on these savings. Much of the Conservative plans for both taxation and spending were based on efficiency savings, and so they were vulnerable to the charge that if they did not carry these out quickly their spending and tax plans would fall down (Chote et al. 2005). There was a conspiracy of silence between the parties and the complexities of Gershon and efficiency savings received little attention.

Attacks on Labour and the budget deficit, inflation and unemployment were difficult because, although all three were rising, they were still at historically low levels (certainly for those whose political memories stretched to the 1970s). Labour did, however, have some vulnerability on the issue of public expenditure. Throughout the period of the Labour government spending had been at about

40 or 42 per cent of GNP. In the 1980s the Conservatives were arguing that such levels of public expenditure were unsustainable and were a drain on the resources of the private sector. In the 2005 election, despite the Thatcherite inheritance of the leader Michael Howard, the Conservatives seemed prepared to maintain similar levels of expenditure. They were hoist on the petard of their commitment to public services which made a programme of expenditure cuts, the basis of much Thatcherite economic rhetoric, unsustainable. Indeed, one of the remarkable events in a generally lacklustre campaign was the rapid deselection of the former Deputy Party Chairman Howard Flight who said in a closed meeting that the cuts outlined in the manifesto were the tip of the iceberg, and the long-term goal of the Conservatives was deep cuts in expenditure. The party leadership clearly wanted to distance itself from any notion of radical cuts in public expenditure. Such a policy moved the Tories to the middle ground on public services but undermined their critique of New Labour. They could not portray Labour as a tax and spend party when their policy was based on maintaining welfare spending and limited tax cuts. Howard did attack Labour on its slow response to the MG Rover situation, but considering his own party's commitment to the market and non-intervention he could hardly criticise Labour's laissez-faire industrial policy – it was taken from the text of Conservative economic solutions.

Labour's initial commitment to Conservative spending plans, market economics and the golden rule led many commentators and academics to accuse Labour of being nothing more than the continuation of the Thatcherite economic agenda. It could be argued that in 2005 economic policy was characterised by a new consensus that marries Conservative fiscal responsibility with Labour's commitments to public spending on welfare and education. However, in Labour's second term there were some very significant differences from the Conservative position. Although during the first term Labour maintained the straightjacket of Conservative spending plans for the first two years as promised, they did increase significantly spending on health and education, in the second term they made considerable increases in public expenditure. The Conservatives under Thatcher and Major were committed to reducing public expenditure as a proportion of GDP, Labour on the other hand consciously and explicitly increased public expenditure to 42 per cent of GDP. On employment the difference is perhaps more significant, the Thatcherite position was that economies had a natural rate of unemployment. If the economy artificially went over that rate by attempting to reduce the level of unemployment then the price of labour would increase, fuelling inflation. The 2005 Labour manifesto explicitly stated: 'Our goal is employment opportunity for all – the modern definition of full employment.'

Despite Tony Blair's continual desire to distance New Labour from Old Labour, economic policy under Blair and Brown had elements of the revision outlined by Tony Crosland in the 1960s and 1970s. Whilst many of the detailed policies are different and the commitment to equality may be much weaker than in the past, Labour's economic policy is based on similar assumptions to those of Crosland. As a *Guardian* leader pointed out, 'Labour's underlying argument ... is that the economy requires nurturing in order to generate the tax receipts required to fund the government's policy goals on health, education and the rest' (*Guardian*, 22 April 2005). Like Crosland, economic growth within the framework of a market economy is central to a strong welfare state. As William Keegan has pointed out Brown has acted like the perfect Keynesian – he tightened fiscal policy in the upswing of the economic cycle and 'left room for the government to loosen fiscal policy when things turned nasty after the collapse of the dotcom bubble and the terrorist attacks on 9/11' (Keegan 2005). Labour has a commitment to full employment, intervention in the supply side and a state-led and well funded welfare state which aims at redistributing wealth to the poorest groups in society. Labour is happy to operate public expenditure at 42 per cent of GDP which is a level many on the right argued was unsustainable. Moreover, as the Keynesian framework suggests, Labour is prepared to support economic growth through expansion of the public sector with 500,000 posts being created in the public sector between 1998 and 2003 (Toynbee and Walker 2005: 156).

In addition to traditional Keynesianism through manipulation of public spending and taxation, we now have a privatised Keynesianism. A key tool in macro-economic policy, although one determined by the Monetary Policy Committee of the Bank of England, is control of interest rates. If interest rates are low in an unregulated credit market, people can borrow more and use that borrowing to fuel economic growth. Much of the economic success of recent years has been fuelled by a combination of credit and the use of equity in homes of rapidly rising value. As Toynbee and Walker (2005: 133) highlight, 'Private households owed £1,000 bn, or the equivalent of 102 per cent of GDP.' Labour have used private and public debt to boost the economy. Whilst many economists would argue that such a policy was unsustainable, the opposition's fear of Labour's economic record meant that this was not an issue they raised during the campaign.

Conclusion

Unlike most previous elections, economic policy received relatively little attention in the campaign. This was partly because Labour managed to sustain the impression that economic policy was its major strength and as a consequence the other parties attempted to keep the campaign agenda away from the economy. It does seem the case that whilst many critics of the New Labour project suggest that it had merely subsumed the Thatcherite economic agenda, the reality is more complex. Labour has accepted the key principles of the market economy and fiscal responsibility but it also has a number of distinctive elements. Labour has maintained relatively high levels of public expenditure, it has renewed a commitment to full employment and it is conceivable that it has maintained elements of Keynesianism in its approach to macro-economic management. Perhaps most significantly, economic policy has been renationalised. Brown seems to maintain the view that national economic policy is within the domain of the government and not international forces. Consequently, Labour's economic policy is not very far from traditional Labour economic policy in that it sees sustaining a thriving market economy as a mechanism for funding the welfare state. However, where it differs from old Labour is that it has abandoned detailed intervention in the economy, and as the MG Rover case illustrates, the bailing out of lame ducks. It is also significant that the main opposition parties have not developed a detailed critique of Labour's economic policy. Both the Liberal Democrats and the Conservatives effectively offered minor modifications of Labour's policy with the Liberal Democrats slightly to the left and the Conservatives slightly to the right of Labour. In many ways the degree of consensus on economic policy seemed much closer in 2005 than it was in the period of the so-called postwar consensus. All parties accepted the market, the golden rule and maintaining public expenditure for public services.

The inability of the opposition to develop an alternative prevented any real attack on Labour's economic policy because they had nothing different to offer. As a consequence Labour's vulnerabilities on the economy were not exploited. Despite evidence that the economy was facing a downturn and people were not feeling so good about their own economic position, the Conservatives and Liberal Democrats made little of it. As a consequence, a myth of Labour's invulnerability on the economy developed.

References

Adam S. and Brewer, M. (2005) 'Proposed tax and benefits changes: winners and losers in the next term', Institute of Fiscal Studies, Briefing Note 11.

Adam, S. and Shaw, J. (2003) 'A survey of the UK tax system', Institute of Fiscal Studies, Briefing Note 9.

Chote, R., Emmerson, C. and Frayne, C. (2005) 'The public finances', 2005 Election Institute of Fiscal Studies, Briefing Note 3.

Elliot, L. (2005) 'Blair banks on economy on final push', *Guardian*, 4 May.

Emerson, C., Frayne, C. and Love, S. (2003) 'A survey of public spending in the UK', Institute of Fiscal Studies, Briefing Note 43.

Hay, C. (2003) 'What's globalisation got to do with it?', Inaugural Lecture, University of Birmingham <www.bham.ac.uk/POLSIS/department/staff/publications/hay_inaugural.htm>, *Government and Opposition*, forthcoming.

ICM (2005) Poll, *Guardian*, 29 April.

Keegan, W. (2005) 'Brown is first chancellor to make Keynes work', *Guardian*, 25 April.

Lawson, N. (1992) *The View from No. 11: Memories of a Tory Radical*, London: Bantam.

Moore, C. and Elliot, L. (2005) 'Labour unfazed by economic gloom', *Guardian*, 4 May.

Sanders, D. (2005) 'Popularity function forecasts for the 2005 UK general election', *British Journal of Politics and International Relations*, 7.

Sanders, D., Ward, H. and Marsh, D. (1987) 'Government popularity and the Falklands War', *British Journal of Political Science*, 17: 281–313.

Toynbee, P. and Walker, D. (2005) *Better or Worse*, London: Bloomsbury.

Milton Keynes North East

The Labour Party might regard the electorate of Milton Keynes as ungrateful. Amid a welter of indicators of economic and social progress, the constituency ejected the Labour incumbent, Brian White, who had presided over these developments since capturing the seat from the Conservatives in 1997.

Milton Keynes could not be viewed as a safe Labour area, but the party could laud a variety of achievements. The Healthcare Commission had awarded Milton Keynes Hospital stars for good performance and its records on patient care and cleanliness placed it among the leading medical centres in the country. Crime was low, with burglary having fallen by 11 per cent in 2003–04, the sixth largest drop in the country (*Guardian*, 12 April 2005). At 1.9 per cent, unemployment was below the UK average (although fractionally above the South East average) whilst annual salaries, at £24,747, exceeded the national and regional averages.

The Conservatives dented the impact of these statistics with a populist campaign, pointing out that crime detection was low, despite an increase in police officers. Moreover, pressure upon housing in the area led to support for the Conservatives' tough line on immigration and sympathy for the party's policies on affordable housing and reductions in stamp duty.

The result of two clearly differentiated campaigns was a swing to the Conservatives slightly below the South East average, but above the national swing and sufficient to deliver victory. Economic success helped Labour increase its majority in 2001, but a 6 per cent fall in vote share this time proved terminal.

Result		%
Lancaster, M. (Con)	19,674	39.3
White, B. (Lab)	18,009	35.9
Carr, J. (LD)	9,789	19.5
Philips, M. (UKIP)	1,400	2.8
Richardson, G. (Green)	1,090	2.2
Vyas, A. (Ind)	142	0.3
Con gain from Lab		
Labour majority	1,829	3.9
Swing: Lab to Con		3.6

Turnout: 62.4%

15
Delivery of Public Services[1]

David Richards

16 May proved to be one of the most memorable days of the 2001 election campaign. The press dubbed it 'Wobbly Wednesday' for Labour, in the aftermath of the Deputy Prime Minister John Prescott punching and grappling with a young man who had thrown an egg at him. On the same day, Sharron Storrer had accosted Tony Blair on the steps of a Birmingham Hospital and harangued the Prime Minister over the standards of medical care received by her partner. Whilst much was made of the Prescott punch, it was the highly frustrated and animated Ms Storrer confronting the Prime Minister which offered the iconic image of that campaign. In the light of the Storrer affair, Labour's woes were further compounded by an article published in the German magazine *Stern*, but receiving widespread coverage in the British media, which spoke of the 'English patient, where its poor live in third-world conditions, a fifth of the adult population is illiterate, its public services are third rate, 25,000 people unnecessarily die annually from cancer and the environment is casually disregarded'. This touched a raw nerve for a Labour government that was perceived as being vulnerable on the issue of the public services. Indeed, delivery subsequently became one of the key themes defining Labour's second term, and it was the government's record on delivery that was to form one of the centrepieces of the 2005 general election campaign.

What was noticeable about the 2005 campaign was the extent to which the ideological debate over public services had moved on over the previous eight years. Throughout the course of the campaign, it appeared at times as though each of the main parties was trying to out-compete with the others in highlighting their commitment to the public sector and public service delivery. Thatcherite-style rhetoric about the need for the market to replace an over-bloated and over-extended public sector was conspicuous by its absence. All three main parties paid constant lip service to their belief in the public services. In the case of Labour and the Conservatives, their spending plans were predicated on separate reviews of public sector efficiency which each party had conducted in the 24 months leading up to the election. For the Labour government, the Gershon Review claimed to have identified over £20 billion in 'efficiency gains' to be made by 2007–08 (Gershon 2004). For the Conservatives, the James Review argued it had identified £35 billion potential savings (James 2005). The Liberal Democrats, despite their rhetoric of tax and spend were not to be outdone, having publishing their own review paper in the autumn of 2002 on the future of public service – *Quality, Innovation and Choice*. By the start of the election campaign, the Liberal Democrats claimed that £5 billion could be annually saved by switching spending from what they regarded as low-priority government programmes to fund their own key proposals (Liberal Democrats 2005).

What symbolised the shift in the ideological terrain that was being fought over in 2005 compared, for example to 1997, was that none of the three parties viewed their proposed 'efficiency gains' as a means to reduce overall government spending. Instead, each claimed the money saved would be spent more effectively elsewhere: Labour claimed the savings would be used to finance a new 'front-line delivery strategy'; the Liberal Democrats argued that by abandoning existing government programmes such as identity cards and university top-up and tuition fees, the money saved could be used to fund their programme of spending on free personal care for the elderly and reducing class sizes; and the Conservatives argued that they would match Labour's spending on the NHS, schools, transport and international development and even increase it above Labour's targets on police, defence and pensions. Indeed, the extent to which the Conservative Party wished to be seen to be committed to public services was evidenced in an incident that erupted less than two weeks before the start of the election campaign; Michael Howard forced through the de-selection of the senior Conservative MP Howard Flight in the Arundel and South Downs Constituency. This followed the leaking of comments Flight had made at a private Conservative function that the £35 billion targeted savings of the James Review would only 'be the start of more radical cuts in the public sector'.[2] The Labour Party were swift to respond, claiming that the Conservatives had a 'hidden agenda' when it came to public services, that would reveal itself only if they gained office. Thus the theme that emerged throughout the campaign was the narrowness of the ideological terrain being fought over, as each party tried to present itself as the most effective manager of public services. This worked to Labour's advantage, despite, as we see below, its sensitivity over issues of delivery. All the main polling companies (ICM, MORI, YouGov, NOP, Populus) indicated that the incumbent government held between a three- and ten-point lead over the other two main parties on the issue of public services throughout the course of the campaign.

If, then, we recognise that a broad convergence had occurred between the three main parties in relation to their commitment to public services, then the focus of the rest of this chapter centres on the issue of delivery. In particular, how had the Labour government in its first two terms addressed the issue of delivery in public services? What I will argue throughout the rest of this chapter is that since 1997, Labour's broad approach to improving delivery has been a reform programme based on a dual-level strategy: it has attempted to sustain and even increase its control over the policy process by concentrating on increasing the size and strength of the 'centre', pursuing a programme of joined-up government and imposing rigorous targets on service delivery agents; concomitantly, it has argued that the most effective way of delivering public policy is to increase the autonomy of the multiple service deliverers responsible for policy implementation. What then follows is an analysis of Labour's reform programme, the criticisms made of it by the other main parties and some of the potential tensions Labour's two-pronged strategy may create in their third term.

New Labour and delivery

One of the themes of the 2001 election campaign was the perception that Labour had failed to deliver in its first term, despite it offering rhetoric of a radical, new agenda. Here the key criticism was that Labour's first term had been a 'missed opportunity', with the government failing to make greater use of its vast Commons majority. Instead, Labour's focus had been too much on political statecraft – for example, trying to demonstrate that it could be trusted to run the economy by adhering to the spending commitments of the previous Conservative administration. Critics argued that this was a strategy to win the trust of ex-Conservative supporters, rather than deliver on a radical, modern, social democratic agenda (Fielding 2002: 33). If, then, criticism of Labour in the 2001 campaign was largely emanating from elements within its own party, in the 2005 campaign, it was from elsewhere, most notably the opposition parties, that Labour's record on delivery was being attacked. The Conservatives argued that people's real needs and priorities under Labour had been overshadowed by centrally imposed targets, the growth in 'Whitehall inspection regimes' and a rapid rise in 'stealth taxes' (Conservative Party 2005: 22). Similar sentiments were expressed by the Liberal Democrats who averred that Labour ministers were trying to 'pull the strings with pointless targets and endless bureaucracy' (Liberal Democrats 2005: 4). But here lay the paradox. When Labour entered the 2005 campaign, it was sensitive to the perception that it had failed to deliver improvements in the public services. Yet more than any previous Labour government, the Blair administration in its first two terms had shown and maintained a greater interest in reforming the machinery of government with a view to improving delivery. Two and a half years into office, Tony Blair complained of having 'scars on my back' from his attempts to get Whitehall departments to improve on policy delivery. His critique centred on the notion that the government's attempts at improving delivery in the public services were being hampered by public servants who were concentrating on operating in 'policy chimneys', protecting their turf and their own interests rather than advancing government programmes (see Kavanagh and Richards 2000; Hyman 2005). There was a lack of central control and co-ordination of policy across Whitehall. Policy was being developed in an isolated and segmented manner, often leading to unintended and unforeseen consequences, most notably when different departments pursued conflicting policy goals. Moreover, Whitehall, from Labour's perspective, was not the Rolls-Royce service that popular myth would have it. The belief within Labour's inner circle was that there was a range of systemic problems within the Civil Service curtailing its ability to deal with change. As one Number 10 insider observed, when Labour came to office, they discovered Whitehall

> ill-equipped to deal with the demands ... Civil servants were still being recruited with far too narrow a set of skills. There were far too few project managers which meant that many government IT projects ran into the ground and wasted vast amounts of taxpayers money. There were few civil servants skilled at drawing up contracts with the private sector which meant that in public finance initiatives and other deals government often got a raw deal ... Most civil servants moved jobs so frequently within departments they were never held accountable for delivering anything. Success was measured by any criteria other than the one that mattered: delivery. (Hyman 2005: 73)

In 2004, Blair reiterated these sentiments:

> The principal challenge is to shift focus from policy advice to delivery. Delivery means outcomes. It means project management. It means adapting to new situations and altering rules and practice accordingly. It means working not in traditional departmental silos. It means working naturally with partners outside of Government. It's not that many individual civil servants aren't capable of this. It is that doing it requires a change of operation and of culture that goes to the core of the Civil Service. (Blair 2004)

Not surprisingly, as with its predecessors, the response of the Labour government since 1997 has been to implement a series of reforms aimed at increasing the power that the centre wields. It has pursued a more holistic or joined-up approach to governing in an attempt to bring together the many, often disparate, elements that constitute the policy arena. Labour argued that 'joined-up-government' would lead to an 'improvement in service delivery' based on a model of strong central control from Number 10 and the Cabinet Office (see HM Government 1999; Cabinet Office 2000; 2002). At the same time, it has put in place what appears to be a countervailing force at 'street level' by continuing to pursue a policy of semi-detaching delivery agencies from government and increasing the local autonomy of the multiple service deliverers (Office of Public Service Reform 2002). This raises the key issue concerning delivery at present: whether or not increasing central control while at the same time attempting to enhance local autonomy creates diametrically opposed goals which are difficult to reconcile. The rest of the chapter argues that Labour's reform programme in the last eight years has produced a dilemma – the success of the delivery agenda for Labour in its third term depends on whether it is possible to rectify increased control at the centre with greater autonomy for agencies and organisations responsible for delivering government policy on the ground.

Improving delivery

After eight years in office and despite Blair's 1999 'scars on my back' speech, by the start of the 2005 election campaign Labour were still addressing issues of restructuring and reform of the machinery of government. A perception persisted within Labour's inner circle that the existing organisational arrangements had limited the government's ability to deliver its core policies, which it regarded as central to re-election. In the first week of the 2005 campaign, such concerns were clearly enunciated by Geoff Mulgan, a Number 10 insider from 1997 to 2004, in an article for *Prospect*:

> In retrospect, New Labour did not go far enough. Its leaders had little experience of running organisations and tended to believe that if only you put the right people in charge, everything would be fine. Whenever there was a clash between the old forms of power based on the major public professions (doctors, teachers, police) and emergent new forms of power, the old tended to win, helped by their champions in Whitehall. The result is that despite some useful experiments, Britain still awaits a radical reformer who can recast the state to cope better with big issues like environmental change, poverty or localism. (Mulgan 2005)

Such sentiments were picked up on by the Conservatives as they attempted to make political capital out of suggestions that the government were 'all talk and no delivery'. The theme formed the centrepiece of the first party conference speech given by Michael Howard, as the new Leader of the Conservative Party, when he declared:

> And why is it that Labour are taxing and spending and failing? The answer is simple. They promised reform. They've talked about reform. But they have failed to deliver reform. Without reform of our public services, the extra money Labour have spent just hasn't made the difference. That is the central failure

of this Government. They have spent the money – taxpayers' money – but they've not carried out the reform. (Howard 2003)

Criticisms concerning Labour's failure to deliver were expressed by both the Conservatives and the Liberal Democrats throughout the course of the campaign. Firstly, over the extent to which Labour were seen to be stifling initiative and curbing entrepreneurship by the excessive use of regulation in business. Michael Howard observed on the 2005 campaign trail:

it is important to cut-back on the hidden costs government imposes on business through regulation. According to the British Chambers of Commerce regulation imposed by Mr Blair is costing British business an extra £40 billion a year. Mr Blair has introduced more regulations than any of his predecessors – 3,459 statutory instruments in 2004 alone. So it's hardly surprising that Britain has fallen from 13th to 30th in the World Economic Forum's league of government regulation since 1998 ... there's a lot of money in regulation – but that's for the regulators themselves. Mr Blair's Britain has created a generation of 'fat regulators' – regulators paid high salaries from your taxes ... The government I lead will act to keep tax low by delivering value for money and by cutting back on regulation and bureaucracy.

At the same time, both main opposition parties focused on what they regarded as the excessive use of targets and bureaucracy in stifling the ability of public services to effectively perform. Charles Kennedy argued in a speech on the reform of public services:

When this government was first elected, it wasn't afraid to talk of 'quality'. We said then that the way to achieve it was through extra investment after years of Conservative cuts. We won that argument and the investment is now going in. But Labour started too late, went about it the wrong way and wasted billions on centralised management and political targets. (Kennedy 2004)

The issue of targets in particular caught the public's imagination during the campaign, following an appearance by Tony Blair on BBC1's *Question Time*. One member of the audience, Diana Church, observed that because of the target regime in the NHS, she was unable to make a doctor's appointment seven days in advance because the existing system only permits a patient to make it 48 hours beforehand. She observed: 'You have to sit on the phone for three hours in the morning trying to get an appointment because you are not allowed to ask for an appointment before that because by making it 48 hours beforehand they are meeting government targets.' An embarrassed Blair conceded he was not aware of the detail in this specific area, but the interpretation of targets in this case did appear 'absurd'. Delivery undoubtedly became a recurrent theme throughout the course of the campaign and it was an issue Labour constantly felt susceptible to. Yet it would be wrong to suggest that it was an issue that the government had paid little attention to over the previous eight years. As we see below, it had put in place an extensive strategy to enhance the performance of the public services.

Increasing central control

On one level, Labour's response to problems of delivery and implementation in the policy process over the last two terms have characterised the standard reaction of previous governments in the form of accruing more powers for the centre. From the outset, the view of the government was that it aimed to 'govern from the centre'. The rhetoric of the Blair government rejected the corporatist, top-down approaches of past Labour governments for achieving its policy goals. Instead the emphasis was to be on 'clearer control over less'. As Blair (2003: 132) observed: 'the era of "big government means better government" is over, – "control" was to become its new mantra ... Leverage, not size, is what counts. What government does, and how well, not how much, is the key to its role in modern society.' Blair's sentiments are not far removed from the 'reinventing government' discourse associated ten years earlier with the American centre-right commentators Osborne and Gaebler (1992: 19–20) and their argument of the need for governments to 'steer not row'.

Strengthening the centre

In order to achieve 'leverage' (control), the Labour government concluded that it should prioritise greater co-ordination. This was captured in one of the slogans of Labour's first term, the need for 'joined-up government'. From this perspective:

> The 'tubes' or 'silos' down which money flows from government to people and localities have come to be seen as part of the reason why government is bad at solving problems. Many issues have fitted imperfectly if at all into departmental slots. Vertical organisation by its nature skews government efforts away from certain activities, such as prevention – since the benefits of preventive action often come to another department. It tends to make government less sensitive to particular client groups whose needs cut across departmental lines. It incentives departments to dump problems on each other – like schools dumping unruly children onto the streets to become a headache for the police ... Over time it reinforces the tendency common to all bureaucracies of devoting more energy to the protection of turf rather than serving the public. (Mulgan 2001)

In response, the government created a range of bodies such as the Social Exclusion Unit, task forces, the Delivery Unit, so-called 'Tsars' and the Strategy Unit to overcome departmentalism. In some ways, this has further extended the reach of Number 10 into departmental affairs under the guise of ensuring a co-ordinated approach.

Changes at Number 10

Initially, pursuing joined-up government was a mechanism for increasing the control of the centre because it was a means of ensuring that strategies developed at Number 10 were not undermined by the conflicting goals of departments. As Blair told the House of Commons Liaison Select Committee in July 2002: 'I make no apology for having a strong centre, particularly in circumstances where, one, the focus is on delivering better services.' This of course laid Blair personally open to a barrage of criticisms from the opposition parties of 'control-freakery', a term regularly heard throughout the 2005 campaign. Yet it is because of the institutional weakness of the centre, Number 10 and the Cabinet Office, which lacks the resources of departments, that Blair chose this particular strategy. Since 1997, the resources of the Prime Minister have increased. Blair expanded the size of the Policy Unit (now the Policy Directorate), almost doubling the personnel compared to the Major years. Crucially, the role of the Policy Directorate has become one not so much of making policy but of ensuring that departments are aware of the Blair agenda and are delivering policy in line with Number 10's wishes. Blair reinforces this policy steer through regular bilateral meetings with ministers to ensure that they are agreed on policy objectives. This is an important development because it means that there is an institutional relationship between departments and Number 10. Also, prime ministerial policy activism does not just rely on the whim or attention span of the Prime Minister. The Prime Minister's office is developing capabilities to direct departments, which are based on the special advisors in Number 10 overseeing and commenting on the policy proposals that are coming from departments. Again, this is an important change in the patterns of dependency between departments and the Prime Minister with departments becoming more dependent on the Prime Minister for policy initiatives. Yet it is also important to recognise the crucial role of the Treasury and, more particularly, the unique relationship between the Prime Minister and his Chancellor Gordon Brown. Over the previous eight years, what amounts to a division of labour between Blair and Brown has developed; Brown and the Treasury are clearly the leaders on economic and welfare issues. Elsewhere, Blair is a more dominant figure. However, this is an understanding based on personal relations and the ebb and flow in the relationship between the two individuals. It is not a recipe for institutionalised, joined-up co-ordination. Nevertheless, there is a dependency relationship between these two central figures in the Labour project. This was amply demonstrated in the 2005 election campaign when at times it appeared that the pair were almost inseparable. Brown recognises his dependence on Blair in order to secure a harmonious and smooth transition to leader of the Party. At the same time, the extensive vocal support that Brown offered Blair, particularly when the Prime Minister was receiving a barrage of criticism over the war in Iraq, was crucial.

Elsewhere in Number 10, strategic policy capability is provided by the Strategy Unit created in 2002. The stated aim of the Strategy Unit is to: 'improve Government's capacity to address strategic, cross-cutting issues and promote innovation in the development of policy and the delivery of the Government's objectives' (Strategy Unit 2005). The unit has three main roles: 'to provide strategy and policy advice, to carry out occasional strategic audits and to help build departments' strategic capability' (Strategy Unit 2005). Again, this can be seen as an attempt to consolidate control over the policy process at Number 10, with the unit reporting to the Prime Minister through the Chancellor of the Duchy of Lancaster, since May 2005 John Hutton, and the Cabinet Secretary, Gus O'Donnell.

The third change introduced by Labour is centred on its distrust of the Civil Service. This is not related to the ideological disposition of officials – that they were politicised in the course of 18 years of Conservative administration – but instead, Labour has questioned Whitehall's ability to develop and deliver policy. The element of distrust was revealed in significant changes in policy-making. Labour looked much more to outside sources for policy advice. This has taken the form of greater use of task forces, 'Tsars' and special advisors: in terms of the former, the government created an array of ad hoc bodies – task forces – with the intention of crossing departmental boundaries and providing a range of sources of advice. Their role remains rather nebulous, but in response to a Parliamentary Question, between May 1997 and October 2000 there were over 200 'live' task forces drawing upon individuals from the private, public and voluntary sector, including academics and civil servants,[3] and the topics they cover are diverse;[4] the second element, that of the creation of Tsars, was a strategy employed by Labour to improve both horizontal and vertical 'joined-upness' within and between departments. Tsars are an eclectic mix of outside appointments, bearing an array of informal titles as 'Drugs Tsar', 'Health Tsar', 'Transport Tsar', 'Anti-Cancer Tsar', 'Children's Tsar', and so on. They are appointed by the Prime Minister but then work within individual Whitehall departments; the third element saw an increased role for special advisors which have more than doubled in number since the last Conservative government (see Table 15.1).

Special advisors offer an alternative source of advice to ministers. Their influence has changed the established pattern of policy-making. For example, in the case of the Treasury, according to a report in the *Guardian* (15 April 2002), the then Treasury Special Advisors, Ed Balls and David Miliband, act as gatekeepers, letting civil servants know what the Chancellor is interested in and acting as a filter for policy ideas coming from below. An official knows that he or she is getting somewhere when they get a half-hour slot with Ed Balls.

The central organisational reforms pursued by Labour have not simply been reflected in the enhanced number of agencies at the centre and increased power at the heart of the Labour government. It has also been about extending the culture of audit and the use of 'governing by targets' to improve delivery initiatives introduced by the previous Conservative administration. Again, the application of such tools of governing should be seen in the context of ensuring Whitehall retains leverage over other actors operating further down the policy-chain.

Table 15.1   Numbers of Government Special Advisors, 1979–2003

Year	Total	Number 10	Departments
1979/80	7	n/a	n/a
1989/90	35	n/a	n/a
1994/95	34	6	28
1995/96	38	8	30
1996/97	38	8	30
1997/98	70	18	52
1998/99	74	25	49
1999/00	78	26	52
2000/01	79	25	54
2001/02	81	26	55
2002/03	81	27	54

Source: Committee on Standards in Public Life (2003).

Improving delivery by target and audit

Targets became a major issue in the course of the 2005 election campaign. Both the main opposition parties were highly critical throughout of what they regarded as the government's excessive use of targets and auditing. In the light of the Diana Church affair, the health service became the key battleground on which the issue of targets was fought out. In an election address to his own party, two days before polling, Charles Kennedy claimed:

It is Tony Blair's Government which ties up our hospitals with targets which just pile problems on doctors and nurses. It is the patients that end up suffering. The Liberal Democrats will end the artificial targets and let doctors and nurses get on with the job. And we will end the hidden waiting lists so that people get diagnosed and treated quickly and efficiently.

The Conservative Party's manifesto claimed targets in the NHS were having a 'very damaging effect', distracting health practitioners from addressing real issues such as the MRSA superbug. Their manifesto cited a National Audit Office report which claimed the impact of targets had increased the volume of NHS activity. This meant that recommendations of professionals to close beds or wards for cleaning had been overruled. Their manifesto concluded: 'We do not believe that patient safety should ever be sacrificed to political targets ...We pledge to abolish all centrally-set targets on hospitals' (Conservative Party 2005: 11).

Ironically it was the previous Conservative administration, while willing to abandon its role of service provider in many areas of public service, that was much less willing to relinquish controlling capacities. A similar approach has been adopted by Labour since 1997, leading to what has been referred to as the development of a new 'regulatory state inside the state' (see Hood et al. 1999). The growth in the use of targets, public service agreements and audit mechanisms reflects an attempt by central government to ensure it maintains control over those agencies delivering services to the public. The regulation of public sector bodies grew substantially in the last two decades coinciding with the perceived fragmentation of the state. For example, individuals employed in 'oversight bodies for public organisations' rose approximately 90 per cent between 1976 and 1995, whilst at the same time Civil Service numbers were cut by about 30 per cent and local government service by 20 per cent (Hood et al. 1999). Moreover, the institutionalisation of this process by central government is reflected elsewhere in such initiatives as the 'Citizen's Charter', introduced by the Major government and then extended and rebranded by the Blair government as 'Service First'. The rationale behind this approach was to shift power away from service providers to consumers. In practice, this has become an explicit process of auditing the public sector – by publishing performance lists for schools, hospitals, universities, and so on. Accompanying this process has been the rise in magnitude of an array of regulatory units including; the Deregulation Unit, also created by the last Conservative administration but again rebranded by Labour – firstly as the Better Regulation Unit, and later the Regulatory Impact Unit; the Better Regulation Task Force; the National Audit Office; the Audit Commission; and the Public Sector Benchmarking Service. There is of course some irony here; the government's quest for better (read less) regulation has led to a profusion of state agencies being set up to address the issue. Clearly, the old Whitehall adage that 'the man [sic] in Whitehall knows best' still has resonance.

Stemming from these government agencies has been the growth of governing by targets and auditing which has taken a variety of forms:

- the creation of numerous regulatory agencies; by the mid 1990s, it was estimated that the number of national-level regulatory organisations ranged from between 135 and 200 with running costs ranging from between £750 million and £1 billion (Hood et al. 1999).
- the appointment of a set of regulatory or inspectorate officials; the figures were estimated in the mid 1990s to be between 14,000 and 20,000. Here there are numerous examples: the Chief Inspector of Prisons for England and Wales created in 1980 to look at the condition of prisons and the treatment of prisoners; or the GM Inspectorate created in 1990 to inspect release sites of GMOs (genetically modified organisms) to ensure that they comply with the terms of the consents granted for trial release or marketing of a GMO. Inspectorates cover almost all areas of social life including health, education, building, the fire service, police, wildlife, vehicles, and so on.
- most importantly, the establishment of a wide array of performance indicators and league tables for services. The most obvious institutional form in which target-setting has been pursued by the present Labour government are public service agreements (PSAs), set up after the 1998 Comprehensive Spending Review. PSAs establish in one document the aims, objectives and performance targets for each of the main government departments. They include value-for-money targets and a statement of who is responsible for the delivery of these targets. PSAs are agreed on by the individual department following discussions with the Treasury and the Prime Minister's Delivery Unit. At present, the Treasury estimates that it has 130 PSAs in place (see HM Government 2002; HM Treasury 2005a). An obvious example would be the Department of Health's PSA, which includes a variety of targets set for the National Health Service: no patient should have to wait longer than six months for an inpatient appointment from 2005; no patient should have to wait longer than 15 months for surgery; no patient should be waiting longer than three months for an outpatient appointment from 2005; patients should not have to wait more than four hours from arrival to admission, transfer or discharge in Accident & Emergency (HM Treasury 2005b). Where organisations fail to meet the targets laid down by government, they can incur an array of prescribed penalties ranging from a simple cut in government funding to the outright closure of an organisation, such as has occurred with a number of 'failed' secondary schools. The practice of target-setting has become the key tool of control now exerted by government, as a report by the Comptroller and Auditor General, focusing specifically on Next Steps Agencies, testifies: 'performance measurement and reporting are intrinsic to the whole process of public management, including planning, monitoring, evaluation and public accountability' (HM Treasury 2000: 2).

At a generic level, Labour's broader reforms of the policy process were originally identified in the 1999 White Paper *Modernising Government*. This committed the Civil Service to six key changes that derived from Labour's modernising government agenda with a clear emphasis on improving delivery: stronger leadership with a clear sense of purpose; better business planning from top to bottom; sharper performance management; a dramatic improvement in diversity; a service more open to people and ideas, which brings on talent; and a better deal for staff. The White Paper suggested that past reforms: 'paid little attention to the policy process and the way this affects the ability of government to meet the needs of the people' (Williams 1999: 452). Labour's concern was not simply about improving efficiency; it wanted to change relationships within government and between government and the citizen.

Labour's first two terms saw some significant changes in the organisation of central government and the way that policy was made. The key changes included the emphasis on joined-up government, the multiplication in sources of advice, an upsurge in the use of targets and auditing tools, the strengthening of the centre and the shifting role of the Civil Service. The goal of joined-up government created tensions within Whitehall. The ability of departments to work together was constrained by the continuation of powerful departmental structures and the notion of ministerial responsibility (see Marsh et al. 2001). Further problems arose because these changes partly built on the reforms introduced by the Conservatives, but also reflected the concerns of Labour and the changing external environment. This produced contradictory demands between, for example, the notion of market mechanisms as a principle of reform through contracting out and empowering managers and centralised notions of reforms through the use of targets. What is clear is that, while Labour was not responsible for initiating a culture of audit, that was the makings of the previous Conservative administration, it has ensured that such a culture has become systematically embedded throughout the public services.

Enhancing 'street-level' autonomy

One of the key criticisms Labour faced in the 2005 election campaign was the extent to which the state had become increasingly extended during the previous eight years. A recurring theme of the Conservatives and Liberal Democrats focused on a supposed explosion of quangos and non-departmental public bodies under Labour. This was coupled to suggestions that the boards of these organisations were populated by so-called 'Tony's cronies'. In February 2005, a centre-right think tank, the Centre for Policy Studies, published *The Essential Guide to British Quangos 2005*, which claimed that 529 quangos were in existence, of which 111 had been set up by Labour. John Redwood, the Conservative Shadow minister for deregulation, commented: 'A Conservative government will axe 162 quangos, as part of its drive for more efficient and more accountable government. That is the way to deliver lower taxes and more democracy to public life.' Whilst Ed Davey, the Liberal Democrat Office of the Deputy Prime Minister spokesman, observed:

> For over two decades, under both Tory and Labour governments, these unaccountable agencies have mushroomed. Liberal Democrats would abolish many, merge others, and make any that remain properly accountable. Labour promised a bonfire of the quangos, but instead delivered an explosion.

The issue of an overextended, interfering state was clearly a sensitive one for Labour throughout the 2005 campaign. Yet it countered by arguing that what they were offering was a solution aimed at freeing-up the autonomy of front-line service deliverers. The government saw the detachment of agencies from government, the development of new management techniques and an increase in local autonomy, as the key mechanisms for improving delivery. It is the latter theme of autonomy that is fundamental to Labour's reform programme. As we saw above, the reform programme was initiated by the *Modernising Government* White Paper, but the key theme of enhanced autonomy at street level is more clearly expounded in the Office of Public Service Reform's (2002: 3) *Reforming Public Services: Principles into Practice*. In its foreword, Tony Blair enunciates four 'Principles for Public Service Reform':

- *National Standards*: mean working with hospitals, schools, police forces and local government to agree tough targets and to see performance independently monitored so people can see how their local services compare.
- *Devolution*: means Whitehall is serious about letting go and giving successful front-line professionals the freedom to deliver these standards.
- *Flexibility*: means removing artificial bureaucratic barriers which prevent staff improving local services.
- *Choice*: acknowledges that consumers of public services should increasingly be given the kind of options that they take for granted in other walks of life.

The notions of choice and flexibility are explicit references made by the government in response to what it regards as an entrenched approach by Whitehall to delivery in public services based on a view that 'one size fits all'. As one Number 10 insider observed: 'To deliver opportunity and security today, public services must be radically recast from monolithic top down public services to personalised public services. Out goes the big state, in comes the enabling state' (Hyman 2005: 255). For Labour, diversity of provision has become the new mantra, a theme that it developed throughout the course of its second term. This is to be achieved through devolution and delegation[5] for front-line professionals who Labour argues are best placed to understand the most appropriate means of delivery in order to meet the specific needs of their individual client groups. Yet here a proviso must be added. Labour is not simply abandoning its state-centric, controlling tendencies. The right to increased autonomy for front-line professionals is not being dispensed carte blanche. Instead, it is based on the 'carrot and stick' principle:

> Better services should get more freedom and flexibility – earned autonomy for schools, hospitals, local government and other public services. Failing services should be given the incentives to improve, and receive intervention in proportion to the risk of damaging under-performance. (Office of Public Service Reform 2002: 17)

The Labour government has argued that it is committed to freeing up those frontline staff that have earned this right through a proven track record in meeting centrally imposed, national standards in the form of PSA agreements. In developing this strategy, Gordon Brown announced in his 2003 Budget Statement a review of: 'new ways of providing departments, their agencies and other parts of the public sector with incentives to exploit opportunities for efficiency savings, and so release resources for front line public service delivery' (HM Treasury 2003). This culminated a year later in the publication of the Gershon Report (2004) which outlined a programme of efficiency savings aimed at financing the increased cost of the government's new front-line delivery strategy.[6] The incentive principle identified in *Reforming Public Services: Principles into Practice* – that street-level bureaucrats who are 'successful' in meeting prescribed national standards are subsequently rewarded with greater autonomy in the form of increased devolution and delegation – ignores existing disparities in levels of autonomy already experienced by different types of street-level bureaucrats within the policy chain. For example, it is clear that depending on the type of organisations, the autonomy of street-level bureaucrats is already of a variable nature. Contrast, for example, the limited autonomy of a teacher in a primary school having to respond to the government's primary national strategy on numeracy and literacy, as opposed to a police officer dealing with crime related to drug misuse, who whilst also in a hierarchical organisation has considerable discretion over, for example, whether to arrest someone or to caution them.

Despite the strategy that Labour has pursued to improve delivery, the issue remained much contested throughout the course of the 2005 election campaign. Both main opposition parties tried to make political capital by constructing an image of a government that had become obsessed with centralisation, state-agency building, target-setting and regulation. Underpinning this particular set of imagery was a clear message that Labour was failing to deliver on public services, while at the same time wasting millions of pounds of taxpayers' money. The tension facing Labour as they enter a third term is trying to strike a balance between the need for some form of central control, holding public services accountable for what they do and how much it costs, whilst also offering greater autonomy to service providers who are best placed to understand the most effective means of product delivery for their clients.

A third term agenda

How should the theme of delivery be understood as Labour enters its third term of government? It is clearly a complex and politically charged issue. As we have seen in this chapter, the 2005 election campaign demonstrated the extent to which an ideological convergence had taken place between the three main parties over the importance of the public services. Gone was the public choice rhetoric from the 1980s and early 1990s of self-interested, overextended and inefficient public services. Instead, the contested issue had become how best to manage them. Yet despite this convergence, the issue of delivery of public services was one which Labour felt less than confident over. On one level, its election campaign centred on the message that Britain had changed for the better over the course of the last eight years. The rhetoric contained in Labour's 2005 manifesto based on the slogan 'Britain: Forward not Back' was that 'the contract has been delivered' and the government had 'fulfilled' its promises (Labour Party 2005: 6–7). When identifying the ambitions for a third-term, Blair observed: 'now we go to the people not only having delivered on our promises, but also setting new and more ambitious goals for our public services and our country' (Labour Party 2005: 6). Rightly, the government could point to both the investments and progress it had made, particularly in the areas of health and education. Yet the public perception was somewhat different. As Toynbee and Walker (2005: 319) observe:

> With growing frustration ministers urged people to open their eyes. Look at their local primary and secondary school, their GP clinic and hospital. Count the police and support officers pounding the streets. Look at the jobs almost everywhere or the colleges and universities beckoning people in. Feel their own wallets. If they didn't believe the official figures, why not believe the evidence of their own eyes?

Not surprisingly, the opposition parties fed off of the public perception to portray a counter-image that Labour had failed to deliver. As we have seen, their focus centred on both the cost and the means of delivery. The perceived use of excessive regulation and targets in particular, were offered up to the electorate as explanations as to why the Labour project was coming unstuck. It is possibly here that we can identify the seeds that might explain the gap between public perceptions of Labour's record on delivery as opposed to its actual record (see Toynbee and Walker 2005). It might be that Labour's use of targets in the public services has raised the expectations of the electorate, elevating the issue of delivery to a level which Labour could never realistically hope to meet. The effect could be to leave the electorate dissatisfied, with government falling somewhat short of individual expectations.

What then of the future, as Labour embarks on its historic third term in office? Presently, the government faces a key dilemma: it has wanted to shift away from the principle of public services predicated on the notion that 'one size fits all'. Labour argues that to achieve this goal entails a degree of devolution and delegation to front-line service deliverers who are best placed to recognise the more specific and variable needs of their client groups. Yet at the same time, to date, Labour has been unwilling to relinquish control over these agencies. How, then, does it ensure control over public services without forcing the agencies to stereotype the needs of their client base and continue to pursue a 'one size fits all' strategy? In Labour's third term, it needs to come to terms with this potential tension and address the culture of audit in the public service spawned from the centre, if it really is committed to creating an enabling state.

Notes

1. This chapter is based on research being conducted as part of the ESRC 'Public Services Programme'. The project is entitled 'Analysing Delivery Chains In The Home Office' (Ref: RES-153-25-00 37).
2. This followed on from a similar incident two weeks earlier, when Danny Kruger, a member of the Conservative Policy Unit and the prospective Conservative Party candidate for Sedgefield, was forced to stand down having suggested that the Conservatives planned 'to introduce a period of creative destruction in the public services' (see Polly Toynbee, *Guardian*, 11 March 2005). Ironically, by speaking of creative destruction, Kruger was reviving a theme associated with Joseph Schumpeter from his analysis of capitalist systems. Schumpeter averred that such economies were only sustainable if they engaged in a process of growth through renewal – with the new replacing the old (Schumpeter 1975). Unfortunately for Kruger, the Conservatives did not construe what was essentially meant as a benign comment on the need for renewal in public services in quite the same light!
3. The Cabinet Office argues that: 'in contrast to NDPBs, which have a long-term activity to discharge, Task Forces, Ad hoc Advisory Groups and Reviews have a short term focus and when their work comes to an end they are disbanded. Their recommendations may of course continue to be taken forward in other parts of government. These groups are usually created to give expert advice to the government on a specific issue and are usually expected to remain in operation for less than two years' (see Cabinet Office 2005).
4. Present examples of task forces include the following: the Prime Minister set up the Commission for Africa, an ad hoc advisory group supported by the Department for International Development. The Commission is taking a look at the challenges Africa faces in the context of the global forces in play in the twenty-first century; the Department for Culture, Media and Sport established a Digital Television Consumer

Expert Group (ad hoc advisory group), to make detailed recommendations in a report on the steps that need to be taken to ensure the public is ready for digital switchover; the Department for Work and Pensions created an Employers' Task Force on Pensions, created to help increase and extend occupational and private pension provision; the Department of Health has set up an A&E Task Force to assist in delivering the target that no patient will spend more than four hours in an emergency department.

5. In this context: 'devolution is defined as the handing over of power from central government to a constituent part (e.g. to local government); delegation means entrusting another with the authority to act as agent' (Office of Public Service Reform 2002: 16).

6. As noted above, the report identified £20 billion in what it refers to as 'efficiency gains' to be made by 2007–08, partly based on cutting 84,000 posts in the Civil Service. From that figure, 60 per cent will be directly released to fund front-line delivery services.

References

Blair, T. (2003) 'The third way: new politics for the new century', in A. Chadwick and R. Heffernan (eds) *The New Labour Reader*, London: Polity.

Blair, T. (2004) 'Speech on the Civil Service', 24 February 2004, <www.number-10.gov.uk/output/Page5401.asp>.

Cabinet Office (2000) *Wiring it Up – Whitehall's Management of Cross-Cutting Policies and Services*, London: Stationery Office.

Cabinet Office (2002) *Organising to Deliver*, <www.cabinetoffice.gov.uk/innovation/2000/delivery/organisingtodeliver/content.htm>.

Cabinet Office (2005) <www.knowledgenetwork.gov.uk/ndpb/ndpb.nsf/0/75E38C72577D2A8E80256FA1003DBBE4?OpenDocument>.

Committee on Standards in Public Life, House of Commons (2003) *Defining the Boundaries within the Executive: Ministers, Special Advisers and the Permanent Civil Service*, Norwich: HMSO.

Conservative Party (2005) *The Conservative Election Manifesto 2005: Are You Thinking What We're Thinking? It's Time for Action*, London: Conservative Party.

Fielding, S. (2002) 'Labour's campaign', in A. Geddes and J. Tonge (eds) *Labour's Second Landslide: The British General Election 2001*, Manchester: Manchester University Press, pp. 28–44.

Gershon, P. (2004) *Releasing Resources to the Frontline: Independent Review of Public Sector Efficiency*, London: Stationery Office.

HM Government (1999) *Modernising Government*, London: Stationery Office, CM4310.

HM Government (2002) *2002 Spending Review: Public Service Agreements*, London: Stationery Office, CM5771.

HM Treasury (2000) *Good Practice in Performance Reporting in Executive Agencies and Non-Departmental Bodies: A Report by the Comptroller and Auditor General*, HC 272, London: Stationery Office.

HM Treasury (2003) *Budget 2003: Building a Britain of Economic Strength and Social Justice*, <www.hmtreasury.gov.uk/budget/bud_bud03/bud_bud03_index.cfm>.

HM Treasury (2005a) *Public Service Performance Index*, <www.hm-treasury.gov.uk/performance/index.cfm>.

HM Treasury (2005b) *Performance: Department of Health*, <www.hm-treasury.gov.uk/performance/Health.cfm>.

Hood, C., Scott, C., James, O., Jones, G. and Travers, T. (1999) *Regulation Inside Government: Waste Watchers, Quality Police and Sleazebusters*, Oxford: Oxford University Press.

Howard, M. (2003) 'Speech to the Conservative Party Conference', <www.michaelhowardmp.com/sp081003.htm>.

Hyman, P. (2005) *1 out of 10: From Downing Street Vision to Classroom Reality*, London: Vintage.

James, D. (2005) *The James Review of Taxpayer Value*, London: Conservative Party.

Kavanagh, D. and Richards, D. (2000) 'Departmentalism and joined-up government: back to the future?', *Parliamentary Affairs*, 54(1).

Kennedy, C. (2004) 'Speech on the reform of public services', Cowley Street, London, 29 June.

Labour Party (2005) *Britain: Forward not Back*, London: Labour Party.

Liberal Democrats (2005) *The Real Alternative*, London: Liberal Democrats.

Marsh, D., Richards, D. and Smith, M.J. (2001) *Changing Patterns of Governance: Reinventing Whitehall*, Basingstoke: Palgrave Macmillan.

Mulgan, G. (2001), 'Joined-up government: past, present and future'. Paper presented at the British Academy Conference on Joined-Up Government, 30 October.

Mulgan, G. (2005) 'Lessons of Power', *Prospect*, May, 110.

Office of Public Service Reform (2002) *Reforming Public Services: Principles into Practice*, March, London: Stationery Office.

Osborne, D. and Gaebler, T. (1992) *Reinventing Government*, Reading, MA: Addison-Wesley.

Schumpeter, J. (1975) *Capitalism, Socialism and Democracy*, New York: Harper.

Strategy Unit (2005) <www.strategy.gov.uk/output/page82.asp>.

Toynbee, P. and Walker, D. (2005) *Better or Worse? Has Labour Delivered?* London: Bloomsbury.

Williams, M. (1999) *Crisis and Consensus in British Politics*, London: Palgrave Macmillan.

Putney

The declaration, shortly after midnight, of a Conservative gain at Putney, on a 6.5 per cent swing, provided confirmation that the BBC/ITN exit poll was correct – Labour's overall majority in Parliament was to be slashed. Indeed, had the swing to the Conservatives in Putney been replicated nationally, a hung Parliament would have resulted. Arguably, Putney represented the rebirth of the Conservative Party, its successful young female candidate, Justine Greening, offering an indication of how, in the South of England at least, it was 'cool to be Conservative' again. The Conservatives, behind in the polls for almost 13 years, had begun to regain credibility and the capture of Putney – 41st on Labour's vulnerability list – offered proof that revival at national elections (Putney was already Labour-free in terms of local councillors) had arrived.

Like so many other seats in the South, Putney had fallen to Labour during the 1997 landslide, having been a Conservative seat since 1979. The 1997 contest was notable for the demise of David Mellor, amid slow-handclapping from the Referendum Party leader, James Goldsmith, and catcalls from the defeated candidate. Although the 2005 result lacked the theatre provided by such an eclectic range of 'characters', its symbolism provided compensation. It was little surprise that the Conservative leader, Michael Howard, offered public congratulations to his victorious candidate the day after the contest.

Howard overlooked the omission of him and his party in the main text of the early campaign literature distributed by Greening. An accountant, Greening stressed how local Conservatives deliver better value: 'People in this area have looked at the low taxes and good services run by their Tory council of Wandsworth and have said "Why can't we have this at national level?"' (*The Times*, 6 May 2005). Indeed Wandsworth charges the lowest council tax in the country. In a diverse constituency embracing affluence and poverty, the successful candidate nonetheless acknowledged different motivations for the switch to the Conservatives, declaring: 'Putney is the electoral equivalent of *Murder on the Orient Express*. Everyone has their reasons but they're all different' (*The Times*, 29 April 2005).

The defending Labour MP, Tony Colman, was widely acknowledged as a diligent constituency MP, but was fighting a strong regional tide. Having unsuccessfully fought Ealing, Acton and Shepherd's Bush in 2001, Greening could testify to the progress made by the Conservatives, but the big swing to the Conservatives in London and the South East proved exceptional.

Result		%
Greening, J. (Con)	15,497	42.4
Colman, T. (Lab)	13,731	37.5
Ambache, J. (LD)	5,965	16.3
Magnum, K. (Green)	993	2.7
Gahan, A. (UKIP)	388	1.1
Con gain from Lab		
Con majority	1,766	4.8
Swing: Lab to Con		6.5

Turnout: 59.5%

16
Foreign Policy and the 'War on Terror'
Gavin Cameron

Compared to previous elections, the 2005 British general election was unusually influenced by foreign policy. This can almost wholly be attributed to the legacy of the terrorist attacks of 9/11, in which nearly 3,000 people, including 67 British citizens, were killed. Following 9/11, further major international attacks occurred in Bali in 2002 and Madrid in 2004, there were a series of thwarted plots to attack targets in the United Kingdom and British overseas facilities were attacked, most notably the British Consulate and a branch of the HSBC in Istanbul in 2003.

In the immediate aftermath of 9/11, the Labour government positioned Britain at the forefront of the developing 'War on Terror'. Prime Minister Blair emerged as US President Bush's most vocal and prominent international ally. Beginning in October 2001, Britain deployed a substantial force to Afghanistan to assist the US-led Operation Enduring Freedom in combat. This was intended to destroy the perpetrators of 9/11, al-Qaeda, and the Afghan regime sponsoring the group, the Taliban. After the combat operations were largely concluded, Britain also contributed to the International Security Assistance Force in Kabul, attempting to provide stability and security in the Afghan capital. British involvement in the campaign was widely supported by the public, with 74 per cent of people, polled before the start of the war, expressing favour. By late October, two weeks after the start of the war, support had fallen to 62 per cent amongst those polled, but was attributable largely to humanitarian concerns over the consequences of the campaign rather than to anti-war sentiment per se, which rose from 16 per cent to 20 per cent in the period (*Guardian*/ICM 2001).

The 'War on Terror' continued when the invasion of Afghanistan was followed, in March 2003, by a US-led invasion of Iraq. Whereas the connection between 9/11 and Afghanistan had been straightforward, that between Iraq and 9/11 was far less so. Moreover, while the Afghan war had received widespread international support, the invasion of Iraq was preceded by ultimately unsuccessful Anglo-American diplomatic efforts to have the impending conflict sanctioned by the UN Security Council. The rationale offered by both the United States and United

Kingdom exacerbated international reservations over the conflict. Although a series of different impetuses were provided, including the need for regime change to protect the Iraqi people and Iraqi sponsorship of al-Qaeda, one explanation remained dominant: that the regime of Saddam Hussein possessed, and intended to use, weapons of mass destruction (WMD). However, by 2004, even the US Iraq Survey Group (ISG) had concluded that there were no WMD in Iraq. From the start, British public opinion was divided on the Iraqi conflict. At the outbreak of hostilities, just over half of Britons polled favoured armed intervention.

Doubts about the war were exacerbated following the July 2003 suicide of British biological weapons expert Dr David Kelly, a Ministry of Defence employee. Kelly had expressed reservations to a BBC journalist about the 'Iraq Dossier', the British government's allegations of Iraq's possession of WMD. Andrew Gilligan, the BBC journalist, used his discussion with the anonymously sourced Kelly to claim that the government had 'sexed up' the dossier beyond the intelligence evidence to provide a more compelling case for war in Iraq. The Hutton Inquiry, convened to examine the circumstances of Kelly's death, excoriated Gilligan and the BBC for making unfounded allegations against the government. Lord Hutton also found that while the intelligence on Iraq was presented in a favourable way to make the government's case, there was no basis to believe that the dossier had been deliberately embellished beyond the intelligence evidence available. Hutton's report had a narrow remit, so made no judgement over the validity or quality of the intelligence on Iraqi WMD, and was widely perceived as a whitewash, favourable to the government. The Butler Inquiry, set up under the chairmanship of a former Cabinet Secretary to investigate the intelligence failure, reported in July 2004 that there had been no deliberate deceit by Tony Blair over intelligence on Iraq's WMD capability. However, it also found that 'Language in the dossier and used by the prime minister may have left readers with the impression that there was fuller and firmer intelligence than was the case. It was a serious weakness' (Oakley 2005).

Public doubts about the war were increased by the highly visible cost of the conflict. Although not all died as a result of enemy action, between March 2003 and the election in May 2005, 1,774 members of the Coalition forces (*Iraq Coalition Casualty Count* 2005), including 88 British troops (Ministry of Defence 2005) were killed. Iraqi civilian casualties were unknown, but reliable estimates ranged into the tens of thousands. By the start of the election campaign, the war in Iraq continued but was unpopular among the British public. A Populus poll for *The Times* tracked net support for the Iraq campaign between July 2003 and February 2005. It found that support for the Iraq war had peaked in August 2003 at +10 per cent, the only month of 15 when over 50 per cent of respondents believed the war was the 'right thing to do'. Net support for the war had been negative since October 2003, and even with the success of the Iraqi elections in January 2005, over 50 per cent of respondents believed that the war was the 'wrong thing to do' (Populus 2005a). The Labour government, and Tony Blair in particular, was perceived as having attached the country too closely to President Bush's policies, and misled Britain into joining a conflict of great cost to both sides and of questionable legitimacy. Even before the revelations of the campaign, polls conducted for the *Daily Telegraph* found over 65 per cent of respondents believed Tony Blair either exaggerated or outright lied about the threat posed by Iraq (*Daily Telegraph*/YouGov 2005a). *The Times* published a Populus poll on 25 April 2005, suggesting that 64 per cent of people believe that, if re-elected as Prime Minister, Tony Blair should be more distant from US President Bush than in the previous four years (Populus 2005b).

The 'War on Terror' encompassed other activities, such as the Antiterrorism, Crime & Security Act (ATCSA) 2001. Although this legislation had widespread support when it was passed in the wake of 9/11, in common with previous anti-terrorism legislation such as the Prevention of Terrorism Act (Temporary Provisions), several of the provisions within the 2001 Act were perceived as sufficiently severe challenges to normal civil liberties as to warrant a sunset clause, requiring the legislation be renewed on an annual basis. The Act, along with the subsequent renewals, caused considerable disquiet amongst those concerned about the balance between security and civil liberties. In March 2005, after the Law Lords had ruled that indefinite detention of foreign terror suspects without trial violated human rights, there was a major political row over the issue of 'control orders', whereby such suspects could be placed under effective house arrest or tagged to monitor their activities. Although the political fight occurred just two months before the general election and involved a stand-off between the House of Lords and the government, requiring a compromise to be brokered, the legislative aspects of the 'War on Terror' appear to have had little impact upon the election. It was the military aspect, the conflict in Iraq, that mattered above all else. The general election of 2005 was, in this respect, a 'khaki' election.

The role of foreign policy and war in previous British general elections

Foreign policy has generally played a relatively minor role in post-1945 British general elections. Even when military conflict was a recent event, domestic, rather than international, politics have tended to be critical in determining the outcome of an election. In the previous two elections, in 1997 and 2001, foreign policy was a non-issue. Although in both elections the issue of Europe was a contentious and even corrosive one, especially for the Conservatives, it is questionable whether this should be regarded as constituting foreign policy in its true sense. Arguments over Europe centred on sovereignty, legal and administrative regulations, and on economic control. As such, European discussions can be seen as more an extension of domestic politics than an aspect of foreign policy in the usual sense. Neither Geddes and Tonge (2002) nor Butler and Kavanagh (2002), in their studies of the 2001 election, include even one reference to foreign policy in the index. Goddard et al. (1998: 156–7) found that Europe and foreign affairs accounted for 8.98 per cent of BBC and 8.28 per cent of ITV political stories during the 1997 campaign, and that represented a significant increase on the coverage of such issues from the 1992 election. Nevertheless, the vast majority of this coverage was on Europe, rather than on broader foreign affairs. As such, Butler and Kavanagh (1997: 84) assert that 'Foreign policy, except for the Europe issue, did not enter the campaign.'

Wars have, historically, played a significant role in just a few of the post-1945 election campaigns. This reflects that it is unusual for a British general election to be fought during a substantial war involving British forces, possibly because the political fortunes of the governing party are likely to be tied to major military successes and failures, an issue over which any government can have only partial control. In 1983 and 1992, election campaigns were fought a year after significant conflicts: the Falklands War and the first Gulf War respectively. The Conservative Party enjoyed a large increase in popularity until March 1991, the end of the Gulf War, but it is questionable whether this reflected the removal of Margaret Thatcher as leader, rather than support arising from the successful conduct of the war. By May 1991, Conservative support had fallen below 37 per cent, suggesting that any political benefits from the conflict were finished nearly a year before the April 1992 election (Sanders 1992: 176). The impact of the Falklands War on the 1983 election is contested. Conservative Party support rose from 33 per cent to 42 per cent within a month of the Argentine invasion of the islands, and remained robust until the election (Sanders 1992: 217). However, while the Falklands conflict clearly indicated a firm Conservative government, the party's major political victory in 1983 owed much to a strengthening economy, a Labour Party riven by in-fighting, especially over the future of Britain's nuclear deterrent (Butler and Kavanagh 1984: 95–7), that fought a disastrous campaign under Michael Foot, and an effective Alliance that further took votes away from Labour (Butler 1989: 36–8).

In fact, with possible exception of the February 1974 election when the Middle East crisis had sparked a major energy crisis, foreign affairs mattered in a British general election only in 1945 and 1951. The 1945 campaign was fought between the military defeats of Germany in May and of Japan in August. The Conservatives campaigned on the basis of Winston Churchill's record as successful war leader. Although Churchill's claim that socialism would mean a Gestapo for Britain was regarded as helpful to Labour, rather than the Conservatives, the Labour Party's victory owed vastly more to their vision for a post-war Britain, and to a lesser extent to some voters' determination to punish the Conservative Party for its pre-war policy of appeasement towards Germany (Butler 1989: 5–9). The 1951 election campaign was conducted during the Korean War. The Labour Party's campaign accused the Conservatives of being socially regressive and warmongers. This even led to the *Daily Mirror* running a front-page election-day headline of 'Whose finger on the trigger?', sparking a successful libel suit by Churchill. The Conservative Party's victory in 1951 was attributed to a reaction against Labour's negative campaign, as well as weariness over the post-war austerity measures that had been enacted under Attlee's government (Butler 1989: 11–13). It is perhaps significant that, as in 2005, and in contrast to all the other examples above, both 1945 and 1951 elections occurred while war remained an ongoing issue.

Initial positions on foreign policy

All three main parties discussed combating terrorism within its election manifesto, and all three manifestos covered much of the same ground in the assessments and proposals for foreign policy, although there were significant differences in emphasis. Although the Labour Party's manifesto ran to over 100 pages, the subsection dealing overtly with terrorism contained just three paragraphs. In it, the party emphasised its plans to protect the country by targeting groups and their fundraising, and by enhancing the authorities' powers of arrest and detention (Labour Party 2005: 53–4). However, an entire chapter of the manifesto was devoted to international policy more broadly, about 10 per cent of the total document (Labour Party 2005: 82–91). Within the chapter on international policy, the Labour Party defended the government's record of dealing with international terrorism without overtly claiming there were WMD in Iraq to justify an invasion, noting that

> We have worked closely with the US and other nations to combat the threat of terrorism in Afghanistan and in Iraq. The threat of the proliferation of chemical, biological and nuclear weapons – and their use by rogue states or terrorist groups – is a pressing issue for the world today. (Labour Party 2005: 85)

The subsequent section of the chapter asserted that terrorism was a threat to British citizens, and offered both validation for, and regrets at, the cost of fighting the war against such violence:

> We mourn the loss of life of innocent civilians and coalition forces in the war in Iraq and the subsequent terrorism. But the butchery of Saddam is over and across Iraq, eight million people risked their lives to vote earlier this year. Many people disagreed with the action we took in Iraq. We respect and understand their views. But we should all now unite to support the fledgling democracy in Iraq. (Labour Party 2005: 85–7)

This section of the manifesto can thus been seen as a means of offering sop to the anti-war wing of the Labour Party and its supporters, while simultaneously claiming that the cause for which the war was fought was justified.

The Conservative Party's manifesto devoted a paragraph to combating terrorism in the context of a wider discussion of law and order. The party promised to 'place the highest possible priority' on the issue, to include 'greater inter-departmental cooperation, increased funding for the intelligence services, tougher anti-terrorism laws, immigration controls and a new Homeland Security Minister to coordinate the response' (Conservative Party 2005:16). Obviously, this final suggestion echoed one of the main US responses to 9/11, to create a Cabinet-level post in charge of a department that consolidated much of the national security architecture under a single entity. The party devoted one section of the manifesto to foreign policy, roughly 10 per cent of the entire document. This included a restatement of the Conservatives' position on the Iraq war, that it was a positive measure, undertaken for the wrong reasons:

> Mr. Blair misrepresented intelligence to make the case for war in Iraq, and failed to plan for the aftermath of Saddam Hussein's downfall. It is nevertheless the case that a democratic Iraq would be a powerful beacon of hope in a troubled part of the world. So we believe that Britain must remain committed to rebuilding Iraq and allowing democracy to take hold. (Conservative Party 2005: 26)

This policy reflected the Conservative position throughout the campaign and captured the party's dilemma in attempting to support the government's Iraq war while distancing itself from the Labour Party (Conservative Party 2005: 25–7).

As with the other parties, the Liberal Democrats' manifesto discussed countering terrorism as part of the justice and crime section of the document, and devoted about 10 per cent of the publication to foreign affairs. Unlike those of the Labour and Conservative Parties, the Liberal Democrats' manifesto emphasised civil liberties over security in dealing with terrorism. It questioned the effectiveness of identity cards, and pledged to overturn the aspects of the government's legislation that curtailed suspects' rights to jury trials or that permitted hearsay evidence or previous convictions to be used at trial, or that permitted control orders at the discretion of a Home Secretary. Instead, the Liberal Democrats proposed more police and a co-ordinated UK Border Force, and to extend the criminal law and some rules of evidence in terrorism trials, but within the framework of a robust reinforcement of the judicial process (Liberal Democrat Party 2005: 8–9).

Unlike the Labour and Conservative Parties, the Liberal Democrats were able to present an unambiguous position on the war in Iraq:

There were no weapons of mass destruction, there was no serious and current threat, and inspectors were denied the time they needed to finish their job. Thousands of soldiers and civilians have been killed and it has cost the UK over £3.5 billion. Britain must never again support an illegal military intervention. But by invading Iraq the Government has imposed on us a moral obligation to work towards a stable, secure and free Iraq. (Liberal Democrat Party 2005: 14)

In a sidebar, Liberal Democrat Shadow Foreign Secretary, Sir Menzies Campbell, noted that 'Britain was taken to war against Iraq without express UN authority and on a flawed prospectus. The Government built its case on unreliable intelligence, in circumstances of doubtful legality' (Liberal Democrat Party 2005: 14). Although pledging to support the rebuilding of Iraq, the Liberal Democrats proposed that the key way to tackle terrorism was through greater international co-operation via the United Nations and the European Union, and by working with the United States to promote respect for international law, democracy and human rights (Liberal Democrat Party 2005: 14–15). All three parties noted the importance of working towards a wider peace in the Middle East, and pledged to provide British assistance in achieving that goal.

The campaign

Although the three main parties showed a high degree of convergence in identifying the principal foreign policy issues, apart from some brief discussion of international development, most of these topics mattered very little in the election campaign. The exception was the war in Iraq. The war was relatively insignificant in the first half of the campaign, but dominated the second half, following the leaking of the Attorney General's advice to the government on the legality of the conflict, the defection of Labour MP Brian Sedgemore to the Liberal Democrats over the issue of the war, and allegations that Tony Blair had committed Britain to military action and regime change in Iraq as early as the summer of 2002. Even relatively innocuous events related to the war became significant. On 2 May, three days before the election, news broke during one of Tony Blair's press conferences of the death of another British serviceman, Anthony Wakefield. Blair's words of sympathy for Wakefield's family were the dominant election story in the media for that day (Morris and Grice 2005).

The three main parties' positions on the war in Iraq were clear from the start of the election, in spite of the lack of emphasis the war initially received in the campaign. The Conservatives argued that although Tony Blair had lied over the reasons for going to war, misrepresenting the intelligence available about Iraqi possession of WMD, the war was nevertheless justified. The Liberal Democrats called for an independent inquiry as 'there is no doubt that we were misled' with regard to 'the threat that we were under as a country' and 'the true aims of government policy' (BBC News Online 2005b). Labour claimed that the other parties were attempting to use the war to distract from the paucity of their own policies, and that the election was not about endorsing the decision to go to war, but rather about domestic policies in the next parliamentary session. Labour also tried to defuse the issue by hinting that the end of the engagement was in sight and that British forces might be home within a year (Ingrams 2005). There was also some limited skirmishing on the fringes of the issue, with the Conservatives attacking Tony Blair over the naming of David Kelly, for example. Reg Keys' campaign against the war in Sedgefield received coverage throughout the campaign (Vulliamy 2005), but initially the war in Iraq was rarely discussed by the main parties, despite being everywhere. The Liberal Democrats had planned to spend the first few weeks of the campaign focusing on their domestic agenda, before finishing the election on Iraq, an issue where they had widespread support (McSmith 2005).

The relative lull changed on 24 April, with the publication in the *Mail on Sunday* of the leaked details of Lord Goldsmith's advice, as Attorney General, to the government on the legality of a war in Iraq. In the *Mail on Sunday*'s version, in his 7 March advice, Lord Goldsmith suggested that the war in Iraq would be illegal, and provided six areas under which the war might be challenged in international law, including that it was only the UN, rather than the United States or United Kingdom that could decide whether Iraq was in contravention of UN Security Council resolutions (White 2005). Until the government published the full version of Goldsmith's advice, on 28 April, the opposition parties appeared justified in claiming that Blair had overridden legal advice in going to war, a claim strenuously denied by both Blair and Goldsmith. The 28 April version of the Attorney General's advice made clear that in his opinion the war was broadly legal, while noting the six caveats under international law. Even then, the issue remained potentially devastating for the Labour campaign because, on 17 March 2003, the Attorney General had provided a written answer to Parliament, shortly before the vote on the Iraq war. In it, Lord Goldsmith's caveats or concerns had been removed, leaving only the apparently unequivocal opinion that the war would be legal. The explosive nature of the allegations was compounded when it was alleged that the Cabinet's decision to go to war was based on the 17 March document, rather than the more nuanced 7 March opinion (BBC News Online 2005c). Clare Short, International Development Secretary at the time, claimed not only that this was so, but that members of the Cabinet had no opportunity to question Goldsmith on his opinion, points disputed by current Cabinet members Gordon Brown and Patricia Hewitt at a press conference with Tony Blair on 28 April (Grice 2005a). Obviously, seeing Goldsmith's 7 March opinion would have decreased the likelihood that Parliament, or possibly the Cabinet, would have approved the start of war in 2003. The rest of the campaign was dominated by questions over the legality of the war in Iraq, whether the government had misled the country about the legitimacy of the conflict, and even whether British ministers and soldiers could be prosecuted in the International Criminal Court for pursuing an illegal campaign. Unsurprisingly, the opposition parties did everything possible to exploit the Labour Party's discomfort over the issue. The first ever live television debate involving the leaders of all three main parties, albeit questioned separately, held on 28 April, was wholly dominated by questions over Iraq. Throughout the rest of the campaign, both the Conservatives and Liberal Democrats sought to tie Iraq to broader questions about the trustworthiness of the Prime Minister. However, Charles Kennedy was at pains to distance himself and his party from both Labour and Conservative Parties, urging voters to punish Labour 'for the government's rush to war', as well as the Conservatives for 'their party's supine support' (BBC News Online 2005e).

A further leaked document, published in the *Sunday Times* on 1 May, alleged that war preparations began at the highest levels of government in July 2002, eight months before there was parliamentary approval for military action in Iraq. The memo, discussing a 23 July meeting, appeared to show that the US administration was committed to regime change in Iraq, and that 'intelligence and facts were being fixed around policy' (an allegation subsequently vehemently denied by the US administration). Furthermore, the memo suggested that in April 2002 Tony Blair had pledged British support for the inevitable US military campaign against Iraq. The minutes of the meeting recorded Foreign Secretary, Jack Straw, suggesting that since the case for war was 'thin', they should 'work up' an ultimatum about weapons inspectors to 'help with the legal justification'. Blair replied that 'it would make a big difference politically and legally if Saddam refused to allow in the UN inspectors'. A secret briefing, separate from the minutes of the 23 July meeting, argued that Britain and the United States had to 'create' conditions to justify war (Smith 2005). Both Tony Blair and Lord Boyce, then Chief of the Defence Staff, insisted that the July 2002 memo should be seen as a 'what if' exercise and not be interpreted as indicating that a firm decision had been taken, but rather that preparations were to be made, in case a war did need to be fought (Evans 2005).

At first, the allegations over Iraq appeared to do little damage to Labour Party support. A *Times*/ITV poll, conducted between the partial leak of the Attorney General's advice and the government's publication of the full opinion, suggested that Labour retained a lead of 8 per cent over the Conservatives, 40 per cent to 32 per cent, with the Liberal Democrats unchanged at 21 per cent. However, the same poll found that 22 per cent had lost their previous trust for Tony Blair as a result of Iraq, and of those, 30 per cent would still support Labour, but 70 per cent would vote for other parties (Riddell 2005a). Moreover, the controversy over Iraq took its toll on later polling numbers. An NOP/*Independent* poll, published on 5 May, showed that Labour's previous ten-point lead had collapsed to three points in the final week of the campaign which was dominated by arguments over the war (Grice 2005b). Labour's campaign ended with Tony Blair pleading with supporters not to endanger progressive politics with a self-defeating protest vote over Iraq (White et al. 2005).

The result – how much did the 'War on Terror' matter?

Overall, the Labour Party suffered a 6 per cent decline in support between the elections of 2001 and 2005. The Liberal Democrats made most gains, in terms of increasing their popular support, from 19 per cent to 23 per cent. The Liberal Democrats were the main beneficiaries of Labour supporters that were supposedly disaffected by the Iraq war. In a pre-election MORI poll, among Labour defectors to the Liberal Democrats, 33 per cent cited Iraq as a key influence on their voting decision. In the 25 most marginal Labour–Liberal Democrat seats, the average swing against Labour in the election was 6.7 per cent (Cowling 2005). However, much of the Liberal Democrats' dramatic increase in support occurred in safe Labour seats. Although the Liberal Democrats gained twelve seats from Labour, it was the Conservative Party that made most gains in marginal constituencies, gaining 31 seats from Labour. This led some in Labour to claim that Conservative MPs had 'got in through the back door' due to people switching to the Liberal Democrats as a result of the war in Iraq (Webster 2005). If true, this would be ironic. The Conservative Party supported the war, and during the election campaign Michael Howard suggested that the war was justified, even if WMD had not been discovered in Iraq (BBC News Online 2005d). However, Howard also campaigned on the basis that since Blair had lied about the legitimacy of the war, he could not be trusted to tell the truth about other issues.

One of the clearest results pertaining to the war was that Respect Party candidate, George Galloway, won a heated battle in Bethnal Green and Bow against the Labour incumbent and prominent supporter of the Iraq war, Oona King. The anti-war Respect Party fielded candidates in 25 constituencies, polling 68,065 votes. However, George Galloway's campaign vote represented one-quarter of the Respect Party's national vote total, so the average total for the remaining 24 seats where a Respect candidate was standing was just over 2,000 votes, suggesting a single issue campaign based on opposition to the war was only a limited success (BBC News Online 2005a). The exceptions were in three seats: East Ham, West Ham, and Birmingham Sparkbrook, where Respect came second, reducing Labour's vote by 19.2 per cent, 18.7 per cent and 21 per cent, and polling 8,000, 6,000 and 10,500 votes respectively. Significantly, all three constituencies, like Bethnal Green and Bow, are seats in the UK top ten for Muslim population. The 2001 census found that there are 40 constituencies within the United Kingdom where Muslims comprise over 10 per cent of the population. Traditionally Labour supporters, although with greater variations among the second and third generations, British Muslims were alienated from the party by the war in Iraq, along with anti-terrorism legislation and a continued backlash from 9/11 that many Muslims felt unfairly targeted them. Labour lost substantial numbers of supporters in all of these top ten seats. Rochdale, not one of the top ten, but still with a population that includes 17,000 Muslims, saw an 8 per cent swing from Labour to the Liberal Democrats, resulting in a defeat for incumbent Lorna Fitzsimmons. Nonetheless, Jack Straw, the Foreign Secretary, held his Blackburn seat comfortably, in spite of a large Muslim population in the constituency and a concerted anti-war campaign. Although there was a 12 per cent swing to the Liberal Democrats, the Conservative Party also lost support, so Straw's majority was only slightly reduced, from 9,000 in 2001 to 8,009 in 2005. Furthermore, it would obviously be a mistake to believe that the Muslim population of the UK acted as a coherent unidirectional political entity during the 2005 election. Muslim candidates won seats for the Labour Party in Birmingham Perry Bar, Dewsbury, and Glasgow Central, and a female Muslim Labour candidate, Yasmin Qureshi, failed to recover Brent East from the Liberal's Sarah Teather (Casciani 2005).

Labour Party rebels, such as Glenda Jackson, also campaigned on the basis of their opposition to the war, arguing that a vote for them was a vote for Labour but against the government (MacIntyre 2005). Jackson retained her seat in Hampstead and Highgate, although she suffered a 6.3 per cent swing in support from Labour to Conservative, with the Liberal Democrats also increasing their support by 6.5 per cent from 2001. It is worth noting, however, that in spite of her opposition to the war, Jackson's 8.6 per cent decline in support was comparable to that experienced by the Labour candidate in Putney (9 per cent) and greater than that of the Labour candidate in Ilford North (6 per cent), both of which were Conservative gains. This experience was replicated across the country, with voters punishing Labour Party candidates, irrespective of their position on the war in Iraq. In Birmingham Ladywood, the fifth most Muslim seat in the UK, former Cabinet minister Clare Short, another vocal opponent of the war, saw a swing of 20.1 per cent from Labour to the Liberal Democrats, although she still received 52 per cent of the votes cast (Casciani 2005). Robin Cook, who resigned from the Cabinet over the war in Iraq, said: 'Even I have people saying to me they can't support Labour … If it's like that for me, it must be at least as strong for others' (Morris and Grice 2005).

Even when they were unsuccessful, independent anti-war candidates attracted attention. In the Prime Minister's own Sedgefield constituency, anti-war candidate and father of a deceased serviceman, Reg Keys, polled 10 per cent of the vote. Keys dedicated his campaign to the 88 servicemen killed in Iraq since 2003, urged Tony Blair to apologise for the war, and said that his result had sent a 'clear and resounding message about the Iraq war' (BBC News Online 2005f). Rose Gentle, whose son was killed in Iraq, contested East Kilbride, Strathaven and Lesmahagow against the Armed Forces Minister, Adam Ingram, receiving only 3.2 per cent of the vote, but extensive local and national coverage.

In his post-election address, Tony Blair acknowledged that the war in Iraq had been a deeply divisive issue. However, while he accepted that it had been 'a big issue', he suggested that people had really voted on other issues, such as public services and the economy (BBC News Online 2005g). Others argued that Iraq was a critical reason why core Labour supporters deserted the party in the 2005 election. In the immediate aftermath of the election, the British press was unanimous in identifying the war as a factor in Labour's reduced majority. The *Sun* suggested that Labour supporters had revolted as 'the anti-war brigade turned nasty and voted for anyone but Labour'. The *Daily Mail* said Blair 'paid a heavy price for his lies over Iraq ... as a voter backlash devastated his Commons', while the *Daily Telegraph* opined that Blair had 'suffered a serious backlash over the Iraq war' (CNN.com 2005).

Iraq certainly played a role in the substantially increased support for the Liberal Democrats, especially in Labour seats and in swinging a number of marginal seats against Labour in 2005. However, the importance of the war should not be exaggerated. Both Labour and Liberal Democrat strategists, speaking after the election, noted that public services, the economy and social issues such as immigration were more important factors in determining the vote of most people. Liberal Democrats found in February that most people had already internalised Iraq within their personal political calculation, so that there were few extra votes to be gained on the issue. The party believed though that its opposition to the war did ensure that they received additional attention from voters who then voted for the party on the basis of their other policies. To that extent, Iraq served as a vehicle for Liberal Democrat gains (Moulitsas 2005).

Those people who felt strongly about the war were not evenly divided among the population. In addition to many Muslims, students and the professional and liberal middle classes (the working class appeared less hostile to the war) were more likely to regard the Iraq war as a substantial issue. Labour's most dramatic losses, Blaenau Gwent excepted, occurred in seats such as Manchester Withington or Bethnal Green and Bow, where there were substantial numbers of students, Muslims or professional middle classes. As well as being a source of indignation in its own right, the Iraq war also served to undermine trust in Labour generally, and Tony Blair more specifically, so, for example, students were less willing to accept the party's position on university tuition fees (Cowling 2005).

The polls about the war tell apparently conflicting stories, partly because the questions being posed were subtly different, some reflecting voting intentions while others merely asked whether the conflict in Iraq was a significant factor. A *Times*/ITV poll by Populus, published on 23 April, asked whether the war in Iraq would be a significant factor in people's decision about how to vote in the general election. Overall, 45 per cent of those surveyed suggested that Iraq would be important in that decision, with 54 per cent saying it would not be a factor. However, there was a major gender difference, with 37 per cent of men and 51 per cent of women saying Iraq mattered. Among the different parties' supporters, the numbers of those for whom the Iraq war was a significant factor were Labour 35 per cent, Conservative 43 per cent, and Liberal Democrat 54 per cent (Riddell 2005b). A BBC poll, published on election day, found that 23 per cent of people surveyed cited opposition to the Iraq war as a reason for being reluctant to vote Labour, while 21 per cent said that they did not trust Mr. Blair, although these two elements overlapped to some degree. This data contrasts with earlier polls which consistently found just 3 per cent of people would make their voting decision purely on the basis of the opposition to the war (MacAskill 2005). As such, it cannot be argued that Iraq was the sole issue that caused voters to desert Labour in 2005. Some traditional Conservative supporters returned to that party over issues such as immigration and asylum. More Labour supporters, especially on the left of the party, moved to the Liberal Democrats, fuelled by a personal anti-Blair movement, along with disenchantment over other Labour policies, such as those on tuition fees and civil liberties. Nonetheless, it is undeniable that, for many, the war in Iraq was a significant additional source of anger, and for some, it certainly was an issue of cleavage with the party. It became the symbol for disenchantment with the government. As a final point though, it is important to remember that Labour did win the 2005 election, more voters stayed with the party than left it for others. For some, this meant doing as the *Guardian* suggested, and holding their noses while they voted for the least bad option, but it is critical to recall that however much anger the war in Iraq caused, it did not prevent 35.2 per cent of voters from supporting Labour.

Conclusion

With his reduced majority, and the perception that the war in Iraq and his foreign policy, more generally, played a role in that, Tony Blair is likely to pursue a more cautious foreign policy. However, since all three main parties support the continued rebuilding of Iraq, it is unlikely that the 2005 election will mean that Britain will cease in its efforts under UN Security Resolution 1546. The election result may mean a policy less overtly Alanticist in direction. Polly Toynbee spoke for many of the left when she asked: 'Will this shock response to the ill-fated Iraqi adventure at last turn us away from the fantasy bridge across the Atlantic, the special relationship that has done us lasting harm over the last half century?' (Toynbee 2005).

Labour's proposals for further anti-terrorism legislation are unlikely to be undermined by the election result. Although before 5 May, House of Lords and Labour backbench rebellions had compelled compromises in the legislation, such as sunset clauses on key aspects of the bill. The terrorist attacks of July 2005 have altered the political climate for such legislation.

Tony Blair's leadership of the Labour Party was undermined by the election, despite his delivery of a third term in office. The conflict in Iraq was widely perceived as 'his' war, and he became an electoral liability, compared to the party as a whole, for the first time. A YouGov poll for the *Daily Telegraph* on 31 January 2005 found that 47 per cent of respondents believed Tony Blair was a liability to the Labour Party, compared to 37 per cent who thought he was an asset (YouGov/*Daily Telegraph* 2005b). A YouGov poll for the *Sunday Times* on 24 April 2005 revealed that 28 per cent of respondents were less likely to vote Labour when they saw Tony Blair on television, compared to 14 per cent who thought they would be more likely to do so, and 48 per cent for whom it would make no difference to their voting (YouGov/*Sunday Times* 2005). Labour dissident Bob Marshall-Andrews, whose majority in Medway was reduced from 3,780 to 213 votes, claimed: 'It is impossible not to draw the conclusion that the war and the Prime Minister have caused a serious haemorrhage in Labour votes.' As such, he called for a change of leader 'sooner rather than later'. A post-election Populus poll suggested that 53 per cent of Labour voters wanted a Labour government with a smaller parliamentary majority (Cowling 2005). This would limit the scope for additional Iraq-style adventurism. Furthermore, 54 per cent of Labour supporters backed their party as a result of negative views about the alternatives, rather than due to holding a positive view of Labour (Cowling 2005). Although Tony Blair's position was strengthened after the July 2005 terrorist attacks, the leader in the *Guardian* on 6 May summarised the election and its aftermath:

> Iraq was not the only reason why these voters deserted Labour ... but there is little doubt that historians will look back on the 2005 election as the Iraq election ... Many voted that Mr. Blair's refusal to listen to the people over Iraq was grounds for divorce. In so doing, they have probably achieved their objects – to cast a vote of conscience, [and] to reduce the Labour majority to a human size.

References

BBC News Online (2005a) 'Election 2005: Full national scoreboard', <http://news.bbc.co.uk/1/shared/vote2005/html/scoreboard.stm>.

BBC News Online (2005b) 'Fact check: Did Blair lie over WMD?', 25 April, <http://news.bbc.co.uk/go/pr/fr/-/1/hi/uk_politics/vote_2005/issues/4481139.stm>.

BBC News Online (2005c) 'Fact check: Was the Iraq war legal?', 29 April, <http://news.bbc.co.uk/go/pr/fr/-/1/uk_politics/vote_2005/issues/4492443.stm>.

BBC News Online (2005d) 'Howard stance on Iraq "unlawful"', 29 April, <http://news.bbc.co.uk/go/pr/fr/-/2/hi/uk_news/politics/vote_2005/frontpage/4497777.stm>.

BBC News Online (2005e) 'Kennedy seeks Iraq war "justice"', 28 April, <http://news.bbc.co.uk/go/pr/fr/-/2/hi/uk_news/politics/vote_2005/frontpage/4479625.stm>.

BBC News Online (2005f) 'Labour acknowledge "Iraq factor"', 6 May, <http://news.bbc.co.uk/go/pr/fr/-1/hi/uk_politics/vote_2005/frontpage/4518785.stm>.

BBC News Online (2005g) 'Tony Blair's third term speech', 6 May, <http://news.bbc.co.uk/go/pr/fr/-/2/hi/uk_politics/vote_2005/frontpage/4522185.stm>.

Butler, D. (1989) *British General Elections Since 1945*, Oxford: Blackwell.

Butler, D. and Kavanagh, D. (1984) *The British General Election of 1983*, Basingstoke: Macmillan.

Butler, D. and Kavanagh, D. (1997) *The British General Election of 1997*, Basingstoke: Macmillan.

Butler, D. and Kavanagh, D. (eds) (2002) *The British General Election of 2001*, Basingstoke: Palgrave Macmillan.

Casciani, D. (2005) 'Muslim vote shifts against Labour', BBC News Online, 6 May, <http://news.bbc.co.uk/1/hi/uk_politics/vote_2005/frontpage/4520527.stm>.

CNN.com (2005) 'UK papers: "Bloody nose" for Blair', 6 May, <http://www.cnn.com/2005/WORLD/europe/05/06/uk.election.press/index.html>.

Conservative Party (2005) *Conservative Election Manifesto 2005*, available at: <http://www.conservatives.com/pdf/manifesto-uk-2005.pdf>.

Cowling, D. (2005) 'Who deserted Labour?', BBC News Online, 10 May, <http://news.bbc.co.uk/go/pr/fr/-/1/hi/uk_politics/vote_2005/issues/4520847.stm>.

Daily Telegraph/YouGov (2005a) www.yougov.com/yougov_website/asp_besPollArchives/pdf/te1050101013_1pdf>.

Daily Telegraph/YouGov (2005b)

Evans, M. (2005) 'Leak shows "Blair set on Iraq war a year before invasion"', *The Times*, 2 May.

Geddes, A. and Tonge, J. (eds) (2002) *Labour's Second Landslide: The British General Election 2001*, Manchester: Manchester University Press.

Goddard, P., Scammell, M. and Semetko, H. (1998) 'Too much of a good thing? Television in the 1997 election campaign', in I. Crewe, B. Gottschalk and J. Bartle (eds) *Political Communications: Why Labour Won The General Election of 1997*, London: Frank Cass.

Grice, A. (2005a) 'Blair's spectacular U-turn on legal advice leaves unanswered questions', *Independent*, 29 April.

Grice, A. (2005b) 'One quarter of voters uncertain as Labour sag at the final post', *Independent*, 5 May.

Guardian/ICM (2001) 'Afghan poll – October 2001', 30 October, <www.icmresearch.co.uk/reviews/2001/guardian-afghan2-poll-oct-2001.htm>.

Ingrams, R. (2005) 'Don't mention the war', *Guardian*, 17 April.

Iraq Coalition Casualty Count (2005) <http://icasualties.org/oif/>.

Labour Party (2005) *Forward not Back: The Labour Party Election Manifesto 2005*, London: Labour Party.

Liberal Democrat Party (2005) *The Real Alternative*, London: Liberal Democrat Party.

MacAskill, E. (2005) 'Poll shows war factor was key issue for many', *Guardian*, 6 May.

MacIntyre, B. (2005) 'Wake up and smell the latte, darling, and vote for Glenda', *The Times*, 2 May 2005.

McSmith, A. (2005) 'Lib Dems to focus on Iraq in campaign's final stretch', *Independent*, 24 April.

Ministry of Defence (2005) 'Operation TELIC: British casualties & fatalities', <www.operations.mod.uk/telic/casualties.html>.

Morris, N. and Grice, A. (2005) 'Labour's dismal performance in London casts a shadow over win', *Independent*, 6 May.

Moulitsas, M. (2005) 'More than war', *Guardian*, 6 May.

Oakley, R. (2005) 'Iraq factor: Blair's 34 words', CNN.com, 25 April, <www.cnn.com/2005/WORLD/europe/04/25/blair.iraq.oakley/>.

Populus (2005a), '*The Times* poll, February 4–6, 2005', <www.populuslimited.com/poll_summaries/2005_02_04_times.htm>.

Populus (2005b) 'Tony Blair and George Bush', available at: <www.populuslimited.com/poll_summaries/2005_04_25_times_tony_georgebush.htm>.

Riddell, P. (2005a) 'Damage limitation keeps Labour on top', *The Times*, 29 April.

Riddell, P. (2005b) 'Women are more likely to be swayed by Iraq war', *The Times*, 23 May.

Sanders, D. (1992) 'Why the Conservative Party won – again', in A. King (ed.) *Britain at the Polls 1992*, Chatham: Chatham House Publishers.

Smith, M. (2005) 'Blair hit by new leak of secret war plan', *The Times*, 1 May.

Toynbee, P. (2005) 'Tony Blair alone bears the blame', *Guardian*, 6 May.

Vulliamy, E. (2005) 'Doing for Tom: Mr Keys takes on the prime minister', *Guardian*, 22 April.

Webster, P. (2005) 'Blair returns to No. 10 but Iraq takes its toll', *The Times*, 6 May.

White, M. (2005) 'Opposition goes on Iraq offensive', *Guardian*, 25 April.

White, M., Watt, N. and Branigan, T. (2005) 'Blair's last plea to waverers over Iraq', *Guardian*, 5 May.

YouGov/*Sunday Times* (2005) 'General Election Survey, April 21–23, 2005' <www.yougov.com/archives/pdf/STI050101005_1.pdf>.

Bethnal Green and Bow

Few constituency contests in British political history can have been so bitterly contested as Bethnal Green and Bow. Representing the Labour Party was sitting MP Oona King; representing Respect – the Unity Coalition was George Galloway, the ex-member for Glasgow Kelvin and an ex-member of the Labour Party expelled for his opposition to the war in Iraq and dubbed the 'member for Baghdad Central' by some of his erstwhile parliamentary colleagues. Allegations of threats, intimidation and even racist abuse marred the campaign. A passion for politics spilled over into real concern for the safety of the candidates.

Bethnal Green would seem natural Labour territory, but the local political mix in the vibrant, cosmopolitan heart of the East End is combustible. Oona King had already had her fingers burned at the 1997 general election, when even in the year of Labour's landslide there was a 7 per cent swing against her as a black woman in a seat where around 40 per cent of the population are non-white. A good many of these were Bengali Muslims who felt that someone from their community should have been selected for the seat. In 1997 as Conservatives fell like nine-pins around the country, the Conservative vote in Bethnal Green for a Bengali Muslim candidate actually rose by 5 per cent.

Even the deployment of Labour's big guns such as Gordon Brown and Ken Livingstone failed to protect King from the consequences of her decision to support the war in an area where the majority of her constituents clearly did not. King's claim that Galloway 'couldn't deliver a pizza', let alone a better record of delivery for constituents, was countered by the impact of the Iraq war. Galloway announced that he would be a one-term candidate and focused his campaign on the war, on Tony Blair and on those he characterised as New Labour 'puppets' such as Oona King. The tactics paid off as Labour's vote crumbled and Respect took their only seat in the House of Commons, although in neighbouring areas of London they also did well.

The acrimony of the campaign continued at the count where Galloway made it clear that the win was all about Iraq, denounced electoral fraud, called for the resignation of the Returning Officer and then angrily broke off an interview with BBC TV's Jeremy Paxman whose first question to Galloway was to ask how it felt to take a seat from one of the very few black women in Parliament.

Result		%
Galloway, G. (Respect)	15,801	35.9
King, O (Lab)	14,978	34.4
Faruk, B.S.	6,244	14.1
Dulu, S.N.I.	4,298	11.1
Foster, J. (Green)	1,950	4.3
Etefia, E. (Alliance for Change)	68	0.1
Pugh, C.	38	0.1
Respect majority	823	1.5

Turnout: 51.2%

Sedgefield

No image quite summed up the 2005 general election more than the tired and drawn face of Prime Minister Tony Blair as he listened to the speech of Reg Keys at the Sedgefield count. Keys, who stood as an independent candidate in Sedgefield, had lost his 20-year-old son Tom, killed while serving in the Military Police in Iraq. Keys had been instrumental in establishing the organisation Military Families Against the War, which called for an independent public inquiry into the decision to go to war in Iraq.

It was always going to be an uphill struggle for Keys in a Labour heartland. Backed by an unlikely collection of supporters including musician Brian Eno and novelist Frederick Forsyth, Mr Keys emerged as the 2005 campaign's 'man in the white suit' standing on a platform of truth and honesty, the role adopted by Martin Bell when he stood against Neil Hamilton in Tatton in 1997. Keys had no political experience and said that 'Unlike Martin Bell, I don't wear a white suit and I'm not used to the media. I've got a Midlands accent and I'm an introvert' … 'I'm not exactly what you'd expect of a politician, but I do know that I can embarrass Tony Blair.' Keys did not come close to winning, but did save his deposit and polled a creditable 4,252 votes in fourth place. When Blair arrived for the election count in the early hours of 6 May, it was becoming clear that Labour was suffering losses, whilst heading for a third term. Blair increased his majority in Sedgefield, but the controversy over the war was stark nationally and locally.

In his speech after the results had been declared Keys said: 'Fighting this campaign has not been an easy task for me, but I had to do it for my son Thomas who was sent to war under extremely controversial circumstances. All the people who have given me their vote tonight have sent out a clear and resounding message about the Iraq war.' An abiding image of the campaign will be the strained look on Blair's face as he listened to Keys' speech and the dignity with which Mr Keys conducted himself in the face of personal loss. Sedgefield, together with Bethnal Green and Bow, were the seats where the Iraq war had its most visible and dramatic effects on the 2005 election.

Result		%
Blair, T. (Lab)	24,429	58.9
Lockwood, A. (Con)	5,972	14.4
Browne, R. (Lib Dem)	4,935	11.9
Keys, R. (Independent)	4,252	10.2
Others (11 candidates)	1,895	4.6
Lab hold		
Lab majority	18,449	44.5
Swing: Con to Lab		0.2

Turnout: 62.2%

17

Nationalism: Immigration and European Integration at the 2005 General Election

Andrew Geddes

Nationalist sentiment has become a more powerful force in British politics since the 1990s. It has been particularly evident with regards to party competition, public discussion and campaign debate centred on two issues that separately or together are often understood as threats to national identity and/or self-government, particularly to English national identity within the United Kingdom. These two issues are immigration and European integration. While immigration and European integration are, of course, separate and distinct issues, they can be analysed alongside each other for three reasons. First, because they both draw into view ideas about the nation, the state and sovereign authority therein and the ways in which understandings of these terms change over time and differ between and within political parties. Second, because immigration and European integration have both been salient themes in campaigns by parties on the political right at general elections since 1997. Third, because they have become linked through movement towards a common EU migration and asylum policy within which the UK participates to some extent.

The issue of European integration was, of course, to the fore in the Conservative campaigns in 1997 and 2001, but was barely mentioned in 2005. Instead immigration – or to be more precise, an immigration system that was allegedly 'out of control' – was a strong Conservative theme. For the United Kingdom Independence Party (UKIP) both European integration and immigration were core themes during the 2005 campaign. One of their campaign posters proclaimed the need to end what they saw as 'mass EU immigration'. On the extreme right the British National Party (BNP) took a hard-line anti-EU and anti-immigration stance. Despite their titles, UKIP and the BNP are parties that barely exist outside England. Labour and the Liberal Democrats have been more concerned to neutralise these issues because of a fear that they will be punished at the ballot box for being either pro-European or 'soft' on immigration, or both. Immigration is a difficult issue for Labour, as it has been for Labour governments in the past. It tends to be an issue on which the Conservatives are seen as the stronger party. Moreover, if we look at immigration to the UK since 1997 we see a steep increase caused by a number of reasons such as increased asylum, but also increased labour migration into a prospering economy. Labour's rhetoric on immigration has often emphasised the need to effectively regulate and to tightly manage immigration. Taken together this can lead to a 'gap' between the rhetoric of immigration control and the reality of increased immigration (Cornelius et al. 1994). This gap could be filled by extremists such as the BNP, but such parties have had little chance of success under the UK electoral system. What would happen if a mainstream party sought to capitalise on concerns about immigration?

This chapter analyses the salience and impact of immigration and European integration on the 2005 campaign. It shows that Europe's salience faded between 2001 and 2005 and that it barely registered as an election issue. This was because the Conservatives under Iain Duncan Smith and Michael Howard stopped talking about it while the government's plan to hold a referendum on the proposed EU constitution and caution on European Monetary Union kicked the EU issue into the long grass, at least in terms of election debate. In contrast, the salience of immigration rose to levels not witnessed in British politics for more than 25 years. In 1978, Margaret Thatcher had spoken in a *World in Action* TV interview of people's fears of being 'swamped' by alien cultures, although the 'winter of discontent' and industrial unrest played a bigger part in Labour's electoral downfall in 1979 than immigration. In 2005, the Conservative election manifesto had ten words written on its cover, two of these were 'controlled immigration'. Could such an approach win back lost support for the Conservatives? Why too was Labour vulnerable on this issue?

Nation, state and sovereignty

To begin with it is useful to briefly clarify some core underlying concepts. Immigration and European integration serve as representations of a broader debate about Britain, the British nation, Englishness therein, the state and sovereignty. Both immigration and European integration expose and question the borders of state and nation. International migration has intensified as an issue across Europe following the geopolitical shake-up at the end of the Cold War (Castles and Miller 2003; Geddes 2003). European integration intensified and expanded too following the end of the Cold War, German reunification, the Maastricht Treaty, the creation of the single currency and enlargement to 25 member states (Hix 2005).

All these developments raise important questions for the UK, which has sought to severely restrict immigration flows since legislation was introduced to that effect in the 1960s and 1970s (Hansen 2000) and has long been seen as an 'awkward partner' within the EU (George 1998). The kinds of questions raised touch upon some of the core issues in politics, such as the idea of the nation, the power and role of the state and political identities within Britain. The nation is a cultural rather than a legal notion. Britain is a multinational nation and a multicultural society. Nationalism can be understood as a

> political principle, which holds that the political and the national unit should be congruent. Nationalism as a sentiment, or as a movement, can best be defined in terms of this principle. Nationalist *sentiment* is the feeling of anger aroused by the violation of this principle, or the feeling of satisfaction aroused by its fulfilment. (Gellner 1983: 1)

State and nation are not congruent in British politics because of distinct English, Scottish, Welsh and, more problematically, Irish, identities within the United Kingdom. Sovereignty can be understood according to the classic definition of Max Weber as the legitimate use of physical violence, or the ability of the sovereign to make and enforce laws. The notion of sovereignty can be broken down into three components: power, authority and capacity (Evans et al. 1985). This distinction suggests that the formal attribution of power to the sovereign may not necessarily entail the effective capacity to exercise this sovereignty. To give practical examples of what this might mean, the British state maintains the sovereign authority to control immigration flows across its borders, but in the exercise of this power is subject to a whole range of domestic and international pressures such as labour market pull effects, the workings of the global economy or the impact of international human rights laws that could constrain its ability to do so. A key element of the Conservative campaign at the 2005 general election was the claim that the Labour government had lost control of immigration and that the system was in chaos.

The remainder of this chapter explores European integration and immigration as campaign issues in 2005. It shows why immigration was an issue and Europe was not. It then analyses immigration as an election issue in 2005 and considers immigration's impact as a campaign issue, on results and on future policy directions. The fact that immigration was highly salient at the 2005 general election, while Europe was not, does not mean that the EU issue has gone away. We only need to look back one year to the 2004 European elections to see that UKIP got 16.2 per cent of the vote and won twelve seats. In June 2004 there was considerable concern amongst Conservative Party strategists that defections to UKIP had the potential to hurt the Conservative Party. If we fast-forward to 2005 then the continued relevance of the European issue was demonstrated when, less than four weeks after the British general election, the French and Dutch delivered crushing blows to 'the European project' when they rejected the EU's new Constitutional Treaty.

The dog that barked and the dog that didn't

This section of the chapter explains why Europe was not a key theme at the 2005 general election and why immigration was. At the 1997 and 2001 general elections Europe was a highly salient issue linked in particular to the decline of the Conservative Party. At the 2005 general election, Europe barely registered as a campaign issue. None of the main parties had much to say about it, preferring to wait for a possible future referendum on the proposed EU constitution (which seemed to become distinctly more unlikely to occur after the French 'non' and the Dutch 'nee' on 29 May and 1 June 2005 respectively). At the 2005 general election only fringe parties such as UKIP and Veritas made European integration a central campaign theme.

There are three reasons why Europe faded as an issue. First, the Conservatives stopped talking about it. This was in stark contrast to 1997 and 2001 when European integration was absolutely to the fore in election debate because of the bitter civil war within the party after the 1992 general election, the Maastricht ratification saga and the 'Black Wednesday' disaster of European Exchange Rate Mechanism exit in September 1992. At the 2001 general election, William Hague veered dangerously close to single-issue politics when he made it clear that the overriding campaign issue for the Conservatives at the 2001 general election was the campaign to 'save the pound' and resist the single European currency (Geddes 2002). While this theme resonated with a considerable proportion of the electorate who also opposed the replacement of sterling by the euro, the salience of the issue lagged far behind concerns such as health care, education and the economy, on all of which Labour held a commanding lead and on all of which it seemed that the Conservatives had little or nothing to say. The triumph of the Eurosceptics within the Conservative Party seemed assured in September 2001 when Iain Duncan Smith won the leadership contest (Garnett and Lynch 2002). However, while Duncan Smith ruled out membership of the euro, he also sought to downplay European integration as an issue within the Conservative Party and to focus Conservative policy across a wider range of issues that could have more appeal to the electorate (for further discussion, see Chapter 4, this volume). The Conservatives showed far less inclination to talk about Europe. The Labour government was prepared to make the case for Britain in Europe, but seemed far less willing to make the case for Europe in Britain (Stephens 2001). The Liberal Democrats preferred to focus on other issues. According to MORI polling data, the number of respondents who saw European integration as one of the most important issues facing the country was at around 24 per cent in June 2001. Yet less than four years later Europe was named as one of the most important issues facing the country by fewer than 10 per cent of respondents for eight months consistently from August 2004 to March 2005.

The second reason that European integration faded as an issue was that it had been organised out of the national election debate by the decision to hold a referendum on the EU constitution. This decision meant that debate about Europe could be postponed until a possible referendum. The Labour government also made it clear that the chances of Britain joining the European single currency were remote. The battle over Europe was thus postponed. This suited the Conservatives too, who were staunch in their opposition to both the constitution and the euro, but preferred to focus their fire on other issues.

The third reason for Europe's lack of resonance at the 2005 general election is linked to the way in which European elections are 'second-order elections'. Second-order elections such as local and European Parliament elections can be distinguished from first-order, national elections in that they do not change governments. In second-order elections there tend to be lower levels of participation than in national 'first-order' elections, there are better prospects for small and new political parties and governing parties tend to do badly. The reason why voters behave in this way is that they know that far less is at stake in a second-order election. Indeed, research has shown that European elections are even more second-order in the minds of British voters than local elections (Heath et al. 1999). This also means that the votes cast at a European election may be more expressive, or from the heart. A vote for UKIP may represent anti-EU sentiment rather than a hard-headed decision that a UKIP government would actually be a good idea.

In terms of issue salience, the picture with regards to immigration provides a stark contrast. In June 2001, 14 per cent of voters thought that race relations, immigration and immigrants were among the most important issues facing the country. By February 2005 this figure had risen to 40 per cent and fell back only slightly to 36 per cent in March 2005. In 2004 the British Social Attitudes Survey had identified 'a rising tide' of anti-immigration sentiment, with 74 per cent of respondents wanting less immigration, up from 65 per cent in 1995. The report's authors went on to conclude that

> The best explanation we could find for this change related to the overall increase in numbers of immigrants, which appears to have stimulated a rise in media coverage of immigration. Perhaps more importantly, [this] produced an increase in government statements and proclamations on the subject that were quite negative in tone and content. (McLaren and Johnson 2004)

This goes to the point already made earlier where a gap between the rhetoric of control and tightly managed migration espoused by government in their official pronouncements may not tally with the on-the-ground reality of increased immigration. This immigration does include many high-skilled people moving directly into employment, but the popular representation of these issues particularly in mid-market tabloids such as the *Daily Mail* and *Daily Express* tends to focus on the 'poor and huddled' masses and the threat that they are supposed to represent to the welfare state, the labour market, national security and/or national identity. This gap between some of the control-oriented rhetoric and reality was the Conservative focus. If we look at migration to the UK over the last ten years or so then we see that there has been a fairly steep increase in the numbers of migrants coming to the UK. Table 17.1 shows trends in immigration and emigration between 1993 and 2003.

Table 17.1   Immigration, emigration and net migration from and to the UK, 1993–2003

Year	Immigration (000s)	Emigration (000s)	Net migration (000s) (immigration–emigration)
1993	265.1	266.3	−1.2
1994	314.4	237.6	76.8
1995	311.9	236.5	75.4
1996	317.8	263.7	54.1
1997	326.1	279.2	46.9
1998	390.3	251.5	138.8
1999	453.8	290.8	163.0
2000	483.4	320.7	162.7
2001	479.6	307.7	171.9
2002	512.8	359.4	153.5
2003	513.0	362.0	151.0

Source: Adapted from HMSO (2004).

Immigration as a campaign issue

The Labour government's alleged failure to control immigration was central to the Conservative campaign. Their manifesto stated that 'It's not racist to impose limits on immigration.' Even though Tony Blair noted in a speech he made in Dover on 21 April 2005 that he knew of no politician who has ever said it was, this was an issue that resonated to the benefit of the Conservative Party. While figures can sometimes vary, immigration was an issue that, according to all polling organisations, was one on which the Conservatives held a commanding lead over Labour. Indeed, it was one of the very few where the Conservatives held such a strong advantage. It was hardly unsurprising that it should be such a strong focus for their campaign. Moreover, as Philip Cowley and Jane Green point out in Chapter 4, this volume, the immigration issue was not one that resonated solely with Conservative voters. A MORI poll published in the *Observer* on 9 April 2005 found that 58 per cent of respondents thought that laws on immigration should be much tougher, with a further 11 per cent endorsing the BNP position and saying that immigration should be stopped altogether. In addition to this, 65 per cent of respondents thought that the government was not being honest about the scale of immigration into Britain with Howard preferred to Blair by a margin of 47 per cent to 29 per cent to deal with the issue, according to a MORI poll for the *Sun* on 22 April.

Labour's vulnerability on immigration was exemplified by two occasions – one before and one during the campaign – on which Tony Blair was 'Paxmanned'. The first of these occurred during a BBC TV *Newsnight* interview with Jeremy Paxman in February 2003 when Blair, to the surprise of some in the Home Office, committed the Labour government to halving the number of asylum applicants arriving in the UK within six months. The second incident occurred during Blair's interview on 20 April 2005 by Paxman on BBC TV during which he faced persistent questioning on the extent of illegal immigration to the UK. This could mean people who enter the UK clandestinely, those who overstay their visa's duration, and those that have had their asylum application rejected but that stay on anyway. When pressed, Blair could not give a number. For Paxman this was taken as a stark admission of failure if the Prime Minister apparently did not have any idea about the number of illegal immigrants in the UK. Blair responded by saying that no other British government (or European government for that matter) has been able to pin down the number of irregular migrants. Paxman was widely seen to have exposed Blair to allegations of not knowing what was happening. This goes back to the point made earlier in this chapter about the distinction between power, authority and capacity in the discussion of sovereignty. Blair's apparent weakness on the issue of irregular migration was taken to expose a weakness in the state's capacity to control its borders and the government's knowledge of what was actually going on. Moreover, this was a serious admission, because an inability to control the national borders can undermine the legitimacy of a government that is seen to have failed in the exercise of one of its core sovereign responsibilities.

For the Conservatives, immigration and asylum were seen as the quintessential 'dog whistle' issues imported to the UK by the Conservative Party's Australian campaign guru Lynton Crosby. This style of conservative politics was famously evident in the run-up to the 2001 Australian federal elections when a boat with more than 400 Afghan refugees was rescued by a Norwegian container ship, the MV *Tampa*. The Australian Liberal Party government refused to let the ship enter Australian territorial waters and demanded that it return to Indonesia with its human cargo (Marr and Wilkinson 2003). Prime Minister Howard had been lagging in the polls, but made great political capital from the *Tampa* incident and his assertion of 'we decide who comes here'. The Australian government then sought to drive a wedge between the proportion of the electorate supporting them on the issue and the rest. In the context of the British debate about immigration, the Conservatives' intention was to pick a fight on immigration, immigrants and asylum and force the Labour Party to defend the minority. The clear incentive for Labour was to do all they could to shut down the issue, decry Conservative scare tactics, and focus on their strengths in areas such as health, education and the economy.

The 'dog whistle' component of the Conservative approach meant putting out a message audible only to those at whom it is aimed so that potential supporters notice but others are not offended. Perhaps a classic – or cynical – example was offered by the Conservative candidate in Woking, Humfrey Malins, who put out one leaflet in Urdu to Muslim voters saying how he had helped with visas and immigration appeals and another in English pleading for toughness on immigration. Sometimes the message could be less subtle. In Castle Point Robert Spink asked, 'What part of send them back don't you understand Mr Blair?' In Croydon Central, Andrew Pelling's leaflets showed a map of the world with an arrow pointing to Croydon (where the Immigration and Nationality Department is based) and the headline 'unlimited immigration'. Nick de Bois, the candidate in Enfield North, warned of 'the strain put on local schools by bogus asylum-seekers'. Anne Main in St Albans stated that five 'illegal immigrants' were arrested and freed in the area, although 'nobody knows if these people were criminals, carrying diseases'. The Conservatives paid for newspaper advertisements in Reading and Wokingham that linked the £17 million spent on supporting asylum to council tax rises (*Independent*, 22 April 2005). Sometimes these tactics could backfire. Conservative candidate Ed Matts, fighting the Conservatives' number one target seat, Dorset South, doctored a photo of himself at a demonstration in support of a family of asylum-seekers' campaign. Originally Ann Widdecombe had been standing next to him with a poster saying 'Let them Stay', but this was changed to 'Not Chaos and Inhumanity' to go with Matts' placard altered to say 'Controlled Immigration'. Matts lost, which shows the potential for cynical campaigning and egregious use of Photoshop technology to rebound. There was also the question of whether immigration was an aspirational issue that could resonate with some of the middle-class voters that the Conservatives needed to win back. It was reported that the victorious Conservative candidate for Putney, Justine Greening, who for many was the symbol of a limited Conservative revival, had put out a campaign leaflet that focused on only four of the five key Tory messages with 'controlled immigration' absent and fought a strong campaign focused almost entirely on local issues such as the District Line, noise from Heathrow airport and policing (*Guardian*, 29 April 2005).

The risk of an anti-immigration stance for the Conservatives was that it could alienate potential supporters and leave the party open to accusations of playing the 'race card'. If the Conservatives were to break from the 32–33 per cent position in the opinion polls at which they had been flatlining for more than ten years, then would immigration be a vote winner? Did a campaign based on fear of immigration and immigrants give a sense of a better tomorrow, or was it likely to induce more negative feelings of fear and reaction? The potential for the approach to go wrong was revealed when Michael Howard appeared on Jonathan Dimbleby's *Ask the Leaders* programme on ITV when audience members challenged Howard's view that immigration could lead to racial unrest. These were scare tactics, some audience members complained. Michael Portillo, who stood down as a Conservative MP in 2005, said that the Conservatives were repeating their errors of 2001 and were in danger of being widely perceived as an unsympathetic party, or in Theresa May's words, the 'nasty party'. The Conservative campaign could be seen as a US-style campaign to press 'anger points' amongst the electorate, but it was not clear how US tactics would work in the UK where voters may be more liberal and more likely to feel alienated by such devices than, say, voters in Iowa. The Confederation of British Industry also expressed its disapproval of the Conservative stance and argued that it was necessary for Britain to keep the most flexible labour markets in Europe and that immigration could help with this.

While the precise impact can be difficult to judge and may vary across constituencies, the story of the immigration issue in the 2005 campaign is the story of the Conservatives trying to increase the salience of one of the few issues on which they were stronger than Labour. The Conservative campaign was predicated on the claims that immigration was out of control, that a politically correct New Labour elite were hiding this fact from the British people and that this represented an abrogation of responsibility by a weak government. This is what the Conservatives meant when they asked 'Are you thinking what we're thinking?' about immigration. The difficulty for Michael Howard was that his own parents were immigrants from Romania who fled Nazism. He admitted that under his proposed changes to the immigration system and the introduction of quotas then they might not have been allowed into the country. Timothy Garton Ash made the point that we can see a real contrast between how these issues were dealt with in the UK and how they would have been dealt with in the US (*Guardian*, 28 April 2005). In the US a politician would have made a tear-jerking election broadcast playing on hardship, struggle and eventual success. In the UK, where attitudes towards immigration have been more cautious and defensive than in North America, the story remained one of migrants as a threat; even, it seemed, Michael Howard's own family.

The aim to portray a system in chaos was evident at the Conservative manifesto launch where it was alleged that people with suspect papers were being allowed into the country for two days in the hope that they would report back after 48 hours. It turned out that this was based on a scheme at Bristol airport which the Home Office said was a long-standing part of the immigration procedures dating back to the 1971 Immigration Act for those not deemed to be a security risk. The Conservative manifesto also pledged:

- An annual immigration and asylum quota set by Parliament
- Round-the-clock surveillance at ports of entry – although when pointed out that there were 650 of these, it was soon cut back to the 35 or so main ports of entry
- A British border control police force
- Points system for work permits (Labour proposed this too)
- Withdrawal from the 1951 Geneva Convention on the status of refugees
- Asylum claims to be 'processed' outside the UK, although it was not clear which countries would process British asylum applications.

If we conduct a rudimentary discourse analysis and explore the language in which the Conservative manifesto was expressed we see that the word 'immigration' was mentioned 15 times, but that the word 'control' or 'controlled' in various contexts was mentioned 33 times. The Conservatives sought to frame the debate in terms of control, set the agenda and control the debate. In addition to this, Migration Watch, a conservative think tank strongly opposed to government immigration policy and with a hot line to the mid-market right-wing tabloids such as the *Daily Mail* and *Daily Express*, was particularly attuned to the Conservative Party agenda. As soon as Blair was seen to slip up in his Paxman interview, Migration Watch's Sir Andrew Green penned a *Daily Mail* article in which he made it clear that in his view the number was about 500,000 and that Blair's obfuscation on the issue was an admission of failure (*Daily Mail*, 22 April 2005).

The debate about immigration was dominated by the Conservatives. Media analysis by Loughborough University academics for the *Guardian* (2 May 2005: 6) showed that immigration was a big campaign issue attracting around 7 per cent of campaign coverage – more than health, education, the economy, Iraq, taxation and crime. Immigration was a particularly salient aspect of the Conservative campaign in weeks two and three. The intention was to be seen as touching upon the concerns of 'ordinary people' because immigration 'breeds a sense of insecurity and that's damaging to good community relations', as Howard put it at the Conservatives' morning press conference on 19 April.

Labour's vulnerability on this issue was compounded by the December 2004 resignation of Home Secretary David Blunkett. Blunkett spoke on issues such as crime, security and immigration in language that resonated with Labour's working-class voters rather than in 'trendy' Islington. His loss before the election was a blow to the Labour campaign, although he had a campaigning schedule as busy as any Cabinet minister, primed, as it turned out, for his re-entry to government. Back in 2002 Peter Mandelson had argued that New Labour needed to be able to take on these issues and find a language that allowed them to confront the right. Mandelson and the Labour campaign guru, Philip Gould, warned that parties of the left across Europe were losing power because they had failed to modernise enough. If New Labour were to avoid this fate then they argued a rethink was needed on immigration policies to reflect the fears and insecurities of some of Labour's core vote (*Guardian*, 13 September 2002). Nevertheless, this was a difficult issue for Labour. Back in 1997 New Labour had borrowed patriotic imagery in 1997 with the bulldog but they also laid great play on their ideas of a 'new Britain', a 'young country' and suchlike, which would seem to imply some comfort with migration and a multicultural society. In his speech in Dover on 22 April 2005, Blair derided Conservative policy as scare tactics and an incoherent babble. Labour proposed an Australian-style points system and continued attempts to restrict asylum within a common EU framework. Britain has formally opted out of EU provisions on a common migration and asylum policy. However, between November 1999 and May 2004, 34 measures on migration and asylum were agreed by the other EU member states, of which the UK opted into 18. The measures that the UK was particularly keen to participate in were those on asylum and the strengthening of border controls on the EU's eastern and southern frontiers. The EU was thus seen as an escape route from some tricky domestic issues if other member states could be used to stop migrants getting to the UK, which also indicates a flexible, non-zero-sum conceptualisation of sovereignty (Geddes 2005).

The precise impact on the election results of the Conservatives' anti-immigration campaign can be difficult to judge. The Conservatives secured only a marginal increase in their share of the vote and picked up an extra 36 seats, but Labour Cabinet minister Margaret Beckett said on election night that she had a 'horrid feeling' that immigration had helped the Conservative effort in the election. Private polling for the Labour Party in the immediate run-up to the election was reported to indicate vulnerability on migration in seats in outer London and the West Midlands (*Guardian*, 1 May 2005). Labour was also concerned about the BNP in the M62 corridor in Lancashire and Yorkshire and some parts of outer London. MORI research in marginal seats suggested that in Con–Lab and Con–Lib marginals, immigration was among the top three issues on voters' minds. The Labour vote did, though, hold up relatively well in some of the most marginal seats (0–10 per cent) with Conservative inroads occurring in some of the less marginal seats (like Putney) where immigration may not have been a core local Conservative campaign theme. The Ed Matts story is also quite instructive where anti-immigration tactics backfired.

One area in which the impact of immigration, racism and xenophobia was very direct was the performance of the BNP, particularly evident in Labour held seats such as Barking, Dagenham, Dewsbury and Keighley. The BNP contested 119 seats and took 192,850 votes in total, compared with 47,129 at the 2001 election with an overall vote share of 0.6 per cent. The best BNP result was in Barking, London, where it took 16.9 per cent of the vote and BNP candidate Richard Barnbrook was only a handful of votes behind the Conservatives. In Dewsbury, West Yorkshire, David Exley polled 5,066 votes (13.1 per cent). In

Keighley, West Yorkshire, the party leader Nick Griffin polled 4,240 votes, 9.1 per cent of the total cast. The BNP lost its deposit in 84 of the seats it contested, failures costing a total of £42,000.

The Labour MP for Dagenham, Jon Cruddas, warned that if New Labour were ever more fixated on Middle England to the neglect of 'Old Labour' areas such as Dagenham, then this could benefit the BNP who could capitalise on a new Labour government 'which has consciously removed class as a political or economic category. It has devised policies to speak to specific swing voters in marginal constituencies.' Cruddas was particularly scathing about government immigration policy, which he saw as integral to flexible labour markets and the delivery of a cheap workforce, but potentially corrosive of a progressive social agenda if attention was not paid to those at the lower end of the labour market who may see migrant workers as a threat. Moreover, if the government's public discourse on migration continues to shift rightwards to a debate about control and security it would thus concede the terms of the debate to the Conservatives (*Guardian*, 20 May 2005).

Europe in the 2005 campaign

Europe barely registered as a campaign issue at the 2005 general election because the Conservatives abandoned the issue as a campaign focus, the possibility of referenda on the constitution and the euro had defused the issue to some extent, and expressive voting of the kind seen at the 2004 European elections was less likely to occur in a first-order national election. Even so, in terms of party positions there was a noticeable divide between the Conservatives, on one side, and Labour and the Liberal Democrats, on the other.

The Conservatives opposed the EU constitution and the European single currency. They also called for a renegotiation of Britain's relationship with the EU and the repatriation of some powers ceded to the EU. If this were not to occur then the Conservatives seemed to be suggesting a fundamental change in Britain's relationship with the EU via a formalised semi-detachment. Metaphorically, Britain would not leave the EU, but would have gone to fetch its coat. Labour supported the constitution, but were more ambivalent about the euro. The Lib Dems supported the euro and the constitution, but were committed to a referendum on both and were, anyway, less keen to talk about these issues because they did not play well in hotbeds of Euroscepticism such as the South West, where the Lib Dems hoped to hold and pick up seats. On the Eurosceptic fringe both UKIP and Veritas called for UK withdrawal from the EU.

Europe was also emblematic of tensions within the Labour Party in government. European policy had effectively been ceded to the Treasury through the establishment of the five economic tests that needed to be satisfied if Britain were to join the euro (Geddes 2004). Whether or not these tests had been met was to be decided by the Treasury. In this key aspect of economic policy it was a Treasury with Eurosceptic tendencies and Gordon Brown that were to hold the power of decision. In June 2003 Brown reported that only one of the five economic tests for membership of the single currency had been met (HM Treasury 2003). In his speech to the British Chambers of Commerce on 25 April 2005 Brown seemed to rule out membership for the next Parliament with his aides spinning the story that as Prime Minister his attitude to the euro would be harder than that of Blair (*Guardian*, 26 April 2005).

The party that fought the strongest campaign on Europe was UKIP, who had enjoyed success at the 2004 European elections and fought the 2005 campaign with the slogan 'We want our country back'. As argued earlier, this performance at a second-order European election was unlikely to be repeated at a first-order national election. UKIP got 2.3 per cent of the vote and lost 451 deposits, costing it £225,500. One candidate, John Whittaker, stood in eight different constituencies. This was a massive fall from UKIP's 16 per cent share in the 2004 European elections where Europe was the issue, where PR favoured smaller parties and where UKIP polled more votes than the Liberal Democrats. The breakaway Veritas Party, led by former television chatshow host Robert Kilroy Silk, pledged to tell the truth, but fared even less well, picking up just over 40,000 votes in the 66 seats where it fielded a candidate. The rather confusing line from these parties was that this was a bogus general election because powers had long since seeped away to Brussels. Why bother voting then? One of the more vivid election broadcasts was that by UKIP which showed a giant green octopus with the EU flag plastered to its forehead engulfing the Houses of Parliament and legal system. Give public esteem for politicians this might not have been seen as an entirely bad thing. The UKIP vote was not even boosted amongst confused environmentalists when Channel 4 ran the UKIP subtitles over the Green Party election broadcast.

Conclusion

Immigration and European integration both symbolise challenges to the nation, the state, national identity and sovereign authority. They have both been prominent features of British electoral politics since 1997. They are issues too where there is a divide between Labour and the Liberal Democrats, on one side, and the Conservatives, on the other. Labour have felt themselves to be particularly vulnerable on the issue of immigration, which is redolent of ex-Cabinet minister Richard Crossman's (1975) remark in his diary made back in the 1960s about immigration's 'powerful political undertow' and its ability to hit Labour's working-class vote. This observation still holds true and indicates a third-term challenge for Labour. The government's five-year plan for immigration and asylum published in 2005 does not envisage quotas. It does make a stronger distinction between skilled and unskilled work and attempts to emphasise the ways in which migration can be made 'to work for Britain' (HMSO 2005). Labour talks the talk of control, restriction and regulation, but may not be seen to walk the walk in terms of delivering tight controls. This can expose a gap between the rhetoric of control and the reality of continued immigration. There is also a potentially more troubling gap for Labour between the rhetoric of labour market 'flexibility', to which immigration contributes, and a public discourse about immigration that is often highly control-oriented and at times very hostile. This is precisely the kind of issue that extreme parties such as the BNP seek to play on in 'Old Labour' areas where senses of vulnerability and insecurity in relation to changes such as those induced by immigration may be high. This is an issue on which the Conservatives hold a strong lead over the government, but for the Conservatives this is an issue that leaves them open to accusations of playing the race card and of scare tactics. Is it an aspirational message for a 'modern' Conservative Party?

Europe barely registered as a campaign issue in the 2005 general election. This does not mean that it is not an important issue or that its challenge to ideas about state, nation and sovereignty have gone away. Rather it shows that Europe was organised out of national election debate and consigned to the second-order domain of European elections. Some big issues loom, not least the fate of the EU constitution. The EU lurched into crisis soon after the British election with the French and Dutch rejection of the proposed constitutional treaty. Whether or not the Treaty will survive in some shape or form is an open question, as too are the implications for European economic reform and enlargement. What is clear is that the leaders who make the decisions on these issues will not be those who were in place at the time of Britain's 2005 general election. The future of Europe will be an issue for Europe's next generation of leaders, which we could assume to include Gordon Brown in Britain and new leaders in post-Schröder Germany and post-Chirac France.

References

Castles, S. and Miller, M. (2003) *The Age of Migration: International Population Movements in the Modern World*, third edn, London: Palgrave.

Cornelius, W., Martin, P. and Hollifield, J. (1994), 'Introduction: the ambivalent quest for immigration control', in W. Cornelius, P. Martin and J. Hollifield (eds) *Controlling Immigration: A Global Perspective*, Stanford, CA: Stanford University Press, pp. 3–42.

Crossman, R. (1975) *Diaries of a Cabinet Minister. Volume 1: Minister of Housing 1964–1966*, London: Cape.

Evans, P., Rueschemeyer, D. and Scokpol, T. (eds) (1985) *Bringing the State Back In: New Perspectives on the State as Institution and Social Actor*, Cambridge: Cambridge University Press.

Garnett, M. and Lynch, P. (2002) 'Bandwagon blues: the Tory fightback fails', *Political Quarterly*, 73(1): 29–37.

Geddes, A. (2002) 'In Europe, not interested in Europe', in A. Geddes and J. Tonge (eds) *Labour's Second Landslide*, Manchester: Manchester University Press.

Geddes, A. (2003) *The Politics of Migration and Immigration in Europe*, London: Sage.

Geddes, A. (2004) *The European Union and British Politics*, London: Palgrave.

Geddes, A. (2005) 'Britain, the EU and migration policy: getting the best of both worlds?', *International Affairs*, forthcoming.

Gellner, E. (1983) *Nations and Nationalism*, Oxford: Blackwell.

George, S. (1998) *An Awkward Partner: Britain in the European Community*, third edn, Oxford: Oxford University Press.

Hansen, R. (2000) *Immigration and Citizenship in Post-War Britain*, Oxford: Oxford University Press.

Heath, A., McLean, I., Taylor, B. and Curtice, J. (1999) 'Between first and second order: a comparison of voting behaviour in European and local elections in Britain', *European Journal of Political Research*, 35(3): 389–414.

HMSO (2004) *Control of Immigration Statistics 2003*, London: HMSO.

HMSO (2005) *Controlling Our Borders: Making Migration Work for Britain. Five Year Strategy Plan for Asylum and Immigration*, London: HMSO.

HM Treasury (2003) *UK Membership of the Single Currency: An Assessment of the Five Economic Tests*, London: HM Treasury.

Hix, S. (2005) *The Political System of the European Union*, second edn, London: Palgrave.

McLaren, L. and Johnson, M. (2004) 'Understanding the rising tide of anti-immigrant sentiment', *British Social Attitudes, 21st Report*, London: Sage.

Marr, D. and Wilkinson, M. (2003) *Dark Victory: The Tampa and the Military Campaign to Re-elect the Prime Minister*, London: Allen and Unwin.

Stephens, P. (2001) 'Blair and Europe', *Political Quarterly*, 72(1): 67–75.

Barking

Two of the most contentious and combustible issues in British society are immigration and ethnic relations. The 2005 general election campaign saw the Conservatives squarely address the issues of immigration, asylum and immigrants while simultaneously denouncing the extreme right-wing British National Party. Indeed, Michael Howard made a connection during the campaign between the relative success of the British National Party in local elections and a Labour government that he claimed was not tough enough on immigration.

The British National Party tends to pick up support in traditional Labour areas and had enjoyed some success in local elections, particularly in the North West of England. At the 2005 general election the BNP candidate Richard Barnbrook trebled the share of the BNP vote and came close to pushing the Conservatives into third place. During the campaign the BNP published the *Barking and Dagenham Patriot* that contained three pictures. The first was entitled 'The way we were' which showed the 'ladies of Barking' at a 1953 Coronation party in 1953. This was contrasted with two photos that were supposed to illustrate 'the way we are now' with photographs of Muslim women in headscarves. This and other kinds of material were clearly designed to stir up bitterness and resentment and to pin the blame for social changes that many residents might find troubling on immigrant newcomers. The myth was spread that the Council had paid African families £50,000 each to move into the borough. This scapegoating approach is a classic far-right strategy and paid off in Barking, particularly in the areas to the east of the constituency where older voters and 'white flight' families reacted angrily to immigrant newcomers from Eastern Europe and Africa.

Result		%
Hodge, M. (Lab)	13,826	47.8
Prince, K. (Con)	4,943	17.0
Barnbrook, R. (BNP)	4,916	16.9
Wickenden, T. (Lib Dem)	3,211	11.1
Jones, T. (UKIP)	803	2.8
Cleeland, L. (Green)	618	2.1
Panton, D. (Ind)	530	1.8
Saxby, M. (WRP)	59	0.2
Lab majority	8,883	30.7
Swing: Lab to Con		3.6

Turnout: 50.1%

18
Conclusion

Andrew Geddes and Jonathan Tonge

The 2005 election was a curate's egg for the three main parties. All could derive some satisfaction from the outcome, but there was also disappointment or concern distributed unequally across each. A dull campaign, albeit one with more drama than was evident in 2001, was followed by an intriguing set of results. The verdict did not preclude the possibility that Labour might become the natural party of government during the twenty-first century in a manner akin to the Conservatives' position during the previous century, yet few would place a great deal of confidence in this interpretation.

For Labour, there was justifiable delight at having secured a third consecutive term for the first time in the party's history. A majority of 66 would normally be considered an excellent result. Indeed it was, although the loss of 47 seats might normally be regarded as a poor showing. The downsizing of the Labour majority might be of less concern had it not been for the rebellious nature of its backbenchers in the 2001–05 Parliament. A repeat of such awkwardness would have far greater implications for the continuation of the Blair (and Brown) project of modernisation of public services, investment in reform and enhanced public–private partnerships.

This was not a difficult election for Labour to win. Given the strong economy, low inflation and low unemployment an alternative verdict might have appeared perverse. Throughout the campaign, the Conservatives barely laid a glove on Labour's economic stewardship. Labour is seen as the party of economic competence, a lead evident since the Conservatives' Exchange Rate Mechanism-exit in 1992. It was away from the economy that Labour displayed vulnerability. The 2005 contest was perhaps the first 'khaki' election since the post-Falklands War election of 1983. Unlike that contest, which bolstered the government, the Iraq war was highly divisive. Survey evidence suggested a nation split almost equally on whether UK intervention was justified. Even more damagingly for Labour, the justification for war raised issues of trust in the government and Prime Minister which dogged Labour's campaign. A defensive Tony Blair, who performed below par in television debates, was, in effect, reliant upon arguments of incompetence rather than deception. His (Blair preferred the use of 'the') intelligence services got it completely wrong on whether weapons of mass destruction were stockpiled in Iraq, but he did not lie to the British public, appeared the basis of the Prime Minister's argument.

The Butler Inquiry appeared to suggest that decision-making in government appeared the opposite of a documented, collective effort. Whilst Butler was far too polite and steeped in civil service language to use the word, the subtext suggested something of a 'chancer' about the Prime Minister's mode of arrival at decisions. Continuing unrest in Iraq, the publication of the initial doubts of the legality of the war held by the Attorney General and the campaigning of an eclectic cast of election characters, ranging from Liberal Democrats to the war-bereaved Reg Keys and the 'colourful' George Galloway, ensured that the Iraq war and the issue of trust formed a big part of the election.

The issue of trust was not confined to the Iraq war, but was also linked to domestic concerns. A Labour government which had apparently ruled out increases in university tuition fees in 2001 had quickly got to work on raising fees after re-election. Moreover, the government considered setting the fees at a higher rate than the £3,000 annual rate introduced, encouraging leading universities to argue for this, before realising that they were at the outer limits of parliamentary tolerance of the measure. Labour ministers toured constituencies promising various items, such as light railway systems, not all of which materialised. Against this, however, a highly favourable economic backdrop, which further strengthened Gordon Brown, had allowed Labour to make genuine improvements to some public services. School class sizes and hospital waiting lists had fallen in size. Labour could even claim a drop in several types of crime, most notably burglary, although the public perception appeared different.

Labour's third term may be dominated (tediously) by discussion of when Brown (surely?) will replace Blair. Whilst the leadership issue is of great importance, the paramount determinants, possible trouble on the European Union aside, of whether the party can secure a fourth term after 2009/10 are more likely to be whether the economy remains stable, with borrowing kept in check, whether further progress can be made in the delivery of public services and, possibly, the impact of terrorism. Given this, the timing of the succession matters less than the development of a coherent post-Blair agenda by Brown which is nonetheless rooted within Blairism; this would be an agenda rooted in pragmatism ('what's best is what works') and reform.

For the Conservatives, the election was, as Cowley and Green record, another case of flatlining. A vote share of 33.2 per cent is not quite as disastrous as it might first seem, given the modern context of such shares. The British electoral system might not see a party form a government with over 40 per cent of the vote ever again, in an era of multiparty politics. To talk of the Conservatives needing to attain such a figure is to exaggerate what is nonetheless a fully-blown crisis. The Conservatives will need to raise their electoral share towards the high 30 per cent mark to form a government. Their crisis lies less in vote share, damagingly low as this is, than in regional variation, although the two are of course strongly related. There are large swathes of northern urban England and most of Scotland where the thought – let alone the actuality – of voting Conservative is not seriously entertained. That the Conservatives outpolled Labour in England owed a great deal to a good performance in the South East, where the Conservatives' share of 45 per cent nearly doubled that acquired by Labour.

Indeed the regional variation in voting was perhaps underplayed in election-night analyses. There were some large swings to the Conservatives in the South East, although these were overwhelmingly the product of a desertion from Labour in seats won outlandishly in 1997 rather than a boost to the Conservative vote. In the North, Labour's vote held up to a greater extent. The erosion of Labour's popularity in the South offers scope for Conservative improvement at the next election, whilst the eradication of seat biases – the overrepresentation of Labour MPs, holding smaller urban northern constituencies with declining populations – by the Boundary Commission, should also assist.

The Conservatives' response to electoral humiliations thus far has been to change leaders. In the case of Iain Duncan Smith (partly rehabilitated by Cowley and Green) the party went further in denying the leader his opportunity for electoral catastrophe. The big vision of what the Conservative Party stands for is still awaited. The criticism of the party's 2005 campaign as too negative was perhaps excessive. Given the state of the economy and Conservative support for the Iraq war, the gravitation towards immigration and asylum was always likely. Whatever the lack of rationality, those issues do resonate with a sizeable section of the electorate, although at times the Conservatives appeared as obsessive as they were on Europe in the 2001 contest. The Conservatives failed to unleash positive or visionary ideas in a minimalist manifesto. The campaign was well-organised, Michael Howard leading from the front (a product, partly, of the feverish defence of their own marginal seats by his colleagues) and the slogan 'Are you thinking what we're thinking?' was by no means the worst election effort ever mustered. Given Howard's own interests and oft-repeated successes on crime as Home Secretary, the lack of concentration on law and order was perhaps surprising. Away from non-traditional concerns, the Conservatives lacked focus or even interest. Tim Yeo's attempt to develop the party's green credentials, which ought to resonate in a party instinctively hostile to brutal urbanisation of the countryside, was undermined by his risible nonsense concerning Labour's (non-existent) 'seven-year war on the motorist'. The facilitation of increased car use appears an intriguing Conservative solution to the problem of global warming.

For the Liberal Democrats, the election represented a real opportunity to make substantial progress. Entering the election flanked by a government in declining popularity and an opposition marooned in the low 30s in the percentage polls, the 2005 contest offered the prospect of a major breakthrough. The party achieved a substantial increase in its vote share, up 3.9 per cent to 22.7 per cent, but this figure was still below that achieved by the SDP–Liberal Alliance of the 1980s and the net increase in seats was disappointing. An increase of eleven was perhaps 15–20 below what might reasonably have been anticipated.

To blame the Liberal Democrats for failing to make a bigger breakthrough, given the preposterous inequities of the voting system, is harsh. However, the party's immediate reappraisal of policy after the election suggests that the positioning to the left of Labour, which lost the party seats to the Conservatives in a number of constituencies in the South, may have a limited shelf-life. A shift to the right could nonetheless jeopardise Liberal Democrat progress in the North, apparent at national and local elections, where Charles Kennedy's party represents the main opposition to Labour in cities. Steven Fielding makes the point that some left-leaning electors were prepared to vote Liberal Democrat in 2005, due to discontent over Iraq, tuition fees or local concerns, but nonetheless were content to see a Labour government elected, albeit of a different type than that evident in the previous term. This suggests softness to the Liberal Democrats' support, vulnerable to erosion from policy shifts from Labour or the Conservatives. As Fieldhouse and Cutts (Chapter 5, this volume) have shown, the Liberal Democrats won seats in places such as Cardiff Central and Manchester Withington, where there was convergence of national-level concerns with local concerns on schools, hospitals and transport. The party cannot be certain of holding these gains next time.

Elsewhere, there were only modest performances by the nationalist parties, as asymmetrical devolution appears to have been accompanied by asymmetrical nationalism. Scotland and Wales remain solidly Labour territory, but the return of Alex Salmond as leader has revived the SNP, which performed respectably. The campaign of Plaid Cymru did not inspire. Northern Ireland remains a dysfunctional polity, marked by electoral polarisation, (notwithstanding the greater moderation evident within the DUP and Sinn Fein), and residential segregation in a form of benign apartheid. Whilst successive secretaries of state have optimistically described the 1998 Good Friday Agreement as the 'only show in town', it remains one boycotted by a sizeable section of the electorate. The stepping down of the IRA will test the commitment of unionists to power sharing.

Overall, the electorate offered a clear verdict in returning Labour with an effective, but reduced, governing majority. In this respect, the result might be judged a vindication of first-past-the-post, but the temptation should be resisted. First-past-the-post, or single plurality, belongs to the two-party era of the 1950s and 1960s, when the governing party could almost achieve an overall majority of votes and the opposition polled a vote share which today's Labour government might envy. Decades on, the system looks archaic, unreflective of the changing tastes of the British electorate. We chime with the *Independent* – easily the most radical paper on a range of concerns, ranging from PR to global warming in calling for serious debate on an overhaul of the voting system. Whilst cognisant of the advantages conferred by single plurality, in terms of single-member constituency representation and governing majorities – although a hung Parliament next time would undermine that argument – a system in which 36 per cent of the vote yields 56 per cent of parliamentary seats, as enjoyed by Labour, needs to be acknowledged as unsatisfactory. For the Liberal Democrats to obtain nearly one-quarter of the vote, yet fewer than one in ten parliamentary seats, is grotesque, an absurd voiding of popular will. This is not to understate the problems of PR, most notably the undue influence given to the third party, as a potential coalition partner. However, the electorate ought to be given a say as to whether they are prepared to countenance this scenario.

Labour's naked self-interest on the issue, preserving an antiquated system and abandoning its 1997 referendum pledge, does not surprise, but does the government little credit. If single plurality is to be legitimised as our voting system for the twenty-first century, this can only be achieved via approval in a referendum. The mechanics of such a contest would not be straightforward. Should electors be offered a multi-option referendum, one that requires a sophisticated electorate, on the merits of first-past-the-post versus additional member system versus single transferable vote? A preferable option might be for a cross-parliamentary group to determine the single mode of PR to be pitted against single plurality in a referendum. Presently, however, the prospect of such a contest is a pipedream.

The election's greatest triumph was surely achieved by exit pollsters, the BBC/ ITN's final prediction of a Labour majority of 66 a spectacular success. Our book on the 2001 election recorded disquiet on the possible impact of the publication of polls during the campaign. We have not abandoned these reservations, whilst recognising that a ban on publication would be illiberal and might have little effect. The widespread poll predictions of a substantial Labour victory would hardly have boosted turnout. As Denver notes, the 2001 turnout of 59 per cent prompted much anguish over a crisis of democracy, yet the modest increase to 61 per cent seems to have relaxed discussion of the issue, as if the problem has been solved. Making the votes of most electors count might be the best means of addressing the issue of turnout, another strong democratic argument for electoral reform. In the meantime, however, Labour start slight favourites for the 2009/10 election, a contest in which it is conceivable that the party may find itself returned to government on an even lower share of the vote.

Index

Compiled by Sue Carlton